Experiencing America: A Smithsonian Tour through American History

Richard Kurin, Ph.D.

Smithsonian®

PUBLISHED BY:

THE GREAT COURSES
Corporate Headquarters
4840 Westfields Boulevard, Suite 500
Chantilly, Virginia 20151-2299
Phone: 1-800-832-2412
Fax: 703-378-3819
www.thegreatcourses.com

Printed in the United States of America

Richard Kurin, Ph.D.

Under Secretary for History, Art, and Culture
Smithsonian

Dr. Richard Kurin is the Smithsonian's Under Secretary for History, Art, and Culture, a position he has held since 2007. He received his B.A. in Anthropology and Philosophy from the State University of New York at Buffalo. He earned both his M.A. and his Ph.D. in Anthropology from the University of Chicago. During his graduate studies, he was awarded a Fulbright-Hays Doctoral Dissertation fellowship and a Social Science Research Council fellowship.

Dr. Kurin first worked for the Smithsonian in 1976 for the Institution's celebration of the Bicentennial of the United States. Since then, he has served in a variety of roles. For decades, he directed the Center for Folklife and Cultural Heritage and was responsible for the Smithsonian Folklife Festival, Smithsonian Folkways Recordings, and other programs representing the diversity and range of American and worldwide cultural traditions. He directed the National Programs of the Smithsonian for several years, enhancing partnerships with museums across the United States. Dr. Kurin has produced many of the large-scale national celebration events on the National Mall including festivals and ceremonies for several presidential inaugurations, the opening of the World War II Memorial, the opening of the National Museum of the American Indian, and the Smithsonian's 150th anniversary. Today, he oversees most of the Smithsonian's national museums, including the National Museum of American History, the National Portrait Gallery, the Smithsonian American Art Museum, the National Museum of the American Indian, the National Museum of African American History and Culture, and other museums and educational and cultural programs.

Dr. Kurin was appointed to the U.S. National Commission for UNESCO by several successive secretaries of state and to an international jury on cultural heritage by the Director-General of UNESCO. He helped UNESCO draft an international treaty on safeguarding the world's living cultural heritage, now ratified by more than 160 nations. He represents the Smithsonian on the President's Committee on the Arts and the Humanities and the White House Historical Association. He has been awarded the Smithsonian Secretary's Gold Medal for Exceptional Service, the Smithsonian American Art Museum Commission's Robert Mills Medal for Scholarship, and the Benjamin A. Botkin Prize for lifetime achievement in public folklore by the American Folklore Society.

Dr. Kurin has taught at the Johns Hopkins School of Advanced International Studies and frequently lectures at The George Washington University, as well as at universities and museums across the country and around the world. He regularly blogs for *Smithsonian* magazine and has led several Around the World expeditions for Smithsonian Journeys. He has given hundreds of speeches, including keynote addresses at Harvard and the International Council of Museums, and has appeared on television and radio programs numerous times.

Dr. Kurin is the author of scores of scholarly articles and several books, including *Hope Diamond: The Legendary History of a Cursed Gem*; *Madcap May: Mistress of Myth, Men, and Hope*; *Reflections of a Culture Broker: A View from the Smithsonian*; *Saving Haiti's Heritage: Cultural Recovery after the Earthquake*; and *Smithsonian Folklife Festival: Culture of, by, and for the People*. His latest book—*The Smithsonian's History of America in 101 Objects*—provides the inspiration for this Great Course. ■

About Smithsonian

Founded in 1846, the Smithsonian Institution is the world's largest museum and research complex, consisting of 19 museums and galleries, the National Zoological Park, and 9 research facilities. The total number of artifacts, works of art, and specimens in the Smithsonian's collections is estimated at 137 million. These collections represent America's rich heritage, art from across the globe, and the immense diversity of the natural and cultural world.

In support of its mission—the increase and diffusion of knowledge—the Smithsonian focuses on four Grand Challenges that describe its areas of study, collaboration, and exhibition: Unlocking the Mysteries of the Universe, Understanding and Sustaining a Biodiverse Planet, Valuing World Cultures, and Understanding the American Experience. The Smithsonian's partnership with The Great Courses is an opportunity to encourage continuous exploration by learners of all ages across these areas of study.

This course, *Experiencing America: A Smithsonian Tour through American History*, presents an audio-visual history of America, based on the Institution's critically acclaimed, best-selling book *The Smithsonian's History of America in 101 Objects*, published by The Penguin Press. Richard Kurin, aided by a team of Smithsonian curators and scholars, has carefully chosen a series of objects that take a unique and compelling approach to American history, life, and culture. As this course makes clear, you can learn the full story of America—from pre-European contact to the digital age—from a curatorial insider's guided tour of the Smithsonian's vast holdings. ■

Table of Contents

INTRODUCTION

LECTURE GUIDES

Table of Contents

Table of Contents

SUPPLEMENTAL MATERIAL

Experiencing America:
A Smithsonian Tour through American History

Scope:

How does one summarize the breadth and diversity of American history and culture? Where does one start? The collections of the Smithsonian—which has been caring for the nation's treasures since 1846—are a great place to begin. Simply, they represent our national memory.

The Smithsonian consists of 19 museums, 9 research centers, and the National Zoo, each a repository of collections reflecting our natural and cultural heritage. The museums usually arrange these collections in exhibits for visitors. But in this course, Smithsonian Under Secretary Richard Kurin and his colleagues have carefully selected some stellar treasures of American history to present directly to you in a stunning lecture tour. The selected objects represent American political, cultural, and scientific achievements, as well as military and social conflicts. They include both natural and man-made objects, as well as the technologies we use to understand these objects. These objects have been grouped in ways that are sometimes obvious, sometimes not so obvious, to offer a unique perspective on American history—a perspective that only the Smithsonian's collections can offer.

This course is arranged thematically, rather than chronologically. It begins with an artifact at the core of the American identity, but one surprisingly unfamiliar to many Americans: the Star-Spangled Banner, the flag that inspired the national anthem. Through it, you will learn about a little-understood war early in the United States' history, as well as the way objects are collected and preserved by the Smithsonian's museums.

From there, you will learn how leadership is established both through actions and through images via the possessions of two great presidents: George Washington and Dwight D. Eisenhower. Next, you will discover America's religious history through four objects that represent the diversity of faith and practice. Then, two lectures will discuss the history of slavery—its causes, its horrors, and the way it was brought to an end—as embodied through objects such as the cotton gin and the Emancipation Proclamation.

The next two lectures consider colonial expansion into the American West, as well as the cultures of the Native Americans who had lived there for more than 10,000 years. As such, you will learn about the gold that drove the settlers west and the art of both European Americans like Albert Bierstadt and Native Americans like Sitting Bull. The following two lectures consider the technologies that assisted this westward expansion, such as the steam locomotive and the telegraph. The next lecture considers the marks that waves of immigration have left on American society.

Technology and science become a stronger theme as the course examines the role of user-friendly design in American industrialization—from sewing machines to computers—and then considers how that same technological know-how took us to the sky and moon. The course also recounts the more solemn moments in our history, with artifacts from the Cold War and the Pearl Harbor and 9/11 attacks.

The course then considers some of the great personalities in American history and the objects through which we remember them: objects associated with Charles Lindbergh and Amelia Earhart and what they achieved as pioneers for flight and for women's rights. Then, you will learn how public images of leaders like Abraham Lincoln and Frederick Douglass—and even "Rosie the Riveter"—can change minds and inspire actions.

In addition, you will learn how popular culture has cemented our common identity, from Benjamin Franklin's presentation of the American image to France, to Kermit the Frog's message of friendship and tolerance. And you will consider how music can be more than just beautiful, but can be a force for good, as you are introduced to Marian Anderson.

In the final two lectures, you will learn how America views itself, both as a physical place and as a group of people. You will discover how we have explored the continent, the skies, and the universe through objects as simple as Lewis and Clark's compass and as complex and the Giant Magellan Telescope. Then, you will learn how we have tried—sometimes stumbling, but ultimately continuing to strive—to achieve the goals set out for us by the Declaration of Independence.

The objects you will learn about in this course were not just witnesses to history; they were a necessary part of history—as essential as the people and ideas that surrounded them. They are only a small part of the 137 objects contained in the Smithsonian's museums, archives, and research centers. Nonetheless, when taken together, they begin to reveal the richness of the tapestry of the American experience. ■

The Star-Spangled Banner—Inspiring the Anthem

Lecture 1

Objects are important because they are the material evidence of history—that's why we put special ones into our museums. Objects have an amazing ability to connect us to history in a powerful, emotional, visceral way. This course will examine American history using the greatest collection of historical artifacts on the planet, drawn from the collection of the Smithsonian Institution and its national museums. In this lecture, the object of attention is the Star-Spangled Banner.

The Defense of Fort McHenry

- No object in the Smithsonian is more inspirational than the Star-Spangled Banner. It is the flag millions of Americans refer to when they sing the national anthem. This flag tells the story of how our fledgling country was in peril in 1814; how the defense of a small fort in Baltimore gave heart to a people; and how we have defined, loved, almost destroyed, and saved a national treasure.

- America's War of 1812 has sometimes been called the United States' second war of independence. The 13 colonies comprised about 2.5 million people—mainly farmers, tradesmen, slaves, merchants, and their families. Occupying a mere sliver of North America, and surrounded by British, French, Spanish and Native American territories, they had just declared their independence as the "United States" in 1776.

- Although the United States was now independent, it was weak by contemporary military standards, particularly at sea. Britain and France were the great powers of the day. They were almost continually at war, vying for territory and trade advantages in Europe and around the world. Naval power was crucial in protecting the transport of raw materials from Asia, Africa, the Caribbean, and the Americas to Europe and for sending finished goods back around the planet.

- Meanwhile, in violation of the Treaty of Paris that had ended the American Revolution, Britain continued to occupy forts in the Northwest Territory on the American frontier. The British wanted to use Indians as a buffer between the United States and their colonies in Canada. They formed alliances with Native American tribes who sought to stop American settlers from encroaching on the natives' traditional lands and natural resources.

- The United States tried desperately to remain neutral in worldwide conflict between Britain and France. But facing a shortage of seafarers due to disease and defection, British admirals detained U.S. merchant vessels, capturing British citizens—including those who had become naturalized Americans—and impressing them into service on their ships. The British also blocked U.S. trade with France. The U.S. government was outraged, but with tiny armed forces and a weak navy, they were powerless to do very much.

- President Thomas Jefferson and his successor, James Madison, at first opted for a trade embargo against the British. They hoped that denial of American raw materials would persuade the British to stop the impressments. But New Englanders depended on Britain for half their trade and undermined the embargo.

- Western war hawks in Congress advocated the U.S. invasion of Canada as an alternative way of pressuring the British. For their part, the British were upset with the Americans for trading with the French and for raking in enormous profits off the war trade. By 1812, finding no other solution to British harassment, President Madison successfully urged Congress to declare war.

- American troops engaged with British troops and their Native American allies, led by such figures as Tecumseh, in a series of indecisive battles in southern Canada and the Great Lakes region. American troops burned Toronto, then called York; British troops took the village of Detroit.

- At this time, the Chesapeake Bay was a hub of the Eastern Seaboard trade. While British ships controlled much of the bay, Baltimore, the United States' fourth largest city, was a center of shipping, a staunchly anti-British city, and it harbored hundreds of privateers—independent ship owners granted the right by Madison to attack and take British ships.

- If British troops captured Baltimore, they could stop the privateers and strangle much of the United States' international commerce. If Baltimore fell, the United States would have to make concessions to Great Britain—its independence could be compromised.

- Before British forces turned their attention to Baltimore, they first struck a dramatic political blow. In August 1814, British General Robert Ross led 4,500 disciplined troops toward Washington DC. In those days, Washington's population was only about 20,000. It wasn't that important economically or even strategically. But it was our nation's capital, the headquarters of the Congress, and home of the president, and, thus, of great symbolic importance.

- At Bladensburg, Maryland, British troops routed a larger force of American regulars and untrained local militia who ran from battle. The city of Washington was now defenseless. First Lady Dolley Madison, servants, and slaves packed up valuables from the president's mansion and fled along with the rest of the government.

- On August 24, British troops set fire to the Capitol building, looted and burned the Executive Mansion, and ransacked the Treasury. Shock reverberated throughout the United States. President Madison returned to a devastated Washington.

- The British attack then turned northward to Baltimore. Only Fort McHenry, guarding the city's harbor, stood in the way of British victory. British Admiral Alexander Cochrane and General Ross had a simple plan: Pound Fort McHenry from ships anchored in the bay and send in troops by land to surround and take the fort. Then, the British could clear out the city's defenders.

- Baltimoreans were determined to defend themselves. Fifteen thousand militiamen protected the land route into the city. They sank junked boats to form a barrier across the inner harbor—the British would have to take the fort. At Fort McHenry, American commander Major George Armistead had 57 artillery pieces and 1,000 troops to face 3 British frigates, 5 bomb vessels, and a rocket-launching ship. Americans would face a tough bombardment.

- The British salvo began on September 13, 1814. Spherical bombs burst deadly shrapnel over Fort McHenry. Whooshing Congreve rockets rained fire. After the daylong, distant bombardment, British ships moved in for the kill. But as they came into range of the fort, the American gunners unleashed their response, knocking the rocket ship out of commission and forcing the bombers to retreat. The British continued the aerial assault. Meanwhile, British land troops, seeking to invade the city, were stalled by the American defenders. Britain's General Ross was killed in the battle.

The Poem and the Song

- Francis Scott Key, a 35-year-old Washington lawyer and amateur poet, observed the onslaught from a boat in the harbor. He was temporarily in British custody. Key had originally opposed the war. Nonetheless, he dutifully served in the militia and sadly witnessed the burning of Washington weeks before.

- Through that night, Key wondered whether Fort McHenry would stand or fall. As dawn approached, which flag would he see over the fort, the American Stars and Stripes or the British Union Jack? The answer would signal the fate of the nation.

- In the dawn's early light, Key could make out the flag flying over Fort McHenry. It was indeed the American flag. Baltimore held. The nation survived. Overcome by emotion, Key penned a four-stanza poem on the back of a letter. Days later, Key's poem was published as "The Defense of Fort McHenry," with instructions that it be sung to the tune of "To Anacreon in Heaven," a British popular song Key had in mind when composing the poem.

- That poem, and that song, are now familiar to all Americans as their national anthem, “The Star-Spangled Banner.” Key’s handwritten poem survived the battle. It is now treasured and cared for by the Maryland Historical Society. The first published copies of the song were distributed for free to veterans of the battle and all around the city of Baltimore. The song was first performed in public at Baltimore’s Holliday Street Theater on October 19, 1814. Mere weeks later, a music publisher released the sheet music under the new title, “The Star-Spangled Banner.”

- The war formally ended with the Christmastime Treaty of Ghent. The U.S. northern borders were settled, and Canada emerged with a stronger sense of national identity. Native Americans were the biggest losers, with the frontier more open than ever for settlement and westward expansion.

- The defense of Fort McHenry became a celebrated event. “The Star-Spangled Banner” soon became the standard patriotic song for national celebrations, banquets, and public performances. It contributed greatly to a growing sense of U.S. national identity and culture.

- The song grew in popularity during the Civil War. By the 1890s, the Army and Navy played “The Star-Spangled Banner” for the daily raising and lowering of the flag; a decade later soldiers and sailors came to attention during its playing and civilian audiences adopted the practice—standing for the song at theaters and baseball games. Congress designated it the national anthem in 1931.

The Story of the Flag

- In the summer of 1813, when Major Armistead took command of Fort McHenry, he ordered two flags from Baltimore flag maker Mary Pickersgill, who had learned her craft from her mother, who had sewn flags and uniforms for George Washington’s Continental Army.

- Armistead ordered a small “storm flag,” measuring about 17 by 25 feet, to be flown in bad weather. He also ordered an enormous

30-by-42-foot-long flag, called the garrison flag. It was made from worsted-wool bunting. It had 15 stars—the original 13 states, plus the new states Vermont and Kentucky. The white cotton stars were 2 feet across and stood out against an indigo background. The flag had 8 red stripes and 7 white ones, as stipulated by the 1794 Flag Act signed by President George Washington. Each stripe was 23 inches wide, sewn together from smaller strips.

- Pickersgill, her 13-year-old daughter Caroline, her two teenaged nieces Eliza and Margaret, and an African American indentured servant named Grace Wisher helped sew the flag by hand. They worked for about seven weeks in Pickersgill's little cottage. They then had to piece the flag together in the larger space of nearby Clagett's brewery. The huge garrison flag cost 405 dollars and 90 cents, more than most Baltimoreans earned in a year. Major Armistead then flew the flag over Fort McHenry so that the British could not miss seeing it.

- Major George Armistead kept the flag after the war. When he died in 1818, it was inherited by his widow, Louisa. For decades, it was carried and displayed during parades and patriotic events. Louisa, and her daughter Georgina, allowed war veterans and prominent people to take snips from the flag. Over time, about 200 square feet had been cut out of the flag. Over the years, the Smithsonian has acquired threads and fragments of the flag.

- The flag was hidden during the Civil War. In 1876, it was sent to the Centennial Exhibition in Philadelphia, but it was not displayed because of its fragility, even though a canvas backing had been added to shore it up.

- Eben Appleton, Armistead's grandson, inherited the flag in 1878 upon the death of his mother. He was besieged with continual requests to display the flag and even cut out fragments of the flag for special keepsakes.

- After Baltimore's sesquicentennial in 1880—when the flag was paraded and the last of the surviving defenders of Fort McHenry were honored, Appleton concluded that the flag was just too fragile for public display. He put it in storage. Decades later, in 1907, to avoid having to deal with requests for its display, the Appleton lent the flag to the Smithsonian. In 1912, Appleton officially donated the flag to the Smithsonian. The Star-Spangled Banner became a treasure in what was then called the National Museum.

The Star-Spangled Banner

- But it was in terrible shape. It was missing pieces, worn, and somewhat forlorn. The Smithsonian immediately hired conservator Amelia Bold Fowler and her team of 10 skilled seamstresses to restore it. They removed the canvas, replacing it with a linen backing attached to the flag with a specially patented interlocking mesh of about 1.7 million stitches. The cost of the project was 1,243 dollars.

- In 1914, with Baltimore officials pressing the Smithsonian to lend it to them for the upcoming centennial celebration of the defense of Fort McHenry, Appleton added a condition to his gift: The flag had to remain at the national museum "forever." The Star-Spangled Banner was then exhibited vertically in a giant glass display case in the Arts and Industries Building, where it was seen by millions over the next half century.

The Restoration of the Flag

- In 1964, the Star-Spangled Banner became the centerpiece of the new Museum of History and Technology, later renamed the National Museum of American History. The Star-Spangled Banner hung vertically on a specially constructed frame, soaring 50 feet high in a monumental open space known as Flag Hall.

- Over the decades, museum conservators realized that hanging was stretching the Star-Spangled Banner out of shape. Changes in temperature and humidity, as well as dust and pollutants, were harming the fibers. Bright light was fading its colors. By the mid-1990s, they devised a plan to preserve the nearly 200-year-old textile born in war and lovingly maltreated as a relic and an icon.

- The project needed major funding. First Lady Hillary Rodham Clinton devised the Save America's Treasures program, and the Star-Spangled Banner was number one on the list. Clothing designer Ralph Lauren helped fund the project, and the restoration began. Museum staff took down the flag and treated it in a temporary laboratory constructed in the museum.

- Visitors could watch conservators working on a scaffold suspended over the flag. The conservators' most painstaking task was carefully removing every one of the 1.7 million stitches sewn in 1914 by Amelia Fowler and her seamstresses and replacing the old backing with Stabiltex—a strong, stable, and sheer material. Per the terms of Appleton's request, the flag remained on display, even as it was being restored. The process took six years.

- Funds from the government, philanthropist Kenneth Behring, and others enabled us to construct a new home for the flag in the museum's central core. It is a special climate- and light-controlled, low-oxygen chamber designed by Smithsonian architects, engineers, and conservators. The flag would be displayed on an adjustable, angled table so that it could be displayed without stressing the fabric. By the time President George W. Bush, General Colin Powell, and others ceremonially opened the renovated museum, nearly 58 million dollars had been spent caring for the flag.

- The allure of the Star-Spangled Banner in America's memory has fueled displays of the flag during poignant moments of our collective national experience: Marines raising it at Iwo Jima, astronauts planting it on the moon, heroic athletes receiving their Olympic gold medals under its gaze, first responders hoisting it over the remnants of the World Trade Center after the attacks of September 11. The flag is also used as a symbol of protest—a call to do better and to realize the highest ideals of our national purpose.

Featured Object

The Star-Spangled Banner

Suggested Reading

Hickey, *The War of 1812.*

Leepson, *What So Proudly We Hailed.*

Taylor, Brodie, and Kendrick, *The Star-Spangled Banner.*

The Star-Spangled Banner—Inspiring the Anthem

Lecture 1—Transcript

Why are objects important? Well, they are simply the material evidence of history. Objects give us something to grab onto, to puzzle over and wonder about; that's why we put special ones into our museums. When we examine them, objects tell stories—sometimes simple, sometimes complex—and not only about the historical past, but also about how they are understood and treated as part of our heritage today. Objects have an amazing ability to connect us to history in a powerful, emotional, visceral way, a way in which verbal and textual accounts do not. This is why more than 30 million people visit the Smithsonian every year and are informed, amazed, and inspired by what they see.

We are about to examine the major developments and themes in our nation's history, not through a chronology of events and a series of names, dates, and places, but rather, through the objects that that have become touchstones—icons, if you will—of the American experience. This is a show and tell of American history using the greatest collection of historical artifacts on the planet, drawn from the collection of the Smithsonian Institution and its national museums.

I'm Richard Kurin, the Under Secretary of the Smithsonian for History, Art, and Culture. As an anthropologist and cultural historian, I have spent the whole of my professional career—the last four decades—working for the Smithsonian researching, exhibiting, caring for and writing about these objects and the people who made and used them. As we view these objects together, I'll not only take you back into American history to understand the development of our country and its people, but also take you behind the scenes at the Smithsonian so you get a sense of how and why we acquire, study, conserve, display, and value these objects in the way we do.

No object in the Smithsonian is more inspirational than the Star-Spangled Banner. I think of it not as an American flag, but rather, the American flag. It is the flag millions of Americans refer to—many unknowingly—when they sing the national anthem. This flag tells the story of how our fledgling country was in peril in 1814; how the defense of a small fort in Baltimore gave heart to a people; and how we have defined, loved, and almost destroyed, and saved a national treasure.

America's War of 1812 has sometimes been called the United States' second war of independence. Although the United States was now an independent country, it was a weak by contemporary military standards, particularly at sea. Britain and France were the great powers of the day; they were almost continually at war, vying for territory and trade advantages in Europe and around the world. Naval power was crucial in protecting the transport of raw materials from Asia, Africa, the Caribbean, and the Americas to Europe, and for sending finished goods back around the planet.

Meanwhile, in violation of the Treaty of Paris that had ended the American Revolution, Britain continued to occupy forts in the Northwest Territory on the American frontier. The British wanted to use Indians as a buffer between the United States and their colonies in Canada. They formed alliances with Native American tribes, who sought to stop American settlers from encroaching on the natives' traditional land and natural resources. This was especially important to Britain after the Louisiana Purchase in 1803. The Louisiana Purchase, obtained from Napoleon for 15 million dollars, nearly doubled the size of the United States, adding over 800,000 square miles of territory west of the Mississippi River.

The United States tried desperately to remain neutral in worldwide conflict between Britain and France. But facing a shortage of seafarers due to disease and defection, British admirals detained U.S. merchant vessels, capturing British citizens, including those who had become naturalized Americans, and impressing them into service on their ships. The British also blocked U.S. trade with France. The U.S. government was outraged, but with a tiny armed forces and a weak navy, they were powerless to do very much.

President Thomas Jefferson and his successor, James Madison, at first opted for a trade embargo against the British. They hoped that denial of American raw materials would persuade the British to stop the impressments. But New Englanders, dependent on Britain for half their trade, undermined the embargo.

Western war hawks in Congress advocated the U.S. invasion of Canada as an alternative way of pressuring the British. For their part, the British were upset with the Americans for trading with the French and for raking in enormous profits off the war trade. By 1812, finding no other solution to British harassment, President Madison successfully urged Congress to declare war.

American troops engaged with British troops and their Native American allies, led by such figures as Tecumseh, in a series of indecisive battles in southern Canada and the Great Lakes region. American troops burned Toronto, then called York. British troops took the village of Detroit. At this time, the Chesapeake Bay was a hub of the Eastern Seaboard trade. While British ships controlled much of the bay, Baltimore, the United States' fourth largest city, was a center of shipping, a staunchly anti-British city, and it harbored hundreds of privateers—independent ship owners granted the right by Madison to attack and take British ships. They were basically legalized pirates. If British troops captured Baltimore, they could stop the privateers and strangle much of the United States' international commerce. If Baltimore fell, the United States would have to make concessions to Great Britain, and its independence could be compromised.

Before British forces turned their attention to Baltimore, they first struck a dramatic political blow. In August 1814, British General Robert Ross led 4,500 disciplined troops toward Washington, D.C. In those days, Washington's population was only about 20,000 people. It really wasn't that important economically or even strategically, but it was our nation's capital, having become the seat of government in 1800. Washington was the headquarters of the Congress, the home of the president, and thus, of great symbolic importance.

At Bladensburg, Maryland, British troops routed a larger force of American regulars and untrained local militia who ran from battle. The city of Washington was now defenseless. First Lady Dolley Madison, servants, and slaves packed up valuables from the president's mansion, including an esteemed version of the Gilbert Stuart painting of George Washington, and fled along with the rest of government.

On August 24th, British troops set fire to the Capitol building, looted and burned the Presidential Mansion, and ransacked the Treasury. Shock reverberated throughout the United States. President Madison returned to a devastated Washington. Repairs on the Presidential Mansion had to wait until war's end, when heavy coats of white paint covered the scorched brick and popularized the building's earlier designation as the White House.

Now, the British turned northward to Baltimore. Only Fort McHenry, guarding the city's harbor, stood in the way of British victory. British Admiral Alexander Cochrane and General Ross had a simple plan—pound Fort McHenry from ships anchored in the bay, and send in troops by land to surround and take the fort. Then the British could clear out the defenders.

Baltimoreans were determined to defend themselves. Fifteen thousand militiamen protected the land route into the city. They sank junked boats to form a barrier across the inner harbor—the British would have to take the fort. At Fort McHenry, American commander Major George Armistead had 57 artillery pieces and 1,000 troops to face three British frigates, five bomb vessels, and one rocket-launching ship anchored two miles away, just beyond the range of his guns. The frigates were about 140 feet long, much larger and much more formidable than any ships the Americans could muster. Americans would face a tough bombardment.

The British salvo began on September 13, 1814. Spherical bombs burst deadly shrapnel over Fort McHenry; whooshing Congreve rockets rained fire. We have some of those bombs and rockets at the Smithsonian. The rockets, in particular, could be launched from far out in the harbor, up to two and a half miles away.

After the daylong, distant bombardment, British ships moved in for the kill. But as they came into range of the fort, the American gunners unleashed their response, knocking the rocket ship out of commission and forcing the bombers to retreat. The British continued the aerial assault; bombs and rockets lit up a tempestuous night sky filled with lightning and torrential rain. Meanwhile, British land troops, seeking to invade the city, were stalled by the American defenders, and Britain's General Ross was killed in the battle.

Francis Scott Key, a 35-year-old Washington lawyer and amateur poet, observed the onslaught from a boat in the harbor. He was temporarily in British custody. He had boarded the ship to negotiate the release of an American civilian prisoner, but he was kept at sea during the battle because he had actually directly witnessed the British preparations. Key had originally opposed the war. He had written to a friend that he would rather see "the American flag lowered in disgrace than have it stand for persecution and dishonor." Nonetheless, he dutifully served in the militia and sadly witnessed the burning of Washington weeks before. Through that night, Key wondered whether Fort McHenry would stand or fall. As dawn approached, what flag would he see over the fort, the American Stars and Stripes, or the British Union Jack? The answer would signal the fate of the nation.

A year earlier, in the summer of 1813, when Major Armistead took command of Fort McHenry, he had written, "We have no suitable ensign to display over the Fort, and it is my desire to have a flag so large that the British will have no difficulty seeing it from a distance." Armistead ordered two flags from Baltimore flag-maker Mary Pickersgill. Pickersgill had learned her craft from her mother, who had sewn flags and uniforms for George Washington's Continental Army.

Armistead ordered a small "storm flag," measuring about 17 feet by 25 feet, to be flown in bad weather. He also ordered an enormous 30-by-42-foot-long flag, called the garrison flag. To give you an idea of how large this was, picture five full-grown men standing on each other's shoulders. The flag is taller than that. It was made from worsted-wool bunting. It had 15 stars; the original 13 plus the new states, Vermont and Kentucky. The white cotton stars were two feet across and stood out against an indigo background. The flag had eight red stripes, and seven white ones, as stipulated by the 1794 Flag Act signed by President George Washington. Each stripe was 23 inches wide—about as wide as my shoulders—sewn together from smaller strips.

Pickersgill; her 13-year old daughter Caroline; her two teenaged nieces, Eliza and Margaret; and an African American indentured servant named Grace helped sew the flag by hand. According to a letter written by Caroline decades later, they often labored until midnight. They worked for about seven weeks in Pickersgill's little cottage. Then they had to piece together the flag in the larger space of nearby Clagett's brewery. The large garrison flag cost $405.90, more than most Baltimoreans earned in a year. Major Armistead then flew the flag over Fort McHenry so that the British could not miss seeing it.

So now, imagine Francis Scott Key aboard the British ship having witnessed the bombardment by day and seen and heard the bombs bursting in air all night. What flag would he see as dawn broke? Would it be that enormous American flag, meaning the defenders would have held the fort? Or would it be a British Union Jack, indicating the fort, the city, and maybe even the country had been defeated?

In the dawn's early light, Key could make out the flag flying over Fort McHenry. It was, indeed, the American flag. Baltimore held. The nation survived. Overcome by emotion, Key penned a four-stanza poem on the back of a letter. Days later, Key's poem was published as "The Defense of Fort McHenry" with instructions that it be sung to the tune of "To Anacreon in Heaven," a British popular song Key had in mind when composing the poem. That poem, and that song, are now familiar to all Americans as the national anthem, "The Star-Spangled Banner." Its famous first verse, which poignantly ends with a question mark, is moving when read, but even more moving when sung. Therefore, to sing it for you now, I'm very pleased to present recording artist Julia Nixon:

O say can you see, by the dawn's early light,

What so proudly we hail'd at the twilight's last gleaming,

Whose broad stripes and bright stars through the perilous fight

O'er the ramparts we watch'd were so gallantly streaming?

And the rocket's red glare, the bombs bursting in air,

Gave proof through the night that our flag was still there,

O say does that star-spangled banner yet wave

O'er the land of the free and the home of the brave?

Thank you, Julia, for that moving performance.

Key's handwritten poem survived the battle. It's now treasured and cared for by the Maryland Historical Society. Those first published copies of the song were distributed for free to veterans of the battle and all around the city of Baltimore. The song was first performed in public at Baltimore's Holliday Street Theater on October 19, 1814. Mere weeks later, a music publisher released the sheet music under the new title, "The Star-Spangled Banner."

The war formally ended with the Christmas-time Treaty of Ghent. The U.S. northern borders were settled, and Canada emerged with a stronger sense of national identity. Native Americans were the biggest losers, with the frontier more open than ever for settlement and westward expansion.

The defense of Fort McHenry became a celebrated event. In Baltimore, punchbowls were even crafted in the form of the bombs that had failed to dislodge the patriotic defenders. "The Star-Spangled Banner" soon became the standard patriotic song for national celebrations, banquets,, public performances, and was performed widely. It contributed greatly to a growing sense of national identity and culture in the United States.

As the song became ever more popular, abolitionists pointed out the irony of the lyrics, particularly the line "the land of the free," because Francis Scott Key was a slaveholder. Interestingly enough, it was Key's law partner and brother in law, Roger Taney, who helped popularize the account of the song's writing, who, as Chief Justice of the United States, later authored the infamous Dred Scott decision in 1857, which solidified the legal status of slavery throughout the United States.

Nonetheless, the song grew in popularity during the Civil War. By the 1890s, the Army and Navy played "The Star-Spangled Banner" for the daily raising and lowering of the flag. A decade later soldiers and sailors came to attention during its playing, and civilian audiences adopted the practice, standing for the song at theaters and baseball games. Congress designated it the national anthem in 1931.

But what of the flag itself? Major George Armistead kept the flag after the war. When he died in 1818, it was inherited by his widow, Louisa. For decades, it was carried and displayed during parades and patriotic events. According to newspapers, it was regarded as "a holy relic never disgraced, and receiving now the homage of friends." Louisa, and her daughter Georgina allowed war veterans and prominent people to take snippings from the flag. One official supposedly got a star. Others were buried with swatches. Over time, some 200 square feet had been cut out of the flag.

Over the years, we at the Smithsonian have sometimes acquired threads and fragments from the flag. Now, let me show you something very special in the Smithsonian's collections. I'll have to put on my curator's gloves so I don't transfer any oils from my hands that might otherwise damage the artifact.

Here in my hand in this framed case is a fragment of the original Star-Spangled Banner; it was clipped in 1880. It later came to us by way of several intermediate owners. Many people ask whether we have found the missing star—we have not. The flag was hidden during the Civil War. In 1876 it was sent to the U.S. Centennial Exhibition in Philadelphia, but it was not displayed because of its fragility, even though a canvas backing had been added to shore it up. Ben Appleton, Armistead's grandson, inherited the flag in 1878 upon the death of his mother. He was besieged with continual requests to display the flag and even cut out fragments of the flag for special keepsakes. In fact, he's the person who cut out this fragment.

After Baltimore's sesquicentennial in 1880, when the flag was paraded and the last of the surviving defender's of Ft. McHenry were honored, Appleton concluded that the flag was just too fragile for public display. He put it in storage. Decades later, in 1907, to avoid having to deal with requests for its display, the somewhat reclusive Appleton lent the flag to the Smithsonian. It arrived in a modest canvas bag.

In 1912, Appleton wrote a letter to Charles Walcott, the Secretary of the Smithsonian, saying "It has always been my intention to present the flag during my lifetime to that Institution in the country where it could be conveniently seen by the public, and where it would be well cared for."

The Star-Spangled Banner became a treasure in what was then called the National Museum.

But it was in terrible shape. Here you can see the formerly proud garrison flag hanging outside on the façade of the Smithsonian's Castle building on the National Mall in Washington, D.C. It's missing pieces; it's worn and somewhat forlorn. The Smithsonian immediately hired conservator Amelia Bold Fowler and her team of ten skilled seamstresses to save the flag. They set up in the Smithsonian Castle and removed the canvas, replacing it with a linen backing attached to the flag with a specially patented interlocking mesh of some 1.7 million stitches. The cost of the project, a little over $1,200.

In 1914, with Baltimore officials pressing the Smithsonian to lend it back to them for the upcoming centennial celebration of the Defense of Fort McHenry, Appleton added a condition to his gift—the flag had to remain at the national museum "forever."

The Star-Spangled Banner was then exhibited in a giant glass display case in the Arts and Industries Building, where it was seen by millions over the next half century. The only time the flag was removed was during World War II, from 1942 to 1944, when President Franklin Roosevelt feared Germany might bomb the National Mall. The flag was packed up and sent for safe keeping, along with other important national collections, to Shenandoah National Park near Luray, Virginia.

In 1964, the Star-Spangled Banner became the centerpiece of the new Museum of History and Technology, later renamed the National Museum of American History. The Star-Spangled Banner hung vertically on a specially constructed frame, soaring 50-feet high in a monumental open space known as Flag Hall. Most of the time, a covering flag blocked it from view. But several times a day, the museum would play a recorded version of the national anthem and lift the covering flag to unveil the historic Star-Spangled Banner to the public.

Over the decades, museum conservators realized that hanging was stretching the Star-Spangled Banner out of shape. Changes in temperature and humidity, as well as dust and pollutants, were harming the fibers. Bright light was fading its colors. By the mid-1990s, they devised a plan to preserve the nearly 200-year-old textile born in war and lovingly maltreated as a relic and an icon.

The project needed major funding. Enter then-First-Lady Hillary Rodham Clinton and her Save America's Treasures program. The Star-Spangled Banner was number one on the list. Clothing designer Ralph Lauren helped fund the project, and the restoration began. Museum staff took down the flag and treated it in a temporary laboratory constructed in the museum. Visitors could watch conservators working on a scaffold suspended over the flag as, inch by inch, they vacuumed and cleaned the flag of oil, mold, dust, and other detritus. Their most painstaking task? Carefully removing every one of the 1.7 million stitches sewn in 1914 by Amelia Fowler and her seamstresses and replacing the old backing with Stabiltex, a strong, stable, and sheer material. Per the terms of Appleton's request, the flag remained on display, even as it was being restored.

The conservation process took six years. Funds from the government, philanthropist Kenneth Behring, and others enabled us to construct a new home for the flag in the museum's central core. This is a special climate- and light-controlled, low-oxygen chamber designed by Smithsonian architects, engineers, and conservators. The flag would be displayed on an adjustable, angled table so it could be displayed without stressing the fabric. By the time President George W. Bush, General Colin Powell, and others ceremonially opened the renovated museum, we'd spent nearly 58 million dollars caring for the flag.

The new installation is striking. You walk along a darkened hallway, seeing painted images of the War of 1812, passing a charred timber from the Presidential Mansion, burned during that invasion of Washington, as well as seeing a rocket and a bomb from the attack on Fort McHenry that night. You imagine Francis Scott Key in the dark out on Chesapeake Bay, his eyes straining to see the fort and the flag flying above it; you turn a corner and then with the light simulating the early dawn, through a wall of glass, you see the Star-Spangled Banner. Every time I see it I get chills.

The threadbare fragility of the physical flag is evident, but it speaks proudly nonetheless. The words of Key's poem are projected onto a back wall. The question mark about the endurance of the country—whether the banner would still be waving after the battle, is answered by the flag's very presence. It is as awe inspiring as a museum experience can be.

The allure of the Star-Spangled Banner in America's memory has fueled displays of the flag during poignant moments of our collective national experience; think of Marines raising it at Iwo Jima, of astronauts planting it on the moon, heroic athletes receiving their Olympic gold medals under its gaze, first responders hoisting it over the remnants of the World Trade Center after the attacks of September 11. And as the exhibition reminds us, the flag is also used as a symbol of protest, a call to do better, to realize the highest ideals of our national purpose.

Among the millions who annually see the flag is a special group. Just outside the Star-Spangled Banner chamber in Flag Hall, the museum periodically holds public swearing-in ceremonies for new naturalized citizens. When it does, there's not a dry eye in the house. Previously naturalized citizens, like former Secretary of State Madeleine Albright, have sworn-in children from Bosnia, refugees from Afghanistan, a serviceman originally from Ghana, and many others.

The ceremony is an affirmation of citizenship and the promise of America as home to those who make the commitment to belong. That affirmation is precisely the act that the British refused to recognize, and the very reason for the War of 1812, and the action—the defense of our freedom, that led to the Star-Spangled Banner becoming the embodiment of the American ideal.

Presidents and Generals—Images of Leadership

Lecture 2

From the inception of the United States, the president has functioned as the head of state and the commander in chief of its military, a role that is enshrined in the U.S. Constitution. American presidents from George Washington onward have been both aware of this vital responsibility and of how they appeared in that role to the public, troops and civilians, and enemies. In this lecture, you will learn how the images of George Washington, Abraham Lincoln, and Dwight D. Eisenhower dealt with and construed symbols of national leadership—how they drew upon symbols of military command to project their role as the elected heads of U.S. democracy.

George Washington's Uniforms and Swords

- As the Commander of the Continental Army in the American Revolution, General George Washington was not only called upon to direct his troops, but also to forge an image of leadership for the new, democratic nation. He was highly attuned to the importance of his military bearing and attire in asserting the rebellious Americans' inherent equality to British.

- At the same time, he knew that he must also portray the dignity of the cause of liberty to a worldwide audience of tottering empires and restive colonies. His uniform at the Smithsonian remains a potent emblem of the strength and authority Washington brought to the Continental Army and to the fledgling nation.

- Washington served as aide to British General Edward Braddock in the Virginia Regiment during the French and Indian War. He was a keen student of the marks of leadership, noting the way a commanding officer conveyed his authority on the battlefield. When he became a colonel and commander of the regiment, he ordered new uniforms from London and was quite attentive to their colors and matters of style.

- In June 1775, a few months after the Revolutionary War began, Washington accepted the commission from the Continental Congress to serve as the commander in chief of the new Continental Army. Washington believed that a commander had to look commanding. He insisted on proper uniforms, not only for himself and other officers, but also for the troops. Washington wanted his army to look like a unified, professional organization, a worthy opponent of the British troops.

George Washington's Uniform

- To contrast with the British redcoats, Washington chose the blue and buff colors of Virginia's Fairfax militia. Washington's design for the uniform was used by the U.S. Army until the beginning of the Civil War, and dress blues are still used by the Army today.

- The pieces that make up Washington's uniform at the Smithsonian were all worn by him, but made at different times. The waistcoat and breeches, made of buff wool, date from the Revolutionary War period. They were worn when he was the commander in chief of the Continental Army, and they are represented in Charles Willson Peale's 1779 painting of Washington after the Battle of Princeton.

- The regimental blue wool coat is part of a uniform made for Washington in 1789, well after the war ended. The coat has a buff wool rise-and-fall wide collar, buff cuffs and lapels, and buff lining; there is a row of distinctive yellow tombac buttons, made of a copper and zinc alloy, on each lapel, as well as on each cuff. Washington periodically wore the uniform until his death in 1799.

- Washington used several swords during the Revolutionary War. His service sword was a simple hunting hanger, also called a couteau, meant to hang from a belt. It has a slightly curved, grooved steel blade, a silver-mounted cross guard and pommel, and a green ivory grip.

- Washington used this sword after 1777. On its scabbard is etched "J Bailey, Fish Kill," because the sword was remounted with a new hilt and silver cross guard in Fishkill, New York, by John Bailey, an immigrant cutler from Sheffield, England. It was Washington's battle sword for much of the Revolutionary War. He may have also used it during his presidency, when he last reviewed the troops in Cumberland, Maryland, and Bedford, Pennsylvania, in 1794 during the Whiskey Rebellion.

- Washington bequeathed five swords to his five nephews. Samuel Washington, who was among the troops reviewed by his uncle in 1794, got to choose first. He chose one with a green grip. He left the sword to his son, Samuel T. Washington, who donated it to the United States; decades later, it was transferred to the Smithsonian.

- The uniform came to the Smithsonian in 1883 and has been on display almost continuously since then. It is perennially one of the most popular of the Smithsonian's holdings, seen by millions of people every year.

Paintings of Washington

- As the nation's first president, Washington was very conscious of making the transition from military leadership to civil rule. He had no desire to be king and was proud to have been elected to serve. But he was well aware that monarchs—from ancient times to his own—had used portraits to shape their image and express their values. Washington made use of this tradition throughout his presidency, most dramatically in a painting by Gilbert Stuart.

- Stuart was a Rhode Island–born artist who moved to England as a young man to make his name. He returned to his country as a mature artist to paint the portraits of many noteworthy and historically important Americans. In November of 1794, Stuart went to Philadelphia, the temporary capital of the United States, to meet Washington and arrange for sittings for a portrait.

***George Washington* (Lansdowne Portrait), Gilbert Stuart, 1796**

- Washington sat for Stuart at least three times in 1795 and 1796. Two of these sessions resulted in two waist-length portraits, including the unfinished painting known today as the *Athenaeum* portrait because of its later ownership by the Boston Athenaeum. Stuart repainted that image on commission more than 75 times, referring to it as his 100-dollar bill, its price per copy. This is the image that appears today on the one-dollar bill.

- In the spring of 1796, Senator William Bingham, then one of America's wealthiest men, and his wife, Anne, commissioned Stuart to paint a third portrait of the president. The painting was a gift for the British Marquis of Lansdowne, in recognition of his support for the American cause during the Revolution.

- The new painting was the first life-size, full-length portrait to depict George Washington as president and civic leader of the nation, rather than as a general in his military uniform. Washington is depicted in the black velvet suit he wore for public appearances as president, demonstrating his citizen status in an age dominated by royal rule and military conflict.

- The setting is entirely fictional, symbolizing the civic republic that the United States aspired to be. Overall, the portrait speaks to Washington's remarkable character and to post–Revolutionary War optimism. It reinforces the idea that the United States, thanks to the leadership of George Washington, faced a bright future.

- The completed painting was shipped to London in the fall of 1796, and it remained in British hands until 1968, passing from owner to owner, occasionally visiting the United States for special exhibitions. In 1968, it was installed in the newly opened National Portrait Gallery on long-term loan. The portrait stayed on public view at the gallery until 2000, when the building closed for a major renovation.

- That year, the painting's owner, Lord Harry Dalmeny, decided to sell the painting for 20 million dollars. Marc Pachter, the director of the National Portrait Gallery at the time, took to the airwaves, appearing on the *TODAY* show with Matt Lauer. Pachter explained the significance of the pending loss of the painting to about 9 million viewers.

- One viewer, Fred W. Smith, chair of the Donald W. Reynolds Foundation, was impressed by Pachter's determination to save the painting for the nation. The Reynolds Foundation made a generous donation to purchase the painting for the American people and present it to the gallery. When the gallery reopened in 2006, the Lansdowne portrait of George Washington was installed in a spectacular new setting.

- Gilbert Stuart was commissioned to paint additional versions of this portrait. Smithsonian scholars have carried out historical research and technical examinations of the several paintings. There are also several derivative paintings in the halls of the United States of Congress and other public buildings.

- There is a healthy debate over whether Stuart or another artist in his studio painted the version that has hung in the White House since 1800. But the Smithsonian has determined that the National Portrait Gallery's Lansdowne portrait is indeed the original.

Abraham Lincoln

- George Washington is not the only president who was concerned about his public appearance, first as a general and then as president. Abraham Lincoln, too, was concerned about how he would look as the nation's leader as he took office during the toughest of times leading up to the Civil War.

- Lincoln was quite cognizant of his gaunt, homey appearance. Nonetheless, he developed an appreciation for how he appeared both to the public and to military and political leaders. Just after his election, he grew out his beard—perhaps in an effort for the incoming president to imitate his future generals and look more like a commander in chief. Most of the military leaders of the time grew whiskers; it was a style that had gained in popularity in the late 1850s and perhaps illustrated male virility and prowess.

- Lincoln was careful to be pictured in particular poses for coverage by *Harper's Weekly*, the newspapers of the day, and for photographers like Civil War documentarian Mathew Brady. In fact, it was one of Brady's assistants, Andrew Berger, who took the image used today on the U.S. five-dollar bill. One of Lincoln's most famous images was among his last, made on February 5, 1865, when he sat for Alexander Gardner, one of Brady's former associates.

- Gardner had already photographed Lincoln half a dozen times, and the two men had great respect for each other. The photo session was to provide *Harper's Weekly* magazine and other publications with images of Lincoln for his second term, which would begin the next month.

- The portrait was shot on an imperial-sized glass-plate negative, 16 by 20 inches. If you wanted a big picture then, you needed a big camera and a large glass plate. Gardner was a photographic artist. For the shot, he focused the camera and set the aperture to a very shallow depth of field. This created an effect where Lincoln's eyes and the front of his face are in very intense focus while the ears and back of his head are fuzzy.

- After exposing the glass plate, Gardner probably followed his usual procedure, using a flame to apply a varnish to finish it. Somehow a crack emerged. It did not break the plate, but it made the image unusable. Gardner made one print, and then, seeing it as a failure, likely destroyed the plate.

- The session turned out to be Lincoln's last formal photographic sitting—though not the last photograph of Lincoln—and it is unknown if anyone saw this print in 1865. Although the portrait is quite sensitive to exposure to light and only rarely exhibited, it quickly became one of the iconic images of the 16th president.

Dwight D. Eisenhower

- The concern for projecting military leadership and presidential bearing has carried over to the modern era. Consider the last president to have been a general, Dwight D. Eisenhower.

- Eisenhower, a Kansan born in 1890, was a five-star general in the United States Army. He served as the Supreme Commander of the Allied Forces in Europe during World War II and was ultimately responsible for planning the invasion of France in 1944.

- Among the huge and various logistical and strategic matters that Eisenhower had to contend with was the Army uniform, the basic dress that soldiers wore every day. Eisenhower thought that the uniform, particularly the long wool jacket, was poorly fitted for combat. Like Washington before him, he was conscious of how he and the military presented itself. He wanted a uniform that would be neater and more flattering.

- In March 1943, Eisenhower called for his tailor, Michael Popp, to take the Army's wool field jacket and modify it to his specifications. Popp took the Army-issued M-1944—also known as the European Theater of Operations, or ETO, jacket—and turned it into the "Eisenhower jacket," or "Ike jacket." He shortened the length, gave the collar a more elegant line, and tailored the shoulders so that they would form a clear outline. The Eisenhower jacket became standard issue for U.S. troops beginning in November 1944.

- The Smithsonian has several Eisenhower jackets in its collections. One is in the form of a portrait of General Eisenhower that was used for the cover of the January 1, 1945, issue of *Time* magazine when he was selected as man of the year for 1944. In the cover art, the top of his well-tailored jacket sets off his four-star Army hat (he was given his fifth star in December of 1944). The flags of the Allies wave behind him.

- Another Ike jacket from the Smithsonian collections belonged to World War II hero Audie L. Murphy, who was one of the most decorated soldiers in the war, fighting in nine campaigns. He was wounded three times and earned about 30 decorations and awards, including the Medal of Honor. Even now, the Ike jacket is an iconic symbol of the World War II GI.

- In 1952, Eisenhower ran for president of the United States, was elected, and then was reelected in 1956. Among his accomplishments were ending the Korean War, signing significant civil rights legislation, and supporting the building of the interstate highway system.

- While Eisenhower's presidency was later characterized by the baby boomers as an era of complacency and cultural conservatism, the jacket reminds us of Eisenhower's leadership—how he modernized the army and the government in both war and in peace—and how he as general and president reassured the nation of its place in the world.

Featured Objects

George Washington's Uniform and Sword

Gilbert Stuart's Lansdowne Portrait of George Washington

The "Ike" Jacket

Suggested Reading

Barratt and Miles, *Gilbert Stuart*.

Chernow, *Washington*.

Eisenhower, *Eisenhower at War*.

Presidents and Generals—Images of Leadership
Lecture 2—Transcript

From the inception of the United States, the president has functioned as the head of state and the commander-in-chief of the military. This office combines under civilian democratic rule two important functions that in other nations are often occupied by two undemocratically selected individuals—a genealogically designated king or queen and an appointed or power-seizing general.

The role of president as Commander-in-Chief of the armed forces is enshrined in the U.S. Constitution, Article II, Section 2, Clause I. American presidents from George Washington onward have been both aware of this vital responsibility and aware how they appeared in that role to the public, to their troops and civilians they led, and the enemies they battled.

As the Commander of the Continental Army in the American Revolution, George Washington was not only called upon to direct his troops, but also forge an image of leadership for the new, democratic nation. He was highly attuned to the importance of his military bearing and attire in asserting the rebellious Americans' inherent equality to British. At the same time, he knew that he must also portray the dignity of the cause of liberty to a worldwide audience of tottering empires and restive colonies. His uniform at the Smithsonian remains a potent emblem of the strength and authority Washington brought to the Continental Army and to the fledgling nation.

Washington was born in 1732 to a wealthy planter family of northern Virginia that raised tobacco with slave labor. At 17, he surveyed the frontier regions of the colonies. He served as an aide to British General Edward Braddock in the Virginia Regiment during the French and Indian War. Washington was a keen student of the marks of leadership, noting the way a commanding officer conveyed his authority on the battlefield. Washington clearly had already formed expectations about the importance of uniforms; in a letter he described the sad state of the regiment's uniforms as "a suit of thin sleazy Cloth without lining, and without Waistcoats except of sorry Flannel." When Washington became a colonel and commander of the regiment, he ordered new uniforms from London and was quite attentive to their colors and matters of style.

In June 1775, a few months after the Revolutionary War began, Washington accepted the commission from the Continental Congress to serve as the commander-in-chief of the new Continental Army. Washington believed that a commander had to look commanding. He had to comport himself in a dignified, professional manner. His uniform had to signal high rank, as well as attract and hold attention. He insisted on proper uniforms, not only for himself and other officers, but also for the troops. Washington wanted his army to look like a unified, professional organization, a worthy opponent of the British troops.

But in 1775, most soldiers wore their everyday clothing, sometimes dyed brown to provide a vague sense of a uniform. This wasn't just an aesthetic problem; without uniforms and insignia, it is nearly impossible to tell soldier from civilian, or sergeant from major. Before Washington's appointment, the army tried various makeshift solutions. Some soldiers would add a cockade to their hats—a rosette or knot of ribbon in a particular color that indicated their rank and regiment. Others wore ribbons of various colors on their epaulettes. High-ranking officers wore their ribbons across their chests.

Obviously, this would not meet Washington's exacting standards, so he designed a new uniform for the Continental Army. To contrast with the British redcoats, Washington chose the blue and buff colors of Virginia's Fairfax militia. Dark blue uniforms were also already in use by militias in New York and in New Jersey. Plus, the color was associated with the Whig party, an anti-royalist party in both Britain and America. Washington's design for the uniform was used by the U.S. Army until the beginning of the Civil War, and dress blues are still used by the Army today.

The pieces that make up Washington's uniform at the Smithsonian were all worn by him, but made at different times. The waistcoat and the breeches were made of buff wool, and they date from the Revolutionary War period. They were worn when he was the commander-in-chief of the Continental Army, and they were represented in Charles Willson Peale's 1779 painting of Washington after the Battle of Princeton.

The regimental blue wool coat is part of a uniform made for Washington in 1789, well after the war ended. The coat has a buff wool rise-and-fall wide collar, buff cuffs and lapels, and buff lining. There is a row of distinctive yellow tombac buttons, made of a copper and zinc alloy, on each lapel, as well as on each cuff. Records reveal that Washington wore this uniform when he visited Philadelphia on Provisional Army duty in 1789.

That uniform may even be depicted in John Ramage's watercolor of the same year, which is now held in the Smithsonian's National Portrait Gallery. This miniature, painted on an ivory amulet, also contains a lock of Washington's hair and was created as a keepsake for his wife, Martha. Washington periodically wore the uniform until his death in 1799.

Washington used several swords during the Revolutionary War. His service sword was a simple hunting hanger, also called a couteau, meant to hang from a belt. It has a slightly curved, grooved steel blade, a silver-mounted cross guard and a pommel, and a green ivory grip. Washington used this sword after 1777. On its scabbard is etched "J Bailey, Fish Kill," as the sword was remounted with a new hilt and silver cross guard in Fishkill, New York, by John Bailey, an immigrant cutler from Sheffield, England. It was Washington's battle sword for much of the Revolutionary War. He may have also used it during his presidency, when he last reviewed the troops in Cumberland, Maryland, and Bedford, Pennsylvania, in 1794 during the Whiskey Rebellion.

Washington bequeathed five swords to his five nephews, instructing them to draw the swords only in self-defense or "in the defense of [the] country and its rights." Samuel Washington, who was among the troops reviewed by his uncle in 1794, got to choose first. He chose this simple sword with the green grip. He left the sword to his son, Samuel T. Washington, who donated it to the United States, and decades later, it was transferred to the Smithsonian.

The uniform came to the Smithsonian in 1883 and has been on display almost continuously since then. It is perennially one of the most popular of the Smithsonian's holdings, seen by millions of people every year, and still, as ever, making an impression. As the nation's first president, Washington was very conscious of making the transition from military leadership to civilian rule. As the nation's first leader, how would he signal the values and sensibilities that should attach to the highest office in the country? Washington had no desire to be king and was proud to have been elected to serve. But he was well aware that monarchs, from ancient times to his own, had used portraits to shape their image and express their values. Washington made use of this tradition throughout his presidency, most dramatically, in a painting by Gilbert Stuart.

Stuart was a Rhode Island-born artist who'd moved to England as a young man to make his name. He returned to his country as a mature artist to paint the portraits of many noteworthy and historically important Americans. While living in New York in 1794, Stuart painted a portrait of prominent patriot John Jay, then the chief justice of the Supreme Court. Jay liked the painting, and he wrote a letter for Stuart introducing him to George Washington.

That November, Stuart went to Philadelphia, the temporary capital of the United States, to meet Washington and arrange for sittings for a portrait. Washington sat for Stuart at least three times in 1795 and 1796. Two of these sessions resulted in two waist-length portraits, including the unfinished painting known today as the Athenaeum portrait, because of its later ownership by the Boston Athenaeum. Stuart repainted that image on commission more than 75 times, referring to it as his $100 bill, its price per copy. This is an image that appears today on the $1 bill.

In the spring of 1796, Senator William Bingham, then one of America's wealthiest men, and his wife, Anne, commissioned Stuart to paint a third portrait of the president. The painting was a gift for the British Marquis of Lansdowne in recognition of his support for the American cause during the Revolution. Bingham called him "a warm friend of the United States," and they both shared a great admiration for Washington.

Timing provided an important context for the particular painting for Lansdowne. The painting was undertaken in April 1796, shortly after the February 1796 ratification of the Treaty of Amity, Commerce, and Navigation, Between His Britannic Majesty and the United States of America, which is known as the Jay Treaty after John Jay, its negotiator.

This treaty resolved several issues that had remained since the signing of the Treaty of Paris at the end of the Revolutionary War. It averted, for a time, anyway, another war between Britain and the United States.

The new painting was the first life-size, full-length portrait to depict George Washington as president and civic leader of the nation, rather than as a general in his military uniform. Washington is depicted in black velvet, his suit he wore for public appearances as president, demonstrating his citizen status in an age dominated by royal rule and military conflict. The setting is entirely fictional, symbolizing the civic republic that the United States aspired to be.

Washington is portrayed in an oratorical stance, though his audience is unseen. The gesture and pose allude to his annual address to Congress, delivered the previous December, which included references to the Jay Treaty. His visage is serious, his jaw rigid, and there's been some speculation that he might have even been pained at the time by a new set of false teeth.

His left hand rests on the hilt of a ceremonial sword, while his right hand is posed near an inkwell. The books on top of his desk refer to the Federalist Papers and the Journals of Congress, and those under the table are titled General Orders, American Revolution, and Constitution & Laws of the United States, referring to his past roles as general and president of the Constitutional Convention of 1787. The papers on the desk may represent the Jay Treaty; no writing is visible on them. The black cockade on his black hat, also on the table, may indicate his loyalty to the Federalist Party, which supported the Jay Treaty.

The architecture of the room is reminiscent of an ancient Roman villa, with its columns and red draperies. The ornate table leg is carved in the shape of a fasces, or bundle of reeds, also a symbol of the Roman Republic, a model of sorts for the United States government. Fasces were carried by ancient Roman officials. A similar symbol can be found on the reverse face of a dime.

These Roman flourishes may also be interpreted as a reference to Washington's character. Washington's contemporaries often compared him to the Roman general Cincinnatus. Cincinnatus is best known for refusing to use his military power to become a dictator over the Roman Republic, instead, he retired to his farm when Rome was at peace. Washington had stepped down from command of the Continental Army. When this portrait was painted, he was about to end his second term as president. Such peaceful yielding of power had few other precedents in history.

The eagles that top each table leg could also be seen as alluding to ancient Roman battle standards, but each of them carries 13 arrows in its claws. In fact, they mimic the Great Seal of the United States. The armchair is elaborately decorated, but, it's not a throne, and hence befitting a president, not a king. The medallion on the back of the armchair, once again, alludes to the Great Seal, showing the Stars and Stripes. It's carved with a laurel and acanthus leaves, another reference to classical Roman decoration. In the distance is the sky. On the left, the clouds signify the turbulence of the American Revolution, while the rainbow is a sign of a positive future for the young republic. Overall, the portrait speaks to Washington's remarkable character and to post-Revolutionary War optimism. It reinforces the idea that the United States, thanks to the leadership of George Washington, faced a bright future.

The completed painting was shipped to London in the fall of 1796, and remained in British hands until 1968, passing from owner to owner, occasionally visiting the United States for special exhibitions. In 1968, it was installed in the newly-opened National Portrait Gallery on long-term loan. The portrait stayed on public view at the gallery until 2000, when the building closed for a major renovation.

That year, the painting's owner, Lord Harry Dalmeny, decided to sell the painting for $20,000,000. Marc Pachter, the Director of the National Portrait Gallery at the time, took to the airwaves, appearing on the Today show with Matt Lauer. Pachter called the pending loss of the painting "a patriotic emergency" and explained its significance to some 9,000,000 viewers. One viewer, Fred W. Smith, chair of the Donald W. Reynolds Foundation, was impressed by Pachter's determination to save the painting for the nation. The Reynolds Foundation made a generous donation to purchase the painting for the American people and present it to the gallery. When the gallery reopened in 2006, the Lansdowne portrait of George Washington was installed in a spectacular new setting.

Gilbert Stuart was commissioned to paint additional versions of this portrait. Smithsonian scholars have carried out historical research and technical examinations of the several paintings. There are also several derivative paintings in the halls of the United States Congress and other public buildings. There is, indeed, a healthy debate over whether Stuart or another artist in his studio painted the version that has hung in the White House since 1800; that's the one that Dolley Madison rolled up and spirited out of the White House when the British attached Washington and burnt the Presidential Mansion in 1814, as discussed in my previous lecture. But the Smithsonian has determined that the National Portrait Gallery's Lansdowne portrait is indeed the original.

George Washington is not the only president who was concerned about his public appearance, first as a general, and then as president. Abraham Lincoln, too, was concerned about how he would look as the nation's leader as he took office during the toughest of times leading up to the Civil War. Lincoln was quite cognizant of his gaunt, homey appearance. In one of his debates, Senator Stephen Douglas called him "two-faced." Lincoln retorted, "If I had another face do you think I'd wear this one?"

Nonetheless, Lincoln developed an appreciation for how he appeared both to the public and to the military and political leaders. Just before the 1860 presidential election, an 11-year-old girl from Westfield, New York named Grace Bedell wrote to Lincoln after seeing his picture and suggested he grow whiskers to look better since his face was so thin. She noted that, "All the ladies like whiskers and they would tease their husbands to vote for you and then you would be President." Incredibly, Lincoln responded asking Grace, "As to the whiskers, having never worn any, do you not think people would call it a piece of silly affectation if I were to begin wearing them now?"

But, Lincoln apparently took this child's advice, and just after his election, he grew out his beard. One of my curatorial colleagues at the Smithsonian believes this was less an act of vanity on Lincoln's part and more an effort for the incoming president to imitate his future generals and look more like a commander-and-chief. Most of the military leaders of the time grew whiskers; it was a style that had gained in popularity in the 1850s and perhaps illustrated male virility and prowess.

The beard would help Lincoln project his seriousness, if not ferocity, and gave him a more mature bearing as he took on the role of commander-in-chief. Lincoln was careful to be pictured in particular poses for coverage by Harper's Weekly, the newspapers of the day, and for photographers like Civil War documentarian Mathew Brady. In fact, it was one of Brady's assistant, Andrew Berger, who took the image used today on the U.S. five dollar bill.

Lincoln was quite conscious of how he looked to the public, his generals, and the troops all during his presidency; he realized that, in some way, he embodied the status of the republic. One of Lincoln's most famous images was among his last; it was made on February 5, 1865, when he sat for Alexander Gardner, one of Brady's former associates. Gardner had already photographed Lincoln half a dozen times, and the two men had great respect for each other. The photo session was to provide Harper's magazine and other publications with images of Lincoln for his second term, which would begin just the next month. The portrait was shot on an imperial-sized glass-plate negative, 16 by 20 inches. If you wanted a big picture then, you needed a big camera and a large glass plate. Gardner was a photographic artist. For the shot, he focused the camera and set the aperture to a very shallow depth of field. This created an effect where Lincoln's eyes and the front of his face are in very intense focus, while the ears and the back of the head are fuzzy.

Lincoln appears to lead with his square chin and beard, projecting firmness, strength, and determination. The image is a soulful one, staged to reveal the man Gardner knew well. It shows Lincoln tired, exhausted by the war effort, but with a hint of a smile, perhaps signaling his optimism about his forthcoming second term and the end of the War, and of course, the rebuilding the Union.

After exposing the glass plate, Gardner probably followed his usual procedure, using a flame to apply a varnish to finish it, and somehow, a crack emerged. It didn't break the plate, but it made the image unusable. Gardner made only one print—this one. And then seeing it as a failure, likely destroyed the plate. The session turned out to be Lincoln's last formal photographic sitting, though not the last photograph of Lincoln, but it's unknown if anyone saw this print in 1865.

Though the portrait is quite sensitive to exposure to light and only rarely exhibited, it quickly became one of the iconic images of the 16th president. Some imputed supernatural meaning to the crack running across the top of Lincoln's head, claiming somehow it foreshadowed his assassination two months later.

The concern for projecting military leadership and presidential bearing has carried over to the modern era. Consider our last president to have been a general, Dwight D. Eisenhower. Eisenhower, a Kansan born in 1890, was five-star general in the United States Army. He served as the Supreme Commander of the Allied Forces in Europe during World War II and was ultimately responsible for planning the invasion of France in 1944. Among the huge logistical and strategic matters that Eisenhower had to contend with was the Army uniform, the basic dress that soldiers wore every day. Eisenhower thought the uniform, particularly the long wool jacket, was poorly fitted for combat; it was too restrictive. The long coat was also shapeless and drab. Like Washington before him, Eisenhower was conscious of how he and the military presented itself. He wanted a uniform that would be neater and more flattering.

In March 1943, Eisenhower called for his tailor, Michael Popp, to take the Army's wool field jacket and modify it to his specifications. Popp, the son of immigrants from the Balkans, had been born in Ohio in 1905 and had joined the U. S. Army in 1942; he'd been assigned as a tailor to Eisenhower's staff during the North African campaign.

According to an aide, Eisenhower wanted the jacket to be "very short, very comfortable, and very natty looking." Popp took the Army-issued M-1944, also known as the ETO, or "European Theater of Operations" jacket, and turned it into the "Eisenhower jacket," or the "Ike jacket." Popp shortened the length; where it had somewhat flared out toward the bottom, now it hugged the waist, giving the collar a more elegant line; and he tailored the shoulders so they would form a clear outline. As an Eisenhower military aide explained, “The Boss was pleased with it and began to wear it, and when we got all of ours, our staff yelled for Popp. He was a good guy and he cut down all of our jackets to make them look as much as possible like the one the Boss wore.” The Eisenhower jacket became a standard issue for U.S. troops beginning in November 1944. Other officers individualized their uniforms according to their needs. Some added a side-slash pocket, or patch pockets, or flaps and buttons. Others modified the waist tabs.

While the jacket built on traditional military issue, it embraced a new style built upon the rationality of battle and contemporary demands, one entirely befitting Eisenhower’s persona. The general regarded it as practical, a value that he would later champion as president of a growing middle-class nation. It was “smart,” and thus mirrored Eisenhower’s military and political savvy. That it was regarded as stylish—or “snappy”—belied any suggestion that Ike was just some naïve farm boy from Kansas. It spoke to his sophistication.

The Smithsonian has several Eisenhower jackets in its collection. One is in the form of a portrait of General Eisenhower that was used for the cover of the January 1, 1945, issue of Time magazine, when he was selected as man of the year for 1944. Eisenhower was chosen because of his leadership of the Allied invasion of the European mainland, beginning with D-day on June 6 on the Normandy coast.

In the cover art, the top of his well-tailored jacket sets off his four-star Army hat—he was given his fifth star in December 1944. The flags of the Allies wave behind him. The uniform speaks to the common identity of a soldier that Eisenhower shared with his troops and the fame and glamour of his elevated command position.

Another Ike jacket from our collections belongs to the World War II hero Audie Murphy. Murphy was one of the most decorated soldiers in the war, fighting in nine campaigns. He was wounded three times, and earned some thirty decorations and awards, including the Medal of Honor. While the Ike jacket was intended for wear in battle, most soldiers preferred to save it for noncombat situations. Following the war, returning veterans wore their jackets as badges of honor, to show neighbors and prospective employers that they had served in the war. Even now, the Ike jacket is an iconic symbol of the World War II GI.

Eisenhower went on to a successful civilian life, and in 1952 he ran for president of the United States with a slogan reflecting America's regard for his character and service—"I like Ike." He was elected and reelected in 1956. Among his accomplishments were ending the Korean War, signing significant civil rights legislation, and supporting the building of the interstate highway system. And under his tenure, the U.S. Postal Service adopted the Ike jacket, albeit in blue, rather than in olive drab, as part of its official uniform. And while Ike's presidency was later characterized by the Baby Boomers as an era of complacency and cultural conservatism, the jacket reminds us of Eisenhower's leadership, how he modernized the army and the government in both war and in peace, and how he as general and president reassured the nation of its place in the world.

Conscience and Conflict—Religious History

Lecture 3

Some of the most challenging questions facing our nation today concern religious freedom and diversity and the degree to which beliefs should influence laws and public policies. As you will learn in this lecture, this question has been raised again and again, throughout American history. Reaching back, deep into colonial times, we find countervailing strains in how settlers in the so-called New World approached religion and how some of these strains played out in the founding and early years of the new republic.

Spanish Hide Paintings

- The earliest European explorers—the Spanish—mainly sought riches in America, but they also pursued a religious mission. Back in Spain, King Ferdinand and Queen Isabella had just defeated the last of the Muslim Moorish rulers in Andalusia, the southern region of the Iberian Peninsula, in 1492. The infamous Spanish Inquisition had begun in 1478 and would accelerate throughout the next century. Spain became a bastion of Catholic Christendom, and America became its frontier. The explorers' attempt to convert Indians to Christianity convinced their sponsors to supply ships, men, and money.

- Conquistadores like Juan de Oñate y Salazar made the eradication of Native spiritual leaders and the mass conversion of Native people part of their colonization program in New Spain, that is, colonial Mexico and the American southwest.

- Oñate crossed the Río del Norte, now the Rio Grande, near present-day El Paso in 1598 and claimed all the land beyond the river for New Spain. His party, which included seven Franciscan friars, continued north up the river valley and established a province he named Santa Fe de Nuevo México—New Mexico. There, Oñate battled Pueblo, Navajo, and Apache groups, and the

Franciscan friars founded the first Spanish mission. The mission and surrounding Spanish encampment were called San Gabriel del Yunque. A few scattered ruins mark the site today.

- Over the next several decades, additional missions were established, including the San Miguel Mission in the city of Santa Fe, which is said to be the oldest church in the United States. The missions would include simple residences and fields. Some missions became rather fortress-like and grew to considerable size.

Spanish Mission Hide Painting of Saint Anthony

- Like their counterpart churches in Spain, some mission chapels featured an ornate altarpiece, or retablo. Although they were similar in themes to European altarpieces, showing scenes from the Bible or the lives of the saints, they were made with local materials and were heavily influenced by native artistic styles and traditions.

- Unlike in a Spanish church, the chapel walls were decorated with buffalo-, elk-, or deer-hide paintings. The Indians of the Southwest didn't really have a hide-painting tradition before the arrival of the Spanish. For the Franciscans, however, the religious hide paintings were practical teaching tools in the conversion process. They were made from inexpensive, local materials, and the paintings themselves could be rolled up and easily transported.

- The Spanish effort to convert the Indians of New Mexico to Christianity took decades and sometimes was met with strong resistance. In 1680, the Pueblos revolted against the Spanish, expelled them from the region for more than a decade, and in the process destroyed most of the missions and many of the hide paintings. After the Spanish reconquered the region in 1692, the hide-painting tradition resumed.

- There is a hide painting from the National Museum of American History that is so delicate that it can no longer be displayed. It was painted in the early 18th century, most likely by a Mexico City–born artist. It depicts Saint Anthony of Padua in Franciscan tonsure, or shaved head, and habit, or robe. He holds an apparition of the baby Jesus, a common motif.

- Hide paintings themselves fell out of favor in the 1800s. New ecclesiastical authorities thought that painting sacred images on animal skins was inappropriate. Furthermore, canvas became more readily available, and buffalo were hunted almost to extinction. But the religious themes of these paintings, founded in colonial Catholicism, provide the touchstones of a long-lived tradition still expressed in art works, paintings, and carvings, forming a vibrant aspect of Latino cultural identity in the American Southwest today.

Plymouth Rock

- Like the Spanish exploration of the Southwest, the English settlement of the Northeast was driven by both political and religious events at home. The difference was that while the missions in the Southwest sought conformity with church doctrines, English settlers sought to practice their own nonconformist ways in America.

- Puritans who founded the Plymouth colony were part of a separatist movement that grew within the Church of England in the late 1500s. They obtained a charter to settle in a region claimed by England that was called Northern Virginia, near the Hudson River, in what is now New York state.

- A group of just over 100 set sail on the *Mayflower* in September 1620. Their two-month journey over rough seas blew them north of their destination, and when they sighted land near Cape Cod, the congregation's leader, William Brewster, led them in prayer. There was some argument about whether to proceed south to their original destination, but in the end, the weather forced them to land.

Fragment of Plymouth Rock

- Because the Puritans were settling outside the bounds of English territory, they were not bound by English law. They discussed their obligations to the group, the colony, and their investors. The result was later called the Mayflower Compact, signed by 41 adult males, including two indentured servants. The Mayflower Compact is often regarded as colonial America's first constitution, a commitment to lawful self-governance.

- A most interesting object in the Smithsonian's collection is a tiny fragment of a much larger rock with an even bigger story. The two-by-four-inch stone has an inscription that reads "Broken from the Mother Rock by Mr. Lewis Bradford on Tues. 28th of Dec. 1830 4 ¼ o'clock p.m." According to legend, it is upon that mother rock—Plymouth Rock—that the *Mayflower* settlers first stepped onto a new land to found their colony so they could freely practice their religion.

- Much of what we know of the Puritans' story comes to us through a memoir called *Of Plymouth Plantation*, written by William Bradford. He was one of the original colonists and a signer of the Mayflower Compact. Plymouth Rock is not mentioned in

Bradford's or any other contemporary account of the colony's founding, though it may have been part of the colony's oral history.

- Over the centuries, Plymouth Rock has been celebrated by authors and artists, patriots and politicians, tourists and marketers, and, like other national icons, subject to numerous elaborations and tales. Some historians have raised questions about both its literal authenticity and its role in mythologizing the narrative of the Pilgrims, which has tended to crowd out the narratives of others—the women and non-Pilgrims of the colony, or the Native Americans of the region.

Jefferson's Bible

- The nation's founders were well aware of how religious conflict had harmed Europe and the importance of establishing freedom of religion as a bedrock principle of the United States. None was probably more focused on the issue than Thomas Jefferson.

- Of his many accomplishments, Jefferson wanted to be remembered for three deeds: authoring the Declaration of Independence, founding the University of Virginia, and writing religious freedom into the Statute of Virginia.

- Jefferson thought of himself as a Christian. During his presidency, he composed a text on the doctrines of Jesus that he distributed only to close friends. He would also cut out selected passages from the Four Gospels and paste them on blank sheets of paper. The result was the 46-page volume *The Philosophy of Jesus of Nazareth Extracted from the Account of His Life and Doctrines as Given by Matthew, Mark, Luke and John*.

- When he retired, Jefferson resumed his passion and meticulously cut up passages from New Testament Bibles in four different languages—English, French, Latin, and Greek—rearranged them, and pasted them onto blank pages. Having studied these languages since his youth, Jefferson was well equipped to make comparisons.

- By about 1820, he was finished; the document now extended to 84 double-page spreads. His title page read "The Life and Morals of Jesus of Nazareth, Extracted textually from the Gospels in Greek, Latin, French, & English." He then sent the pages to Frederick Mayo, a bookbinder in Richmond, who stitched the pages together and covered the book in a red leather binding adorned with gold lettering. The short title *Morals of Jesus* was tooled in gold on the spine. Jefferson handwrote "A Table of the Texts from the Evangelists employed in this narrative and of the order of their arrangement" to provide a table of contents of sorts.

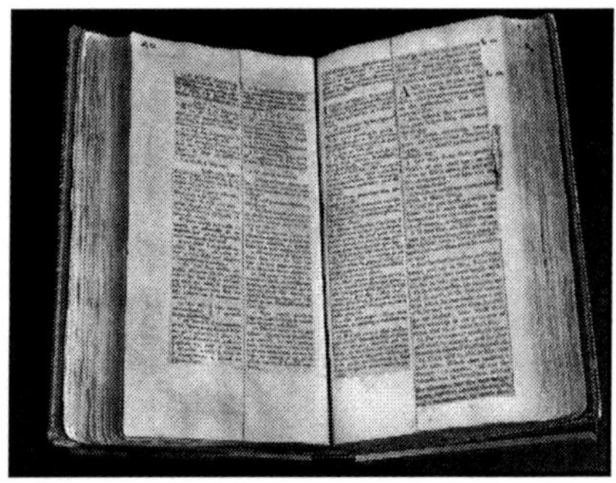

Thomas Jefferson's Bible

- The book is noteworthy for what it reveals about Jefferson's beliefs. He thought that the Gospels had been tainted by Jesus's followers—that the main teachings of Jesus's life had suffered from misunderstandings, historical accretions, elaborations, supposition, and even superstition. He was convinced that Christ was a great teacher of universal moral truths. It was unnecessary to clothe those truths in the miraculous, especially when, in Jefferson's view, Jesus never claimed to be divine.

- Jefferson kept his Bible at his Monticello home, read it before bed, and drew lessons and wisdom from it. He had no plans to publish it or distribute it broadly, knowing that many would take exception to his approach. After Jefferson died, the book stayed in his family and remained a private document. It came to the Smithsonian in the 1890s through the efforts of the Institution's librarian, Cyrus Adler.

- Jefferson's Bible had already suffered some damage. Over the next century, the book became increasingly fragile. Extensive conservation treatment would be needed. The National Museum of American History's paper conservator Janice Ellis and curator Harry Rubenstein tested, analyzed, and photographed the book, painstakingly documenting every page.

- Conservation involved taking the volume apart page by page, cleaning and repairing each leaf, replacing the stubs forming the spine, and resewing the book into its original covers using as much original material as possible while keeping the methods and materials sympathetic to the original.

- The result was a marvelous success, and the Jefferson Bible went back on display in 2011 in the museum's Albert H. Small Documents Gallery. A fully digitized version and two new print editions, including a leather-bound facsimile of the original, were also produced.

The Nauvoo Temple

- It's not surprising that a nation whose citizens and leaders were so devoted to religious principles would produce many powerful and influential religious movements. The first of these movements was an evangelical revival called the First Great Awakening. It was a sort of counterreaction to the philosophy of the Enlightenment. It emphasized emotion and divine revelation. Among other important developments, it led to the founding of many great schools, such as Princeton University.

- The second important movement took place right around the time Jefferson had completed pasting together his Bible. Beginning in the 1790s and continuing through the 1830s, this time, the movement's values reflected the values of the Revolution. Its adherents emphasized the equality of all people in God's eyes and the ability of all people to achieve salvation. Historians call this movement the Second Great Awakening.

- The center of the Second Great Awakening was in the towns, cities, and villages that developed along the Erie Canal, in central New York state. It was a place and time of tremendous national growth, early industry, and expansion. It gave birth to new, uniquely American religious movements. The Church of Jesus Christ of Latter-day Saints, colloquially known as Mormonism to outsiders, is perhaps the best known of these.

Nauvoo Sun Stone

- The church grew from the reports of Joseph Smith Jr., who said that he'd had a vision of the divine near his western New York home. He drew some early converts and dictated its scripture, the Book of Mormon, which he claimed was a translation of buried ancient golden plates that he had uncovered through the guidance of an angel.

- Although the nation's founding documents specifically promised religious tolerance, most Americans at the time equated religion with established European Protestantism. Thus, new native-born religious movements were viewed with suspicion. To avoid persecution in New York, Smith led his followers west in 1831.

- Smith and his followers first settled in Kirtland, Ohio, where they built a temple between 1833 and 1836. The architecture shows a mixture of Federal, Greek Revival, and Gothic Revival styles. The building still stands today. The group also established an outpost in Jackson County, Missouri. Both settlements faced local bias and ridicule, and sometimes violent opposition; Smith and his followers were forced out of Missouri and fled Ohio.

- In 1839, they settled in western Illinois, in a town called Commerce that they renamed Nauvoo, which means "beautiful place" in Hebrew. The town grew from about 2,400 settlers in 1840 to about 11,000 five years later. Once again, they built a temple, this one much larger than the Kirtland temple, placing it on the bluff overlooking the city and the Mississippi River.

- Drawn from a dream vision of Joseph Smith's, the Nauvoo temple was designed by architect William Weeks in a Greek Revival style and was elaborately adorned. His design was based on celestial themes, with star stones, sun stones, and moon stones symbolizing the relationship between the church and the divine.

- Smith was not only a religious leader but also Nauvoo's mayor. He ran for president of the United States as an independent in 1844. As Smith's political voice became more radical, so did some of his theological revelations. His attempt to consolidate power caused a split in the community and also exacerbated extant anti-Mormon sentiment in surrounding towns. Smith was jailed on the orders of the Illinois governor, and on June 27, 1844, he was killed by an anti-Mormon mob that stormed the jail.

- Brigham Young took over as the leader of the main body of the community. But the Mormons faced increasing violence. Young led much of the community west yet again, eventually settling in the Salt Lake Valley, then part of Mexico. By the fall, mobs had run the remaining Mormons out of Nauvoo and vandalized the temple. In 1848, it was set afire and badly gutted. Damage from a tornado two years later rendered the structure unsafe and unsound.

- In 1865, what remained of the temple was demolished, and stones were salvaged for other buildings—including the town jail and a school. A century later, two moon stones were retrieved from Nauvoo and sent to Salt Lake City, Utah, which had become the seat of the church. Two of the surviving sun stones were moved around a lot, with one of them finally going to the Smithsonian in the 1980s.

- In 1999, the Church of Latter-day Saints announced plans to rebuild the Nauvoo temple on its original site and broke ground for the construction. The interior was designed to reflect current church styles and practices, but the exterior replicated the original architecture. The new Nauvoo temple was dedicated in 2002, and a sunstone was borrowed for public display in order to connect the structure to its storied history.

Featured Objects

Spanish Mission Hide Painting of Saint Anthony

Fragment of Plymouth Rock

Thomas Jefferson's Bible

Nauvoo Sun Stone

Suggested Reading

Bradford, *Of Plymouth Plantation.*

Jefferson, *The Jefferson Bible.*

Kimbro, Costello, and Ball, *The California Missions.*

Pykles, *Excavating Nauvoo.*

Conscience and Conflict—Religious History

Lecture 3—Transcript

Some of the most challenging questions facing our nation today concern religious freedom and diversity, and the degree to which beliefs should influence laws and public policies. This question is not a new one. It has been raised again and again, throughout American history. Reaching back, deep into colonial times, we find countervailing strains in terms of how settlers in the so-called New World approached religion and how some of these strains played out in the founding and early years of the new republic.

The earliest European explorers—the Spanish—mainly sought riches in America, but they also pursued a religious mission. Back in Spain, King Ferdinand and Queen Isabella had just defeated the last of the Muslim Moorish rulers in Andalusia—the southern region of the Iberian Peninsula—in 1492. The infamous Spanish Inquisition had begun in 1478 and would accelerate throughout the next century. Spain became a bastion of Catholic Christendom, and America became its new frontier. The explorers' attempt to convert Indians to Christianity convinced their sponsors to supply ships, men, and money.

Conquistadores like Juan de Oñate y Salazar made the eradication of native spiritual leaders and the mass conversion of native people part of their colonization program in New Spain, that is, colonial Mexico and American southwest. Oñate crossed the Río del Norte, now the Rio Grande near present-day El Paso, in 1598 and claimed all the land beyond the river for New Spain. His party, which included seven Franciscan friars, continued north up the river valley and established a province he named Santa Fe de Nuevo México—New Mexico. There, Oñate battled Pueblo, Navajo, and Apache groups, and the Franciscan friars founded the first Spanish mission. The mission and surrounding Spanish encampment were called San Gabriel de Yunque-Ouinge; a few scattered remains mark the site today.

Over the next several decades, additional missions were established, including the San Miguel Mission in the city of Santa Fe, which is said to be the oldest church in the United States. San Miguel is typical of Spanish mission architecture. The chapel is constructed of adobe brick and rough-hewn wood, though, some were built of stone. The chapels would have no pews or seating; supplicants would stand or kneel on the earthen floor. Typically, chapels would have one or two towers, often several stories tall. A large wooden cross would top the tower, and some had bells installed to call people to prayer. The chapel would usually have a walled yard, which sometimes also served as a burial ground. The mission would include simple residences and fields. Some missions became rather fortress-like and grew to considerable size.

Like their counterpart churches in Spain, some mission chapels featured an ornate altarpiece, or retablo. Most of these were imported from workshops in Mexico. Although they were similar in themes to European altarpieces, showing scenes from the Bible or the lives of the saints, they were made with local materials and were heavily influenced by native artistic styles and traditions.

Unlike in a Spanish church, the chapel walls were decorated with buffalo-, elk-, or deer-hide paintings. Now, it's worth noting that the Indians of the Southwest didn't really have a hide-painting tradition before the arrival of the Spanish. Painting on hides, especially buffalo hides, was common among the Plains Indians of central North America for both religious spiritual purposes as well as for record keeping. But before the colonial period, the Pueblo, Hopi, and Navajo generally did not paint on hides.

For the Franciscans, however, the religious hide paintings were practical teaching tools in the conversion process. They were made from inexpensive local materials, and the paintings themselves could be rolled up and easily transported. The Spanish effort to convert the Indians of New Mexico to Christianity took decades and sometimes met with strong resistance. In 1680, the Pueblos revolted against the Spanish, expelled them from the region for more than a decade, and in the process, destroyed most of the missions and many of the hide paintings. After the Spanish re-conquered the region in 1692, the hide-painting tradition resumed.

This hide painting from the National Museum of American history is a delicate object, so delicate, in fact, that we can no longer display it. It was painted in the early 18th century, most likely by a Mexico City-born artist. It depicts Saint Anthony of Padua in Franciscan tonsure, or shaved head, and habit, or robe. He holds an apparition of the baby Jesus, a common motif. Saint Anthony was a well-respected contemporary of Saint Francis of Assisi, the founder of the Franciscan order.

Hide paintings themselves fell out of favor in the 1800s. New ecclesiastical authorities thought painting sacred images on animal skins inappropriate. Furthermore, canvas became more readily available, and the buffalo were being hunted almost to extinction. But the religious themes of these paintings, founded in colonial Catholicism, provide the touchstones of a long-lived tradition still expressed in art works, paintings, and carvings, forming a vibrant aspect of Latino cultural identity in the American Southwest today.

Like the Spanish exploration of the Southwest, the English settlement of the Northeast was driven by both political and religious events at home. The difference was, while the missions in the Southwest sought conformity with Church doctrines, English settlers sought to practice their own, non-conformist ways in America. Puritans, who founded the Plymouth colony, were part of a separatist movement that grew within the Church of England in the late 1500s. They obtained a charter to settle in a region claimed by England that was called "Northern Virginia, near the Hudson River.

A group of just over a hundred set sail on the Mayflower in September 1620. Their two-month journey over rough seas blew them north of their destination, and when they sighted land near Cape Cod, the congregation's leader, William Brewster, led them in prayer. There was some argument about whether to proceed south to their original destination, but in the end, the weather forced them to land.

Because the Puritans were settling outside the bounds of English territory, they were not bound by English law. They discussed their obligations to themselves, the group, the colony that they were to form, and their investors. The result was later called the Mayflower Compact, signed by forty-one adult males, including two indentured servants. In it, they pledged "for the general good of the Colony unto which we promise all due submission and obedience" to form a "civil body politic," through which issues would be settled by majority vote. The Mayflower Compact is often regarded as colonial America's first constitution, a commitment to lawful self-governance.

The signers also declared that their colony was "undertaken for the glory of God and advancement of the Christian faith, and honor of our King and Country." Although they dissented from the Church of England, they were still loyal Englishmen. Of course, there's a sort of a paradox here; they had fled one state religion, and yet their faith would dominate their civil laws for many generations to come in America, but as I said at the outset, it's a question we still grapple with today.

Now let's take a look at a most interesting object in the Smithsonian's collection. It's a tiny fragment of a much larger rock with an even bigger story. The two-by-four-inch stone has an inscription that reads "Broken from the Mother Rock by Mr. Lewis Bradford on Tues. 28th of Dec. 1830 4 ½ o'clock p.m." According to legend, it is upon that mother rock—Plymouth Rock—that the Mayflower settlers first stepped onto a new land to found their colony so they could freely practice their religion.

Much of what we know of the Puritans' story comes to us through a memoir called *Of Plymoth Plantation*, written by William Bradford. He was one of the original colonists and a signer of the Mayflower Compact. Plymouth Rock is actually not mentioned in Bradford's or any other contemporary account of the colony's founding, though, indeed, it may have been part of the colony's oral history.

The first written reference to the rock actually comes in 1741. The town historian, 94-year-old Thomas Faunce, identified the boulder where his father had told him the settlers had set foot to found the colony. The granite boulder weighed about ten tons. In 1774, the townspeople tried to move the rock from the shore to the village square, but the rock split in two. The top portion was removed to the town meetinghouse, with the bottom of the, so called, mother rock remaining in place near the wharf.

A canopy was installed over the wharf rock, and in 1880 the two pieces of the rock were reunited at the shore. They were cemented together, and the date of the landing, 1620, was carved into it at that time. By then, souvenir takers had considerably reduced the size of the mother rock. For its 300th anniversary, the rock was set under a new canopy designed by the famed architectural firm McKim, Mead, & White.

Over the centuries, Plymouth Rock has been celebrated by authors and artists, patriots and politicians, tourists and marketers, and, like other national icons, subject to numerous elaborations and tales. Some historians have raised questions about both its literal authenticity and its role in mythologizing the narrative of the Pilgrims, which has tended to crowd out the narratives of others—the women and non-Pilgrims of the colony, and the Native Americans of the region.

But whether celebrated as a symbol of the quest for liberty and self-determination, or held up as a reminder of the times that we've failed to fulfill those ideals, Plymouth Rock remains a powerful reminder of freedom of religious belief and practice in America. And that freedom was important to those of other religious faiths who also found a home in colonial America. Roger Williams was exiled from Puritan Massachusetts to found a new community in Rhode Island more tolerant of Christian diversity. Maryland became an early home for Catholic colonists. Jewish immigrants, traders, and merchants founded their first synagogues in Charlestown, South Carolina and in Newport, Rhode Island. Quakers, Mennonites, Moravians, and other groups found a home in Pennsylvania, and so on.

The nation's founders were well aware of how religious conflict had harmed Europe and they were aware of importance of establishing freedom of religion as a bedrock principle of the United States. None was probably more focused on the issue than Thomas Jefferson. Jefferson was an unusually accomplished man, even among his many remarkable peers. But, of his many accomplishments, he wanted to be remembered for three deeds: authoring the Declaration of Independence, founding the University of Virginia, and writing religious freedom into the Statute of Virginia. By his own request, those are the only three accomplishments that appear on his tombstone.

Jefferson typically avoided discussing his religious beliefs publicly. As a result, he was sometimes accused of being anti-Christian and antireligious. The truth is far more nuanced that that. Jefferson believed profoundly that the relationship between man and God was a matter of individual belief and that the government had no business being involved in such an intimate activity.

Jefferson, nonetheless, thought of himself as a Christian, though he wrote that "I am a sect by myself, as far as I know." In broad terms, Jefferson was a Deist; he believed in God as the creator, even the endower of human and natural gifts, but believed that God did not interfere with human actions or the laws of nature.

During his presidency, Jefferson composed a text on the doctrines of Jesus that he distributed only to very close friends. He would also cut out selected passages from the Four Gospels and paste them down on blank sheets of paper. The result was the 46-page volume *The Philosophy of Jesus of Nazareth* extracted from the account of his life and doctrines as given by Matthew, Mark, Luke, and John. Jefferson would read passages from this volume before sleep to gain inspiration.

When he retired, Jefferson resumed his passion and meticulously cut up passages from New Testament Bibles in four different languages—English, French, Latin, and Greek. And he had rearranged them and pasted them onto blank pages. Having studied these languages since his youth, Jefferson was well equipped to make comparisons. He needed two Bibles of each language so that he could use both the front and back sides of their pages. He would line up the extracted verses in each column, so that when he put two pages side by side, he could read and compare, from left to right, the Greek version in the first column, the Latin in the second column, the French in the third, and the English in the fourth.

By about 1820, Jefferson was finished. The document now extended to 84 double-page spreads. His title page read, "The Life and Morals of Jesus of Nazareth, Extracted textually from the Gospels in Greek, Latin, French, & English." He then sent the pages to Frederick Mayo, a bookbinder in Richmond, who stitched the pages together and covered the book in a red leather binding adorned with gold lettering. The short title, *Morals of Jesus*, was tooled in gold on the spine. Jefferson handwrote "A Table of the Texts from the Evangelists employed in this narrative and of the order of their arrangement" to provide a table of contents of sorts.

The book is noteworthy for what it reveals about Jefferson's beliefs. He thought that the Gospels had been tainted by Jesus's followers; that the main teachings of Jesus' life had suffered from misunderstandings, historical accretions, elaborations, supposition, and even superstition. Jefferson purged the material he judged "contrary to reason." He was convinced that Christ was a great teacher of universal moral truths. It was unnecessary to clothe those truths in the miraculous, especially when, in Jefferson's view, Jesus never claimed to be divine. Jefferson's arrangement of the extracts provides a chronological narrative of Christ's life, from his birth on this very first page to his death on the last. Jefferson did not include the resurrection.

Jefferson kept this book at his Monticello home, read it before bed, and drew lessons and wisdom from it. He had no plans to publish it or distribute it broadly, knowing that many would take exception to his approach. Various clergymen had previously declared that Jefferson would bring down God's wrath on the New Republic; revealing this work would only fan such sentiments. After Jefferson died, the book stayed in his family and remained a private document. It came to the Smithsonian in the late 1890s through the efforts of the Smithsonian's librarian, Cyrus Adler.

Jefferson's Bible had already suffered some damage. Over the next century, the book became increasingly fragile. Extensive conservation treatment would be needed. The National Museum of American History's paper conservator, Janice Ellis, and curator, Harry Rubenstein, tested, analyzed, and photographed the book, painstakingly documenting every page. Conservation involved taking the volume apart page by page, cleaning and repairing each leaf, replacing the stubs forming the spine, and re-sewing the book into its original covers using as much original material as possible, while keeping the methods and materials sympathetic to the original.

The result was a marvelous success, and the Jefferson Bible went back on display in 2011 in the museum's Albert H. Small Documents Gallery. A fully digitized version and two new print editions, including a leather-bound facsimile of the original, were also produced. I have one of the print facsimiles with me today, and the level of detail is just incredible. I'll just start with this page. The book begins with the Gospel of Luke, chapter 2; that's "the decree from Caesar Augustus that all the world should be taxed." And you can see all the cut edges and the glue marks from each individual passage that was cut out and pasted down on the page. The page numbers in the upper corner are in Jefferson's handwriting. And the book even reproduces little smudges of mold and decay.

This page, toward the end of the book, shows a bit of Jefferson's decision-making process. This is Jesus in the Garden of Gethsemane, and it's been edited together from Mathew, Mark, and John, as you can see from these annotations in the margin. And lower down in the margin we have two extra verses right down here that Jefferson went back and inserted after his first edit. So, you can really see and get a sense of how this was an ongoing process, something that Jefferson painstakingly mulled over, reread, and revised. When scholars study primary sources, in other words, an original work of art or scholarship, nothing really compares to getting your hands on the authentic manuscript. While that's not possible with books as fragile as Jefferson's original Bible, reproductions like this can get us very, very close.

Jefferson's bible is an amazing artifact. It provides insight into Jefferson's views and his handiwork, an amazing illustration of how this founding father himself practiced the freedom of religion so avidly sought for all Americans.

It's not surprising that a nation whose citizens and leaders were so devoted to religious principles would produce many powerful and influential religious movements. The first of these movements in America was an evangelical revival called the First Great Awakening. It was a sort of counter reaction to the philosophy of the Enlightenment. It emphasized emotion and divine revelation. Among other important developments, it led to the founding of many great schools, such as Princeton University.

The second important movement took place right around the time Jefferson had completed pasting together his Bible. Beginning in the 1790s and continuing through the 1830s, this time, the movement's values reflected the values of the Revolution. Its adherents emphasized the equality of all people in God's eyes and the ability of all people to achieve salvation. As you might guess, historians call this movement the Second Great Awakening.

The center of the Second Great Awakening was in the towns, cities, and villages that developed along the Erie Canal, in central New York State. It was a place and time of tremendous national growth, early industry, and expansion. The area became a hotbed of Protestant evangelical revival, and with its emphasis on equality, nurtured the growth of the abolitionist and women's rights movements as well. It also gave birth to new, uniquely American religious movements. The Church of Jesus Christ of Latter-day Saints, colloquially known as Mormonism to outsiders, is perhaps the best known of these. Its early history and a fascinating artifact at the Smithsonian illustrate some of the tensions between religious freedom and tolerance in American history.

The church grew from the reports of Joseph Smith Jr., who said he'd had a vision of the divine near his western New York home. He drew some early converts and dictated its scripture, the Book of Mormon, which he claimed was a translation of buried ancient golden plates that he had uncovered through the guidance of an angel. This testament offered an account of ancient American civilizations. Native Americans, for example, were cast as Lamanites. These were descendants of Israelites who had settled in the New World and had been visited by Christ after the Resurrection but had rebelled against Christian teachings. In this way, Mormonism holds America to be the successor to the ancient Holy Land, and Smith's aim was to reestablish the true Church of Christ in the United States.

Though the nation's founding documents specifically promised religious tolerance, most Americans at the time equated religion with established European Protestantism. Thus, new native-born religious movements were viewed with suspicion. To avoid persecution in New York, Smith led his followers west in 1831. Smith and his followers first settled in Kirtland, Ohio, where they built a temple. This building, intended to be part of a complex dedicated to education and worship, was built between 1833 and 1836. The architecture shows a mixture of Federal, Greek Revival, and Gothic Revival styles. The building still stands today. The group also established an outpost in Jackson County, Missouri. Both settlements faced local bias and ridicule, and sometimes violent opposition. Smith and his followers were forced out of Missouri and fled Ohio.

In 1839 they settled in western Illinois in a town called Commerce that they renamed Nauvoo, which means "beautiful" in Hebrew, and according to Joseph Smith's own translation, also implies "the idea of rest." The town grew from about 2,400 settlers in 1840 to some 11,000 people five years later. Once again, they built a temple, this one, much larger than the one in Kirtland, placing it on a bluff overlooking the city and the Mississippi River. A traveler described the 165-foot-tall structure, huge at the time, as "a noble marble edifice, whose high tapering spire was radiant with white and gold."

Drawn from a dream vision of Joseph Smith's, the Nauvoo temple was designed by architect William Weeks in a Greek Revival style and elaborately adorned. His design was based on celestial themes, with star stones, sun stones, and moon stones, symbolizing the relationship between the church and the divine. The sunstones had a radiant sun face rising out of a bank of clouds, with a pair of hand-held trumpets above them. Hand carved out of limestone, thirty of these two-and-a-half-ton stones formed capitals, crowing pilasters that defined the temple's perimeter. The interior of the temple was designed progressively, from basement to attic, in terms of life's spiritual journey from baptism through terrestrial and celestial rooms to a sealing room for marriages.

Smith was not only a religious leader, but also, Nauvoo's mayor. He ran for president of the United States as an independent in 1844, arguing aggressively for the country's western expansion and for ending slavery. As Smith's political voice became more radical, so did some of his theological revelations. His attempt to consolidate power caused a split in the community and also exacerbated extant anti-Mormon sentiment in surrounding towns. Smith was jailed on the orders of the Illinois governor, and on June 27, 1844, he was killed by an anti-Mormon mob that stormed the jail.

Though there was some doubt and disagreement over succession, Brigham Young took over as the leader of the main body of the community. But the Mormons faced increasing violence. Young led much of the community west yet again, eventually settling in the Salt Lake Valley, which was then part of

Mexico. By the fall, mobs had run the remaining Mormons out of Nauvoo and vandalized the temple. Those who remained tried to sell the temple over the next two years. In 1848 it was set afire and badly gutted, its finely carved wooden interior furnishings destroyed. Damage from a tornado two years later rendered the structure unsafe and unsound.

In 1865 what remained of the temple was demolished, and the stones were salvaged for other buildings, including the town jail and school. A century later, two moon stones were retrieved from Nauvoo and sent to Salt Lake City, Utah, which had become the seat of the church. Two of the surviving sun stones were moved around from a college to the state capital, to the fairgrounds, a park, and the governor's mansion, with one of them eventually coming to the Smithsonian in the 1980s.

In 1999, the Church of Latter Day Saints announced plans to rebuild the Nauvoo Temple on its original site and broke ground for the construction. The interior was designed to reflect current church styles and practices, but the exterior replicated the original architecture. The new Nauvoo Temple was dedicated in 2002, and a sunstone borrowed for public display in order to connect the structure to its storied history.

The sunstone helps represent the complexity of our nation's religious identity, relating to both the flourishing of the country's diverse communal faiths, as well as to the persecution and intolerance that many have faced. That complexity continues, and the Smithsonian today continues to collect items documenting the experience of Christians, Jews, Muslims, Hindus, Sikhs, Buddhists and those of other faiths in America today.

The Growth and Spread of Slavery

Lecture 4

Artifacts like the ones you will learn about in this lecture—slave shackles, Eli Whitney's cotton gin, and Harriet Tubman's hymnal and shawl—help humanize and personalize the story of slavery in the United States. These objects tell us the true human cost of slavery and freedom and the power of humankind to overcome it.

Slave Shackles

- Modern slavery had its roots in the 1400s during an era of sea exploration. The Portuguese and Spanish sought sea routes to India and the rest of Asia to acquire and trade luxury goods, such as porcelain, spices, pearls, diamonds, ivory, silk, and jade. They did this to avoid the long and uncertain land routes through the Middle East and territories controlled by the Ottoman Empire. The sea routes meant sailing around Africa.

- Portuguese and Spanish seafarers generally hugged the African coast. They built forts and small ports and traded with local rulers for gold, peppers, ivory, copper, cowrie shells, textiles, and other goods. Among Portugal's trade partners were the rulers of Benin. Some of Benin's rulers had slaves who were generally captured in warfare and regional skirmishes. But African slavery was a small-scale, local phenomenon, with nothing like the scope, scale, and institutional form of the later trans-Atlantic slave trade.

- Benin's slave trade was intimately entwined with its artistic tradition. Benin's artists, then and now, are famous for making truly magnificent sculptures from bronze. The figures in these sculptures are often depicted wearing elaborate bronze or brass bracelets called *manillas*.

- Slaves were bought and sold in exchange for *manillas*. The *manillas* would then be melted down and crafted into bronze artwork. A few slaves, on the other hand, were transported back to Portugal to become personal or household servants, while most were sold or exchanged for goods in other African coastal markets.

- Over the course of the next several decades, the slave trade and use of slave labor was to change in scale and scope. The Cape Verde islands, off the coast of West Africa in the Atlantic Ocean, became an early testing ground for plantation agriculture. Large numbers of African slaves were procured to work on the plantations and produce goods for a European market.

- Christopher Columbus found the Caribbean islands of Cuba, Hispaniola, and Puerto Rico already inhabited by native people called the Taino, who were initially welcoming and generous to the European explorers. But Columbus and the Spanish colonists who followed conquered and enslaved the Taino. Some Taino rose up in revolt, and many of them were slaughtered in the fighting. Many others died of European diseases. By the early decades of the 1500s, the Taino natives had mostly died out.

- The colonists, therefore, needed another large source of labor to pursue their building, mining, and agricultural ambitions. Bartolomé de las Casas, a Dominican friar serving in the Caribbean and then Mexico, suggested the importation of African slave labor as a solution.

- The first African slaves were transported to Hispaniola, the island that comprises modern-day Haiti and the Dominican Republic, in the early 1500s. Although the Spanish never found large amounts of gold—and, thus, didn't need massive numbers of slaves—the idea of slavery took root nonetheless. Over the course of the next century, several hundred thousand slaves were sent, largely through Portuguese traders, to Portuguese and Spanish colonies in the Caribbean and South America. The horrendous voyage across the Atlantic in specially modified ships designed to carry humans as cargo came to be called the Middle Passage.

- Slaves were put to work growing food, as construction laborers, and as domestic servants. Occasionally, slaves would escape, often fleeing to the mountains or swamps and sometimes learning from and intermarrying with Native peoples. They became known as Cimaroons, or, later, Maroons.

- Slavery in the Americas expanded substantially in the 17th and 18th centuries, because of the development of sugar plantations and the production of molasses and rum. Plantations also needed slaves to work fields of indigo, rice, tobacco, coffee, cocoa, and cotton. These agricultural enterprises drove the infamous "triangular trade."

- As slavery became a thriving international business, ship owners and captains economized the loading and transport of slaves, which they considered cargo. Specialized ships were constructed and designed to hold hundreds of people. Slaves were crowded together and suffered from poor sanitation, lack of fresh air and food, and devastating epidemics caused by the appalling conditions.

- In the 1600s, the Dutch and French supplanted the Portuguese as the leaders of the slave trade. In the 1700s, with the establishment of their American colonies, it was the English who dominated the slave trade.

- The first enslaved Africans in British North America arrived in Jamestown in 1619. Although sold at market, they were initially regarded as indentured servants, a European custom in which a poor person—white or black—was bound for a fixed term of labor. But in practice, the distinction hardly mattered, because few people managed to outlive the term of their indenture, and those who did had little recourse when owners refused to free them.

- In 1654, the Virginia colony recognized slavery as an officially sanctioned condition. Enslaved people had no legal protection, no human rights, nor any hope of liberation. Within a century, slavery was legal in all 13 colonies.

Eli Whitney's Cotton Gin

- The economy in Jamestown, Virginia, and the colonial South initially developed around the cultivation of tobacco. Although it was lucrative, intensive tobacco cultivation depleted soils fairly quickly, and growers increasingly faced competition from around the world. Planters began looking for an alternative cash crop.

- Rice, indigo, and sugarcane were cultivated in the semitropical low-country regions of South Carolina and Georgia but faced strong competition from widespread Caribbean plantations with better land and climate conditions. Growers in the upland South needed a crop that would thrive in the hot, dry summers and in relatively poor soil with limited rainfall.

Cotton Gin

- Cotton was a possible answer. Grown natively in India and Mexico for thousands of years, cotton first became known to Europeans in the 14th century as a kind of wool that grew on trees or shrubs. It produced pods or bolls of fiber that when processed could be turned into yarn and threads and woven into textiles and clothing. By the 18th century, England's developing textile mills began using Indian cotton, employing considerable labor, and turning out new cloth for domestic consumption and export.

- There were two basic types of cotton: short-staple and long-staple cotton, where "staple" means the length of the individual fibers. Short-staple Mexican cotton was a good horticultural fit with the American South. Unlike long-staple cotton, it did not need a semitropical environment and could be widely planted.

- There was, however, a big problem: It required too much labor to be economically profitable. Picking cotton—that is, removing the bolls from the shrubs—took a lot of time and labor in the fields. In addition, the short-staple cotton bolls were full of seeds intricately attached to fibers.

- A technology—the roller gin—had long before been developed to remove the seeds from long-staple cotton. But the roller gin was ineffective for the short-staple variety of cotton. The seeds had to be removed by hand. This was a slow, tedious procedure. One person working all day could perhaps separate out about four to eight pounds of usable cotton fiber from the seeds.

- A number of inventors attempted to tackle the problem by trying to develop a workable and efficient cotton "engine" to separate the fiber from the unwanted seeds. Several found varying degrees of success, but it was Eli Whitney who broke through.

- Eventually, he constructed a small device in a wooden housing. At its core was a hand-turned wooden cylinder, or drum. Attached to the drum were wire hooks, or teeth, to catch onto the boll and pull the fibrous material through a slatted screen. The seeds would not fit through the slats and, thus, dropped out, leaving the seeded cotton fiber to pass through. Brushes then removed the fiber from the teeth and moved the cotton along to be collected.

- Using the device, one could process 50 to 60 pounds of cotton per day, about a tenfold increase over the previous hand-removal method, dramatically increasing efficiency. The only drawback was that many more of the fibers were cut in the process than would have been by hand processing. This would result in an inferior yarn, with more knots and rougher to the touch. Nonetheless, the vast improvement in the quantity of cotton processed provided the opportunity for considerable economic gain.

- Whitney submitted a model, description, and drawing of the cotton gin as part of his application for a patent to the federal government. But other mechanics easily and cheaply produced their own cotton gins. It was not until 1807 that Whitney's patent was firmly established, and while it made him famous, it did not make him wealthy.

- Meanwhile, the mass proliferation of cotton gins had consequences that went far beyond the mechanical seeding of cotton. Because cotton processing could now proceed on a whole new scale, much more land could be devoted to cotton cultivation.

- Because cotton was easy to transport and did not spoil, it could be sent to textile mills in Europe. In 1793, before the cotton gin, the United States exported 500,000 pounds of cotton. This grew to 93 million pounds by 1810. In the ensuing decades, cotton became America's chief export, accounting for more than half of all exported goods.

- Cotton also headed to New England, where immigrant British entrepreneur Samuel Slater had developed a machine to spin cotton thread. As mechanical textile looms were established in Rhode Island and Massachusetts in the following decades, they acquired almost unlimited capacity to turn raw materials into finished textiles, stoking demand for Southern cotton.

- Profits from the enterprise fueled large plantations. Cotton cultivation also supported small-farm owners and slavery for their operations. This drove settlers west, into what had been native territory, and brought white farmers into direct conflict with Native tribes once again. Ultimately, this led to the forced removal of Cherokee, Choctaw, and Seminole Indians from their Southern homelands to Oklahoma in the 1830s—a migration we now refer to as the Trail of Tears.

- The costs and stakes of managing and controlling the huge slave population led to increasing regulations and harsher treatments in the period from the 1830s to the 1860s. Slaveholding states made legal gains, but worsening conditions led to a rise in slave rebellions, such as Nat Turner's brutal, and brutally suppressed, uprising in Virginia in 1831.

- These conditions also stoked the fires of abolitionism in the North. Efforts by northern abolitionists—black and white—to point to the horrors of plantation slavery and the institution as a whole grew with the efforts of people like Frederick Douglass, William Lloyd Garrison, Henry Ward Beecher, Harriet Beecher Stowe, and many others.

- The new technology of photography helped spread the abolitionist message. In addition, the abolitionist movement was fueled by a new, very popular genre of literature: the slave narrative. These autobiographies, written by escaped slaves, laid bare the harsh realities of slavery for readers on both sides of the Atlantic. Harriet Beecher Stowe's 1852 novel *Uncle Tom's Cabin* was one of the best-selling novels of the 19th century and probably the most significant piece of abolitionist literature.

Harriet Tubman's Hymnal and Shawl

- The fight against slavery had many such heroes and heroines, perhaps none better known or admired than Harriet Tubman. Enslaved for the first quarter of her life, Tubman found her way to freedom and then dedicated herself to saving others. She earned her renown as a "conductor" for the Underground Railroad, an illegal network of people who assisted and sheltered escaped slaves along routes to Canada, Mexico, or Spanish Florida, where they would be free under law and exempt from extradition.

- The Underground Railroad network expanded rapidly after 1850, in spite of the greater legal risk for those assisting escaped slaves. An estimated 1,000 enslaved people per year made it to freedom along the Underground Railroad. While this was a statistically small percentage, it nonetheless gave people hope and helped dramatize the terrible injustice of the federal laws that supported slavery.

- Undeterred by law and physical danger, Tubman ventured into Maryland at least a dozen times in the 1850s; most historians believe she conducted 13 missions. She helped rescue scores of people, guiding them to safe houses in the North and to freedom in Canada. She developed a friendship with abolitionist William Seward, later President Lincoln's secretary of state, who helped her relocate to Auburn, New York.

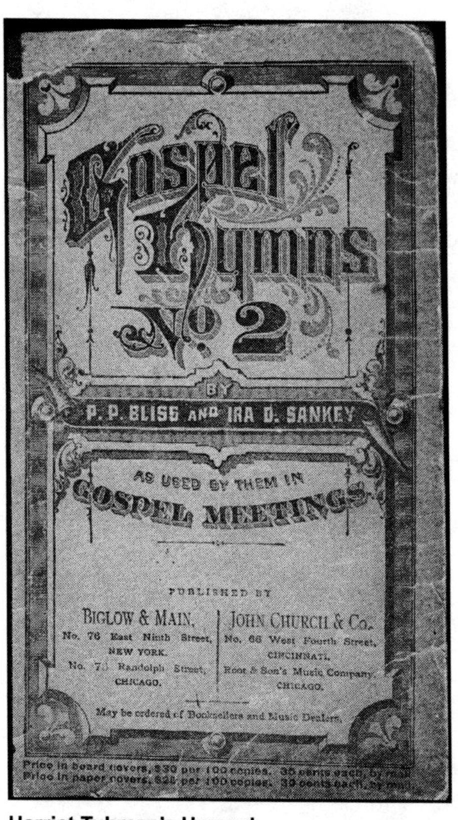

Harriet Tubman's Hymnal

- During the Civil War, Tubman served as a cook, nurse—possibly a spy—and scout for the Union Army. In 1863, she accompanied Union troops on gunboat raids on plantations along the Combahee River near Beaufort, South Carolina, raids that rescued more than 700 fleeing slaves. Tubman is reputed to have calmed and encouraged many of them by singing hymn and encouraging them to "Come along! Come along! Don't be alarmed."

- After the war, Tubman settled in Auburn. She befriended Susan B. Anthony and became an advocate for women's rights and suffrage. She was active in her church, with the Salvation Army, and with freedman schools. Following the death of her second husband, she helped establish an African American nursing home. When she died, she was buried with military honors at Auburn's Fort Hill Cemetery.

- Tubman was a devout Christian and throughout her life was inspired by divine visions. Harriet Tubman's copy of P. P. Bliss and Ira D. Sankey's *Gospel Hymns No. 2* now rests in the Smithsonian's National Museum of African American History and Culture. Although Tubman could not read, she loved singing.

- Tubman also cherished a silk lace and linen shawl sent to her by Queen Victoria in 1897, also part of the Smithsonian's collection. The shawl was a gift to Tubman on the occasion of the queen's Diamond Jubilee—her 60th year of rule. Invitations were sent to rulers and prominent people around the world, including Tubman, to join in the celebration in England. Although Tubman could not attend, Queen Victoria sent her the shawl as well as a silver medal.

Featured Objects

Slave Shackles

Cotton Gin

Harriet Tubman's Hymnal and Shawl

Suggested Reading

Clinton, *Harriet Tubman.*

Horton and Horton, *Slavery and the Making of America.*

O'Malley, *Final Passages.*

The Growth and Spread of Slavery

Lecture 4—Transcript

These are slave shackles on display at the Smithsonian's National Museum of African American History and Culture. Made of iron, they are heavy, and they look terribly uncomfortable. They were designed to hobble, physically constrain, and psychologically dispirit those who wore them. They were worn by children—Africans who were captured on their continent, often separated from their parents and loved ones, and brought over by ship to the Caribbean and to the Americans during the infamous slave trade.

Holding these shackles, feeling their heft, you also feel the weight of an instrument of bondage that afflicted millions of slaves, as well as the societies that participated in slavery. Scholars estimate that approximately 12,000,000 men, women, and children crossed the Atlantic Ocean in shackles for some 350 years—from the early 1500s until the widespread abolition of slavery in the 19th century. Numbers like those can be overwhelming. The mind simply can't process the enormity of the suffering. That's why artifacts like the ones we are about to discuss—these slave shackles, Eli Whitney's cotton gin, and Harriet Tubman's hymnal and shawl—are so important. They help to humanize and to personalize the story of slavery in the United States.

Let's begin with the shackles and the story of how slavery came to the Americas. Modern slavery had its roots in the 1400s during an era of sea exploration. The Portuguese and Spanish sought sea routes to India and the rest of Asia to acquire and trade luxury goods, like porcelain, spices, pearls, diamonds, ivory, silk, and jade. They did this to avoid the long and uncertain land routes through the Middle East and territories controlled by the Ottoman Empire. The sea routes meant sailing around Africa.

Portuguese and Spanish seafarers used a compass and astrolabe to navigate and generally hugged the African coast. They explored Africa's Atlantic Islands and its coastal regions. They built forts and small ports and traded with local rulers for gold, peppers, ivory, copper, cowrie shells, textiles, and other goods.

Among Portugal's trade partners were the rulers of Benin. Some of Benin's rulers had slaves who were generally captured in warfare and regional skirmishes. But African slavery was a very small-scale, local phenomenon, with nothing like the scope, scale, and institutional form of the later trans-Atlantic slave trade. Benin's slave trade, strangely enough, was intimately entwined with its artistic tradition. Benin's artists, then and now, are famous for making truly magnificent sculptures from bronze. The figures in these sculptures are often depicted wearing elaborate bronze or brass bracelets called manillas. Manillas, such as this one from the National Museum of African Art, were used as a form of currency.

Slaves were bought and sold in exchange for these manillas. An adult slave might have cost 11 manillas in the 1490s. The manillas, once exchanged, would be melted down and crafted into bronze artwork, such as bronze trophy heads, to be kept and treasured. A few slaves, on the other hand, were transported back to Portugal to become personal or household servants, while most were sold or exchanged for goods in other African coastal markets. Much of the Portuguese trade was conducted in the West African coastal region from today's Senegal to Nigeria, part of which came to be known as the Slave Coast, and then later in the Angola region.

Over the course of the next several decades, the slave trade and the use of slave labor was to change in scale and scope. The Cape Verde islands, off the coast of West Africa in the Atlantic Ocean, became an early testing ground for plantation agriculture. Large numbers of African slaves were procured to work on the plantations and produce goods for a European market.

This model crossed the Atlantic with Christopher Columbus's voyages to the Americas, particularly the Caribbean islands of Cuba, Hispaniola, and Puerto Rico. Columbus found these islands already inhabited by native people, called the Taino, who were initially welcoming and generous to the European explorers. But Columbus and the Spanish colonists who followed conquered and enslaved the Taino. They were forced to look for gold, to build forts, and to grow food. Some Taino rose up in revolt, and many of them were slaughtered in the fighting. Many others died of European diseases to which they had no immunity. By the early decades of the 1500s, the Taino natives had mostly died out.

The colonists, therefore, needed another, large source of labor to pursue their building, their mining, and agricultural ambitions. Bartolomé de las Casas, a Dominican friar serving in the Caribbean and then Mexico, suggested the importation of African slave labor as a solution, a position he later recanted.

The first African slaves were transported to Hispaniola, the island that comprises modern-day Haiti and the Dominican Republic, and that was in the early 1500s. Although the Spanish never found large amounts of gold, and thus didn't really need massive numbers of slaves, the idea of slavery took root nonetheless. Over the course of the next century, several hundred thousand slaves were sent, largely through Portuguese traders, to Portuguese and Spanish colonies in the Caribbean and South America. The horrendous voyage across the Atlantic in specially modified ships designed to carry humans as cargo came to be called the Middle Passage.

Slaves were put to work growing food, as construction laborers, and as domestic servants. Occasionally slaves would escape, often fleeing to the mountains or swamps, and sometimes learning from and intermarrying with native peoples. They became known as Cimaroons or, later, Maroons.

Slavery in the Americas expanded substantially in the 17th and 18th centuries because of the development of sugar plantations and the production of molasses and rum. Plantations also needed slaves to work fields of indigo, rice, tobacco, coffee, cocoa, and cotton. These agricultural enterprises drove the infamous triangular trade. African slaves were imported to labor in colonial plantations, largely in the Caribbean. They produced massive amounts of valuable raw materials that were then processed and sent to Europe for trade, for sale, for consumption. European merchants, made rich as a result, financed their own industrial and entrepreneurial pursuits and purchased additional slaves using precious metals, luxury goods, textiles, and firearms as currency, trading with rulers and merchants along Africa's western coast.

In West Africa, the growth of the slave trade resulted in close alliances and cooperation with African rulers, who supplied the European markets by procuring large numbers of slaves through warfare, kidnapping, punishment, and internal trade. Their agents would force-march slaves to the coast in coffles—human caravans. Captured slaves were bound with chains and ropes and Y-shaped branches around their necks, as depicted in carvings like this one from the National Museum of African Art. On this ivory tusk from the Loango coast of the Congo region you see the line of chained slaves.

Slaves would be herded into barracoons, or pens, at coastal slave forts or depots, where their bodies would be washed, shaved, and oiled to give them a robust appearance. Prices were negotiated in currencies and in kind. The forts, compounds, and slave castles that developed along the slave coast gave rise to so-called doors of no return, places where slaves looked out over an ocean that would forever separate them from their homes and their families. There is a dramatic door of no return on present-day Gorée Island, one of the slave compounds off of the coast of Dakar, Senegal.

As slavery became a thriving international business, ship owners and captains economized the loading and the transport of slaves, which they considered cargo. Specialized ships were constructed and designed to hold hundreds of people, usually about 450, sometimes many more captives, unwilling, desperate, and terrified; people would be packed into these ships. You can see from this historical illustration of the slave ship Brookes, the methodical engineering that went into loading and packing human beings as cargo in the most economical way. It is truly sobering to imagine the mindset that went into doing that.

Slaves were stripped naked and often branded. Men were shackled, the right leg of one to the left leg of the next, lying in tight rows next to one another. Women and children were sometimes shackled, sometimes not. Nonetheless, they were crowded together and suffered from poor sanitation, lack of fresh air and food, and devastating epidemics caused by the appalling conditions.

Slaves were typically led up to the main deck to be fed one meal a day—beans, corn, yams, rice, and water—before being taken back down to the hold. Conditions were foul and unsanitary, with scurvy, measles, smallpox, dysentery, and other infectious diseases rampant, taking the lives of an estimated one in every six people. Experiencing a five- to eight-week trip under these conditions led some slaves to commit suicide by jumping ship or starving themselves. Ship crews then installed nets to prevent the former and would torture slaves into eating.

In the 1600s, the Dutch and French supplanted the Portuguese as the leaders of the slave trade. In the 1700s, with the establishment of their American colonies, it was the British who dominated the slave trade. The first enslaved Africans in British North America arrived in Jamestown in 1619. Though sold at market, they were initially regarded as indentured servants, a European custom in which a poor person—white or black—was bound for a fixed term of labor. But in practice, the distinction hardly mattered, as few people managed to outlive the term of their indenture, and those who did had little recourse when owners refused to free them.

In 1654, the Virginia colony recognized slavery as an officially sanctioned condition. Enslaved people had no legal protection, no human rights, nor any hope of liberation. Within a century, slavery was legal in all 13 colonies. The economy in Jamestown, Virginia and the colonial South initially developed around the cultivation of tobacco. Though it was lucrative, intensive tobacco cultivation depleted soils fairly quickly, and growers increasingly faced competition from around the world. Planters began looking for an alternative cash crop. Rice, indigo, and sugarcane were cultivated in the semitropical low-country regions of South Carolina and Georgia but faced strong competition from widespread Caribbean plantations that, frankly, had better land and better climatic conditions. Growers in the upland South needed a crop that would thrive in the hot, dry summers and in relatively poor soil with limited rainfall.

Cotton was a possible answer. Grown natively in India and Mexico for thousands of years, cotton first became known to Europeans in the 14th century as a kind of wool that grew on trees or shrubs. It produced pods, or bolls, of fiber that looked like this. When processed, the fiber could be turned into yarn and threads and woven into textiles and clothing. By the 18th century, England's developing textile mills began using Indian cotton, employing considerable labor, and turning out new cloth for domestic consumption and export.

There were two basic types of cotton, short-staple and long-staple, where "staple" means the length of the individual fibers. Short-staple Mexican cotton was a good horticultural fit with the American South. Unlike long-staple cotton, it did not need a semitropical environment and could be widely planted. There was, however, a big problem; it required too much labor to be economically profitable. Picking cotton, that is, removing the bolls from the shrubs, took a lot of time and labor in the fields. The pods had sharp points; they cut up the picker's hands. Plus, the short-staple cotton bolls were full of seeds, about 25 per boll. Removing the seeds is an extremely difficult process and very time consuming. Even the best pickers could only de-seed about five pounds of cotton per day.

A technology—the roller gin—had long before been developed to remove the seeds from long-staple cotton. But the roller gin was ineffective for the short-staple variety of cotton. The seeds had to be removed by hand. This was a very slow and tedious process. One person working all day could perhaps separate out about four to eight pounds of usable cotton from the seeds. A number of inventors attempted to tackle the problem by trying to develop a workable and efficient cotton "engine" to separate the fiber from the unwanted seeds. Several found varying degrees of success, but it was Eli Whitney who broke through.

Whitney was a New Englander and Yale graduate who moved to Georgia in 1792 in search of a teaching job. He ended up living at the Mulberry Grove plantation of Catharine Greene, the widow of Continental Army General Nathanael Greene. Whitney's background in farming and his penchant for mechanical tinkering and engineering primed his interest in the challenge of processing cotton. Eventually, and maybe with Greene's help, he constructed a small device in a wooden housing, like this one.

At its core was a hand-turned wooden cylinder, or drum. Attached to the drum were wire hooks, or teeth, to catch onto the boll and pull the fibrous material through a slatted screen. The seeds would not fit through the slats, and thus dropped out, leaving the seeded cotton fiber to pass through. Brushes then removed the fiber from the teeth and moved the cotton along to be collected.

This is a model of a saw gin invented about two years after Whitney's, but it's a good example of the difference these machines made. Watch how it works. I put the cotton in here. A simple turn of the handle moving these gears and the cotton gets caught on the teeth of the saw blades. The teeth pull the fibers through; the brushes remove the fibers; and here it is. The cotton is de-seeded and ready to be spun, just like that.

However, the machine's simplicity belies its impact. A machine this size could process 50 to 60 pounds of cotton a day, about a tenfold increase over the previous hand-removal method, dramatically increasing efficiency. The only drawback was that many more of the fibers were cut in the process than would have been done by hand processing. Spinning machines had to be adapted to deal with the shorter fibers. It also produced a rougher yarn. Nonetheless, the vast improvement in the quantity of the cotton processed provided the opportunity for considerable economic gain.

Whitney submitted a model, description, and a drawing of the cotton gin as part of his application for a patent to the federal government. But other mechanics easily and cheaply produced their own cotton gins. Some came up with their own designs, while others copied Whitney's invention or made modifications and improvements on his design, as did Whitney himself. This kept Whitney very busy filing some two dozen patent-infringement lawsuits over the next decade, which drained his profit. But it was not until 1807 that Whitney's patent was firmly established, and while it made him famous, it did not make him wealthy.

Meanwhile, the mass proliferation of cotton gins had consequences that went far beyond the mechanical seeding of cotton. Because cotton processing could now proceed on a whole new scale, much more land could be developed and devoted to cotton cultivation. As cotton was easy to transport, it did not spoil; it could be sent to textile mills in Europe. In 1793, before the cotton gin, the United States exported 500,000 pounds of cotton. This grew to 93 million pounds by 1810. In the ensuing decades, cotton became America's chief export, accounting for more than half of all exported goods.

Cotton also headed to New England, where immigrant British entrepreneur Samuel Slater had developed a machine to spin cotton thread. As mechanical textile looms were established in Rhode Island and Massachusetts in the following decades, they acquired almost unlimited capacity to turn raw materials into finished textiles, stoking demand for Southern cotton.

Paradoxically, Whitney's labor-saving invention helped to preserve and expand slave labor through the South. Other forms of Southern slave-based agriculture were of declining import before the expansion of cotton growing, but cotton agriculture required a huge expanding labor force for planting and picking. So this device helped make cotton king, and it led to the expansion of slavery, and inadvertently, contributed to America's most costly conflict—the Civil War.

Thanks to King Cotton's dominance of the Southern economy, the number of enslaved people in the Southern states grew rapidly. In 1790, just under 700,000 slaves were reported in the first U.S. census. The number grew to almost 900,000 in 1800, and even though the importation of slaves was abolished in 1808, there were about 2 million slaves in 1830 and 4 million by 1860, as cotton production reached a staggering almost 2 billion pounds.

Profits from the enterprise fueled large plantations, with their Greek Revival mansions, as well as the lavish, almost aristocratic lifestyles of the antebellum South's white, landowning elite. Cotton cultivation also supported small-farm owners and slavery for their operations as well. This drove settlers west, into what had been native territory and brought white farmers into direct conflict with native tribes once again.

Ultimately, this led to the forced removal of Cherokee, Choctaw, and Seminole Indians from their Southern homelands to Oklahoma in the 1830s, a migration we now refer to as the Trail of Tears. Though we often consider how slavery ravaged the lives, family, and culture of African Americans, it's important to note that the economics of cotton production was profoundly destructive to Native American culture in the South as well.

The costs and the stakes of managing and controlling the huge slave population led to increasing regulations and harsher treatments in the period from the 1830s to the 1860s. Slaveholding states made legal gains, such as the Fugitive Slave Act of 1850 and the Supreme Court's Dred Scott Decision of 1857. But as you might expect, worsening conditions led to a rise in slave rebellions, like Nat Turner's brutal, and brutally suppressed, uprising in Virginia in 1831. Turner was inspired by Biblical teachings to seek freedom and an end to slavery. We have his Bible in the collections of the Smithsonian's National Museum of African American History and Culture.

These conditions also stoked the fires of abolitionism in the North. Efforts by northern abolitionists—black and white—to point to the horrors of plantation slavery and the institution as a whole grew with the efforts of people like Frederick Douglass, William Lloyd Garrison, Henry Ward Beecher, Harriet Beecher Stowe, and many others. The abolitionist movement was fueled in part by a new, very popular genre of literature, the slave narrative. These autobiographies, written by escaped slaves, like Frederick Douglass, Solomon Northup, Sojourner Truth, laid bare the harsh realities of slavery for readers on both sides of the Atlantic. Harriet Beecher Stowe's 1852 novel, *Uncle Tom's Cabin*, was one of the best-selling novels of the 19th century, and probably, the most significant piece of abolitionist literature. It was based in part on the published narrative of escaped slave Josiah Henson.

The new technology of photography helped spread the abolitionist message as well. In 1863, a slave named Gordon fled captivity in Mississippi and joined up with a Union Army regiment stationed in Baton Rouge. A photographer visiting the regiment heard his story and asked his permission to photograph the terrible scars on his back. This graphic image was widely published, and as a journalist for the *New York Independent* wrote, "It tells the story in a way that even Mrs. Stowe cannot approach, because it tells the story to the eye."

The fight against slavery had many such heroes and heroines, perhaps none better known or admired than Harriett Tubman. Harriet Tubman was an unlikely heroine. Petite, sickly, and enslaved for the first quarter of her life, she found her way to freedom and then dedicated herself to saving others. Tubman earned her renown as a "conductor" for the Underground Railroad, an illegal network of people who assisted and sheltered escaped slaves along routes to Canada, Mexico, or Spanish Florida, where they would be free under the law and exempt from extradition.

Born into slavery as Araminta Ross on Maryland's Eastern Shore and nicknamed "Minty," Tubman worked first as a house servant and then as a field hand. As a teen, she suffered a severe head injury at the hands of a brutal overseer when she tried to help a fellow slave. This abuse might have caused subsequent spells of unconsciousness, seizures, and vivid dreams throughout her lifetime. In 1844, she married a free black man, John Tubman, and in 1849 ran away for the first time, accompanied by her brothers. Tubman's owner placed an advertisement in a local newspaper, the Cambridge Democrat, offering a $100 reward for her capture. Her brothers, missing the family they'd left behind and fearing the slave-catchers, returned to the plantation, forcing Tubman to come with them.

Later, she fled again, this time reaching Philadelphia. The city, with its large Quaker and free black population, was a center of abolitionist sentiment. It had an active Underground Railroad led by William Still and the Vigilance Society. Despite the danger of capture, Tubman returned to Maryland's Eastern Shore in secret and began to guide enslaved people to their freedom via the series of safe houses known as the Underground Railroad, and she began with her niece and other members of her family.

The Underground Railroad expanded rapidly after 1850 in spite of the greater legal risk for those assisting escaped slaves. An estimated 1,000 or so enslaved people a year made it to freedom along the Underground Railroad. While this was a statistically small percentage, it nonetheless gave people hope and helped dramatize the terrible injustice of the federal laws that supported slavery.

Undeterred by law and physical danger, Tubman ventured into Maryland at least a dozen times in the 1850s; most historians believe she conducted 13 missions. She helped rescue scores of people, guiding them to safe houses in the North and to freedom in Canada. Frederick Douglass hailed her work, and insurrectionist John Brown called her "General Tubman." She developed a friendship with abolitionist William Seward, later, President Lincoln's secretary of state, who helped her relocate to Auburn, New York.

During the Civil War, Tubman served as a cook, nurse, spy, and scout for the Union Army. In 1863, she accompanied Union troops on gunboat raids on plantations along the Combahee River near Beaufort, South Carolina, raids that rescued more than 700 fleeing slaves. Tubman is reported to have calmed and encouraged many of them by singing hymns and encouraging them to "Come along! Come along! Don't be alarmed."

After the war, Tubman settled in Auburn and married a younger black man, Nelson Davis, a Union Army veteran. She befriended upstate New York neighbor Susan B. Anthony and became an advocate for women's rights and suffrage. She was active in her church, with the Salvation Army, and with freedman schools. Following the death of her second husband, she helped establish an African American nursing home. When she died, she was buried with military honors at Auburn's Fort Hill Cemetery. Tubman was a determined individual who, in an age that enshrined passivity as a virtue in women and slaves, took on a leading role in helping people seek their freedom.

Tubman was also a devout Christian and throughout her life was inspired by divine visions. We see the evidence of this in one of Tubman's prized personal possessions that we have with us today. This small book now rests in the Smithsonian's National Museum of African American History and Culture. It is Harriet Tubman's copy of P. P. Bliss and Ira D. Sankey's Gospel Hymns No. 2. The book is too fragile to manipulate, but if you did, it would naturally fall open to a certain hymn, the hymn most often read to her, and the ones she loved to sing, like "Swing Low, Sweet Chariot," which was sung at her funeral.

Tubman also cherished this silk lace and linen shawl sent to her by Queen Victoria in 1897, also part of the Smithsonian's collection. The shawl was a gift to Tubman on the occasion of the queen's Diamond Jubilee, her sixtieth year of rule. Queen Victoria was perhaps the world's most powerful leader at the time. Invitations were sent to rulers and prominent people around the world, including Tubman, to join in the celebration in England. Although Tubman could not attend, Queen Victoria sent her the shawl as well as a silver medal. When I look at and get close to Tubman's hymnal and shawl I can feel her presence and get a sense of the vision that motivated her bravery and cause. This is the power of objects, to put us in touch with the people who changed the world.

We started this lecture by looking at and feeling the slave shackles, so weighty and confining, so viscerally limiting one's freedom and humanity. And we end with considering Tubman's hymn singing, cast in a spiritual light, metaphorically, and in her case, actually, freeing human beings from the bondage of slavery.

These objects tell us the true human cost of slavery and the power of humankind to overcome it through freedom. Enshrining such objects in the National Museum of African American History and Culture provides the means by which this important aspect of our history will continue to be told and felt for future generations.

Emancipation and the Civil War

Lecture 5

The drive to end slavery in the United States was a long one—from being debated in the writing of the Declaration of Independence to exposure of its ills in literature, from rebellions of slaves to the efforts of people like Harriet Tubman to transport escaping slaves along the Underground Railroad. We as a nation have come a long way, but for the longest time, African American accomplishments were not documented and poignant stories were not told in the national museums. As you will learn in this lecture, the National Museum of American History includes Christian Fleetwood's Medal of Honor and other artifacts for precisely this reason.

The Emancipation Proclamation

- Abolitionists had urged President Abraham Lincoln to free the slaves in the Confederate states from the very outset of the Civil War. By mid-1862, Lincoln had become increasingly convinced of the moral imperative to end slavery, but he hesitated. As commander in chief of the Union Army, he had military objectives to consider.

- On one hand, emancipation might undermine support for the Union cause in the border states—Delaware, Maryland, Kentucky, and Missouri. Those were the slave states that had not joined the Confederacy, and their loyalty was crucial for the Union's military success. White communities in these states were strongly divided over the issue. If abolition upset slave owners in these states and tipped the scales toward secession, the Union would be dealt a major blow.

- But on the other hand, emancipation also had strategic advantages. A promise of freedom for enslaved African Americans in the South could seriously undermine Confederate power. These slaves might actively sabotage the Southern war effort or weaken its fragile economy by withholding their labor.

- In fact, thousands of slaves had already escaped to sanctuary in Union territory, to places like Fort Monroe in Virginia. These refugees aided the war effort by providing information on Confederate movements and supply lines. But they were not yet eligible for protection under the law. Instead, they were classified as contraband—enemy property subject to seizure. Emancipation would offer them civil rights.

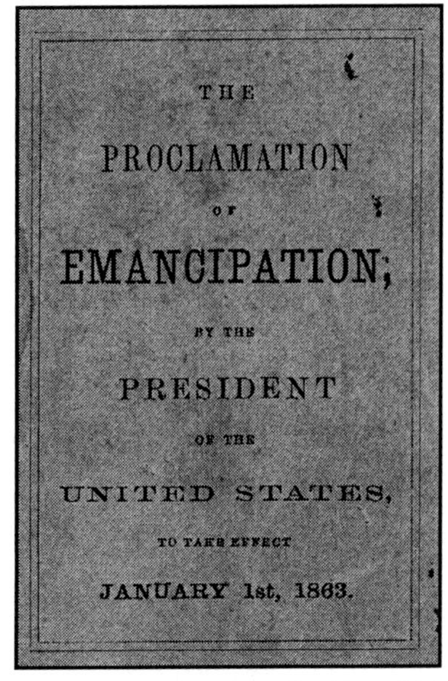

THE
PROCLAMATION
OF
EMANCIPATION;
BY THE
PRESIDENT
OF THE
UNITED STATES,
TO TAKE EFFECT
JANUARY 1st, 1863.

Emancipation Proclamation Pamphlet

- Lincoln also hoped that emancipation of Southern slaves would persuade African Americans in the Northern states to enlist in the Union Army. Finally, an abolitionist course might dissuade Britain and France from lending military support to the Confederate states. Both nations had ended slavery in their own countries but retained economic interests in Southern goods and plantation crops. Overall, emancipation seemed not only the right moral decision, but also the right military decision.

- Lincoln's first step was to sign the District of Columbia Compensated Emancipation Act on April 16, 1862. About 3,000 enslaved people who had been living in the shadows of the Capitol and the White House were freed. Their former masters were compensated from a government fund. They received up to 300 dollars per slave—at the time considered very generous.

- On April 19, three days after Lincoln signed the act, the District's African American population celebrated with a huge parade.

Historians estimate that half the city's black population participated, and 10,000 people lined the streets to watch the joyous marchers. Emancipation Day is still a holiday in Washington DC. Overall, Lincoln's first step toward emancipation was a success. He now believed that freeing the Southern slaves was the correct course.

- During the summer of 1862, Lincoln visited the War Department's telegraph office almost daily, exchanging messages with his Union generals. Finally, as summer faded into autumn, the president sat at the desk of its chief, Major Thomas Eckert. Using the officer's pen and ornate brass inkstand, he drafted the Emancipation Proclamation. Then, he waited for good news from the battlefields to issue it from strength, not weakness.

- On September 22, 1862, five days after Union troops turned back the northern charge of the Confederate Army at Antietam, Maryland, Lincoln issued the Emancipation Proclamation. Lincoln presented the proclamation as an executive order based on his presidential powers as commander in chief. Because it was not a law, it did not require congressional approval or review.

- It proclaimed as free the enslaved people in states and regions that remained in the Confederacy as of January 1, 1863. It did not free the remaining slaves in northern or border states, nor did it free enslaved people in Tennessee, parts of Virginia, or parts of Louisiana where Union forces had already assumed control.

- The proclamation did not abolish slavery throughout the United States, but it did make the abolition of slavery a war aim. But the Emancipation Proclamation gave hope to African Americans across the country, who now saw their dreams of freedom clearly linked to a Union victory.

- Lincoln's proclamation was widely publicized and reproduced in the next few months. A clause about compensating slave states for the loss of their "property" was dropped, as was a repatriation clause. The preliminary draft did not mention military service, but the final proclamation allowed former slaves to join the United States armed forces.

- On December 30, 1862, Secretary of State William Seward brought the final version to the White House for the president to sign on the morning of January 1, 1863. Lincoln signed it, but then noticed a small technical error. Seward had it changed, and later that day, Lincoln signed the corrected final copy.

- By day's end, the proclamation was distributed to the press and brought to the telegraph office for transmission across the nation. Four copies were made of the original final draft. A "clean" official document was kept by the State Department, and that copy is now in the National Archives.

- Pocket-sized copies of the Emancipation Proclamation were designed for distribution by soldiers on the front lines. One such pamphlet is in the National Museum of African American History and Culture. It was from these pamphlets that Lincoln's proclamation was read aloud in the field by Union officers in Confederate territory. Eyewitness accounts describe celebrations on January 1, 1863, as thousands of blacks in Confederate states were informed of their new legal status as freedmen.

African Americans in the Military

- Among its many benefits, the Emancipation Proclamation encouraged African Americans to join the Union Army, just as Lincoln had hoped. African Americans had fought in the Revolutionary War and the War of 1812, but by the mid-19th century, that service was often publicly ignored. Since 1820, the U.S. Army had prohibited "Negroes or Mulattoes" from serving in uniform.

- When the Civil War broke out in April 1861, President Lincoln called for 75,000 volunteers to join the army. A number of Northern blacks offered their services but were rebuffed. The War Department was opposed to arming blacks for fear it would induce the loyal slave-holding border states to join the Confederacy.

- By the fall of 1862, the situation had changed. The Union faced heavy battlefield losses, and enrollments were declining. It was clear that winning the war would take more time, and more troops, than anyone expected.

- After the Emancipation Proclamation legalized black enlistment, the 54th Massachusetts Infantry was born. Frederick Douglass was buoyed by the new policy and encouraged two of his sons to serve. Other black regiments, designated U.S. Colored Troops, were quickly raised, with help from Douglass and others who issued the call "Men of Color, to Arms!" Douglass knew that military service provided a route to freedom.

- The first regiments were formed in Massachusetts, South Carolina, and Tennessee. They served as artillerymen and infantrymen. They also served in support positions such as scouts, surgeons, and chaplains. About 19,000 men served in the Navy. Almost 80 African American men were commissioned officers across the armed services, although more often, due to prejudice, black regiments were led by white commissioned officers.

- African American women served as well, albeit in a less official capacity. Many were nurses; some were the Union's most important spies. Mary Bowser, a slave in Jefferson Davis's presidential mansion, was a spy for the North. Harriet Tubman, along with her Underground Railroad work, acted as both a scout and a spymaster for the Union. By war's end, approximately 180,000 men and women had answered the call. About 40,000 had given their life for the cause. African Americans comprised about 10 percent of all Union forces.

Christian Fleetwood's Medal of Honor

- Christian Fleetwood was born a free man in Baltimore, Maryland. He attended the Ashmun Institute in Pennsylvania, one of the first colleges in the nation dedicated to educating African Americans. At the age of 23, Fleetwood enlisted in Company G of the Fourth Regiment, U.S. Colored Infantry. Given his education, he was assigned the rank of sergeant and was promoted to sergeant major days later. His unit was assigned to fight in North Carolina and Virginia.

Christian Fleetwood's Medal of Honor

- In September 1864, Fleetwood's unit was part of the massive siege of Petersburg, Virginia, a pivotal campaign that would help end the war. Union troops under General Ulysses S. Grant were trying to break the network of trenches and garrisons protecting the route between the southern Virginia supply center and Richmond, the capital of the Confederacy.

- On September 29, 1864, Fleetwood's Fourth Regiment participated in the Battle of Chaffin's Farm on the outskirts of Richmond, south of the James River. About 26,000 Union troops faced about 15,000 Confederate troops. Several thousand black troops led the charge through rough forests and swamps.

- Fleetwood led one flank of his unit's attack. More than half of the black soldiers were killed or wounded. During his unit's charge, all save one of the flag-bearing color guards were killed. Fleetwood grabbed the American flag from a soldier who had been hit and continued forward, leading his men into heavy fire. Although they could not breach the defense line, the flag-brandishing Fleetwood again rallied the troops to continue the fight.

- Fleetwood and two of his fellow flag bearers were issued Medals of Honor on April 6, 1865, three days before Confederate General Robert E. Lee surrendered to Grant. Congress had approved such Medals of Honor in 1861 for the Navy and a year later for the Army. The central figures are Minerva, the goddess of wisdom, repulsing a snake-clutching figure of discord. The 34 stars that encircle them represent the 34 states, both Union and Confederate.

- Although the war was over and the Emancipation Proclamation freed enslaved people in the South, slavery remained the law of the land in some of the border states. Only Maryland, Missouri, Tennessee, and West Virginia had enacted emancipation during the war. About 40,000 people remained in bondage in Delaware and Kentucky, as well as a handful of unfortunate people in the North, trapped under decades-old legal provisions. Only with the passage of the Thirteenth Amendment in December 1865 would all Americans be free.

- After Fleetwood won his medal, all of the white officers of his regiment petitioned for him to be commissioned an officer, but Secretary of War Edwin Stanton refused. The respect African American soldiers had earned from their fellows in the field could not overcome the age-old prejudice at the higher levels of command. He was issued an honorable discharge at the war's end and never saw active duty again.

- After the war, Fleetwood worked in several government positions in the Freedman's Savings and Trust Company and in the War Department in Washington DC. He organized a battalion of National Guardsmen as well as the Colored High School Cadet Corps, which established a high standard of military service for African American soldiers. He died in 1914.

- In 1947, Fleetwood's elderly daughter, Edith, offered his Medal of Honor to the U.S. National Museum. She noted that, at the time, the museum did not have or display any African American collections. Her father's medal would be the first. She also said it was important because of the "nation's renewed and determined emphasis upon true democracy." She was referring to President Harry S Truman's recent decision to integrate the armed forces.

- In principle, her gift to the museum fit within the collecting framework espoused by Theodore Belote, then the Smithsonian's curator of historical collections. Belote focused on what he described as "eminent Americans," by which he generally meant men who served in some capacity in government or the military.

- Fleetwood was one of only 24 African Americans to be awarded the Medal of Honor in the Civil War. While the associate curator, Charles Casey, who handled military medals, recommended that the material be accessioned to the permanent collection, Belote objected.

- Belote argued that the collection lacked adequate storage and display space, a patently false claim. He was more concerned with the inclusion of African American historical collections as a political statement. The secretary of the Smithsonian, Alexander Wetmore, overrode his curator's decision and accepted the donation.

- But when Belote put the medal on display, he omitted any reference on the label to Fleetwood's membership in the Fourth Colored Troops. Edith Fleetwood objected, saying that no one would ever know that her heroic father was black. She said that, one day, she hoped that would be superfluous. But for the present, it was necessary to achieve a "true democracy." This time, the head of the museum, Remington Kellogg, overruled Belote, and Fleetwood's service was accurately recognized.

Featured Objects

Emancipation Proclamation Pamphlet

Christian Fleetwood's Medal of Honor

Appomattox Courthouse Furniture

Suggested Reading

Berlin, Reidy, and Rowland, *Freedom's Soldiers*.

Masur, *Lincoln's Hundred Days*.

Varon, *Appomattox*.

Emancipation and the Civil War

Lecture 5—Transcript

The drive to end slavery in the United States was a long one, from being debated in the writing of the Declaration of Independence to exposure of its ills in literature, from rebellions of slaves to the efforts of people like Harriett Tubman to transport escaping slaves along the Underground Railroad, as we heard in our last lecture. Abolitionists had urged President Abraham Lincoln to free the slaves in the Confederate states from the very outset of the Civil War. By mid-1862, Lincoln had become increasingly convinced of the moral imperative to end slavery, but he hesitated. As commander-in-chief of the Union Army, he had military objectives to consider.

On one hand, emancipation might undermine support for the Union cause in the border states—Delaware, Maryland, Kentucky, and Missouri. Those were slave states that had not joined the Confederacy, and their loyalty was crucial for the Union's military success. White communities in these states were strongly divided over the issue. If abolition upset slave owners in these states and tipped the scales toward secession, the Union would be dealt a major blow. But on the other hand, emancipation also had strategic advantages. A promise of freedom for enslaved African Americans in the South could seriously undermine Confederate power. These slaves might actively sabotage the Southern war effort or weaken its fragile economy by withholding their labor. In fact, thousands of slaves had already escaped to sanctuary in Union territory, to places like Fort Monroe in Virginia. These refugees aided the war effort by providing information on Confederate movements and supply lines. But they were not yet eligible for protection under the law. Instead, they were classified as contraband—enemy property subject to seizure. Emancipation would offer them civil rights.

Lincoln also hoped emancipation of Southern slaves would persuade African Americans in the Northern states to enlist in the Union Army. Finally, an abolitionist course might dissuade Britain and France from lending military support to Confederate states. Both nations had ended slavery in their own countries but retained economic interests in Southern goods and plantation crops. So, overall, emancipation seemed not only the right moral decision, but the right military decision.

Lincoln's first step was to sign the District of Columbia Compensated Emancipation Act on April 16, 1862. About three thousand enslaved people who had been living in the shadows of the Capitol and the White House were freed. Their former masters were compensated from a government fund. They received up to $300 per slave, at the time, considered very generous.

The act had three very interesting provisions. One, anyone who had fought for the Confederacy or given "aid and comfort" to Confederate soldiers, could not make a claim for compensation. Two, kidnapping a citizen of the District back into slavery was deemed a felony; anyone found guilty of that crime would serve a sentence of 5 to 20 years in prison. And three, a separate fund was set up to help newly freed persons emigrate to Liberia, Haiti, or "such other country beyond the limits of the United States as the President [might] determine."

Liberia was a new nation, carved out of the former slave coast of Africa. It was founded in 1820 by members of the American Colonization Society as a refuge for freed slaves. The society was composed of a group of strange bedfellows—Abolitionist Quakers from the North and slaveholders from the Chesapeake Bay region. These abolitionists generally believed that African Americans faced too much prejudice in the United States and would have greater economic opportunity in Africa. The slaveholders generally believed that free blacks were a danger to white society and simply wanted them gone. On April 19th, three days after Lincoln signed the act, the District's African American population celebrated with a huge parade. Historians estimate that half the city's black population participated, and 10,000 people lined the streets to watch the joyous marchers. Emancipation Day is still a holiday in Washington DC.

Overall, Lincoln's first step toward emancipation was a success. He now believed that freeing the Southern slaves was the correct course. The only question was, when? During the summer of 1862, Lincoln visited the War Department's telegraph office almost daily, exchanging messages with his Union generals. Finally, as summer faded into autumn, the president sat at the desk of its chief, Major Thomas Eckert. Using the officer's pen and ornate brass inkstand, he drafted the Emancipation Proclamation. Then, he waited for good news from the battlefields, so as to issue it from strength, not weakness.

On September 22, 1862, five days after Union troops turned back the northern charge of the Confederate Army at Antietam, Maryland, Lincoln issued the Emancipation Proclamation. Lincoln presented the proclamation as an executive order based upon his presidential powers as commander in chief. It was not a law, it did not require congressional approval or review. It proclaimed as free the enslaved people in states and regions that remained in the Confederacy as of January 1, 1863. It did not free remaining slaves in northern or border states, nor did it free enslaved peoples in Tennessee, parts of Virginia, or parts of Louisiana where Union forces had already assumed control. The proclamation did not abolish slavery throughout the United States, but it did make the abolition of slavery a war aim. But the Emancipation Proclamation gave hope to African Americans across the country, who now saw their dreams of freedom clearly linked to a Union victory. Lincoln's proclamation was widely publicized and reproduced in the next few months.

A clause about compensating slave states for the loss of their "property" was dropped, as was a repatriation clause like the one in the District Emancipation Act. This preliminary draft, issued by Lincoln in September 1862, did not mention military service, but the final proclamation allowed former slaves to join the United States armed forces. On December 30, 1862, Secretary of State William Seward brought the final version of the Emancipation Proclamation to the White House for the president to sign on the morning of January 1, 1863.

Lincoln signed it, but then he noticed a small technical error, and so Seward had it changed, and later that day, Lincoln signed the corrected final copy, saying as he did, "I never, in my life, felt more certain that I was doing right than I do in signing this paper." By day's end, the proclamation was distributed to the press and brought to the telegraph office for transmission across the nation. Four copies were made of the original final draft. A "clean," official document was kept by the State Department, and that copy is now in the National Archives.

Now come and take a look at this tiny, pocket-sized pamphlet, which is from the collections of the National Museum of American History. It's tiny for a reason. This copy of the Emancipation Proclamation had to be small, because it was designed for distribution by soldiers on the front lines. One of the most interesting things about it is that it was actually printed a few weeks before the proclamation was signed by Abraham Lincoln. It was printed in Boston by the abolitionist John Murray Forbes, sometime in December 1862. We don't know how many copies like these were printed, but they were an important part of the war effort. It was from these little pamphlets that Lincoln's proclamation was read aloud in the field by Union soldiers in Confederate territory. This allowed former slaves to hear for themselves the official words of the president, words that transformed their hopes and prayers for freedom into the law.

Eyewitness accounts describe the celebrations on January 1, 1863, as thousands of blacks in the Confederate states of North Carolina, South Carolina, Florida, and other locales were informed of their new legal status as free men. Booker T. Washington, who was just a boy at the time, recalled the event:

"Some man who seemed to be a stranger (a United States officer, I presume) made a little speech and then read the Emancipation Proclamation, I think. After the reading, we were told that we were all free and could go when and where we pleased. My mother, who was standing by my side, leaned over and kissed her children, while tears of joy ran down her cheeks. She explained to us what it all meant, that this was the day for which she had been so long praying, but fearing that she would never live to see."

The effect of reading these cheaply printed "pocket" copies of the Emancipation Proclamation was stunning. Read countless times, these unassuming little booklets communicated a new spirit of freedom for enslaved people. And among its many benefits, the Emancipation Proclamation encouraged African Americans to join the Union Army, just as Lincoln had hoped.

African Americans had fought in the Revolutionary War and the War of 1812, but by the mid-19th century, that service was often publicly ignored.

Since 1820, the U.S. Army had prohibited "negroes or mulattoes" from serving in uniform. When the Civil War broke out in 1861, Abraham Lincoln called for 75,000 volunteers to join the army. A number of Northern blacks offered their services but were rebuffed. The War Department was opposed to arming blacks for fear it would induce the loyal slave-holding border states to join the Confederacy.

By the fall of 1862, the situation had changed. The Union faced heavy battlefield losses and enrollments were declining. It was clear that winning the war would take more time and more troops than anyone expected. After the Emancipation Proclamation legalized black enlistment, the 54th Massachusetts Infantry was born. Frederick Douglass was buoyed by the new policy and encouraged two of his sons to serve. Other black regiments, designated U.S. Colored Troops, were quickly raised with help from Douglass and others who issued the call, "Men of Color, to Arms!" Douglass knew military service provided a route to freedom. He said: "Once, let the Black man get upon his person the brass letters 'U.S.,' let him get an eagle on his button, and a musket on his shoulder, and bullets in his pocket, and there will be no power on earth which can deny that he has earned the right to citizenship in the United States."

The first regiments were formed in Massachusetts, South Carolina, and Tennessee. They served as artillery men and infantry men. They also served in support positions such as scouts, and surgeons, and chaplains. About 19,000 men served in the Navy. Almost 80 African American men were commissioned officers across the armed services, although more often, due to prejudice, black regiments were led by white commissioned officers.

African American women served as well, albeit in a less official capacity. Many were nurses. Some of them were the Union's most important spies. Mary Bowser, a slave in Jefferson Davis's presidential mansion, was a spy for the North. And Harriet Tubman, along with her Underground Railroad work, acted as both a scout and a spymaster for the Union. By war's end, approximately 180,000 men and women had answered the call. Some 40,000 had given their life for the cause. African Americans composed about 10% of all Union forces.

One man who served was Christian Fleetwood. Fleetwood was born a free man in Baltimore, Maryland. He received an excellent early education and visited Liberia as a teenager. He attended the Ashmun Institute in Pennsylvania, one of the first colleges in the nation dedicated to educating African Americans. He promoted the emigration of free blacks in the United States to Liberia and founded and published the Lyceum Observer, a newspaper in Baltimore during the beginning of the Civil War.

He joined the army with "A double purpose," as he said, "to assist in abolishing slavery and to save the country from ruin." At the age of 23, Fleetwood enlisted in Company G of the 4th Regiment, U.S. Colored Infantry. Given his education, he was assigned the rank of sergeant and was promoted to sergeant major only days later. His unit was assigned to fight in North Carolina and in Virginia.

In September 1864, Fleetwood's unit was part of the massive siege of Petersburg, Virginia, a pivotal campaign that would help end the war. Union troops under General Ulysses S. Grant were trying to break the network of trenches and garrisons protecting the route between the southern Virginia supply center and Richmond, the capital of the Confederacy.

On September 29, 1864, Fleetwood's 4th Regiment participated in the Battle of Chaffin's Farm on the outskirts of Richmond, south of the James River. Some 26,000 Union troops faced about 15,000 Confederate troops. Several thousand black troops led the charge through the rough forests and swamps.

Fleetwood led one flank of his unit's attack. More than half of the black soldiers were killed or wounded. During his unit's charge, all, save one of the flag-bearing color guards, were killed. Fleetwood grabbed the American flag from a soldier who had been hit and continued forward, leading his men into heavy fire. Though they could not break the defensive line, the flag-brandishing Fleetwood, again, rallied the troops to continue the fight. Fleetwood and two of his fellow flag bearers were issued Medals of Honor on April 6, 1865, three days before Confederate General Robert E. Lee surrendered to General Grant. Fleetwood's official citation reads, "Seized the colors, after two color bearers had been shot down, and bore them nobly through the fight."

Congress had approved such Medals of Honor in 1861 for the Navy, and a year later, for the Army. The central figure in the Medal of Honor is Minerva, the goddess of wisdom, repulsing a snake-clutching figure of discord. The 34 stars that encircle them represent the 34 states, both Union and Confederate.

A few days after Fleetwood received his medal of honor, on Palm Sunday, April 9, 1865, Confederate General Robert E. Lee, commander of the Army of Northern Virginia, entered the home of Wilmer McLean in the village of Appomattox Court House, Virginia. He was there to discuss the terms of surrender that would effectively end the Civil War. A few hours earlier, Lee had told General James Longstreet, "There is nothing left for me to do but to go and see General Grant, and I would rather die a thousand deaths."

The son of a Revolutionary War general Lee had served as an engineer in the U.S. Army in the Mexican-American War; he'd served as superintendent of the U.S. Military Academy at West Point and had put down John Brown's uprising at Harpers Ferry. Lee had married into the family of George Washington, and, though he supported the preservation of the Union, he'd resigned his commission to remain loyal to his home state of Virginia, even though President Lincoln had asked him to lead the Union Army. Instead, he became the military adviser to Jefferson Davis, and a head of the Confederate Army of Northern Virginia, and ultimately, the leader of all Confederate forces.

By 1865, with his army boxed in, cut off from supply lines, and exhausted from the Siege of Petersburg and the Appomattox Campaign, Lee had no choice but to surrender. Dressed in a notably clean dress uniform with sword, Lee arrived first in the McLean parlor and took the more comfortable high-backed cane chair. He reportedly waited about a half an hour.

Ulysses S. Grant, in contrast to Lee, entered the parlor clad in a mud-spattered battle uniform with no sword. Grant was about 15 years younger than Lee but also had been West Point graduate. The two had actually met in 1848 when both fought in the Mexican-American War. Grant had since retired from the military and failed at farming, bill collecting, the tannery business, and so on, before rejoining the Army at the outset of the Civil

War. He rose in rank and command, eventually becoming head of the Union forces. He took the lower-backed leather chair.

Lee was joined by just one aide while Grant brought with him more than a dozen, including Robert Todd Lincoln, the son of the president. After a brief exchange of personal reminiscences, Lee and Grant got down to business. Lee objected to the surrender provision that the troops' horses and arms be confiscated. Soldiers often supplied their own weapons and mounts, and they'd need these horses back in their civilian lives. Grant agreed to this and added a stipulation that all troops agree not to take up arms against the government again. Leaning over the small, oval, spool-legged table between them, Grant drafted the final terms, and Lee leaned on a marble table and wrote his surrender letter.

While there were still Confederate troops in the field under other commanders, Lee's surrender ensured the freedom of his key military leaders and thus effectively marked the end of the Civil War. Great cities like Atlanta and Richmond lay in ruins. Millions of lives had been disrupted; homes and crops destroyed; and families devastated by the loss of sons, fathers, and husbands—about 700,000 in total.

Grant would go on to become president of the United States for two terms. Lee would, in many quarters, gain ever more respect as a university president, reconciler between North and South, and in retrospect, a brilliant general who had loyally served the "Lost Cause of the Confederacy." Both men would be celebrated with statues and other memorials, Lee throughout the South, and Grant throughout the North.

Shortly after the treaty was signed, Union officers, recognizing the significance of the event, took pieces of furniture as souvenirs. These became increasingly valuable relics of American history in the decades that followed. They were passed through the veterans' families to the Smithsonian. The McLean house, home to the surrender furniture, was purchased in 1891 by a New York State investor who hoped to dismantle and reconstruct it as an exhibit at the 1893 World's Columbian Exposition in Chicago. This effort failed. A subsequent scheme to move the McLean house to Washington, DC, as the "surrender" centerpiece of a Civil War museum progressed far enough along that the building was completely disassembled. But those plans, again, fell apart, and the materials fell prey to scavengers. In 1941, an act of Congress created the Appomattox Court House National Monument to reconstruct the McLean House. The furnishings at that site are replicas, based on the originals at the Smithsonian.

Although the war was now over, and the Emancipation Proclamation freed enslaved peoples in the South, slavery remained the law of the land in some of the border states. Only Maryland, Missouri, Tennessee, and West Virginia had enacted emancipation during the war. About 40,000 remained in bondage in Delaware and Kentucky, as well as a handful of unfortunate people in the North, trapped under decades-old legal provisions. Only with the passage of the Thirteenth Amendment in December 1865 would all Americans be free.

But as we know, "freedom" is not a synonym for "equality." The fight for civil rights for African Americans was far from over. In future lectures, we'll turn to the story of this struggle. But before we move on, let's take a look at how that struggle played out in the story of Christian Fleetwood's medal of honor. That Medal of Honor went on to have a fascinating second life as a museum artifact.

Every Medal of Honor awarded by the U.S. government is extraordinary, and this one is especially so given the context. But also compelling is the tale of how his descendants fought for justice long after his death on a very different kind of battlefield. After Fleetwood won his medal, all the white officers of his regiment petitioned for him to be a commissioned an officer, but Secretary of War Edwin Stanton refused. The respect African American soldiers had earned from their fellows in the field could not overcome the age-old prejudice at the highest levels of command.

Fleetwood was issued an honorable discharge at war's end and never saw active duty again. After the war, Fleetwood worked in several government positions in the Freedman's Savings and Trust Company and in the War Department in Washington, DC He organized a battalion of National Guardsmen, as well as the Colored High School Cadet Corps, which established a high standard of military service for African American soldiers. He died in 1914.

In 1947, Fleetwood's elderly daughter, Edith, offered his Medal of Honor to the United States National Museum. She noted that at the time the museum did not have or display any African American collections. Her father's medal would be the first. She also said it was important because of the "nation's renewed and determined emphasis on true democracy." She was referring to President Harry S. Truman's recent decision to integrate the armed forces. In principle, her gift to the museum fit within the collecting framework espoused by Theodore Belote, then the Smithsonian's curator of historical collections. Belote focused on what he described as "eminent Americans," by which he generally meant men who served in some capacity in government or the military.

Fleetwood was only one of only 24 African Americans to be awarded the Medal of Honor in the Civil War. While the associate curator at the Smithsonian, Charles Casey, who handled military medals, recommended that the material be accessioned to the permanent collection, Belote objected. Belote argued that the collection lacked adequate storage and display space, which was a patently false claim. He was more concerned with the inclusion of African American historical collections as a political statement. While he said he would be "the last one to recommend that relics of colored soldiers should be excluded from a national military museum," he maintained that the United States National Museum's collection was not the proper place for Fleetwood's Medal of Honor.

The secretary of the Smithsonian, Alexander Wetmore, overrode his curator's decision and accepted the donation. But when Belote put the medal on display in the museum, he omitted any reference on the label to Fleetwood's membership in the Fourth Colored Troops. Edith Fleetwood, his daughter, objected, saying that no one would never know that her heroic father was a black man. She said that one day she hoped that that would be superfluous. But for the present, it was necessary to achieve a true democracy. This time, the head of the museum, Remington Kellogg, overruled Belote, and Fleetwood's service was accurately recognized.

We as a nation have come a long way since 1947, but the truth is that for the longest time African American accomplishments were not documented and poignant stories not told in the national museums. The National Museum of African American History and Culture includes these and other artworks and artifacts for precisely this reason. We need to not only tell the story of African Americans, but a larger American story of how our country struggled with and went from slavery to freedom and a broader, more inclusive view of who we are as a people.

Gold, Guns, and Grandeur—The West

Lecture 6

For Americans of many generations, "the West" has conjured up images of the unknown, of opportunity beyond the frontier, of the promise of a new life. But the West is more complicated and nuanced than that. As you will learn in this lecture, the West was the home to diverse groups of native people for thousands of years. You will learn how far the country has come in recognizing and honoring the rights of Native Americans in the face of historical injustice and what was the winning and the losing of the West.

The California Gold Rush

- Perhaps most emblematic of the Westward drive was a nation-changing discovery on January 24, 1848, along the South Fork of the American River at Coloma, California. California was at that moment, officially, Mexican territory, because the Treaty of Guadalupe Hidalgo ending the Mexican-American War of 1846 to 1848 had not yet been signed.

- The war had been prompted by America's admission of Texas into the United States and a dispute over this new border. The treaty signed on February 2, 1848, ceded the entire Southwest to the United States: today's New Mexico, Arizona, Utah, Nevada, California, and a bit of Colorado. In exchange, former Mexican citizens in the territory were guaranteed protection, and the United States paid the Mexican government 15 million dollars, a bargain price, as it turned out.

- On the morning of January 24, carpenter James Marshall was overseeing the construction of a sawmill for Colonel John Sutter. Marshall noticed something glittering in the water of the mill's tailrace and bent down to pick it up. Marshall and Sutter tested the flake and were confident that what Marshall had found was a flake of pure gold.

- In the summer of 1848, Colonel Sutter presented Marshall's gold flake to Captain Joseph Folsom, U.S. Army assistant quartermaster at Monterey. Folsom was in northern California to verify the gold claim for the U.S. government. He gave the weight of Marshall's flake as less than nine hundredths of a gram.

- After Marshall's first find, other nuggets were discovered, and Folsom estimated that about 4,000 men were mining gold by the time he arrived. Folsom took samples, and U.S. Army Lieutenant Lucien Loeser took them back to Washington to give to President James Polk.

- In his State of the Union address on December 5, 1848, Polk formally told Congress that gold had been discovered in California. Polk called for a mint to be established in California—for them to be able to make coins there—and he argued that the discovery of gold would be good for everyone in the country and for the country itself.

- It was for the good of the country that the nation had to acquire California, New Mexico, and the settlement of the Oregon boundary, in addition to annexing Texas. This was the vindication of the Mexican-American War. In fact, it was a vindication of an idea that journalist John L. Sullivan had recently called "Manifest Destiny."

- Polk pursued an expansionist vision in waging war, and this vision was captured in the painting *Westward the Course of Empire Takes Its Way* by Emanuel Gottlieb Leutze. It shows a historical amalgam of explorers, pioneers, and settlers, with guns and wagons having made their way through dark and treacherous mountains grandly and dramatically eyeing their progress toward the sun-filled, colorful California coast.

The Colt Revolver

- One of the main reasons for victory in the Mexican-American War was the development of the Colt revolver. A born inventor, Samuel Colt was particularly enamored of firearms and eventually seized on the idea of a single-barrel gun with a revolving cylinder that would lock into place, automatically aligning lead balls with the barrel. He sought and secured patents for the revolver in both England and the United States in the 1830s and started manufacturing the Colt Paterson as a commercial firearm.

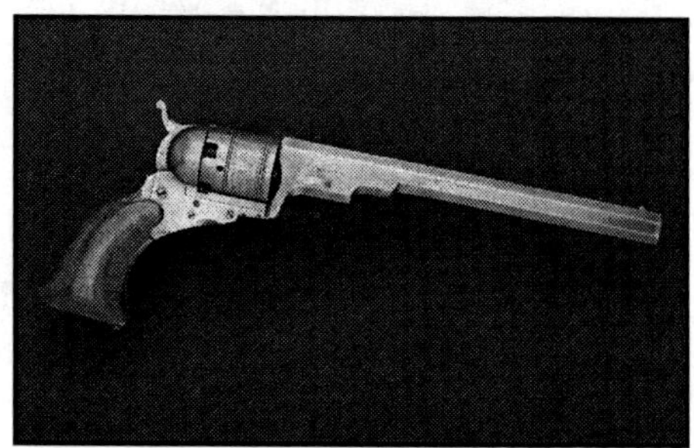

Colt Revolver

- Colt sold an early version to the Republic of Texas, whose Rangers used the revolver in their fights with the Comanches. The gun evolved when the United States went to war with Mexico in 1846. Former Ranger Captain Samuel Walker became an officer in the U.S. Mounted Rifles. He visited Colt, seeking a more powerful weapon that could be used by horse-mounted troops. The result was the Colt Walker, a long, heavy six-shooter that could stop a horse and win battles.

- The Colt revolver was used by soldiers on both sides of the Civil War and afterward by settlers, family members, cowboys and Indians, homesteaders, ranchers, and lawmen and outlaws. The Colt Single Action Army Model revolver was incredibly popular and is sometimes called "the gun that won the West"—it made possible the realization of Manifest Destiny.

The Sutter's Mill Gold Flake

- The discovery of gold in California became widely known in 1849, and this kicked off the Gold Rush. About 300,000 Americans from the East and the Midwest headed to California. So did many immigrants from Latin America, Europe, China, and even Australia. They became known as '49ers, ready to prospect for gold and gain boundless wealth. Some of the '49ers grew wealthy, but many either left in despair or simply stayed in the region as farmers or menial laborers.

- The influx of prospectors from all nations set up the foundation for a culturally diverse California populace. It wasn't necessarily harmonious, though. In fact, the Native population dropped drastically; most died of disease, many were killed, and others were forced from their land. California was quickly organized as a U.S. territory and admitted to the Union as a "free" state in 1850—this was required by the terms of the Missouri Compromise.

- There was a lot of fear, however, that the Gold Rush was attracting free blacks and other immigrants, so the state constitution denied the right to vote to all except white male inhabitants. The legislature passed the Foreign Miner's License law and, to make sure it was followed, imposed taxes on all foreign miners. Because many could not pay, they looked for other work. Chinese prospectors and laborers in particular became targets of systematic discrimination.

- As the mines prospered and wealth increased, California's great urban centers developed. San Francisco, which was closest to the mines, grew from 1,000 people in 1848 to 25,000 in 1850 and 150,000 in 1870. The federal mint was established there in 1854, and the mint quickly outgrew initial expectations.

- Within decades, the rapidly modernizing West fueled both the need and the desire to connect with the rest of the country. The transcontinental railroad sprung forth partly as a result. The railroad helped transport Western resources to Eastern cities, which in return provided manufactured products and luxury goods. The railroad also spurred the growth of Midwestern centers like Chicago, St. Louis, and Kansas City as railroad hubs.

- By 1862, the Sutter's Mill gold flake had made its way to the Smithsonian. Over the ensuing decades, the Smithsonian received many requests to send the flake back to California, either for temporary or for permanent display.

- In 1925, the Pioneer Society of California requested that the Smithsonian return the gold nugget to California so that it could be displayed at the state museum. A few years later, the Smithsonian made a mold, cast a gold facsimile, and sent it to California for an exhibit at the California State Fair. Finally, in 1998, for the 150th anniversary of the original discovery, the tiny gold flake returned to California—temporarily—and was exhibited at the James Marshal Gold Discovery Center, near where it was first found.

Albert Bierstadt's Paintings

- The Gold Rush aroused the curiosity of the entire nation and fueled the idea of Manifest Destiny as the divinely ordained expansion of the United States across the continent, to the Pacific Ocean—and even beyond.

- It also opened the door of the American imagination. Among those who turned the ideal of the West into a concrete vision were artists like Thomas Moran and Albert Bierstadt, whose paintings offer majestic, glowing, panoramic visions of the American West. The 10-foot-wide painting *Among the Sierra Nevada, California* was created by Bierstadt in 1868.

- Bierstadt was born in Germany in 1830 and immigrated to New Bedford, Massachusetts, with his parents when he was an infant. As a young man, he studied in Germany, where he mastered a dramatic style of landscape painting that he practiced first in Europe and later after he returned to New Bedford.

- In 1859, he traveled to the Rocky Mountains with a land-surveying party. Their mission was to scout a route for the first continental railroad. Bierstadt was awestruck by the landscape's visual beauty and grandeur. He made several such trips over the next decade and was paid by the Union Pacific Railroad to paint scenes of California that would lure tourists and eventually investors to the West.

- In 1863, Bierstadt came upon the imposing Sierra Nevada mountain range and then Lake Tahoe and the borders of the Golden State. In a studio in Rome four years later, Bierstadt would reenvision the moment he first saw this scene, transferring it to this canvas.

***Among the Sierra Nevada, California*, Albert Bierstadt, 1868**

- He painted the serene, luminous landscape with a range of emotions—awe-inspiring mountain scenery and a theatrical sky contrasted by small fragile flowers. Bierstadt painted not what he actually saw but an inspired, visionary mountain landscape. The overall effect is that of a national anthem in visual form that pays homage to the American West.

Sitting Bull

- Bierstadt and other artists of his day promoted a vision of the West as a divinely inspired land of unbridled opportunity. Especially in the decade following the Civil War, these imaginative, aggressively American landscapes were seen as redemptive. They represented a new West—an unbelievably rich and strikingly beautiful Eden where the nation might start over, where the wounds of a terrible Civil War could be healed.

- Unfortunately, these artists also tended to leave out evidence of the Native inhabitants and cultures that had also marked and affected the landscape. Those inhabitants were being squeezed out of the landscape as the United States and its frontier moved westward. Not only were the lands of American Indians taken, but they were also being killed in massive numbers. It was imperative not only to fight to hold onto their land, freedom, and lives, but for some, it also became critical to capture in some way who they were and what they valued before it was lost.

- Among the greatest Native American leaders was Sitting Bull, who had a reputation as a fierce warrior in the Lakota Sioux, or Dakota Sioux, tribe. These tribes were originally based in the Dakotas, Minnesota, and Wisconsin, but they migrated frequently to other Midwestern states and even to Canada.

- Sitting Bull was renowned for his fearlessness. We often think of him primarily as a warrior, but he was also a dedicated leader, holy man, and tribal chief. As a warrior, he was aggressive about expanding the territory of his tribe and also fought against intruders to Lakota territory—both Indians and non-Indians.

- In the 1860s, Sitting Bull participated in raids against U.S. Army forts and small settlements in the region. One by one, other tribal leaders, like Red Cloud, relented and agreed to settle on reservations. But Sitting Bull continued to urge his people and those of other tribes to resist the encroaching U.S. government in the northern plains of the American West.

- He realized early on that straight-out battles weren't going to be as successful as guerrilla-style fights. He targeted survey parties like the one Bierstadt had traveled on, as the intent grew to establish a Northern Pacific Railway line through the Dakotas.

- Meanwhile, the Gold Rush had been changing the West. The fever for gold hadn't died down when in 1874, a brash U.S. Army Lieutenant Colonel, George Armstrong Custer, led military escorts into the Black Hills to look for gold. It didn't matter to Custer that this was Lakota Sioux territory. He was hoping that it would become the next California.

- Indeed, when Custer announced that he had found gold, there was a rush of speculators to the area. To ensure unrestricted access to the gold, all resident tribes were ordered to move onto reservations. The conditions were deplorable, and food was scarce. Those who resisted were declared hostiles, and that included Sitting Bull and his band of warriors.

- Ever the strategist, Sitting Bull quickly made alliances with other tribal groups. Bands of Indians and fighters seeking refuge joined his camp, and by mid-1876, it's thought to have grown to about 10,000 people. Custer's Seventh Cavalry attacked the camp, but Sitting Bull and several thousand Sioux, Cheyenne, and Arapaho warriors fought back. They forced Custer's retreat.

- On June 25, 1876, at the Battle of the Little Bighorn, Indian warriors decimated the Army, killing Custer and more than 260 under his command. Custer's defeat shocked many Americans who were convinced that they were superior to Indians and that all U.S. territory belonged under their control. The federal government counterattacked against Sitting Bull and his allies, and the Indians were forced to break up into smaller bands and retreat to isolated areas.

- Sitting Bull withdrew into Canada. Eventually, the scarcity of buffalo pushed his people nearly to starvation, and he surrendered. With about 200 others, he presented himself at Fort Buford in Montana in 1881. Sitting Bull and his group were eventually transferred to Fort Randall in South Dakota.

- While he was there, Sitting Bull used the pages of a blank ledger book to draw scenes from his life as a warrior. He had learned to write his name in English while in Canada, and he signed each of the drawings. He explained each of the episodes in his native language, which was then translated into English and written down. The book came to the Smithsonian through the family of an officer posted at Fort Randall.

- In 1883, Sitting Bull and his band were allowed to rejoin their people. He wouldn't convert to Christianity, lived with two wives, and refused to embrace white settlement in the area. He did send his children to reservation schools to learn to read and write.

- By 1890, the Ghost Dance movement had spread among the Lakota. This was both a ceremony and a movement, it was a way for Indians to summon supernatural powers to help them reclaim their freedom and independence.

- Sitting Bull was asked to lead a Ghost Dance at Standing Rock. Authorities worried that his involvement would lead to full-scale rebellion on the reservation, so a federal agent sent Lakota police to his cabin to "arrest" him. They dragged Sitting Bull outside, and a battle ensued. Sitting Bull was killed as his warriors tried to rescue him.

- Government officials demanded that bands of Ghost Dancers surrender their weapons. In one atrocious confrontation, the Seventh Cavalry attacked the band of Big Foot, a Lakota Ghost Dance leader, at Wounded Knee Creek on December 29, 1890. Several hundred Lakota men, women, and children were slaughtered. Both Wounded Knee and Sitting Bull became symbolic rallying points for the American Indian Movement in the 1970s.

Featured Objects

Gold Flake from Sutter's Mill

Colt Revolver

Albert Bierstadt's Among the Sierra Nevada, California

Sitting Bull's Drawing Book

Suggested Reading

Anderson and Ferber, *Albert Bierstadt.*

Brands, *The Age of Gold.*

LaPointe, *Sitting Bull.*

Utley, *Sitting Bull.*

Gold, Guns, and Grandeur—The West
Lecture 6—Transcript

The West. For Americans of many generations, "the West" has conjured up images of the unknown, of opportunity beyond the frontier, of the promise of a new life. But the West is more complicated and nuanced than that, and as we'll hear in the next lecture, the West was home to diverse groups of native people for thousands of years.

Perhaps most emblematic of the Westward drive was a nation-changing discovery on January 24, 1848, along the South Fork of the American River at Coloma, California. California at that time was officially Mexican territory, since the Treaty of Guadalupe Hidalgo, ending the Mexican-American War of 1846 to 1848 had not yet been signed. The war had been prompted by America's admission of Texas into the United States and a dispute over this new border. The treaty signed on February 2, 1848, ceded the entire Southwest to the United States—today's New Mexico, Arizona, Utah, Nevada, California, and even a bit of Colorado. In exchange, former Mexican citizens in the territory were guaranteed protection, and the United States paid the Mexican government 15 million dollars, a bargain price, as it turned out.

On the morning of January 24th, carpenter James Marshall was overseeing the construction of a sawmill for Colonel John Sutter. Marshall noticed something glittering in the water of the mill's tailrace and bent down to pick it up. According to Sutter's diary, Marshall "found that it was a thin scale of what appeared to be pure gold." Marshall and Sutter tested the flake and were confident that they were right. In the summer of 1848, Colonel Sutter presented Marshall's gold flake to Captain Joseph Folsom, U.S. Army assistant quartermaster at Monterey. Folsom was in northern California to verify the claim for the U.S. government.

Though it was already a thin piece of metal, Folsom noted that Marshall had hammered it perfectly flat for easier identification. It now looked like this. Folsom gave its weight at less than nine hundredths of a gram. It might look large on the screen, but in reality, it's smaller than the fingernail on my pinky.

After Marshall's first find, other nuggets were discovered, and Folsom estimated that some four thousand men were mining gold by the time he arrived. Folsom took samples, and U.S. Army Lieutenant Lucien Loeser took them back to Washington to give to President James Polk. Folsom cataloged this flake as "Specimen #1, the first piece of gold ever discovered in this Northern part of Upper California, found by J. W. Marshall at the Saw Mill of John A. Sutter."

In his State of the Union address on December 5, 1848, Polk formally told Congress that gold had been discovered in California. He lamented that crews were abandoning their ships and soldiers were deserting their posts, because almost all the men in the territory were consumed with the search for gold. Prices were skyrocketing. Polk called for a mint to be established in California for them to be able to make coins there, and he argued that the discovery of gold would be good for everyone in the country and for the country itself.

It was for the good of the country, he said, that the nation had to acquire California, New Mexico, and the settlement of the Oregon boundary, in addition to annexing Texas. This was, for Polk, a vindication of the Mexican-American War. In fact, it was a vindication of an idea that journalist John L. O'Sullivan had recently called "Manifest Destiny." O'Sullivan had written, "it is our manifest destiny to overspread the continent allotted by Providence."

Some thought that idea folly. Here's a quote from the time, sometimes attributed to Senator Daniel Webster, questioning the idea. It goes, "What do we want with this vast worthless area, this region of savages and wild beasts, of desert, or shifting sands and whirlwinds of dust, of cactus, and prairie dogs?" But undeterred, Polk had pursued an expansionist vision in waging war, and this vision was captured in the painting, Westward the Course of Empire takes its Way, by Emanuel Gottlieb Leutze. It shows a historical amalgam of explorers, pioneers, and settlers, with guns and wagons having made their way through dark and treacherous mountains grandly and dramatically eyeing their progress toward the sun-filled, colorful California coast.

One of the main reasons for victory in the Mexican-American war was the development of the Colt revolver. Samuel Colt seems to have been born an inventor. While growing up in Connecticut, he was particularly enamored of firearms and eventually seized on the idea of a single-barrel gun with a revolving cylinder that would lock into place, automatically aligning lead balls with the barrel. He sought and secured patents for the revolver in both England and the United States in the 1830s and started manufacturing the Colt Paterson as a commercial firearm.

Colt sold an early version to the Republic of Texas, whose Rangers used the revolver in their fights with the Comanches. The gun evolved when the United States went to war with Mexico in 1846. Former Ranger Captain Samuel Walker became an officer in the U.S. Mounted Rifles. He visited Colt, seeking a more powerful weapon that could be used by horse-mounted troops. The result was the Colt Walker, a long, heavy six-shooter that could stop a horse and win battles.

The Colt revolver was used by soldiers on both sides of the Civil War, and afterward by settlers, family members, cowboys, Indians, homesteaders, ranchers, lawmen, and outlaws. The Colt Single Action Army Model revolver was incredibly popular and is sometimes called "the gun that won the West;" it made possible the realization of manifest destiny.

But if manifest destiny was the "push" for winning the West, the discovery of gold was the "pull." The discovery of gold in California became widely known in 1849, and this kicked off the Gold Rush. Some 300,000 Americans from the East and the Midwest headed to California; so did many immigrants from Latin America, Europe, China, and even Australia. They became known as 49ers, ready to prospect for gold and gain bundles of wealth.

It's true that some of the 49ers grew wealthy, but it's also true that many either left in despair or simply stayed in the region as farmers or menial laborers. The influx of prospectors from all nations set up the foundation for a culturally diverse California populace. It wasn't necessarily harmonious, though. In fact, the Native population dropped drastically, from about 150,000 in 1848 to about 30,000 a dozen years later. Most native people died of disease, many were killed, and others were forced from their land. California was quickly organized as a U.S. territory and admitted to the Union as a "free" state in 1850; this was required by the terms of the Missouri Compromise.

There was a lot of fear, however, that the Gold Rush was attracting free blacks and other immigrants, so the state constitution denied the right to vote to all, except white male inhabitants. The legislature passed the Foreign Miner's License law, and, to make good and sure it was followed, imposed a tax of 20 dollars a month on all foreign miners. As many could not pay, they looked for other work. This had the unintended effect of creating competition with white workers. Chinese prospectors and laborers, in particular, became targets of systematic discrimination. A law passed in 1852 levied a 50 dollars-per-person tax on Chinese immigrants. The governor defended it by claiming that Chinese immigrants undercut other laborers and resisted assimilation. On top of everything else, he claimed they didn't contribute to the economy because they sent their pay back home to China.

As the mines prospered and wealth increased, California's great urban centers developed. San Francisco, which was closest to the mines, grew from just 1,000 people in 1848 to 25,000 in 1850, and 150,000 in 1870. The federal mint was established there in 1854, and the mint quickly outgrew initial expectations. Within decades, the rapidly modernizing West fueled both the need and the desire to connect with the rest of the country. The transcontinental railroad sprung forth partly as a result.

Here's an example of how badly something like the railroad was needed. When Folsom sent those initial gold samples back to Washington, his agent, Lieutenant Loeser, had to take a ship to Panama's Pacific coast, travel by horseback across the isthmus to the Atlantic coast, board a ship to New Orleans, and then continue overland to the Nation's capital. The discovery of California gold created an urgent need for a better transport system and provided the money to create it. Kind of as a punctuation mark of sorts, the transcontinental railroad was completed with the final, symbolic joining of track with a golden spike!

The railroad helped transport western resources to Eastern cities, which in return provided manufactured products and luxury goods. The railroad also spurred the growth of Midwestern centers, like Chicago, St. Louis, and Kansas City as railroad hubs. Later in the century, the need for efficient shipping would help drive the demand for the Panama Canal.

Back in Washington, the Sutter Mill gold flake faced its own developments. By 1862, it had made its way to the Smithsonian. Over the ensuing decades, the Smithsonian received many requests to send the flake back to California, either temporarily or for permanent display. In 1925, the Pioneer Society of California requested that the Smithsonian return the gold nugget to California so that it could be displayed at the state museum. George Merrill, the museum's curator of geology protested, writing, "How long would a museum last if each and every city or state were to withdraw its choice materials?"

A few years later, the Smithsonian made a mold, cast a gold facsimile, and sent it to California for an exhibit at the California State Fair, where it was a big hit. Finally, in 1998, for the 150th anniversary of the original discovery, this tiny gold flake returned to California—albeit temporarily—and it was exhibited at the James Marshal Gold Discovery Center near where it was first found. Governor Pete Wilson noted how this little flake had started it all, not just the Gold Rush, but the State of California!

The Gold Rush aroused the curiosity of the entire nation and fueled the idea of manifest destiny as the divinely ordained expansion of the United States across the continent, to the Pacific Ocean and even beyond. It also opened up the door of the American imagination. Among those who turned the ideal of the West into a concrete vision were artists like Thomas Moran and Albert Bierstadt. Their work inspired Americans to imagine the West as an almost biblical "promised land," endowed by the Creator with abundant resources and destined to be occupied and settled by intrepid pioneers assumed to be of European backgrounds.

Their paintings offer majestic, glowing, panoramic visions of the American West. Take a look at this amazing 10-foot-wide painting, called Among the Sierra Nevada, created by Bierstadt in 1868. Bierstadt was born in Germany in 1830 and immigrated to New Bedford, Massachusetts with his parents when he was an infant. As a young man, he studied in Germany, where he mastered a dramatic style of landscape painting that he practiced first in Europe and later, after he returned to New Bedford, with the Hudson River School artists in the East.

The Hudson River School, as the name implies, was a group of artists based in and around upstate New York. They were landscape painters, and philosophically, they were drawn to the ideals of Romanticism, and particularly the idea of the Sublime, the idea that what was most fearsome in nature was also what was most beautiful. It's an idea almost perfectly suited to what happened to Bierstadt next.

In 1859, he traveled to the Rocky Mountains with a land-survey party. Their mission was to scout a route for the first continental railroad. Along the way, they encountered brutal trail conditions and Indian attacks. Despite these challenges, Bierstadt was awestruck by the landscape's visual beauty and grandeur. He made several such trips over the next decade, and was paid by the Union Pacific Railroad to paint scenes of California that would lure tourists, and eventually investors, to the West.

In 1863 Bierstadt came upon the imposing Sierra Nevada mountain range along a route his companion described as "the most horrible desert conceivable by the mind of man … the most frightful nightmare of my existence." Then they came to Lake Tahoe and the borders of the Golden State, where they felt "transported into heaven." In a studio in Rome four years later, Bierstadt would re-envision that moment, transferring it to the canvas. He painted the serene, luminous landscape with a range of emotions—awe-inspiring mountain scenery and a theatrical sky contrasted with small, fragile flowers.

Bierstadt painted not what he actually saw, but an inspired, visionary mountain landscape. He freely dramatized and romanticized flora, fauna, topography, and sky to create a transcendent image. Most striking of all is the celestial light that falls on the spectacular mountain peaks. The overall effect is that of a national anthem in visual form that pays homage to the American West.

We tend to think of paintings like this as something you'll see only in the rarified setting of a museum. But that's not how they were first shown. Bierstadt was a natural showman and a self-promoter. He unveiled his canvases like theatrical events. He sold tickets and planted news stories. One critic described this approach as " a vast machinery of advertisement and puffery."

But remember, this was also an age without much entertainment, a time when P. T. Barnum used his museum to both educate and entertain. In some cases, a Bierstadt canvas, elaborately framed, might be installed in a darkened room and hidden behind luxurious drapes. At the appointed time, the work would be revealed to thunderous applause. The theatrics typified other spectacles of artistic and historical display, such as large-size cycloramas. A cyclorama, at the time, was a device that covered the back and sometimes the sides of a stage. With special lighting, the cyclorama could convey the illusion of great space, open sky, or depth. Eleanor Harvey, a Smithsonian curator and art historian, has said that Bierstadt's displays were like "an IMAX theater experience for the 19th century."

Bierstadt and other artists of his day promoted a vision of the West as a divinely inspired land of unbridled opportunity. Especially in the decade following the Civil War, these imaginative, aggressively American landscapes were seen as redemptive. They represented a new West, an unbelievably rich and starkly beautiful Eden, where the nation might start over, where the wounds of a terrible Civil War could be healed.

Unfortunately, these artists also tended to leave out evidence of native inhabitants and cultures that had also marked and affected the landscape. These inhabitants were being squeezed out of the landscape as the United States and its frontier moved westward. Not only were the lands of American Indians taken, American Indians themselves were being killed in massive numbers. It was imperative not only to fight to hold onto their land, their freedom, and their lives, but for some, it also became critical to capture, in some way, who they were and what they valued before it was lost.

Among the greatest Native American leaders was Sitting Bull, and the Smithsonian has an amazing artifact documenting his exploits and demonstrating his artistry. Sitting Bull had a reputation as a fierce warrior in the Lakota Sioux tribe. As a quick side note, you may have also heard him called a Dakota Sioux. Lakota and Dakota are just different pronunciations of the same tribal name, meaning allies. Oddly enough, Sioux isn't from their language but from Ojibway, and it means little snakes.

The Lakota/Dakota tribes were originally based in the Dakotas, Minnesota, and Wisconsin, but they migrated frequently to other Midwestern states and even to Canada. Sitting Bull participated in his first war party at only 14 and was soon renowned for his fearlessness. We often think of him primarily as a warrior, but he was also a dedicated leader. He was active in several men's warrior societies, including the Strong Hearts society. Just as important, he was also known as a holy man and tribal chief. He participated in dream societies, such as one called the Buffalo, and in groups, such as the Silent Eaters, who dedicated themselves to the good of the tribe, rather than the benefit of the individual. He was a complex man. But as a warrior, he was aggressive about expanding the territory of his tribe and also fought against intruders to Lakota territory—both Indians and non-Indians.

In the 1860s, Sitting Bull participated in raids against U.S. Army forts and small settlements in the region. One by one, other tribal leaders, like Red Cloud, relented and agreed to settle on reservations. But Sitting Bull continued to urge his people and those of other tribes to resist the encroaching U.S. government in the northern plains of the American West. He realized early on that straight-out battles weren't going to be as successful as a guerrilla-style fight. He targeted survey parties, like the one Bierstadt had traveled on, as the intent grew to establish a Northern Pacific Railway line through the Dakotas.

Meanwhile, the Gold Rush had been changing the West. The fever for gold hadn't died down when in 1874, a brash U.S. Army Lieutenant Colonel, George Armstrong Custer, led military escorts into the Black Hills to look for gold. It didn't matter to Custer that this was Lakota Sioux territory. He was hoping it would become the next California. And indeed, when Custer announced he'd found gold, there was a rush of speculators into the area. To ensure unrestricted access to the gold, all resident tribes were ordered to move onto reservations. The conditions there were deplorable, and food was scarce. Those who resisted were declared hostiles, and that included Sitting Bull and his band of warriors.

Ever the strategist, Sitting Bull quickly made alliances with other tribal groups. Bands of Indians and fighters seeking refuge joined his camp, and by mid-1876, it was thought to have grown to about 10,000 people. Custer's 7th Cavalry attacked the camp, but Sitting Bull and several thousand Sioux, Cheyenne, and Arapaho warriors fought back. They forced Custer's retreat.

At his camp by the Little Bighorn River, Sitting Bull performed a ritual known as the Sun Dance and entered a trance induced by self-torture. When he emerged from his state, he shared his vision that soldiers fell into the camp like grasshoppers from the sky. On June 25, 1876, at the Battle of the Little Bighorn, Indian warriors, inspired by Sitting Bull's vision, decimated the army, killing Custer and more than 260 under his command. Custer's defeat shocked many Americans who were convinced they were superior to Indians and that all U.S. territory belonged under their control. The federal government counterattacked against Sitting Bull and his allies, and the Indians were forced to break up into smaller bands and retreat to isolated areas.

Sitting Bull withdrew into Canada. Eventually, the scarcity of buffalo pushed his people nearly to starvation, and he surrendered. With about 200 others, he presented himself at Fort Buford in Montana in 1881. Legend has it that he said, "I wish it to be remembered that I was the last man of my tribe to surrender my rifle." Sitting Bull and his group were eventually transferred to Fort Randall in South Dakota. While he was there, Sitting Bull used the pages of a blank ledger book to draw scenes from his life as a warrior. He had learned to write his name in English while in Canada, and he signed each of the drawings with his name. He explained each of the episodes in his native language, which was then translated into English and written down. The book of his drawings came to the Smithsonian through the family of an officer posted at Fort Randall.

Sitting Bull's 22 pencil and watercolor sketches record, in his own terms, his exploits as a warrior and the deeds that established him as a leader. It preserves as no later writer or artist could what life was like in this particular time and this particular place. The Plains Indians had long recorded events through pictures. At one time, drawings were made on buffalo and other hides with natural pigments. Sometimes, in drawings called winter counts, the images documented the history of a tribe or band. Other drawings memorialized exploits of individuals. Sitting Bull wasn't the only warrior to adapt this tradition to drawing with new materials. Another Lakota, Red Horse, made incredible pictographs of the Battle of the Little Bighorn. They provide a rare glimpse of an Indian perspective on this engagement.

I'm going to share some of Sitting Bull's drawings with you now. Sitting Bull's drawings, done at Fort Randall, will focus on his exploits against other Indian tribes, such as the Assiniboine and the Crow. The drawings are revealing in both style and detail. Notice that Sitting Bull portrays human figures as flat—they lack dimension. There's not much facial detail. But take a look at the horses! They're drawn with almost three-dimensional perspective. You can see volume and musculature; many of these horse depictions have distinctive hide patterns and coloring so you can identify them individually. Sitting Bull depicts himself in seven or eight different headdresses in the 1882 drawings. They signal his status, power, and accomplishments. Here, as a youthful warrior, he wears a horned headdress. In others, he's shown as a more mature chief, and he wears elaborate eagle-feathered headdresses. In one picture, he's wearing a long sash. Masterful warriors staked themselves to the ground with the sash during a fight and wouldn't retreat unless released by a comrade.

In this drawing Sitting Bull displays the spiritual powers that protected him in battle. Paint on his body was part of the protection, and here he has Buffalo hooves on his hands and at his ankles. His horse is painted to embody a bird of prey; it might be a hawk. The eye and beak of the bird overlap with the eye of the horse, and the bird's talons are painted on the hind quarter. Due to his extraordinary power, Sitting Bull can vanquish his opponent with only a coup stick, a decorated, ritual weapon.

In 1883, Sitting Bull and his band were allowed to rejoin their people. He wouldn't convert to Christianity; he lived with two wives; and refused to embrace white settlement in the area. He did send his children to reservation schools to learn to read and write. In 1885, Buffalo Bill persuaded Sitting

Bull to join his Wild West Show. For 50 dollars a week, Sitting Bull paraded in front of packed arenas of largely white audiences, including in Washington, D.C. The show romanticized and mythologized the West, even though real-life Indians, cowboys and other historical figures performed in the shows. After four months, Sitting Bull quit the show and returned to the reservation.

By 1890, the Ghost Dance movement had spread among the Lakota. This was both a ceremony and a movement; it was a way for Indians to summon supernatural powers to help them reclaim their freedom and independence. Sitting Bull was asked to lead a Ghost Dance at Standing Rock. Authorities worried that his involvement would lead to full-scale rebellion on the reservation, so a federal agent sent Lakota police to his cabin to arrest him. They dragged Sitting Bull outside, and a battle ensued, and Sitting Bull was killed as his warriors tried to rescue him.

Government officials demanded that bands of Ghost Dancers surrender their weapons. In one atrocious confrontation, the 7th Cavalry attacked the band of Big Foot, a Lakota Ghost Dance leader, at Wounded Knee Creek on December 29, 1890. Several hundred Lakota men, women, and children were slaughtered. Official accounts claimed that this prevented a potential rebellion, but many, particularly Native Americans, saw it as revenge for Custer's defeat at Little Bighorn.

Both Wounded Knee and Sitting Bull became symbolic rallying points for the American Indian Movement in the 1970s. In 2010, the Smithsonian's National Museum of the American Indian projected the image of Sitting Bull, among other elders, onto the façade of its building on the National Mall, located in the shadow of the U.S. Capitol. It was a dramatic juxtaposition and a statement of how far the country had come in recognizing and honoring the rights of Native Americans in the face of historical injustice and what was the winning and the losing of the West.

The First Americans—Then and Now
Lecture 7

Native Americans are a diverse group of tribes and communities, speaking hundreds of languages and occupying every corner of the Western Hemisphere. Each native group—from the far northern polar climes to the Great Plains, from the Amazonian rainforests to the southernmost tip at Tierra del Fuego—had its own account of its own origins. In some stories, their ancestors had emerged from underground, descended from the sky, or migrated from other lands. European priests, settlers, and scholars applied their own cultural assumptions. In this lecture, you will discover why scholarly research on the question of who first came to America—and when—provokes scientific debate.

Clovis Points

- It was only in the 20th century that we developed the tools to answer the question of Native American origins in a truly scientific way. One of the most important and extraordinary discoveries toward this understanding was made in 1929 in the desert near Clovis, New Mexico, where 19-year-old Ridgely Whiteman found what he called warheads together with extinct elephant bones.

- Convinced of the significance of his discoveries, Whiteman sent a letter and a fluted flint spear point to Alexander Wetmore, the assistant secretary of the Smithsonian. Charles Gilmore, the Smithsonian's vertebrate paleontologist, went to Clovis to meet up with Whiteman and inspect the site. He found bison bones and the tooth of a mammoth—an extinct elephant-like species—but no human artifacts.

- Smithsonian anthropologists of the time were generally skeptical that the Americas had a Stone Age prehistory anything like that of Europe or the Middle East, where troves of stone tools had been found. To be sure, the Smithsonian had many stone and flint arrowheads and spear points; they just did not have any concrete evidence of their age, nor were any found in direct proximity to extinct remains. They returned Whiteman's original spear point.

- But in the years that followed, more finds came to light, and other archaeologists became interested in them. Finally, Edgar Howard, an archaeologist from the University of Pennsylvania Museum of Anthropology and Archaeology, joined with Whiteman to uncover the decisive artifacts in New Mexico.

- By 1933, Howard had accumulated evidence to support the existence of at least two prehistoric cultures: In the upper, newer layer of earth, he found bison remains and a type of artifact called Folsom points. Below this layer, he found what years later came to be called Clovis points in close association with the remains of mammoths and other extinct animal species.

- These points, Howard concluded, indicated the presence of a big-game hunting people in the American Southwest. Because mammoths were extinct, the existence of the man-made tools for hunting these beasts indicated that human habitation had occurred long ago. Howard couldn't be sure how old the Clovis points were. Clovis became the generic name for similar finds—first in the West, but later in other parts of North America—and scores of them came to the Smithsonian.

Clovis Points

- The age of Clovis points was not determined with any certainty until two decades after Whiteman's discovery. In 1949, University of

Chicago chemist Willard Libby and his team invented a process called radiocarbon dating, which later won him a Nobel Prize.

- Archaeologists collected burned or decayed organic remains found in close proximity to stone points, and by dating the remains could thus extrapolate the time the tool was used. Testing of material associated with Clovis points from different parts of the United States, Canada, and Mexico have now yielded dates up to about 13,500 years ago.

- The identification and dating of Clovis points raised questions about their makers. Because the earliest archaeological discoveries were made in the western plains, most anthropologists believed that the first Americans migrated over land bridges across the Bering Strait from northeastern Asia into Alaska about 14,000 years ago, when the sea levels were lower due to the last ice age. They would then have moved southward, following ice-free corridors along the Pacific Coast and east of the Rocky Mountains, eventually moving south and eastward through Central and South America.

- Questions about when and how the first Americans came are far from settled, however. In the late 1970s, archaeologist Tom Dillehay's discoveries in South America at Monte Verde, near Chile's west coast, included evidence of shelters and stone tools. Carbon dating suggested human occupation about 15,000 years ago. This finding was initially controversial, but rigorous examination confirmed Dillehay's results and prompted speculation that there were probably multiple waves of migration from Asia, including at least one that predated Clovis.

- Many now believe that early migrants to the Americas did not generally follow large mammalian prey, such as mammoth, overland into the North American interior, but more likely moved southward along the West Coast by boat, surviving on seafood.

- The habitation sites of these early migrants would now be under water, off America's Pacific coastline. Non-Clovis remains dating from about 13,000 years ago found on the Channel Islands just off the coast of Santa Barbara, California, might be evidence of one such migration.

- Dennis Stanford at the Smithsonian has come to a very different and controversial conclusion. He has studied numerous Clovis finds in the eastern United States. Their dating corresponds to Clovis finds in western Canada, suggesting that the technology may not have originated in the northwestern part of the continent, as previous scholars had thought.

- Stanford also points to the lack of extensive finds of Clovis-like points in northeastern Asia and notes that Clovis points bear a striking resemblance to, and seem to be made in the same way as, stone and bone artifacts identified with Solutrean culture from the Iberian Peninsula in Europe.

- From this resemblance, Stanford hypothesizes that 20,000 years ago, early Solutrean peoples hunted marine animals along the frozen edge of the North Atlantic ice shelf that connected Europe and North America during the last ice age, perhaps using primitive boats.

- With the advent of DNA studies, scientists have been able to examine the connections between populations. However, DNA studies tend to link Native American populations to those of Siberia and eastern central Asia, not Europe. These analyses also suggest a divergence of the two populations between 15,000 and 22,000 years ago.

- Linguistic evidence—another method for identifying long-lost links between peoples—is inconclusive. Depictions in rock art of such culturally distinctive symbols as large game animals, shamanistic drums, and turtles suggest linkage between America and Asia, though dating such evidence remains an issue. Several other professionally excavated and studied sites throughout North and South America now suggest possible pre-Clovis and multiple migration theories.

Rogan Plates

- While the study of Native American origins has long fascinated scholars, so, too, have their civilizations. European conquistadors encountered the Aztec of Mexico and the Inca of Peru directly. The grand architecture and complex sociopolitical organization of these empires were well known, so that Europeans could consider them civilizations.

- Colonial explorers and settlers in the expanding United States tended to think of Native North Americans as less culturally developed and often characterized them in disparaging terms. There were, though, features on the landscape that puzzled them. They came upon enormous earthen works mounds in Ohio, Tennessee, Alabama, Georgia, and, most of all, Cahokia, Illinois, near present-day St. Louis, Missouri. French explorers traveling along the Mississippi River in the 1600s found more than 100 mounds spread over an area of six square miles near Cahokia. The largest was about 100 feet high.

- Even though 16th-century Spanish explorer Hernando de Soto had encountered Native Americans who built and used earthen works for defensive and ritual purposes, speculation abounded about the original mound builders. Most settlers, viewing Native Americans as lacking in "civilization," could not imagine them building such sophisticated structures. As a result, well into the 19th century, the lost tribes of Israel, Egyptians, Greeks, Mesopotamians, and Hindus were suggested as the architects of these mounds.

- Thomas Jefferson suspected otherwise when, in the 1780s, he excavated several skeletons and artifacts from a burial mound with a 40-foot diameter of his Monticello, Virginia, home. His conviction that the mounds were made by indigenous Americans was reinforced when he observed local Monacan Indians periodically returning to the mound to perform mortuary rituals and venerate ancestors.

- An important breakthrough occurred in the mid-1880s, when Smithsonian researcher James Rogan was excavating an earthen works mound at Etowah, Georgia. He came across stone sepulchers containing the skeletal remains of several adults and children. Among them were thin copper plates, two of which were exceptionally exquisite and depicted human birdman characters.

Mississippian Copper Birdman Plates

- The workmanship startled anthropologists at the Smithsonian. The embossed copper sheets, typically known as Rogan plates, would help change the way scholars thought about the native cultures of North America.

- Archaeological research since has revealed that Native American mound building is a tradition well over 5,000 years old. By A.D. 1000, tens of thousands of mounds had proliferated in a region that stretched from west of the Mississippi River to the Atlantic Ocean and from the Gulf of Mexico to the Great Lakes.

- Settlements of mound-building people were established on a scale comparable to the massive cities of the Aztecs of Mexico, the Maya of the Yucatán, and the Incas of the Andes. Cahokia, the largest urban center in North America, supported a population estimated at 20,000 to 40,000 people at its peak in the 12th century. Archaeological excavations have unearthed residential units near the mound composed of sod blocks, wooden posts, skins, and natural fibers, with hearths for cooking.

- Cahokia was the major center for a culture termed "Mississippian" by archaeologists. It was characterized by large chiefdoms and an important spiritual and religious tradition. Mississippian people believed in the so-called birdman, depicted on stone tablets, pottery, shell pendants, and hammered copper plates that were worn as headdresses.

- Because of Cahokia's importance in shaping this tradition and some limited evidence of a copper workshop there, several scholars believe that the Rogan plates, although discovered in Etowah, originate from Cahokia.

- Some researchers believe that the copper plates were a means of not only representing the birdman's powers, but also imparting them to those who wore them. Mississippian rulers would have prominently displayed birdman plates to associate themselves with powerful gods and legitimize their power. People would see in their leader's connection to the spiritual realm enhanced powers to protect the community and fight off enemies.

- As the Rogan plates and subsequent research have borne out, there's no doubt that Mississippian society was highly sophisticated and complex, defying later popular assessments. But Cahokia, Etowah, and other mound settlements declined in the 14th and 15th centuries—right before European exploration. We don't know why; it could have been invasion, environmental degradation, or even disease.

- Whatever the cause of Mississippian collapse, the remaining Native American communities did not fare well with the coming of explorers and settlers from Europe. Despite a variety of truces and treaties—first with the colonists and later with the government of the United States—Native Americans faced tough circumstances and threats to their survival. Many succumbed to European-introduced diseases. Others were wiped out in battle, assimilated and converted, or increasingly pushed west.

- Yet, through it all, Native people persevered. Native Americans serving in World War I prompted the passage of an act of Congress in 1924 granting citizenship to American Indians. Although native people had to fight for the right to vote and to uphold treaty rights, many succeeded in the full range of both personal and community endeavors.

Tsimshian Totem Pole by David Boxley

Totem Poles

- American Indians in the 21st century proudly say, "We are still here!" That was the rallying cry of the grand opening of the Smithsonian's National Museum of the American Indian on September 21, 2004. The museum had as its basis a marvelous collection of 800,000 artworks and artifacts assembled by George Gustave Heye. The museum not only has old items, but also collects and commissions new ones that show the continuity and vitality of Native American knowledge and insight, artistry and talent.

- Totem poles among the coastal tribes of the Pacific Northwest have long been recognized for their traditional importance in conveying the identity of a family or a clan through carved and painted images, typically of animals supernaturally related to the kinship group. The poles would stand outside a communal house and usually tell a story, like an origin myth, or a particularly poignant episode in the history of the group.

- Although much of the historical means and reasons for making totem poles receded over the past century, the tradition of making them has nonetheless continued. The director of the National Museum of the American Indian thought that the institution needed a contemporary totem pole in order to show the continuity of that living tradition. He commissioned the sculptor David Boxley to make one.

- Boxley is a highly reputed Native artist and carver of the Tsimshian tribe who lives on the island of Kingston in Alaska, near Ketchikan. He learned totem pole carving largely on his own by studying old designs and visiting museums.

- Boxley's Smithsonian totem pole started out as a 3,000-pound, 22-foot-long log of a 500-year-old red cedar that Boxley and his son prepared, carved, and transported to Washington to finish and paint in the museum's atrium in front of the visiting public. The carved motifs on the totem pole tell a story from Boxley's clan.

- Just as Boxley creates designs for his totem poles based on traditional motifs, he also adapts tools and supplies to serve similar cultural purposes. He uses store-bought latex paints rather than making them from natural pigments. Store-bought paints are easier to obtain, and the color lasts longer. Boxley recognizes the important role his carving plays in encouraging Tsimshian youth to embrace their culture.

Featured Objects

Clovis Points

Mississippian Copper Birdman Plates

David Boxley's Tsimshian Totem Pole

Suggested Reading

Halpin, *Totem Poles*.

Page, *In the Hands of the Great Spirit*.

Pauketat, *Cahokia*.

The First Americans—Then and Now

Lecture 7—Transcript

As we discussed in the previous lecture, Sitting Bull's brave but unsuccessful efforts to hold off the settlement of the American West were not just about preserving the political sovereignty of the Sioux nation. He was trying to preserve cultures that had resided on the continent for millennia.

Sitting Bull had spent part of a year touring with Buffalo Bill Cody's Wild West Show in 1885. That show famously romanticized the origins, character, and fate of American Indians. Long after Sitting Bull's departure, the show was a featured attraction on the Midway at Chicago's famed Columbian Exposition. This 1893 World's Fair was intended in part to celebrate Christopher Columbus's so-called "discovery" of the Americas 400 years before. Of course, his discovery of native peoples was a part of that.

We now have solid archaeological evidence of Norse settlements in Newfoundland several centuries before Columbus's voyages. And many scholars have made claims of contacts between Native Americans and other European, African, and Asian explorers, with varying levels of evidence. What made Columbus's effort different, and important, was its result. The eastern and western hemispheres would never be divided again.

Columbus's first contact with the people of the Americas, as significant as it was, also established an unfortunate pattern of misapprehension and misunderstanding. Convinced he was in Asia, Columbus called the natives Indios, or Indians. They called themselves Tainos. Columbus was also convinced the islands were rich with gold; they were not. Finally, he and many other Europeans did not recognize the full humanity of the Tainos. Columbus himself ordered as many as 200,000 Native people enslaved. Some Europeans argued that natives were basically beasts of burden and not truly human, lacking souls and incapable of accepting Christianity. Others disagreed, including Pope Paul III, who in 1537 issued a papal bull asserting the humanity of America's Native inhabitants.

Native Americans are a diverse group of tribes and communities, speaking hundreds of languages, and occupying every corner of the western hemisphere. Each native group, from the far northern polar climes to the great plains, from the Amazonian rainforests and to the southern-most tip of the continent at Tierra del Fuego, had its own account of its own origins. Some of their stories suggested that they were the first, or even the only true humans. In some stories, their ancestors had emerged from underground, or descended from the sky, or migrated from other lands.

European priests, settlers, and scholars applied their own cultural assumptions. Perhaps Native Americans were one of the lost tribes of Israel described in the Bible or even survivors from the vanished, mythical island of Atlantis. One Spanish Jesuit, José de Acosta, who lived in Peru, arrived at an explanation close to modern conventional scientific understanding. In 1590, he suggested that most of the Indians had arrived by migrating overland near the northern extremities of North America, an amazing guess, since no Western European had, at that time, seen Bering Strait.

But all of this was, really, just speculation. It was only in the 20th century that we developed the tools to answer the question of Native American origins in a truly scientific way. One of the most important and extraordinary discoveries toward this understanding was made in the desert near Clovis, New Mexico, in 1929. There, 19-year-old Ridgely Whiteman found what he called "warheads," together with extinct elephant bones. Whiteman, active in the Boy Scouts, was interested in Indian lore and familiar with arrowheads from an extensive collection of artifacts his mother had accumulated in her native Ohio. Convinced of the significance of his discoveries, he sent a letter and a fluted flint spear point to Alexander Wetmore, the assistant secretary of the Smithsonian. Charles Gilmore, the Smithsonian's vertebrate paleontologist, went to Clovis, New Mexico to meet up with Whiteman and inspect the site. He found bison bones; he found the tooth of a mammoth—an extinct elephant-like species—but no human artifacts.

Smithsonian anthropologists of the time were generally skeptical that the Americas had a Stone Age prehistory anything like that of Europe or the Middle East, where troves of stone tools had been found. To be sure, the Smithsonian had many stone and flint arrow heads and spear points; they just did not have any concrete evidence of their age, nor were any found in direct proximity to extinct remains. They returned Whiteman's original spear point. But in the years that followed, more finds came to light, and other archaeologists became interested in them. Finally, Edgar Howard, an archaeologist from the University of Pennsylvania Museum of Anthropology and Archaeology, joined with Whiteman to uncover the decisive artifacts in New Mexico.

By 1933, Howard had accumulated evidence to support the existence of at least two prehistoric cultures. In the upper, newer layer of Earth, he found bison remains and a type of artifact called Folsom points. Below this layer, he found what years later came to be called Clovis points, in close association with the remains of mammoths and other extinct animal species. These points, Howard concluded, indicated the presence of a big game–hunting people in the American Southwest. Since mammoths were extinct, the existence of the man-made tools for hunting these beasts indicated that human habitation had occurred long, long ago. But how old were the Clovis points? Well, Howard couldn't be sure. Clovis became the generic name for similar finds, first in the West, but later in other parts of North America, and scores of them came to the Smithsonian.

I have some of these here with me today. These are really nice examples of Clovis points showing the important features of how these tools were made. Clovis points were made out of several different types of rock, typically flint, jasper, or chert. The point was made by flaking and chipping, a technique archaeologists call knapping. Basically, the mother rock was held in one hand on a horizontal surface, such as the maker's thigh. The maker wields another rock—the percussor—in his or her other hand and strikes, chips, and flakes off the mother stone, fashioning it into shape. Edges are made sharp by applying careful pressure to break off fine chips rather than striking. See each of these little grooves? Each of these represents a place where a chip of stone was struck off, making that nice, fine edge. I have tried knapping, and it is a lot more difficult than it looks.

The shape of the Clovis point likely arose through much trial and error. See how the sides of the stone bow from roughly parallel at the bottom here toward a fine tip. It is decidedly thicker in the midsection, which gives it weight, and is sharp at the sides and the tip. The base is typically concave and dull edged, and it's fluted, that is, there's a channel chipped out on one or both sides of the point so that a stick can be hafted to it, that is, can be attached by wrapping the point in a wooden shaft. Given that Clovis points range from about 2 to 8 inches long, they were likely used at the tip of a number of different kinds of hunting devices for hunting, carving, and cutting tools—like spears, darts, or knives.

The age of Clovis points was not determined with any certainty until two decades after Whiteman's discovery. In 1949, University of Chicago chemist Willard Libby and his team invented a process called radiocarbon dating, which later won him a Nobel Prize. Archaeologists collected burned or decayed organic remains found in close proximity to stone points, and by dating the remains, they could thus extrapolate the time the tool was used. Testing of material associated with Clovis points from different parts of the United States, Canada, and Mexico have now yielded dates up to about 13,500 years ago.

The identification and dating of Clovis points raised questions about their makers. Since the early archaeological discoveries were made in the western plains, most anthropologists believed that the first Americans, indeed, migrated over land bridges across the Bering Strait from northeastern Asia into Alaska about 14,000 years ago, when the sea levels were lower due to the last ice age. They would then have moved southward following ice-free corridors along the Pacific Coast and east of the Rocky Mountains, eventually moving south and eastward through Central and South America.

Questions about how and when the first Americans came are far from settled, however. In the late 1970s, archaeologist Tom Dillehay's discoveries in South America at Monte Verde, near Chile's western coast, included evidence of shelters and stone tools. Carbon dating suggested human occupation about 15,000 years ago. This finding was initially controversial, but rigorous examination confirmed Dillehay's results and prompted speculation that there were probably multiple waves of migration from Asia, including at least one that preceded Clovis.

Many now believe that early migrants to the Americas did not generally follow large mammalian prey, such as mammoth, overland into the North American interior, but rather, more likely, moved southward along the West

Coast by boat, surviving on seafood. The habitation sites of those early migrants would now be under water, off America's Pacific coastline. Non-Clovis remains dating from about 13,000 years ago found on the Channel Islands just off the coast of Santa Barbara, California, might be evidence of one such migration.

Dennis Stanford, a colleague of mine at the Smithsonian, has come to a very different conclusion, and a controversial one. He has studied numerous Clovis finds in the eastern United States. Their dating corresponds to Clovis finds in western Canada, suggesting the technology may not have originated in the northwestern part of the continent, as previous scholars had thought. Stanford also points to the lack of extensive finds of Clovis-like points in northeastern Asia and notes that Clovis points bear a striking resemblance to, and seem to be made in the same way as, stone and bone artifacts identified with Solutrean culture from the Iberian Peninsula in Europe. From this resemblance, Stanford hypothesizes that 20,000 years ago, early Solutrean peoples hunted marine animals along the frozen edge of the North Atlantic ice shelf that connected Europe and North America during the last ice age, perhaps using primitive boats.

With the advent of DNA studies, scientists have been able to examine the connections between populations. However, DNA studies tend to link Native American populations to those of Siberia and eastern central Asia, not Europe. These analyses also suggest a divergence of the two populations between 15,000 and 22,000 years ago. Linguistic evidence, another method for identifying long-lost links between people, is inconclusive. Depictions in rock art of such culturally distinctive symbols as large-game animals, shamanistic drums, and turtles suggest linkage between America and Asia, though dating such evidence remains an issue. With several other professionally excavated and studied sites through North and South America now suggesting possible pre-Clovis and multiple migration theories, I expect that scholarly research on the question of who first came to America and when will heat up over the next few years and provoke vigorous scientific debate.

While the study of Native American origins has long fascinated scholars, so too have their civilizations. European conquistadors encountered the Aztec of Mexico and the Inca of Peru directly. The grand architecture and complex socio-political organization of these empires were well known, so the Europeans could consider them civilizations. But what of North America? Colonial explorers and settlers in the expanding United States tended to think of Native North Americans as less culturally developed and often characterized them in disparaging terms.

There were, though, features on the landscape that puzzled them. They came upon enormous earthen works mounds in Ohio, Tennessee, Alabama, Georgia, and most of all, Cahokia, Illinois, near present-day St. Louis, Missouri. French explorers traveling along the Mississippi River in the 1600s found more than 100 mounds spread over an area of six square miles near Cahokia. The largest was some 100 feet high. The size of its base, measuring more than 900 feet long and more than 800 feet wide, rivals that of the Great Pyramid in Egypt. Other mounds, like Great Serpent Mound in Ohio, were designed and constructed in figurative shapes.

Even though 16th-century Spanish explorer Hernando de Soto had encountered Native Americans who built and used earthen works for defensive and ritual purposes, speculation abounded about the original mound builders. Most settlers, viewing Native Americans as lacking in "civilization," could not imagine them building such sophisticated structures. As a result, well into the 19th century, the lost tribes of Israel, Egyptians, Greeks, Mesopotamians, and Hindus, basically, anyone but Native Americans, were suggested as the architects of these mounds.

Thomas Jefferson suggested otherwise, when, in the 1780s, he excavated several skeletons and artifacts from a burial mound with a 40-foot diameter near his Monticello, Virginia, home. His conviction that the mounds were made by indigenous Americans was reinforced when he observed local Monacan Indians periodically returning to the mound to perform mortuary rituals and venerate their ancestors. An important breakthrough occurred in the mid-1880s, when Smithsonian researcher John Rogan was excavating an earthen works mound at Etowah, Georgia. He came across stone sepulchers containing the skeletal remains of several adults and children. Among them were thin copper plates, two of which were exceptionally exquisite and depicted human birdman characters.

The workmanship startled anthropologists back at the Smithsonian. The embossed copper sheets, typically known as the Rogan plates, would help change the way scholars thought about the native cultures of North America. Archaeological research since has revealed that Native American mound building is a tradition well over 5,000 years old. By 1000 A.D., tens of thousands of mounds had proliferated in a region that stretched from west of the Mississippi River to the Atlantic Ocean, and from the Gulf of Mexico to the Great Lakes.

Settlements of mound-building people were established on a scale comparable to the massive cities of the Aztecs of Mexico, the Maya of the Yucatán, and Incas of the Andes. Cahokia, the largest urban center in North America, supported a population estimated at 20,000 to 40,000 people at its peak in the 12th century; that's comparable to London at the time. Archaeological excavations have unearthed residential units near the mound composed of sod blocks, wooden posts, skins, and natural fibers, with hearths for cooking.

Cahokia's economy depended upon planting and harvesting expansive fields of maize, supplemented by gardening, hunting, and fishing. This Midwestern metropolis was a bustling multiethnic hub populated by immigrants, pilgrims, and locals. Its largest mound included a plaza for large civic gatherings, perhaps for sports and religious rituals. Other structures included a stockade fence with watchtowers, a possible astronomical observatory, and earthen works, where members of important lineages were likely buried. Artifacts found at the site indicate that Cahokia was trading goods and information with sites throughout the Great Lakes, the Southeast, and the Gulf of Mexico.

Cahokia was a major center for a culture termed Mississippian by archaeologists. It spread over a large region of what later became the central and southeastern United States. It was characterized by large chiefdoms and important spiritual and religious traditions. Mississippian people believed in the so-called birdman, depicted on stone tablets, on pottery, shell pendants, and hammered copper plates that were worn as headdresses. Because of Cahokia's importance in shaping this tradition and some limited evidence of a copper workshop there, several scholars believe that the Rogan plates, although discovered in Etowah, Georgia, actually originate from Cahokia.

This plate, about 13-inches long and 9½-inches wide, is made of sheet copper on which the birdman was carefully hammered out. Its details are tooled and finely chased, probably with a tool made of bone or antler, using a technique that we call repoussé. It depicts the large-winged birdman in an active stance, possibly dancing. His upraised arm holds a stone mace; his lowered arm holds a severed head. The birdman is richly costumed, wears an elaborate headdress, and possesses what seemed to be a medicine bundle. Rogan found the plate in a mound built somewhere between 1250 and 1400 A.D., though the plate could have been crafted well before that. Etowah was the political and trade center of a regional Mississippian chiefdom, and the mound served as a burial site for the elite. Individuals were buried there with regalia and ornamentation illustrated in the repoussé plate.

Ethnohistoric documents and oral traditions indicate that the birdman was a powerful deity who embodied several different incarnations represented by symbols on the copper plate. Archaeologists, art historians, and specialists in Native culture have offered varied interpretations of the iconography. Part falcon, the birdman was associated with the upper world of the sky but, holding a mace and human head, also a guide for war. Some have associated the mythic creature with death, fertility, and rebirth.

Some researchers believe that the copper plates were a means of not only representing the birdman's powers but imparting them to those who wore them. Mississippian rulers would have prominently displayed these birdman plates to associate themselves with powerful gods and legitimate their power. People would see in their leader's connection to the spiritual realm enhanced powers to protect the community and fight off enemies.

As the Rogan plates and subsequent research have borne out, there's no doubt that Mississippian society was highly sophisticated and complex, defying later popular assessments. But Cahokia, Etowah, and other mound settlements declined in the 14th and 15th centuries, right before European exploration. Why? We don't know. It could have been invasion, environmental degradation, or even disease.

Whatever the cause of Mississippian collapse, the remaining Native American communities did not fare well with the coming of explorers and settlers from Europe. Despite a variety of truces and treaties, first with the colonists and later with the government of the United States, Native Americans faced tough circumstances and threats to their survival. Many succumbed to European-introduced diseases. Others were wiped out in battle, assimilated, or converted, or increasingly pushed westward. War, forced resettlement, and the loss of buffalo as a food source drastically reduced Native populations and lands. Even on reservations, government policies tended to exacerbate cultural loss, like the 20th-century practice of taking Native children away from their families and sending them to missionary schools for their "own good."

Yet, through it all, Native people persevered. Native Americans serving in World War I prompted the passage of an act of Congress in 1924 granting citizenship to Native Americans. Though Native people had to fight for the right to vote and to uphold treaty rights, many succeeded in the full range of both personal and community endeavors. American Indians in the 21st century proudly say, "we are still here!"

That was the rallying cry of the grand opening of the Smithsonian's National Museum of the American Indian on September 21, 2004. The museum was the result of legislation that had been introduced by Senator Daniel K. Inouye of Hawaii and Congressman Ben Nighthorse Campbell of Colorado, and signed by President George H. W. Bush in 1989.

The museum had as its basis a collection of some 800,000 artworks and artifacts assembled by George Gustave Heye. Many in the Indian country and in Congress were convinced that Native people needed a museum to tell their uniquely American story from their own perspective. The Heye treasures of Indian life from across the centuries and across the Americas, under the umbrella of the Smithsonian, could help them do that. So on that beautiful September morning, more than 25,000 Native people from more than 600 tribes and communities, from Inuit in the north of Canada to Suya of the Amazon rainforest and every place in between, strode in celebration down the Mall from near the Washington Monument to the foot of the U.S. Capitol.

They were joined by about 60,000 other supporters and well-wishers to mark the occasion, including the president of Peru, a Quechua Indian, and as well as representatives and spokespeople of other native peoples as far away as New Zealand and India. Those rejoicing in the opening viewed the creation of the museum as a mark of respect for the resiliency, heritage, and accomplishments of indigenous people everywhere. I have never been prouder as a Smithsonian staffer and scholar for having played a role in producing that museum's opening.

The museum not only has old items but collects and commissions new ones that show the continuity and vitality of Native American knowledge and insight, artistry, and talent. I'd like to share one of those items with you now. Totem poles among the coastal tribes of the Pacific Northwest have long been recognized for their traditional importance in conveying the identity of a family or a clan through carved and painted images, typically of animals supernaturally related to the kinship group. The poles would stand outside a communal house and usually tell a story, like an origin myth, or a particularly poignant episode in the history of the group.

Though much of the historical means and reasons for making totem poles receded over the past century, the tradition of making them has nonetheless continued. The director of the National Museum of the American Indian thought the institution needed a contemporary totem pole in order to show the continuity of that living tradition. He commissioned the sculptor David Boxley to make one.

Boxley is a highly reputed and regarded Native American artist and carver of the Tsimshian tribe who lives on the island of Kingston in Alaska, near Ketchikan. Raised largely by his grandparents, he became a schoolteacher and learned totem pole carving largely on his own by studying old designs and visiting museums. Asked why, he says that the culture was disappearing and he had to help make sure it survived. He said, "My mother's generation was punished for speaking their own language, sent off to boarding schools and made to feel ashamed of who they were." He says, "I have to reach back, past my mother's generation to my grandfather's and even past that."

Boxley has made about 70 totem poles and acquired an international reputation. He's made totem poles for fellow Tsimshian, and is also most proud of the ones he made for his grandfather's house. But in a shift from the traditional context, he has also made them for organizations and collectors. Boxley's Smithsonian totem pole started out as a 3,000-pound, 22-foot-long log of 500-year-old red cedar that Boxley and his son prepared, carved, and transported to Washington to finish and paint in the museum's atrium in front of the visiting public. The carved motifs on the totem pole tell a story from Boxley's own clan.

The story goes like this: A young boy was walking along a beach when he came upon an eagle entangled in a fishnet. The boy freed the eagle and it flew away. The boy grew up to become the chief of his village, which was then struck by a famine that threatened its people. As he walked along the same beach, wondering what to do, a salmon fell out of the sky and landed at his feet, providing sustenance for his people. He looked up and he saw the eagle he had rescued years before, who was a naxnox—or spirit guardian. Boxley says, "The moral of the story is that one good turn deserves another."

Just as Boxley creates designs for his own totem poles based upon traditional motifs, he also adapts tools and supplies to serve similar cultural purposes. He uses store-bought latex paints, rather than making them from natural pigments, which were traditionally composed of copper oxide and charcoal mixed with salmon eggs and fixed with urine. Store-bought paints are easier to obtain, and the color lasts longer.

Boxley recognizes the important role his carving plays in encouraging Tsimshian youth to embrace their culture. He's seen a real upswing in Native attitudes over the years. "There's few of us," he says, "but we're alive and well." To underscore the point, as he was carving the totem pole, members of his community back home were actually watching his work via Webcam on the museum's Web site. It was an amazing cultural commentary on the accessibility of Native culture in a digital age, and a sure sign that even America's most ancient traditions can find meaning in and inspire our nation's future.

Planes, Trains, Automobiles … and Wagons

Lecture 8

North America is a vast continent. For centuries, as the United States has taken shape, it has spread westward and beyond, toward new frontiers. That spread occurred because Americans used and invented mechanized forms of transportation so that large numbers of people and a huge amount of raw materials and finished goods could reach every corner of a growing, dynamic nation. In this lecture, you will examine four key artifacts that tell the story of America on the move: the Conestoga wagon, the John Bull steam locomotive, the Ford Model T, and Charles Lindberg's airplane—the *Spirit of Saint Louis*.

Conestoga Wagons

- Conestoga wagons originated in the mid-1700s, maybe a little earlier, near Lancaster, Pennsylvania, and the Conestoga River. The frame and suspension were made of wood, while the wheels were typically iron-rimmed for greater durability.

- Wagons needed to be sturdy, because they had to cross streams and shallow rivers, navigate steep mountain passes, and deal with rutted roads and deep mud. The body of the wagon was curved so that as the wagon traversed hills and mountains, cargo would shift toward the center—rather than slide toward the sides and destabilize the wagon. Wagons combined utility with Pennsylvania German folk art.

- Six horses pulled the wagon. Passengers rarely rode in it. The wagoner, or driver, typically rode on the horse nearest the wagon on the left side, or sat on the "lazy board," which extended from the wagon, or walked alongside it. A stretched tough white canvas cover provided protection from the weather. In good weather, the wagon would travel about 10 to 15 miles per day.

- The American colonies and the young United States were rich in resources. Conestoga wagons transported supplies and finished goods from eastern towns like Baltimore to settlers in the interior and returned with flour, whiskey, tobacco, furs, coal, iron, and other products that could be processed in coastal cities or sold abroad.

Conestoga Wagon

- But these wagons weren't only used for shipping goods. They were a major part of colonial migration. An ancient pathway that the Indians called "Jonontore" and the colonists eventually called "the Great Wagon Road" stretched from Philadelphia through Virginia's Shenandoah Valley and on to Augusta, Georgia.

- Between 1700 and 1775, 100,000 German and Scots-Irish immigrant settlers made their journey southwestward along the Western Appalachian foothills using this road, seeking land on the colonial frontier. Today, Interstate highway 81 runs along a good part of the route—and the settlements grew like a strand of beads along the roadway.

- Settlers' routes also took them further inland. Until the year 1700, European colonists had mostly settled along the coast. By the 1750s and the start of the French and Indian War, around the time the Conestoga Wagon was invented, the colonists had pushed into the Eastern Appalachian foothills, but not much further. After that war, treaties with the defeated Indians allowed the colonists to push through the mountains and begin to settle on the other side.

- Then, the War of 1812 put the Northwest Territory—what we now call the Midwest—firmly in American hands. This lured settlers into the Ohio River Valley, and the Conestoga wagon helped them get there. Good roads became essential; upgraded byways linked Philadelphia to Pittsburgh and Baltimore to Wheeling.

- The first federally funded road, known as the National Road, was constructed between 1811 and 1838. It stretched from Cumberland, Maryland, to Wheeling, and then through Ohio and Indiana to Vandalia, Illinois. Much of it still exists today as U.S. Route 40.

Steam Engines

- What eventually put the wagons out of business was the steam engine, developed by James Watt and his contemporaries in mid-18th-century England. A coal- or wood-burning fire would create the steam within an enclosed chamber, creating pressure. That pressure was then channeled to push pistons back and forth to power pumps, wheels, gears, blowers, and other mechanical devices to move and turn things.

- The earliest steam engines ran at extremely low pressures and were terribly wasteful of fuel; it took years of experimentation to develop more compact engines with higher working pressures that had enough power to move things like boats and locomotives.

- In America, the potential of steam-powered transportation was dramatically demonstrated in 1807, when Robert Fulton sailed his steamboat *Clermont* up the Hudson River from New York City. Traveling at a steady 5 miles per hour upriver, the huge, 142-foot ship amazed all who saw it defying the river's flow.

- Before long, steamboats were plying the Mississippi, the Ohio, the Hudson, the Mohawk, the Erie Canal, and the Great Lakes, bringing lumber, furs, coal, minerals, and foodstuffs from the interior to the coastal cities and returning to the hinterlands with manufactured goods. And just as towns had grown up along the Great Wagon Road, they now grew along the western waterways.

Railroads

- Steamboats relied on extant rivers, but also on expensive canal building at the hands of both governments and private entrepreneurs. Another innovation—the railroad—had an advantage over canal building: Track could be laid anywhere and relatively cheaply.

- The John Bull locomotive, located in the National Museum of American History, helped lead the growth of the railways and what turned out to be America's industrial revolution. Assembled in 1831, it is one of the first successful locomotives to run in the United States; it heralded the new form of transportation that would within decades stretch across the continent.

- The John Bull was built in England by Robert Stephenson, the foremost engine designer of the time. He was the son of George Stephenson, who in 1825 had built the first successful steam-powered railroad, the Stockton & Darlington Railway in the north of England.

- The success of the English railroad excited an American engineer and entrepreneur named Robert Stevens. He decided to build a railway through his home state of New Jersey that could help connect the two biggest U.S. cities of the time, New York and Philadelphia.

- Stevens saw this route as an important and lucrative one for the nation. He'd have to lay about 76 miles of track between Camden—which lay a short ferry ride across the Delaware to Philadelphia—and South Amboy, another longer ferry ride across the mouth of the Hudson River to Manhattan.

- The locomotive was built in England and then taken apart for shipment to the United States. It was reassembled in New Jersey by a team led by a young steamboat mechanic named Isaac Dripps. In 11 days, he and his crew put the locomotive back together on a short length of track. Two years later, in 1833, once enough money

John Bull Steam Engine

had been raised, a route surveyed, and tracks laid, the Camden and Amboy Railroad began service.

- But the locomotive had a tendency to derail over the hastily laid, uneven track, so Stevens and Dripps added an extra pair of guide wheels carried in a frame out in front. This innovation became an American hallmark.

- Camden and Amboy eventually built its own locomotive workshops and bought 15 additional American-made copies of the locomotive, all with the added guide wheels. It was by far the most prosperous of all the railroad lines in America between the 1830s and 1850s.

- The Camden and Amboy Railroad inspired the development of other railroads, as well as American locomotive and railway car manufacture. By the end of the 1830s, American manufacturers were building locomotives and exporting them to other countries.

- Railways soon began to transform the country. Land had to be purchased and cleared for rail routes and rail yards; bridges and tunnels had to be constructed. Railroad construction stimulated waves of new immigration by hiring hundreds of thousands of people coming from Ireland, Italy, eastern Europe, and Asia.

- Railroads stimulated new agriculture, especially wheat growing in the upper Midwest. A big stimulus to the industry was supplying the ore and finished iron needed to manufacture millions of rails and supplying the wood and coal needed to operate the ever-growing fleet of locomotives. Locomotive manufacturing became a leading U.S. industry.

- These developments led to the dream of a true transcontinental railroad. Two companies, chartered by Congress in the early 1860s, built the line. The Central Pacific Railroad built eastward from Sacramento, and the Union Pacific Railroad built westward from Council Bluffs, Iowa. The two met at Promontory Summit—an arid spot north of the Great Salt Lake in Utah Territory—on May 10, 1869, to ceremonially drive the last spike, which was made of California gold.

- Railways generated subsidiary industries and spawned towns as hubs of commerce. Railroads encouraged internal migration and tourism, reduced the perils of overland travel, and allowed for the rapid movement of troops, treasure seekers, and reporters. Rail travel changed conceptions of distance and time.

- The John Bull ended active use in 1866. It was featured at the U.S. Centennial Exhibition in 1876, and then was acquired by the Smithsonian. Years later, a train crew took the little engine from Washington DC to Chicago for the 1893 Columbian Exposition.

Automobiles

- By the end of the 19th century, the success of railroads in moving masses of people and goods across the United States led to the pursuit of another even more ambitious technology: the development of mechanical, engine-powered vehicles to replace the horse-drawn wagons, buggies, and carriages used by individuals and families.

- A number of German, French, British, and American inventors made progress toward such a self-propelled vehicle in the 1870s. Karl Benz, a German engineer, won a patent in 1879 for an internal-combustion two-stroke gasoline engine. In 1886, he built a "Motorwagen," arguably the first automobile. It had three wire wheels and was powered by a gasoline engine mounted horizontally in the rear of a tubular steel-frame body. Over the next few years, Benz and his partners built and sold several dozen of these motorcars.

- By the 1890s, inventors were experimenting with electricity-, steam-, and petrol-powered vehicles, most with two axles and four wheels. Steam-powered vehicles needed large, heavy boilers and a lot of time to build up sufficient pressure to propel motion. The real competition was between electric cars, which needed frequent recharging, and petroleum engines—using kerosene, alcohol, benzene, and gasoline.

- Charles and Frank Duryea, brothers and bicycle engineers from Illinois, were America's first successful automobile builders. They built their first successful vehicle in 1893. It is now in the Smithsonian. It added a four-horsepower single-cylinder gasoline engine to an adapted two-axle, four-wheel, horse-drawn buggy.

- The brothers organized the first American automobile manufacturing company—the Duryea Motor Wagon Company—in 1896 in Springfield, Massachusetts. There, they hand-assembled 13 identical vehicles. That same year, in a workshop home in Detroit, Michigan, Henry Ford built a gasoline-powered motorcar he called the Quadricycle.

- Ford, like other entrepreneurs, sought to produce commercially successful motorcars. Ransom Olds, for example, sold more than 400 cars in 1901, the first large-scale gasoline automobile enterprise. Ford started and failed in his first forays before putting together a group of partners to form the Ford Motor Company in 1903. The company produced the Model A and, in ensuing years, the models K, N, and S.

- The Model K was known as the Gentleman's Roadster and sold for about 2,800 dollars, making it accessible to only very wealthy customers. By contrast, Olds' least-expensive cars were selling for less than a quarter of that price, thanks to his use of a stationary assembly line. Instead of a team of workers assembling one vehicle at a time from beginning to end, specialized groups would concentrate on performing specific sets of tasks to install particular components of the automobile.

- In 1908, Ford adopted this manufacturing strategy to produce the Model T, selling it for 850 dollars. Popularly known as the Tin Lizzie, it was a roaring success. Ford sold about 10,000 the first year, and by 1926, the last year of its manufacture, it had sold over 15 million, making it one of the most popular models ever—transforming America into a car-producing and car-driving nation.

- Electric cars with batteries outsold gasoline-powered cars until 1910. But they cost two to three times as much as the Model T, had limited range, and needed frequent recharging. Even though gasoline cars generated noxious, smelly fumes and noisy knocking sounds, gasoline's lower price, greater availability, and superior range proved decisive.

Airplanes

- The final leg of the mass transportation story in America—air travel—got off the ground with the Wright Brothers. But flight as a form of mass transit was made possible by the first nonstop transoceanic flight in history, made by Charles Lindbergh, safely flying the *Spirit of Saint Louis* 3,610 miles, from New York to Paris, in 1927.

- Lindbergh began his flying career as a wing walker, parachutist, and mechanic on barnstorming tours across the Midwest and West. He later purchased his own plane and received his training as a reservist in the Army Air Service.

- Meanwhile, private entrepreneurs were trying to develop the possibilities of transatlantic flight. A Franco-American hotel owner named Raymond Orteig was offering a 25,000-dollar prize to anyone who could make the crossing.

- Lindbergh rose to the challenge. Using his own money and that of several backers—including sponsors in Saint Louis, hence the name of the plane—he purchased a craft from Ryan Air in San Diego. The plane needed many technical modifications in order to carry enough fuel for the flight.

- Lindberg took off from Long Island. During the flight, Lindbergh encountered terrifying obstacles, including storm clouds at 10,000 feet and whitecap waves as he skimmed the ocean at 10 feet, plus ice and fog that left him flying blind for several hours. But finally, he landed in Paris, where he was greeted by a wildly enthusiastic crowd of more than 100,000 people.

- Lindbergh claimed the prize and instantly became a world hero. He subsequently flew around Europe in the *Spirit of Saint Louis* receiving honors and accolades. Upon his return to the United States, President Calvin Coolidge awarded him the Distinguished Flying Cross. A ticker-tape parade down Fifth Avenue in New York City followed.

- Lindbergh was quickly and often pictured in newspapers and on plates, medallions, and other memorabilia—and, later, on stamps—wearing a flight helmet. The Smithsonian has several of Lindbergh's flight helmets, which are very simple canvas and leather skull caps held on with a chin strap.

- After returning home, Lindbergh toured the United States with the *Spirit of Saint Louis*, visiting every state as well as countries in Central America and the Caribbean. Seen by more than a quarter of the U.S. population and many internationally, the plane generated such massive publicity that it boosted the aviation industry and led to an explosion of air travel.

- The *Spirit of Saint Louis* made its final flight from Saint Louis to Washington DC, where Lindbergh presented the aircraft to the Smithsonian. Now that plane is seen by more than 8 million visitors a year to the National Air and Space Museum.

Featured Objects

Conestoga Wagon

John Bull Steam Engine

Model T Ford

Spirit of St. Louis

Suggested Reading

Berg, *Lindbergh.*

Rouse and Rouse, *The Great Wagon Road.*

Snow, *I Invented the Modern Age.*

Wolmar, *The Great Railroad Revolution.*

Planes, Trains, Automobiles … and Wagons

Lecture 8—Transcript

North America is a vast continent. For centuries, as the United States has taken shape, it has spread westward and beyond, toward new frontiers. That spread occurred because Americans used and invented mechanized forms of transportation so that large numbers of people and a huge amount of raw materials and finished goods could reach every corner of a growing, dynamic nation. In this lecture, I want to examine four key artifacts that tell the story of America on the move—the Conestoga wagon, the John Bull steam locomotive, the Ford Model T, and Charles Lindberg's airplane, the *Spirit of St. Louis*. They take us from the colonial era of horse-drawn transport to the modern era of intercontinental air travel.

The first of these, the Conestoga wagon, is not what many people think it is. If you've watched a lot of Westerns with scenes of covered wagons moving across the great prairies, this wagon probably appears quite familiar. Actually, the Conestoga wagon is the forerunner of those 19th century prairie schooners, which were smaller, lighter, and usually drawn by oxen.

Conestoga wagons originated in the mid-1700s, maybe even a little earlier, near Lancaster, Pennsylvania and the Conestoga River. This one, from the National Museum of American History, was probably built and used in the 1840s and 50s, a little after the heyday of the Conestogas. It is unusually large, 18 feet long, and almost 8 feet wide, indicating its intended use, hauling large, heavy consignments of freight.

The frame and suspension were made of wood, while the wheels were typically iron-rimmed for greater durability. Wagons needed to be sturdy; they had to cross streams and shallow rivers, navigate steep mountain passes, and deal with rutted roads and deep mud. Notice how the body of the wagon is shaped; it's curved. This is so as the wagons traversed hills and mountains, cargo would shift toward the center, rather than slide toward the sides and destabilize the wagon.

Wagons combined utility with Pennsylvania German folk art, like you see here, with a blue body, red running gear, and decorative ironwork. Six horses pulled the wagon. Passengers rarely rode in it. The wagoner, or driver, typically rode on the horse nearest the wagon, on the left side, or sat on the lazy board, which extended from the wagon, or, they walked alongside it. Finally, a stretched tough white canvas cover provided protection from the weather. In good weather, the wagon would travel about 10 to 15 miles a day.

So, if these weren't the wagons taking pioneers to the West, where exactly were they going? Well, in a sense, they were going West, just not in the way you were probably visualizing. Recall from earlier lectures that the American colonies and the young United States were rich in resources. Conestoga wagons transported supplies and finished goods from eastern towns, like Baltimore, to settlers in the interior, and returned with flour, whiskey, tobacco, furs, coal, iron, and other products that could be processed in coastal cities or sold abroad. An interesting historical note, the slang term "stogie," for a cheap cigar, comes from the Conestoga wagon.

But these wagons weren't only used for shipping goods; they were a major part of colonial migration. An ancient pathway that the Indians called "Jonontore" and the colonists eventually called "the Great Wagon Road" stretched from Philadelphia through Virginia's Shenandoah Valley and on to Augusta, Georgia. Between 1700 and 1775, some 100,000 German and Scots-Irish immigrant settlers made their journey southwestward along the Western Appalachian foothills using this road, seeking land on the colonial frontier. In North Carolina, for example, the population rose from approximately 35,000 to almost 210,000 people. Today, Interstate highway 81 runs along a good part of the route, and the settlements grew like a strand of beads along the roadway.

Settlers' routes also took them further inland. Up until the year 1700, European colonists mostly settled along the coast. But by the 1750s and the start of the French and Indian War, around the time the Conestoga wagon was invented, the colonists had pushed into the Eastern Appalachian foothills, but not much further. After that war, treaties with the defeated Indians allowed the colonists to push through the mountains and begin to settle on the other side.

Then, as we saw in the first lecture, the War of 1812 put the Northwest Territory, what we now call the Midwest, firmly in American hands. This lured settlers into the Ohio River Valley, and the Conestoga wagon helped them get there. Good roads became essential; upgraded byways linked Philadelphia to Pittsburgh and Baltimore to Wheeling. The first federally funded road, known as the National Road, was constructed between 1811 and 1838. It stretched from Cumberland, Maryland, to Wheeling, and then through Ohio and Indiana to Vandalia, Illinois. Much of it still exists today as U.S. Route 40.

What eventually put the wagons out of business was the steam engine, developed by James Watt and his contemporaries in mid-18th century England. A coal- or wood-burning fire would create the steam within an enclosed chamber, creating pressure. That pressure was then channeled to push pistons back and forth to power pumps, wheels, gears, blowers, and other mechanical devices to move and turn things. The earliest steam engines ran at extremely low pressures and were terribly wasteful of fuel. It took years of experimentation to develop more compact engines with higher working pressures that had enough power to move things like boats and locomotives.

In America, the potential of steam-powered transportation was dramatically demonstrated in 1807 when Robert Fulton sailed his steamboat, Clermont, up the Hudson River from New York City. Traveling at a steady five miles per hour upriver, the huge, 142-foot ship amazed all who saw her defying the river's current. Before long, steamboats were plying the Mississippi, the Ohio, the Hudson, Mohawk, the Erie Canal, and the Great Lakes, bringing lumber, furs, coal, minerals, and foodstuffs from the interior to the coastal cities and returning to the hinterlands with manufactured goods. And just as towns had grown up along the Great Wagon Road, they now grew along western waterways.

Steamboats relied on extant rivers, of course, and also on expensive canal building at the hands of both governments and private entrepreneurs. Another innovation, the railroad, had an advantage over canal building: track could be laid anywhere and relatively cheaply.

This artifact, the John Bull locomotive, which you can visit in the National Museum of American History, helped lead the growth of the railways and what turned out to be America's industrial revolution. Assembled in 1831, it is one of the first successful locomotives to run in the United States; it heralded a new form of transportation that within decades would stretch across the continent.

The John Bull was built in England by Robert Stephenson, the foremost engineer and designer of the time. He was the son of George Stephenson, who in 1825 had built the first successful steam-powered railroad, the Stockton & Darlington Railway in the north of England. The success of the English railroad excited an American engineer and entrepreneur named Robert Stevens. He decided to build a railway through his home state of New Jersey that could help connect the two biggest U.S. cities of the time, New York and Philadelphia. Stevens saw this route as an important and lucrative one for the nation. He'd have to lay about 76 miles of track between Camden, which lay a short ferry ride across the Delaware river to Philadelphia, and South Amboy, which was another, longer ferry ride across the mouth of the Hudson River to Manhattan.

Stevens cultivated state legislators and investors to literally pave the way for his enterprise. The locomotive was built in England, taken apart, and shipped to the United States. It was reassembled in New Jersey by a team led by a young steamboat mechanic named Isaac Dripps. Dripps had never seen a locomotive before! In eleven days, he and his crew put the locomotive back together on a short length of track. A fire was lit, steam rose, and the locomotive moved. Two years later, in 1833, once enough money had been raised, a route surveyed, and tracks laid, the Camden & Amboy Railroad began service.

But the locomotive had a problem, a tendency to derail over the hastily laid, uneven track, and so Stevens and Dripps added an extra pair of guide wheels carried in a frame out in front of the locomotive. That innovation became an American hallmark. Interestingly enough, we have in the collections of the Smithsonian's Archives of American Art a first-hand description of what it was like to ride this train. John Frazee, one of America's first professional sculptors, described his trip in a letter to his wife in 1834. He wrote, "A few minutes, and we were off like a shot, at the rate of 15 miles an hour." The sensation of "high speed train travel [was] at first quite disagreeable." And wrote Frazee, "I was chuck full of fears, fits, and starts!" Frazee never got used to what he called "the eternal and deafening roar" of the train's locomotive, which bombarded his ears like a "continual thunder" and gave him a headache.

That speed of 15 miles an hour might not seem too impressive to us now, but remember, the first steamboats had a top speed of about 5 miles per hour upriver, and the Conestoga wagon, under ideal conditions, could make about 15 miles per day. In just a few decades, the speed of commerce in the United States had increased almost incomprehensibly. Frazee included an illustration of the train with his letter. He draws the locomotive, which he calls the engine car, belching steam, followed by 11 other cars, the last, he notes, is for baggage. He draws a finger pointing to his car, designated for passengers, he writes.

Camden & Amboy eventually built its own locomotive workshops and bought 15 additional American-made copies of the locomotive, all with the added guide wheels. It was by far the most prosperous of all the railroad lines in America between the 1830s and the 1850s. The C&A Railroad inspired the development of other railroads, as well as American locomotive and railway car manufacture. By the end of the 1830s, American manufacturers were building locomotives and even exporting them to other countries.

Railways soon began to dominate and transform the countryside. Land had to be purchased and cleared for rail routes and rail yards; bridges and tunnels had to be constructed. Railroad construction stimulated waves of new immigrants by hiring hundreds of thousands of people coming from Ireland, Italy, Eastern Europe, and Asia. Railroads stimulated new agriculture, especially wheat-growing in the upper Midwest. A big stimulus to industry was supplying the ore and finished iron needed to manufacture millions of rails and supplying the wood and the coal needed to operate the ever-growing fleet of locomotives. Locomotive manufacturing became a leading U.S. industry.

Railcars transported massive amounts of timber, ore, cattle, and grain to mills and stockyards; delivered finished metals and component parts to manufacturing plants; and carried produce, dressed meat, and consumer goods of all kinds to markets across the nation. These developments led to the dream of a true transcontinental railroad. In an earlier lecture, we discussed the dangers and difficulties of crossing the continent, when Lieutenant Loesser had to bring that first California gold flake all the way back to Washington. During the Civil War, a transcontinental railroad took on a new political urgency, as a way to keep California, and its gold, in the Union.

Two companies, chartered by Congress in the early 1860s, built the line. The Central Pacific Railroad built eastward from Sacramento, and the Union Pacific Railroad built westward from Council Bluffs, Iowa. The two met at Promontory Summit, an arid spot north of the Great Salt Lake in Utah Territory, on May 10, 1869, to ceremonially drive the last spike, which was made of California gold. Bells rang in celebration all across the country.

Railways generated subsidiary industries and spawned towns as hubs of commerce. Railroads encouraged internal migration and tourism, reduced the perils of overland travel, and allowed for the rapid movement of troops, treasure seekers, and reporters. Rails carried money and mail, connected people and communities across the continent. Rail travel changed conceptions of distance and time; journeys became predictable, with schedules, timetables, and even standard time calculations. "Railroads carried everything and everybody everywhere."

The John Bull ended active use in 1866. It was featured at the U.S. Centennial Exhibition in 1876 and then acquired by the Smithsonian Institution. Years later, a train crew took the little engine—under its own steam!—from Washington, D.C. to Chicago for the 1893 Columbian Exposition. Brass bands greeted the locomotive and its two-car train at stops all along the way. And then, on September 15, 1981, for the 150th anniversary of its first test run in America, the Smithsonian's curators, John White, John Stine, and Bill Withuhn, did something really special. They arranged a crane and a flatbed truck and hauled the John Bull out of the museum and over to the old Georgetown Branch rails beside the Chesapeake and Ohio Canal in

Washington, D.C. They fired up her steam engine, and they went for a once-in-a-lifetime locomotive ride. They got a kick out of it, and they also learned a great deal about the engine's operation.

By the end of the 19th century, the success of railroads in moving masses of people and goods across the United States led to the pursuit of another, even more ambitious technology, the development of mechanical, engine-powered vehicles to replace the horse-drawn wagons, buggies, and carriages used by individuals and families. A number of German, French, British, and American inventors made progress toward such a self-propelled vehicle in the 1870s. Karl Benz, a German engineer, won a patent in 1879 for an internal-combustion, two-stroke gasoline engine. In 1886, he built a "Motorwagen," arguably the first automobile. It had three wire wheels and was powered by a gasoline engine mounted horizontally in the rear of a tubular steel-frame body.

There were no foot pedals on the Motorwagen. The driver, with his feet resting on a buckboard, operated a tiller connected by a rack-and-pinion mechanism to a single front wheel. The back wheels were rotated by chains that connected them to the engine with a gear mechanism similar to that of a bicycle. Benz's vehicle could go about eight miles an hour. Over the next few years, Benz and his partners built and sold several dozen of these motor cars.

By the 1890s, inventors were experimenting with electricity-, steam-, and petrol-powered vehicles, most with two axles and four wheels. Steam-powered vehicles needed large, heavy boilers and a lot of time to build up sufficient pressure to propel motion. The real competition was actually between electric cars, which needed frequent recharging, and petroleum engines using kerosene, alcohol, benzene, and gasoline.

Charles and Frank Duryea, brothers and bicycle engineers from Illinois, were America's first successful automobile builders. They built their first successful vehicle in 1893. It's now in the Smithsonian. It added a four-horsepower, single-cylinder gasoline engine to an adapted two-axle, four-wheel, horse-drawn buggy. The brothers organized the first automobile company, the Duryea Motor Wagon Company, in 1896 in Springfield,

Massachusetts. There they hand-assembled 13 identical vehicles. That same year, in a workshop home in Detroit, Michigan, 32-year-old Henry Ford built a gasoline-powered motor car he called the Quadricycle.

Ford, like other entrepreneurs, sought to produce commercially successful motor cars. Ransom Olds, for example, sold more than 400 cars in 1901, the first large-scale gasoline automobile enterprise. Ford started and failed in his first forays before putting together a group of partners to form the Ford Motor Company in 1903. The company produced the Model A, and in ensuing years, the models K, N, and S.

The Model K was known as the Gentleman's Roadster and sold for about $2,800, making it accessible to only very wealthy customers. By contrast, Olds's least-expensive cars were selling for less than a quarter of that price, thanks to his use of a stationary assembly line. Instead of a team of workers assembling one vehicle completely at a time from beginning to end, specialized groups of workers were concentrating on performing specific sets of tasks to install particular components of the automobile, and then repeat those procedure for the next unit. In 1908, Ford adopted this manufacturing strategy to produce the Model T, selling it for $850. Popularly known as the Tin Lizzie, it was a roaring success. Ford sold about 10,000 the first year, and by 1926, the last year of its manufacture, it had sold over 15 million, making it one of the most popular models ever, and transforming America into a car-producing and car-driving nation.

The Model T had several things going for it. First, it was a good product. It had a four-cylinder engine, manufactured in a block that gave it 20-horsepower performance and allowed speeds of 40 miles an hour. Ford produced several varieties of the Model T, a two-seat runabout, a five-seat touring car, a seven-seat town car, so, he could accommodate everything from a single individual or a couple to an entire family. Second, Ford's stationary assembly line, and then after 1913, a moving assembly line, cut the cost of production. The method used interchangeable parts, stressed speed, worker efficiency, and quality, and meant a good buy for the money. A new Model T went for as little as $260 in 1925. Third was the fact that the Model T engine could run on just about anything—kerosene, gasoline, or ethanol. Car owners could even distill their own fuel. With the advent of large, commercially viable oil wells in Texas and decreasing prices for gasoline, that meant lower operating costs for car owners. Now, electric cars with batteries actually outsold gasoline-powered cars until 1910. But they cost two to three times as much as the Model T; they had limited range; and they needed frequent recharging. Even though gasoline cars generated noxious, smelly fumes and noisy, knocking sounds, gasoline's lower price, greater availability, and superior range proved decisive. Henry Ford democratized personal mobility by making an exceedingly popular product affordable to millions.

The dramatic expansion of Model T use stimulated Ford's competitors and fueled the growth of the massive U.S. automobile industry. Ford began losing sales to General Motors in the mid-1920s when GM introduced yearly model changes for their cars; that ended the Model T. Nonetheless, hundreds of thousands of jobs were created directly through Ford's innovation, and millions more through secondary occupations and services.

The automobile had tremendous consequences for American culture, from the development of the drive-in theater to fast-food restaurants in the 1960s to its continuing celebration in song, film and the race-car circuit. Driving has come to symbolize personal freedom, and individual models have achieved iconic status.

The final leg of the mass transportation story in America—air travel—literally got off the ground with the Wright Brothers, whom we will discuss in a later lecture. But it was flight as a form of mass transit that was made possible by the first nonstop transoceanic flight in history, made by Charles Lindbergh. Lindbergh was safely flying the *Spirit of St. Louis* 3,610 miles from New York to Paris in 1927. In a way, the sky was the last frontier Americans had to conquer, at least, the last earthly barrier. The continent was now linked by rail and road, and the 48 United States—remember, Alaska and Hawaii were not yet part of the Union—were all connected. Where else did we have to go?

Even so, flight was still seen as a novelty, the provenance of soldiers and acrobats. Planes had been flown successfully in combat in World War I, and 122 men had earned the title "Flying Ace." In the post-war era, many retired military pilots returned to barnstorming, that is, stunt flying exhibitions.

Lindbergh began his flying career as a wing walker, parachutist, a mechanic on barnstorming tours across the Midwest and the West. He later purchased his own plane and received his training as a reservist in the Army Air Service.

Meanwhile, private entrepreneurs were trying to develop the possibilities of transatlantic flight. A Franco-American hotel owner named Raymond Orteig was offering a $25,000 prize to anyone who could make the crossing, a prize that had eluded more experienced pilots than Lindbergh for years. Lindbergh rose to the challenge. Using his own money and that of several backers, including sponsors in St. Louis, hence, the name of the plane, he purchased a craft from Ryan Air in San Diego. The plane needed many technical modifications in order to carry enough fuel for the flight. Lindbergh made a particularly risky decision to depend upon just a single engine. He also designed the plane with a single seat, so he would fly solo, even though it was not a requirement for the prize.

Lindberg took off from Long Island wearing his flight gear. This included a leather flying helmet with a set of goggles, which was the standard pilot headgear since the First World War. It provided protection from the wind and cold in an era of open-cockpit flying. During the flight, Lindbergh, who always jointly referred to himself and the *Spirit of St. Louis* as "we," encountered terrifying obstacles, including storm clouds at 10,000 feet and whitecap waves as he skimmed the ocean at 10 feet, plus ice and fog that left him flying blind for several hours. But finally, he landed in Paris where he was greeted by a wildly enthusiastic crowd of more than 100,000 people. They swarmed the plane and Lindbergh himself, literally tearing the flying helmet off of his head. Lindbergh claimed the prize and instantly became a world hero. He subsequently flew around Europe in the *Spirit of St. Louis*, receiving honors and accolades. Returning to the United States, President Calvin Coolidge awarded him the Distinguished Flying Cross. A ticker-tape parade down Fifth Avenue, New York, followed.

Lindbergh was quickly and often pictured in the newspapers, on plates, medallions, and other memorabilia, and later stamps, wearing a flight helmet. It came to signify his identity as a flyer. And in the collection at the Smithsonian, we have several of Lindbergh's flight helmets, very simple canvas and leather skull caps, really, covering the hair and ears, and held on with a chin strap.

After returning home, Lindbergh toured the United States with the *Spirit of St. Louis*, visiting every state, as well as countries in Central America and the Caribbean. Flags of the countries he visited were later painted on the Spirit's cowling. Seen by more than a quarter of the United States population, and many internationally, the plane generated such massive publicity that it boosted the aviation industry and led to an explosion of air travel.

Before Lindbergh's flight, the public viewed air travel as rare and dangerous. But now people trusted "Lucky Lindy." They began to see airplanes as a safe and reliable means of transport. Airlines grew dramatically in the decades after World War II and now transport the vast majority of long distance passengers to their destinations.

The plane that built that confidence, the *Spirit of St. Louis*, made its final flight from St. Louis to Washington DC, where Lindbergh presented the aircraft to the Smithsonian. Now that plane is seen by more than eight million visitors a year to our National Air and Space Museum.

Of course, the story of transatlantic flight was not the end of America's adventures into new frontiers. But we'll return to that story in a few lectures.

Communications—From Telegraph to Television
Lecture 9

The United States grew and developed in the industrial revolution, when communications quickly went electric—a process that continues to this day. Reliable, rapid, and extensive systems of communication have proved their economic value. As you will learn in this lecture, they have helped bring together a huge population dispersed over a continent stretching from the Atlantic to the middle of the Pacific Ocean, and, indeed, around the planet. Most importantly, they have been vital to the free exercise of democracy.

Telegraph

- The revolution in communications began on May 24, 1844, with an innovation in one-to-one communications and a brief message: "What hath God wrought?" This simple sentence from the Bible was tapped out on a device by Samuel Morse and sent to Alfred Vail. Through their exchange, Americans and the world entered a new age of widespread rapid communication via the telegraph. Before this moment, the only means of communicating over long distances was the mail.

- Morse and Vail were not the first to experiment with sending electrical messages, and these early machines took many forms. The eventual success of the Morse-Vail system lay in its simplicity. It used one wire to transmit a message over great lengths using the earth as a ground to complete the circuit. The encoding technology—the keying or tapping device—allowed an easily transmitted and easily read pulse code.

- In 1837, Morse developed a prototype of a recording telegraph that printed messages on a ribbon of paper. This prototype can be seen in the Smithsonian. Morse partnered with a fellow professor and inventor, Leonard Gale, to experiment with transmissions of electric current and with Alfred Vail to produce the model telegraphs.

Morse thought that he would encode words as numbers, send pulses indicating numbers over the electric line, and then decode the numbers at the receiving end.

- It was Vail who came up with a better system, one we now call Morse code. Each letter of the alphabet was assigned a unique pattern of dots and dashes formed by short and long key taps. Vail analyzed the frequency of letter use in the English language, and the more common letters were assigned the simplest taps.

Morse-Vail Telegraph

- In 1838, Morse sent a telegraph message, now in the Smithsonian collections—"Attention the universe, by kingdom's right wheel"—over a distance of two miles. This inspired Congress to allot him 30,000 dollars to build an electric telegraph line between Washington DC and Baltimore. He tried to lay the line in trenches, but poorly insulated wires forced him to switch to overhead lines.

- Months later, he was ready for the famous transmission. On May 24, 1844, Morse sat in the Supreme Court Chamber—then located in the U.S. Capitol building in Washington, while Vail waited at the Mount Clare depot in Baltimore.

- Morse tapped out the message on his key. The taps closed an electric circuit, sending pulses of electric current from a battery down a wire that ran north along railroad tracks to the receiving machine 40 miles away. Electric relays along the course helped send the pulses along.

- When received by Vail, the pulses activated an electromagnet that caused a stylus to indent a paper tape. Short pulses made dots; long pulses made dashes. The paper tape moved forward powered by a clockwork mechanism or register.

- When interrupted, the stylus retracted, creating space on the tape as the device waited for the next pulse to indent the next coded letters. When Vail then sent the message back down the line as confirmation, the two men had successfully demonstrated that instantaneous long-range communication was possible and practical.

- The Smithsonian has the strip of paper on which the message was recorded. Above the message, Morse handwrote the date and circumstances of the transmission, while below he transcribed the message. The Library of Congress has the paper message from Vail's Baltimore telegraph register.

- Investors rapidly appreciated the economic potential of the telegraph. By 1850, dozens of different telegraph companies operated more than 20,000 miles of line across the United States. The first transatlantic cable was in operation by 1858. By 1861, telegraph lines stretched from the Atlantic to the Pacific. Uses of the telegraph proliferated. But as with all great technologies, the days of the telegraph were numbered.

Telephone

- Alexander Graham Bell became fascinated with the possibilities of electromagnetic communication. He studied developments in acoustic theory and conducted his own experiments. He created a phonautograph, a device that translated sound waves into patterns on a smoked-glass plate. Bell realized that it was a short leap from translating sounds into patterns to translating them back into sounds again.

- In the summer of 1874, he sketched out a plan for a harp-like apparatus composed of a series of steel reeds. A voice projected at the reeds would cause them to vibrate over a magnet, inducing a variable current in the coils of an electromagnet. That current would then be transmitted over a wire to a receiver that would turn the variable current back into sound. Bell termed this proposed device an articulating telephone.

- Several months later, Bell traveled to Washington to see Smithsonian Secretary Joseph Henry, who encouraged Bell to further pursue electricity and electromagnetism studies. With the help of an assistant, the mechanic and electrician Thomas Watson, Bell developed a primitive mechanism for acoustic telegraphy, a device to convey the human voice over an electric line.

- Bell and competitor Elisha Gray both filed papers at the U.S. Patent Office in February of 1876 for a similarly designed device, but Bell had built a prototype, while Gray submitted only a concept. Bell got the patent for an "improvement in telegraphy" a few weeks later.

- Within days of receiving the patent, Bell made the world's first, legendary telephone transmission, summoning his assistant: "Mr. Watson, come here. I want to see you!"

- The device could barely convey a conversation, and Bell and Watson continued to experiment, seeking a viable and efficient design. They developed several models that Bell then showed in Philadelphia at the 1876 U.S. Centennial Exhibition. A pair of units that could function as both transmitter and receiver proved immensely popular.

- Bell continued to experiment through the summer and fall and developed what came to be called the box telephone. Critical features are the iron diaphragm, two electromagnets, and a horseshoe-shaped permanent magnet pressed against the electromagnets.

- When used as a transmitter, sound waves at the mouthpiece caused the diaphragm to move, inducing the fluctuating current in the electromagnets. That current was conducted over wires to a similar instrument that acted as a receiver. There, the current in the electromagnets caused the diaphragm to move, producing air vibrations that could be heard by the listener.

- Bell, in Boston, and Watson, 16 miles away in Salem, connected two telephones to the telegraph wires of the Eastern Railroad Company. Their voices, even when whispered, were clearly heard. They routed the conversation through lines over hundreds of miles and could still be heard. People could now converse over long distances.

- The telephone proved immediately popular. This time-saving, convenient improvement on the telegraph did away with trips to a telegraph station, intermediaries for transcribing and transmitting messages, and waiting for a response. The number of users went from 5 million in 1910 to virtually all households and businesses by the year 2000.

- Bell Telephone, founded by Bell, Watson, and a group of colleagues in 1877, would become the American Telephone and Telegraph Company (AT&T), which was the byword in American communications prowess through most of the 20th century.

- Although Thomas Edison had already invented the first phonograph, a machine that recorded and played back sound on a foil-wrapped cylinder, in 1877, Bell continued to experiment with sound-related technology, forming the Volta Laboratory in 1880 with his relatives and associates.

- By 1887, this grew into the Volta Bureau, which developed numerous inventions, including the wax-coated cylinder used in the Graphophone, a type of record player that competed with Edison's. Bell and Volta also experimented with magnetic and other types of recordings.

- Bell donated a number of important objects and early recordings to the Smithsonian. Shortly after his death, Bell's company donated originals and models of early experimental telephones. The 400 or so recordings Bell left to the Smithsonian remained inaccessible for decades, due to the lack of a technology for their playback.

- In 2011, scientists and scholars from the Lawrence Berkeley National Laboratory, the Library of Congress, and the Smithsonian cooperated on a project to optically read the grooves in Bell's early recording disks and turn them back into sound.

Radio

- For all their differences, the one thing telephones and telegraphs had in common was wires. In 1895, the Italian inventor Guglielmo Marconi became the first person to "cut the cord" of electronic communications, sending wireless signals across the Italian countryside. In 1900, he patented this invention: radio.

- The shipping trade was the first industry to adopt Marconi's technology. Radio was also quickly adopted for military use. Wireless communications had obvious advantages for reaching ships at sea and planes in the air.

- Because radio communications were so important to the war effort, commercial development ground to a halt during World War I in both Europe and the United States. The first commercial radio station in America—KDKA in Pittsburg—wasn't licensed until November 2, 1920.

- Radios were hugely expensive at first, but their costs came down as their popularity mushroomed. About one-third of U.S. households owned a radio in the late 1920s, compared to about 60 percent by 1933. Thanks to installment plans, people could keep buying radios even during the Depression.

- Radio broke new ground for the country. People all over the United States could hear the same news broadcast, music, and radio shows at the same time. Suddenly, we had a medium to develop a nationwide culture. Radio was, therefore, the most powerful medium yet invented for spreading information and shaping public opinion.

- The first U.S. president to try to take advantage of this was Herbert Hoover. Unfortunately, Hoover was not cut out for radio. His speaking style was condescending and stilted. He came across to listeners as distant and impersonal; the inferior quality of broadcast and radio reception did not help.

- Franklin Delano Roosevelt fared much better. On the evening of Sunday, March 12, 1933, only eight days after his swearing in as the 32nd president of the United States, he took to the airwaves for the first time. The nation was in the throes of its worst economic depression in history, and Roosevelt had to reassure the nation. Radio was the means to do so.

- That broadcast was the first of 31 informal "fireside chats" that Roosevelt would deliver through a bevy of microphones from different stations and networks to an audience of millions of Americans brought together by the radio.

- The microphone that Roosevelt used to deliver this fireside chat is part of the collection at the National Museum of American History. This particular microphone is special, because it recalls a watershed moment in American politics, a moment that personalized the presidency for a vast number of Americans. It is estimated that by the time of his last address, two-thirds of American households had listened to his voice.

Television

- A few years later, Roosevelt became the first sitting president to appear on another new technology that would revolutionize communications: television. The occasion was the opening ceremony of the 1939 New York World's Fair. Roosevelt delivered a speech to about 200,000 fair attendees. That speech was also transmitted by RCA to the very few people who owned the TRK-12 television.

- The TRK-12 was developed for limited commercial service in the New York area. Its experimental nature and high price, about 600 dollars, made it a very exclusive product. Still, RCA began broadcasting some programs and, on May 17, televised a baseball game for the very first time. It was a college match between Princeton and Columbia, viewed through a single camera, but it was a start.

First Commercial RCA Television

- Over the next two years, RCA sold about 7,000 television sets, mainly in New York and Los Angeles. Broadcasts were crude, and audiences were tiny, even after RCA's competition, the Columbia Broadcasting System (CBS), began two 15-minute daily newscasts. These news shows featured difficult-to-discern commentators running pointers over impossible-to-decipher maps.

- Television was a dream of many inventors and engineers in the closing decades of the 19th century, and the invention of movies, telephone, and radio seemed to put it within reach. As with so many inventions, it took a number of advances by inventors and engineers in many countries—in this case Germany, Russia, Japan, Scotland, and Hungary—to make the technology practical and economically viable.

- The first true working television was essentially the work of two inventors and one savvy businessman. Philo Taylor Farnsworth, an American inventor, developed a method for scanning images with a beam of electrons and transmitting them with what he called an image dissector—essentially, a primitive television camera—in 1927.

- In 1931, RCA head David Sarnoff hired a Russian immigrant named Vladimir Zworykin, who was a former Westinghouse employee who had patented a television transmitting and receiving system. At RCA, Zworykin developed the use of cathode-ray tubes and came up with a new form of camera called the iconoscope. Working with Zworykin, Sarnoff sought, contested, and purchased various patents—including Fransworth's—to develop a commercially and technologically viable television transmission and reception system.

- Just as World War I slowed the development of radio, World War II slowed the development of television, as companies like RCA turned their attention to military production. Six experimental television stations remained on the air during the war: one each in Chicago; Philadelphia; Los Angeles; and Schenectady, New York, and two in New York City.

- New companies gradually came into being, but full-scale commercial television broadcasting did not begin in the United States until 1947. The number of television sets rose from 6,000 in 1946 to 12 million by 1951. Up to that point, no new invention had entered American homes faster than black-and-white television sets. By 1955, half of all U.S. homes had one.

- With the proliferation of television sets and broadcasting came programs and advertising in the form of commercials to pay for them. Television became a new center of home life as well as cultural life. Television news added a new, visual dimension to sharing information.

- The televised presidential debate between Senator John F. Kennedy and Vice President Richard Nixon showed the power of the medium to influence viewers when Nixon's appearance, as much as his performance, shaped the television audience's reaction.

- The Smithsonian has a rich collection of the artifacts of television history, from the iconic stopwatch from *60 Minutes*, to the Fonz's leather jacket from *Happy Days*, to the judges' desk from the musical talent show *American Idol*.

Featured Objects

Morse-Vail Telegraph

Early Bell Telephone

FDR's Fireside Chat Microphone

First Commercial RCA Television

Suggested Reading

Buhite and Levy, eds., *FDR's Fireside Chats*.

Gray, *Reluctant Genius*.

Kisseloff, *The Box*.

Standage, *The Victorian Internet*.

Communications—From Telegraph to Television

Lecture 9—Transcript

Scholars conventionally date the beginning of history to the inception of writing. Writing allowed a person to communicate their thoughts to someone distant in space or time through a carving in wood, an inscription in stone, or marks on paper. History grows out of these ancient traditions of communication and the societies that made them possible.

America, though, was born in the age of mass communications. The printing press was already hundreds of years old when the United States was founded. Printing made copying a text fast and inexpensive, which made information available to the masses. The United States grew and developed in the industrial revolution, when communications quickly went electric, a process that continues to this day. Reliable, rapid and extensive systems of communication have proved their economic value. They have helped bring together a huge population dispersed over a continent stretching from the Atlantic to the middle of the Pacific Ocean, and indeed, around the planet. Most importantly, they have been vital to the free exercise of democracy.

This revolution in communication began on May 25, 1844 with an innovation in one-to-one communications and a brief message: "What hath God wrought?" This simple sentence from the Bible, Numbers chapter 23, verse 23, was tapped out on what now looks like a very primitive device by Samuel Morse and sent to his partner, Alfred Vail. Through their exchange, Americans and the world entered the new age of widespread rapid communication via the telegraph!

Now, before this moment, the only means of communicating over long distance was the mail. The United States Postal Service was established in the Constitution—Article I, Section 8, Clause 7, to be exact. It carried, the mail service did, both personal letters and newspapers using stagecoaches and steamboats. But as we discussed in a previous lecture, overland travel was very slow. Before the intercontinental railroad, the overland mail route between Tipton Missouri and San Francisco was supposed to take 24 days. More often, the mail took months to arrive. The land-and-sea route over the Isthmus of Panama was only a little faster.

The emerging science of electricity offered a potential alternative. In late 18th and early 19th centuries, Benjamin Franklin demonstrated the electrical nature of lightning; Alessandro Volta developed the battery; Hans Christian Ørsted and André-Marie Ampère made the connection between electricity and magnetism. In 1821, Michael Faraday invented the electric motor. A few years later, William Sturgeon developed the electromagnet and Georg Ohm analyzed the electric circuit. A world of possibilities had opened.

Morse and Vail were the first to experiment with sending electrical messages, and these early machines took many forms. Some of them seem quite impractical today. For example, one invention featured dozens of wires leading into glass tubes of acid, each representing a letter or a number. When current was transmitted along one of the wires, it caused a reaction in the tube, creating bubbles. Wire by wire, bubble by bubble, a message could be tediously sent and read. William Cooke and Charles Wheatstone developed an electrical telegraph in Britain. It consisted of multiple lines and ran for 13 miles along a railroad. Pulses of electricity made needles point to different letters. Later, they used wheels of typescript to decode messages. Their system failed to catch on.

The eventual success of the Morse-Vail system lay in its simplicity. It used one wire to transmit a message over a great length using the earth as a ground to complete the circuit. The encoding technology—the keying or tapping device—allowed an easily transmitted and read pulse code. So, how did this system come to be? Well, in 1837, Morse developed a prototype of a recording telegraph that printed messages on a ribbon of paper. We have that prototype in the Smithsonian. Morse partnered with a fellow professor and inventor, Leonard Gale, to experiment with transmissions of electric current and with Alfred Vail to produce model telegraphs. Morse thought that he could encode words as numbers, send pulses indicating numbers over an electric line, and then decode the numbers at the receiving end.

But it was Vail who actually came up with a better system, one we now call the Morse code. Each letter of the alphabet was assigned a unique pattern of dots and dashes formed by short and long key taps. Vail analyzed the frequency of letter use in the English language, and the more common letters were assigned the simplest taps. The letter E is a single dot, for example, and the letter T, a single dash.

In 1838, Morse sent a telegraph message, also now in the Smithsonian collections, “Attention the universe, by kingdom’s right wheel,” over a distance of two miles. This inspired the Congress to allot him $30,000 to build an electric telegraph line between Washington, D.C. and Baltimore. He tried to lay the line in trenches, but poorly insulated wires forced him to switch to overhead lines. Months later, he was ready for the famous transmission. Annie, the daughter of the Patent Office Commissioner, Henry Leavitt Ellsworth, chose the message. So on May 25, 1844, Morse sat in the Supreme Court Chamber, then it was located in the U.S. Capitol building, in Washington, while Vail waited at the Mount Clare depot in Baltimore. Morse tapped out the message on his key—short quick taps and slower long ones. The taps closed the electric circuit, sending pulses of current from a battery down a wire that ran north along railroad tracks to the receiving machine some 40 miles away. Electric relays along the course helped send the pulses along. When received by Vail, the pulses activated an electromagnet that caused a stylus to indent a paper tape. Short pulses made dots, long pulses made dashes. The paper tape moved forward powered by a clockwork mechanism, or a register. When interrupted, the stylus retracted, creating space on the tape as the device waited for the next pulse to indent the next coded letters. When Vail then sent the message back down the line as confirmation, the two men had successfully demonstrated that instantaneous, long-range communication was possible and practical.

At the Smithsonian we have the strip of paper, 28 inches long and 1½ inches wide, recording the message. Above the message, Morse handwrote the date and the circumstances of the transmission, while below the message, the transmission, he transcribed the actual message. The Library of Congress has the paper message from the Vail transmission from Baltimore’s telegraph register.

Investors rapidly appreciated the economic potential of the telegraph. By 1850, dozens of different telegraph companies operated more than $20,000 miles of line across the United States. In 1852, a wire under the English Channel successfully connected London and Paris, and the first transmission cable was in operation by 1858. By 1861, telegraph lines stretched from the Atlantic to the Pacific. You could now send a message almost halfway around the world in mere minutes.

Uses of the telegraph proliferated. Police departments used it to convey information to catch criminals. Railroad companies could send information about schedules and delays. The telegraph required correspondents to use short sentences, so our public use of language itself became "telegraphic." Thanks to the telegraph, the "news" was really new, and print newspapers flourished. Reporters flocked to the Mexican-American War and filed reports every few hours, engaging the public as never before in world events. In 1848, six newspapers in New York established the Associated Press to help defray the costs of long-distance telegraphy. During the Civil War, President Lincoln frequently used the telegraph to communicate with his battlefield generals while the public closely followed the war's progress.

Starting in the 1840s, Joseph Henry, one of the early scientists working on electro-magnetism, became the Secretary of the Smithsonian. He developed a system of some 600 volunteer "citizen scientists" across the United States who would daily record their observations of the weather and mail their reports to the Smithsonian. The project eventually evolved into the National Weather Service.

But as with all great technologies, the days of the telegraph were numbered. Alexander Graham Bell became fascinated with the possibilities of electronic communication. Born in Scotland, he immigrated to Canada and then to Boston as a young man. He followed in his father's footsteps as a teacher to the deaf. He also studied developments in acoustic theory and conducted his own experiments. He created a phonautograph, a device that translated sound waves into patterns on a smoked-glass plate. It helped Bell's deaf students improve their elocution by helping them to "see" the sounds their voices were producing.

Bell realized that it was a short leap from translating sounds into patterns to translating them back into sounds again. In the summer of 1874, he sketched out plan for a harp-like apparatus composed of a series of steel reeds. A voice projected at the reeds would cause them to vibrate over a magnet, inducing a variable current in the coils of an electromagnet. That current would then be transmitted over a wire to a receiver that would turn the variable current back into sound. Bell termed this proposed device, an articulating telephone.

Several months later Bell traveled to Washington to see Smithsonian Secretary Joseph Henry. Henry was enthused by Bell's work and encouraged him to further pursue electricity and electromagnetism studies. With the help of an assistant, the mechanic and electrician Thomas Watson, Bell developed a primitive mechanism for acoustic telegraphy, a device to convey the human voice over an electric line. He and competitor Elisha Gray both filed papers at the U.S. Patent Office in February 1876, for a similarly designed device, but Bell had built a prototype, while Gray submitted only a concept. Bell got the patent for an "improvement in telegraphy" a few weeks later.

Within days of receiving the patent, Bell made the world's first, legendary telephone transmission, summoning his assistant with the words, "Mr. Watson, come here. I want to see you!" The device could barely convey a conversation, and Bell and Watson continued to experiment, seeking a viable and efficient design. They developed several models that Bell then showed in Philadelphia at the 1876 U.S. Centennial Exhibition. A pair of units that could function as both transmitter and receiver proved immensely popular.

Bell continued to experiment through the summer and fall and developed what came to be called the box telephone. The object here is one of the first commercial Bell telephones. It is used as both a transmitter and as a receiver. When used as a transmitter, sound waves at the mouthpiece cause the diaphragm to move, inducing the fluctuating current in an electromagnet. That current was conducted over wires to a similar instrument that acted as a receiver. There, the current in the electromagnets caused the diaphragm to move, producing air vibrations that could be heard by the listener.

When Bell conducted experiments with telephones like this, he connected to telephones to telegraph wires at the railroad companies. Their voices, even when whispered, were clearly heard, and then the press would describe such conversation as "free and easy." Conversation through lines over hundreds of miles could be heard, and people could now converse over long distances.

It's hard to imagine that this modest device is the precursor of the ubiquitous cell phone of today—but it is.

The telephone proved immediately popular. This time-saving, convenient improvement on the telegraph did away with trips to the telegraph station, intermediaries for transcribing and transmitting messages, and the waiting time for a response. Civic services benefited, as people gained the ability to call police and fire departments. Household users were able to communicate with doctors, merchants, relatives, and friends. The number of users went from five million in 1910 to virtually all households and businesses by the year 2000. Bell Telephone, founded by Bell, Watson, and a group of colleagues in 1877, would become the American Telephone and Telegraph Company, AT&T, or Ma Bell, as it was sometimes called, And this was the byword in American communication prowess through most of the 20th century.

Though Thomas Edison had already invented the first phonograph in 1877, a machine that recorded and played back sound on a foil-wrapped cylinder, Bell continued to move forward and experiment with sound-related technology, forming Volta Laboratory in 1880 with his relatives and associates. By 1887, this grew into the Volta Bureau, which had as its mission "the increase and diffusion of knowledge relating to the deaf." The mission mirrored the more generalized mission of the Smithsonian, on whose board of regents Bell served for more than two decades. Volta developed numerous inventions, included the wax coated cylinder used in the Graphophone, a type of record player that competed with Edison's. Bell and Volta also experimented with magnetic and other types of recordings.

Bell donated a number of important objects and early recordings to the Smithsonian. Shortly after his death, Bell's company donated originals and models of early experimental telephones. The 400 or so recordings Bell left to the Smithsonian remained inaccessible for decades, due to the lack of a technology to play them back. In 2011, scientists and scholars from the Lawrence Berkeley National Laboratory, the Library of Congress, and the Smithsonian cooperated on a project to optically read the grooves in Bell's early recording disks and turn them back into sound. Let's take a listen to a recitation of Mary Had a Little Lamb.

Though the children's poem is not very profound, that hard-to-decipher recording is. This is a medium in its very infancy. The voice is coming to us from more than a century ago. It's this past speaking to us through that barely discernable voice thanks to an inspired inventor illustrating his quest to create electronic speech.

For all their differences, the one thing telephones and telegraphs had in common was wires. In 1895, the Italian inventor Marconi became the first person to "cut the cord" of electronic communications, sending wireless signals across the Italian countryside. In 1900 he patented this invention, calling it tuned, or syntonic, telegraphy. We simply call it the radio.

The shipping trade was the first industry to adopt Marconi's technology. Ships at sea used radio to communicate with each other and to get news and weather reports from the shore. These radio operators were not employed by the ships but were, rather, independent contractors. In fact, the radio operators who signaled for help from on board the sinking Titanic were employees of the Marconi International Marine Communication Company. Radio was also quickly adopted for military use. Wireless communications had obvious advantages for reaching ships at sea and planes in the air. Ironically, during World War I, the United States Navy began broadcasting its nightly radio news summaries...in Morse code!

Because radio communications were so important to the war effort, commercial development ground to a halt during World War I in both Europe and in the United States. But the first commercial radio station in America—KDKA in Pittsburg—wasn't licensed until November 2, 1920. Radios at that time were usually expensive. But their costs came down as their popularity mushroomed. About one-third of U.S. households owned a radio in the late 1920s, compared to some 60 percent by 1933. Thanks to installment plans, people could keep buying radios even during the Depression.

Radio broke new ground for the country. The telegraph had sped up the spread of information from a few days or weeks or months to a few hours. Reporters could receive the news, write it up, send it to print in a newspaper, and people would read about it, perhaps, half a day later. Now, people all over the United States could hear the same news broadcast at the same time, and not only news, music and radio shows as well. Suddenly, we had a medium to develop a nation-wide culture. Radio was, therefore, the most powerful medium yet invented for spreading information and shaping public opinion.

The first U.S. president to take advantage of this, or, I should say, to try to take advantage of this, was Herbert Hoover. Unfortunately, Hoover was not cut out for radio. His speaking style was condescending and stilted. He came across to listeners as a distant and impersonal leader; the inferior quality of broadcast radio and radio reception did not help. He used the medium poorly, and, therefore, rarely.

Franklin Delano Roosevelt fared much, much better. On the evening of Sunday, March 12, 1933, only eight days after his swearing in as the 32nd president of the United States, he took to the airwaves for the first time. The nation was in the throes of its worst economic depression in history. Unemployment was at about 25 percent. Industrial production was down by about a third from pre-crash levels. The banking system was collapsing. No president, with the exception of Abraham Lincoln, ever entered the White House facing such a severe crisis.

Roosevelt had to speak to his fellow citizens and reassure the nation. Radio was the means to do this. That broadcast was the first of 31 informal "Fireside Chat" radio addresses that Roosevelt would deliver through a bevy of microphones from different stations and networks to an audience of millions of Americans brought together by the radio. A radioman had the idea of calling them fireside chats, which Roosevelt approved, feeling they captured the informality, and even more the intimacy, of what he thought to convey.

Roosevelt opened the first of these chats with the words, "My friends, I want to talk for a few minutes with the people of the United States about banking," and it was, for the most part, a quite technical economic talk. But then he noted that to solve the crisis something more important than gold, was needed, and that was the confidence of the people themselves. Let's listen to a particularly powerful except of that historical talk:

> "Confidence and courage are the essentials of success in carrying out our plan. You people must have faith; you must not be

stampeded by rumors or guesses. Let us unite in banishing fear. We have provided the machinery to restore our financial system, and it is up to you to support and make it work. It is your problem, my friends, your problem no less than it is mine. Together we cannot fail."

Listening to broadcasts such as this one, many Americans felt as if the president were speaking to them personally. One wrote, "last evening as I listened to the President's broadcast I felt that he walked into my home, sat down and in plain and forceful language explained to me how he was tackling the job."

This microphone, now part of the collection at the National Museum of American History, was one that Roosevelt used to deliver this fireside chats. This particular microphone is special, because it recalls a watershed moment in American politics, a moment that personalized the presidency for a vast number of Americans. It is estimated that by the time of his last address, some two-thirds of American households had listened to Roosevelt's voice. As family members gathered around a radio in a living room or kitchen and turned a dial, they literally invited the president into their homes.

A few years later, Roosevelt became the first sitting president to appear on another new technology that would revolutionize communications. The occasioning was the opening ceremony of the 1939 World's Fair. Roosevelt delivered a speech to about 200,000 fair attendees. That speech was also transmitted by RCA to the very few people who owned this television, the TRK-12. RCA showcased the TRK-12 at the World's Fair, displaying it in what they called "the living room of the future." They could not have been more prescient!

The TRK-12 was developed for very limited commercial service in the New York area. Its experimental nature and high price, about $600, made it a very expensive and exclusive product. Still, RCA began broadcasting some programs, and on May 17 televised a baseball game for the very first time. It was a college match between Princeton and Columbia, viewed through a single camera, but it was a start. Over the next two years, RCA sold about 7,000 television sets, mainly in New York and Los Angeles. Broadcasts were crude and audiences were tiny, even after RCA's competition, the Columbia Broadcasting System, or CBS, began two 15-minute daily newscasts. These news shows featured hard-to-discern commentators running pointers over impossible-to-decipher maps.

Television had been a dream of many inventors and engineers in the closing decades of the 19th century, and the invention of movies, telephone, and radio seemed to put it all within reach. As with so many inventions, it took a number of advances by inventors and engineers in many countries, in this case, Germany, Russia, Japan, Scotland and Hungary, to make the technology practical and economically viable.

But the first true working television—this television—was essentially the work of two inventors and one savvy businessman. Philo Taylor Farnsworth, an American inventor, developed a method for scanning images with a beam of electrons and transmitting them with what he called an image dissector, essentially, a primitive television camera; he did this in 1927. In 1931, RCA head, David Sarnoff, hired a Russian immigrant named Vladimir Zworykin. Zworykin was a former Westinghouse employee who had patented a television transmitting and receiving system. At RCA, Zworykin developed the use of cathode-ray tubes and came up with a new form of camera called the iconoscope. Working with Zworykin, Sarnoff sought, contested, and purchased various patents, including Fransworth's, to develop a commercially and technologically viable television transmission and reception system.

The TRK-12 doesn't look like much to us now. The picture tube was only 5 inches in diameter by 12 inches tall, and it was mounted inside the top of the unit. A hinged lid held a mirror, and the audience actually saw the image as a reflection. The unit also came with a radio receiver, so if you couldn't yet get television in your area, well, at least it was still useful. The beautiful Art Deco design here was the work of Greek-born John Vassos, RCA's lead industrial designer.

Just as World War I had slowed the development of radio, World War II slowed the development of television as companies like RCA turned their attention to military production. Six experimental television stations remained on the air during the war, one each in Chicago; Philadelphia; Los Angeles; and Schenectady, New York; and two in New York City. New companies gradually came into being. But full-scale commercial television broadcasts did not begin in the United States until 1947. The number of television sets rose from 6,000 in 1946 to some 12,000,000 by 1951. Up to that point, no new invention had entered the American home faster than black-and-white television sets. By 1955, half of all U.S. homes had one.

With the proliferation of television sets and broadcasting came programs and advertising in the form of commercials to pay for them. Television became a new center of home life, as well as cultural life. Television news added a new, visual dimension to sharing information. The televised presidential debates between Senator John F. Kennedy and Vice President Richard Nixon showed the power of the medium to influence viewers, when Nixon's appearance, as much as his performance, shaped television audience's reaction.

The Smithsonian has a rich collection of the artifacts of television history, from the iconic stopwatch of 60 Minutes, to the Fonzie's leather jacket from Happy Days, to the judges' desk from the musical talent show American Idol. The last of these represents the trend that really brings us full circle in this lecture. In reality television shows like this one, the audience is asked to participate by voting. One of the ways of voting is by sending in a cell phone text message, a short, dare I say, telegraphic form of communication. Mass communication and personal communications merge in determining the outcome of a television show, an amazing, if refracted, illustration of our absorption with grassroots democracy.

Immigrant Dreams and Immigrant Struggles
Lecture 10

This lecture will examine three objects from the Smithsonian's collections, each of which raises intriguing questions and offers interesting perspectives on the history of immigration in the United States. One is an original model of the Statue of Liberty, which, years after being built, became a symbol for immigrants. The second is a painting made by a Japanese American artist during World War II that tells a painful story about immigration and citizenship. The last is a farmworker's back-bending hoe that teaches us about the complexities of the Mexican American population.

The Statue of Liberty

- In the mid-1850s, visiting the Pyramids and the Great Sphinx of Giza in Egypt, French sculptor Frédéric Bartholdi was transfixed by the power and romance he found in the large-scale public monuments. A decade later, back home in France, he attended a dinner party hosted by Édouard René Lefebvre de Laboulaye, a lawyer, professor, and chairman of the French antislavery society.

- The Civil War had just ended, and Laboulaye was rejoicing at the defeat of slavery. He rhapsodized about the historic connections between France and the United States. He proposed that a grand monument to liberty be built in time for the American Centennial in 1876, several years hence.

- The idea of a monument struck a chord with Bartholdi. Returning to Egypt in 1869, he proposed building a massive statue at the entrance to the newly constructed Suez Canal. His design was of a robed woman with a headdress holding a torch. She would double as a lighthouse. He called his vision "*Egypt Bringing Light to Asia*."

- The Egyptians were uninterested in Bartholdi's proposal and unwilling to pay for it. So, the artist changed course. He set sail for America in 1871. Entering New York Harbor, Bartholdi was struck by Manhattan's beauty and symbolic power as the gateway to America. Bedloe's Island, a tiny islet owned by the federal government, seemed perfect for a monument.

Model of Frédéric Bartholdi's *Liberty*

- The Frenchman compared his proposal to the Colossus of Rhodes, a bronze statue erected on a Greek island more than 2,000 years ago and described as one of the Seven Wonders of the World. While the brief-lived Colossus was emblematic of power, Bartholdi's lady would signify liberty. She would be modeled after the Roman goddess Libertas and would reflect America's faith in its citizenry.

- With the help of his old friend Laboulaye, the sculptor formed the Franco-American Union in 1875 to raise money. Through Levi Morton, the American minister to France at the time, Laboulaye urged President Ulysses Grant to support the endeavor. To succeed, it needed the American government to donate the underlying land.

- The design featured a robed lady in spiked crown, clutching a tablet inscribed "July 4, 1776," and standing atop broken chains and shackles. In her right hand, she is lifting a torch. Bartholdi needed a first-class engineer for the project. He enlisted Eugène Viollet-le-Duc, who suggested the *repoussé* method of metalwork. Three hundred thin sheets of copper would be hammered into the form of the statue's skin. They would then be connected by iron-bar armature.

- Bartholdi built progressively larger-scale models—4-, 9-, and 36-foot versions. From these, he could develop plaster casts and wooden forms for shaping the copper. In 1876, he was able to send Liberty's right arm and torch to Philadelphia to be shown at the Centennial Exposition, after which it was displayed at New York's Madison Square Garden.

- Although contributions did not pour in as expected, President Grant signed a bill authorizing the construction of a statue on Bedloe's Island before he left office in 1877. In 1878, Bartholdi displayed the completed head and shoulders at the Paris Exposition.

- French architect and structural engineer Alexandre-Gustave Eiffel took over the statue's internal design after the death of le-Duc in 1879. This was slightly less than a decade before Eiffel would begin construction of the lattice tower named for him in Paris.

- Eiffel praised le-Duc's designs but, instead of relying on the outer shell for support, envisioned a 120-ton inner skeletal structure anchored by a 98-foot pylon composed of four huge iron posts to hold up the statue. It would be tied to another anchor sunk in the 154-foot high pedestal. This marvel of relatively lightweight trusses and flexible suspension would enable the statue to adjust to weather conditions and would allow visitors to walk to the top via an interior staircase.

- By 1882, the French committee had raised all the money needed to build the statue —250,000 dollars—and Bartholdi and Eiffel were on track to complete work the following year. But American efforts were lagging, so Bartholdi had to slow down. Meanwhile, he shipped his 4-foot model of the Statue of Liberty from Paris to Washington DC to persuade Congress to help fund the project. The terra-cotta model, painted to appear bronze with a touch of tin in the crown, was used by architect Richard Morris Hunt to design the pedestal.

- Bartholdi's model was displayed in the Capitol Rotunda, where it attracted its fair share of attention, including notice by Hungarian immigrant Joseph Pulitzer, a newspaper publisher who that same year moved to Manhattan and acquired the mass-circulation *New York World.*

- Pulitzer's newspaper exhorted Americans to donate money for the cause and criticized the wealthy for failing to contribute. The public rallied to his call. By 1885, Pulitzer had helped raise the last one-third of 300,000 dollars needed to complete the pedestal and its anchor through fund-raising sporting events, plays, and performances.

- The statue was shipped from Paris to New York and was assembled to its full height of 151 feet. Given Thomas Edison's recent triumph of electrifying Pearl Street in Lower Manhattan, the decision was made to light the torch with electric bulbs.

- On October 28, 1886, with President Grover Cleveland presiding, Bartholdi pulled a rope that released the French tricolor flag covering Lady Liberty's face. Following the statue's dedication, Bartholdi's 4-foot model was transferred from the Capitol Rotunda to the Smithsonian, where today it is on display in the American Art Museum.

- In 1903, words from a poem, "The *New Colossus*," were added on a tablet to the base of the Statue of Liberty in New York Harbor. The poem was written by Emma Lazarus in 1883 and was donated to the Bartholdi Pedestal Fund for the Statue of Liberty. The sight would greet some 12 million newcomers to America until Ellis Island's closing in 1954.

Henry Sugimoto's Painting

- In 1917, Congress passed a literacy requirement to restrict the numbers of low-skilled and unskilled Jews, Italians, Poles, Swedes, Greeks, and others flocking to America from their homelands. Concerns with maintaining a homogeneous national identity—

tinged with racial theories of eugenics—led to the Emergency Quota Act of 1921 and the Immigration Act of 1924.

- These laws limited immigration from southern and eastern Europe by setting quotas through a "national origins formula" and denied the possibility of citizenship to Arabs, Indians, Chinese, Japanese, and others.

- A few backdoors, though, remained for restricted populations: The legislation that tightened the sluice gates of immigration excluded the Western Hemisphere. Therefore, immigrants could still enter the United States from Mexico and the Caribbean. And with America's annexation of Hawaii in 1898, many people of Asian descent had become residents of the United States and internal migrants to the West Coast.

- By the early 1940s, Japanese Americans had established thriving communities in Hawaii and California. Most had roots in agriculture, having been recruited beginning in the 1860s to work in Hawaiian sugarcane fields and then later on California's fruit and vegetable farms. Gradually, they took up trades and businesses and built schools, churches, and cultural organizations. People of Japanese ancestry accounted for almost 40 percent of Hawaii's residents by 1940.

- While earlier generations were prohibited from becoming citizens and owning property, many nevertheless purchased homes, farms, and businesses through their American-born and assimilated children, called *nisei*, a Japanese-language term meaning "the second generation."

- The attack on Pearl Harbor was a catalyst for questioning the loyalty of all people of Japanese descent in the United States. On February 19, 1942, President Franklin Roosevelt signed Executive Order 9066, authorizing military authorities to uproot ethnic Japanese living on the West Coast and confine them in isolated, heavily guarded camps. The order included citizens and noncitizens alike and was based on deep and widespread suspicions about their identity as Americans and their loyalty to the United States.

- Justice Department officials questioned the constitutionality of such an order, and there was no such directive covering Americans of German or Italian decent, whose native countries were also at war with the United States.

- About 120,000 West Coast Japanese Americans—two-thirds of them American citizens—were rounded up by the U.S. government and designated as "evacuees." They had to leave their home communities, with only as many possessions as they could carry. Many had to sell their homes and businesses quickly and at a loss.

- They were sent first to temporary "assembly centers" in California, Arizona, Oregon, and Washington state and then to jails, prisons, military installations, and "relocation" camps, quickly and poorly constructed by the War Relocation Authority.

- These camps were isolated geographically and socially. Due to a wartime shortage of critical building materials, some "evacuees" were forced temporarily to live in barracks without lights, laundry facilities, or adequate toilets. Mess halls designed to accommodate several hundred people handled two and three times that number for short periods of time.

- The internees lived behind barbed-wire fences, watched over by military police. One of their few opportunities for self-expression was through art. Painters, artists, and craftspeople employed naturally occurring materials and scraps to express their feelings about confinement.

- Japanese-born artist Henry Sugimoto was interred halfway across the country in 1942 under government order—first in Jerome, Arkansas, and later at adjacent Rohwer—more than 20 years after arriving in America as a boy.

- While in confinement, Sugimoto completed about 100 paintings. One, called *Thinking of Loved One*, depicts a Japanese American mother and her newborn child. The irony of the painting is clear: A baby born in America, the land of the free, is comforted by its mother within sight of a watchtower.

- Although Japanese Americans were initially classified as "enemy aliens," for the purpose of military service, that changed in late 1942. Hawaiian nisei formed the 100th Infantry Battalion, later incorporated into the 442nd. About 25,000 Nisei served in the war effort, enduring high-casualty rates and rewarded with many decorations of honor.

- The system of interment ended in December 1944, with the Supreme Court ruling that claims of military necessity could not justify holding American citizens against their will. The camps were closed. Each internee received a 25-dollar payment and transportation home.

- In 1988, President Ronald Reagan issued a formal apology on behalf of the American people and granted each former internee a largely symbolic payment of 20,000 dollars, under belated civil liberties legislation passed by Congress and signed by the president.

Cesar Chavez's Short-Handled Hoe

- A similar struggle for recognition and respect occupied Cesar Chavez, a Mexican American founder and leader of the United Farm Workers union. During World War II, the U.S. government established the Bracero Program, extending an opportunity for Mexican guest workers to temporarily work on American farms, fields, and orchards to help alleviate agricultural labor shortages and feed American families.

- *Braceros*—a Spanish-language term that refers to manual laborers—were often willing to work for less money than most Americans and frequently accepted substandard working conditions. After the program ended in 1964, millions of Mexican workers continued to pass back and forth across the border illegally, responding to seasonal labor demands.

Cesar Chavez's Short Hoe

- This sparked a conflict with naturalized Mexicans and their American-born offspring, many of whom depended on jobs in Texas's cotton fields and California's orchards. Aggressive border-enforcement campaigns, such as "Operation Wetback" in 1954, heightened tensions.

- Cesar Chavez was a labor organizer and conciliator whose methods of nonviolent protest were remarkably effective, given the lack of leverage farm workers traditionally possessed. Born near Yuma, Arizona, in March 1927, Chavez and his parents worked as migrant laborers. After attending dozens of schools as a boy, Chavez dropped out to work in the fields and then joined the U.S. Navy in 1946, after World War II had ended.

- Migrant farmworkers made the equivalent of about 90 cents per hour in the early 1960s, at a time when the federal minimum was a dollar and 25 cents. They paid daily rent for housing, often with no power or plumbing. Farmworkers also had few benefits and virtually no security. For all that, they did backbreaking work using implements like short-handled hoes. Because these were only a little more than a foot long, workers had to virtually kneel and crab walk in the hot sun.

- Chavez's big effort was aimed at unionizing workers so that they could demand and receive the minimum wage, basic benefits, and decent treatment. He modeled his initiatives—including marches and boycotts of table grapes and lettuce—on the burgeoning civil rights movement.

Cesar Chavez's Union Jacket

- Chavez identified closely with the Reverend Dr. Martin Luther King Jr. Following Mahatma Gandhi's example, he also fasted in the pursuit of justice. In 1972, during a 24-day fast in Arizona, Chavez adopted the Spanish-language slogan "*Sí, se puede*"—"Yes, it can be done," or "Yes, we can"—a rallying cry for farmworkers, later adapted by Latino civil rights and immigration advocates.

- After years of struggle, Chavez gained support from consumers and other labor unions to form the United Farm Workers of America and, with it, the right to organize agricultural workers.

- The Smithsonian has Chavez's union jacket, donated after his death in 1993 by his widow and fellow activist, Helen Chavez. It bears the union's logo—a stylized eagle with wings in the shape of an inverted Aztec pyramid—and the colors black (for struggle), red (for sacrifice), and white (for hope), all symbols that resonated with Mexican Americans.

- In 1975, California banned the use of the hated short-handled hoe under an administrative order that found that they were unsafe and constituted an occupational hazard. The Smithsonian has one that once belonged to Cesar Chavez and to his father.

Featured Objects

Frédéric Bartholdi's Liberty

Henry Sugimoto's Thinking of Loved One

Cesar Chavez's Short Hoe and Union Jacket

Suggested Reading

Binder, *All the Nations under Heaven.*

Hirasuna, Heffernan, and Hindrichs, *The Art of Gaman.*

Levy, *Cesar Chavez.*

Muller, ed., *Colors of Confinement.*

Immigrant Dreams and Immigrant Struggles
Lecture 10—Transcript

We often think of the United States as a nation of immigrants. Native Americans had North America to themselves for millennia. But the most diverse country in human history was largely populated during the last 400 years, and by people from every corner of the planet. Spanish explorers, soldiers, and friars came seeking gold and religious glory, and sometimes dealt with native inhabitants in brutal ways.

The English constituted the vast majority of the early colonists; it was a quest for religious freedom that propelled the Puritans, and many immigrants, particularly the Irish, came as indentured servants. From Jamestown on, hundreds of thousands of Africans arrived in shackles and chains, as they would for the next 200 years.

The first Europeans in the New World typically did not think of themselves as immigrants. British, French, Spanish, they identified with their home countries and conceived of life in the colonies as outposts, and indeed, extensions, of European life. That would change, in time.

The pageant of American immigration was mostly unplanned. It was sometimes disorderly and full of surprises. And we're about to examine the three objects from the Smithsonian's collection, each of which tells a story about immigration. Each artifact raises intriguing questions and offers interesting perspectives on the history of immigration in the United States.

One is the original model of the Statue of Liberty, which, years after being built became a symbol for immigrants. The second is a painting made by a Japanese American artist during World War II, and it tells a painful story about immigration and citizenship. The last is a farmworker's back-bending hoe that teaches us about the complexities of the Mexican American population.

The first U.S. Census, taken in 1790, records a population of almost four million, over half of whom came from England. About 20 percent of those early Americans were of African origin, equal to the combined totals of Scotch, Irish, Germans, and Dutch. Taking effect the same year, the Naturalization Act of 1790 prescribed that only free white persons of "good character" could become naturalized citizens. By statute, this excluded Native Americans, slaves, indentured servants, and many others.

English was America's predominant language, and Protestantism its dominant form of spiritual expression. Most population growth in the United States from the 1700s to the mid 1800s was due to natural increase, rather than immigration. Several developments in the 1840s and the early 1850s started to change both the character and conceptions of America.

One catalyst was the Irish Potato Famine, which began with crop failure in 1845, caused by a common fungus. It went on to claim at least 750,000 lives over the next decade, while catapulting two million migrants to Great Britain, Canada, and the United States.

Out west, the Mexican-American War ended with the 1848 Treaty of Guadalupe Hidalgo and resulted in our southern neighbor relinquishing its claims to Texas and ceding much of the present-day Southwest. This opened vast new territories to resident Americans and immigrants alike. The California gold rush drew tens of thousands more; gold-seeking 49ers, as they were called, came as far away as from China and Australia.

In Europe, the Industrial Revolution from about 1760 to 1850 produced still more social foment, subjecting workers to harsh conditions while powering the rise of a nascent middle class. Old aristocracies crumbled as popular movements sought social reform and even toppled governments. Out of this pressure cooker, many Europeans saw America as a potential haven of peace and prosperity, offering cheap land, plenty of jobs, and a chance to start life afresh.

These waves of immigration, modest as they were, nonetheless provoked some strong reactions. California discriminated against its Chinese immigrants through taxes, denying them the prosperity of the Gold Rush. The Know-Nothing Party arose on a platform of limiting immigrants, particularly of Irish and German Catholics, whom they saw as undermining the Protestant-oriented civic values underlying American society of the time.

After the Civil War, the pace of immigration quickened with America's rapid industrialization and the 14th Amendment to the Constitution. Ratified by Congress in July 1868, this amendment granted citizenship to "all persons born or naturalized in the United States." This included former slaves. It also provided a path to citizenship for the families of naturalized immigrants.

The Statue of Liberty is a symbol of freedom, recognized around the world, and it heralded this wave of immigration that gave America a much more diverse face, though it didn't start out that way, or with that purpose in mind. The Liberty statue's story begins in Egypt in the mid 1850s. Visiting the Pyramids and the Great Sphinx of Giza, young French sculptor Frédéric Bartholdi was transfixed by the power and romance he found in the large-scale public monuments. A decade later, back home in France, he attended a dinner party hosted by Édouard Laboulaye. Laboulaye was a lawyer, a professor, and chairman of the French antislavery society. The Civil War had just ended, and Laboulaye was rejoicing at the defeat of slavery; he rhapsodized about the historic connections between France and the United States. The names of Benjamin Franklin, Thomas Jefferson, and the Marquis de Lafayette rolled off his tongue as he proposed a grand monument to liberty that should be built in time for the American Centennial in 1876, several years hence.

The idea of a monument struck a chord with Bartholdi. Returning to Egypt in 1869, he proposed building a massive statue at the entrance to the newly constructed Suez Canal. His design was of a robed woman with a headdress holding a torch. She would double as a lighthouse. He called his vision Egypt Bringing Light to Asia. Well, the Egyptians were uninterested in Bartholdi's proposal and unwilling to pay for it. So the artist changed course. He set sail for America in 1871, and entering New York Harbor, Bartholdi was struck by Manhattan's jewel-like beauty and its symbolic power as the gateway to America. Bedloe's Island, a tiny islet owned by the federal government, seemed a perfect place for a monument in that harbor.

The Frenchman compared his proposal to the Colossus of Rhodes, a bronze statue erected on a Greek island more than 2,000 years ago and described as one of the Seven Wonders of the World. While the brief-lived Colossus was emblematic of power, Bartholdi's lady would signify liberty. She would be modeled after the Roman goddess Libertas and would reflect America's faith in its citizenry. With the help of his old friend Laboulaye, the sculptor formed the Franco-American Union in 1875 to raise money. He hoped the French would generate funds to build and ship the statue through private donations; and that individual Americans could raise the money to construct the statue's rather large pedestal. Through Levi Morton, the American minister to France at the time, Laboulaye urged President Ulysses Grant to support the endeavor. To succeed, it needed the American government to donate it the underlying land.

The design that Bartholdi came up with featured a robed lady in spiked crown, clutching a tablet inscribed "July 4, 1776" and standing atop broken chains and shackles. In her right hand, she is lifting a torch. Bartholdi needed a first-class engineer for the project, as the massive statue would be buffeted by rain, snow and wind. He enlisted Eugène le-Duc, who suggested the repoussé method of metalwork; 300 thin sheets of copper would be hammered into the form of the statue's skin. They would then be connected by iron-bar armature to a structure. Bartholdi built progressively larger-scale models—4-, 9-, and 36-foot versions of the Statue of Liberty. From these, he could develop plaster casts and wooden forms for shaping the copper skin. In 1876, he was able to send Liberty's right arm and torch to Philadelphia to be shown at the Centennial Exposition, after which, it was displayed at New York's Madison Square Garden.

American fund-raising got off to a slow start, however; and many wondered whether the French would come through on their part. Though contributions did not pour in as expected, President Grant signed a bill authorizing the construction of a statue on Bedloe Island before he left office in 1877. And in 1878, Bartholdi displayed the completed head and shoulders of the statue at the Paris Exposition.

French architect and structural engineer Alexandre Eiffel took over the statue's internal design after the death le-Duc in 1879. This was slightly less than a decade before Eiffel would then begin construction of the lattice tower named for him in Paris. Now, Eiffel praised le-Duc's designs, but instead of relying on the outer shell for support, he envisioned a 120-ton inner skeletal structure that would be anchored by a 98-foot pylon composed of four huge iron posts to hold up the statue. It would be tied to another anchor sunk in 154-foot-high pedestal. This marvel of relatively lightweight trusses and flexible suspension would thus enable the statue to adjust to the weather conditions, and also, allow visitors to walk right up to the top via an internal staircase. These ideas, cutting-edge at the time, would again be put to use in the construction of the Eiffel Tower.

By 1882, the French committee had raised all the money needed to build the statue—250,000 dollars—and Bartholdi and Eiffel were on track to complete the work the following year. But American fund-raising efforts were lagging, and so Bartholdi had to slow down. Meanwhile, he shipped his four-foot model of Liberty from Paris to Washington, DC in order to persuade Congress to help fund the project. He didn't succeed, at least not right away. But this terracotta model, painted to appear bronze, with a touch of tin in the crown, was used by architect Richard Morris Hunt to design the pedestal. Hunt, the son of a congressman, was the first American to study architecture at the École des Beaux-Arts in Paris; and he had just helped design a new façade for the Louvre, and he'd worked on the construction of the U.S. Capitol dome.

Bartholdi's model was displayed in the Capitol Rotunda, where it attracted its fair share of attention, including notice by a Hungarian immigrant named Joseph Pulitzer, a newspaper publisher who that same year moved to Manhattan and acquired the mass-circulation New York World. Pulitzer's newspaper exhorted Americans to donate money for the cause and criticized the wealthy people for failing to contribute. The public rallied to his call. By 1885, Pulitzer had helped raise the last one-third of 300,000 dollars needed to complete the pedestal and its anchor through his fund-raising activities; these included sporting events, plays, and performances. Even Mark Twain donated goods for auction for the purpose.

The statue was shipped from Paris to New York and assembled to its full height of 151 feet. Given Thomas Edison's recent triumph of electrifying Pearl Street in Lower Manhattan, the decision was made to light the torch with electric bulbs. And on October 28, 1886, with President Grover Cleveland presiding, Bartholdi pulled a rope that released the French tricolor flag covering Lady Liberty's face. Following the statue's dedication,

Bartholdi's four-foot model was transferred from the Capitol Rotunda to the Smithsonian, where today it's on display in the American Art Museum.

In 1903, words from a poem, "The New Colossus," were added on the tablet at the base of the Statue of Liberty in New York Harbor. The poem was written by Emma Lazarus in 1883 and donated to the Bartholdi Pedestal Fund for the Statue of Liberty. Lazarus's poem had originally addressed anti-Semitism toward Jews who had fled pogroms in Russia to come to the United States in the early 1880s. But with the opening of nearby Ellis Island in 1892 as the processing station for millions of immigrants from all of Europe, the sight of the Statue of Liberty and the last verse of Lazarus's poem took on special meaning:

> Give me your tired, your poor
>
> Your huddled masses yearning to breathe free,
>
> The wretched refuse of your teeming shore.
>
> Send here, the homeless, tempest-tost to me,
>
> I lift my lamp beside the golden door!

The sight of the Statue of Liberty and the words of that poem would greet some 12 million newcomers to America until the Ellis Island closed for immigration in 1954.

The notion of America as a composite, or fusion, of Old World characteristics has been expressed in literary and historical accounts since at least the independence era. But the idea of the country as somehow a melting pot took popular expression in 1908 with a play, The Melting Pot, by Israel Zangwill. Zangwill was an Anglo-Jewish writer and political activist whose parents had emigrated from eastern Europe to England. In his play, as in actuality, the Statue of Liberty serves as a visual metaphor, unifying people from diverse backgrounds. However, in this play "God's Crucible" of America only melded European immigrants. The English playwright left out African Americans, Asians, Latin Americans, and Native Americans.

Even European immigrants faced increasing pushback in the decades to follow. Congress passed a literacy requirement in 1917 to restrict the numbers of low-skilled and unskilled Jews, Italians, Poles, Swedes, Greeks, and others flocking to America from their homelands. Concerns with maintaining a homogeneous national identity, tinged with racial theories of eugenics, led to the Emergency Quota Act of 1921 and the Immigration Act of 1924.

These laws limited immigration from southern and eastern Europe by setting quotas through what they called a national origins formula and denied the possibility of citizenship to Arabs, Indians, Chinese, Japanese, and others. A few backdoors, though, remained for restricted populations. The legislation that tightened the sluice gates of immigration excluded the Western Hemisphere. Therefore, immigrants could still enter the U.S. from Mexico and the Caribbean. And with America's annexation of Hawaii in 1898, many people of Asian descent had become residents of the United States and internal migrants to the West Coast.

By the early 1940s, Japanese Americans had established thriving communities in Hawaii and California. Most had roots in agriculture, having been recruited beginning in the 1860s to work in Hawaiian sugarcane fields and then later on in California's fruit and vegetable farms. Gradually, they took up trades and businesses, and built schools, churches, and cultural organizations. People of Japanese ancestry accounted for almost 40 percent of Hawaii's residents by 1940.

While earlier generations were prohibited from becoming citizens and owning property, many, nevertheless, purchased homes, and farms, and businesses through their American-born and assimilated children, called nisei, a Japanese language term meaning "the second generation."

The attack on Pearl Harbor was a catalyst for questioning the loyalty of all people of Japanese descent in the United States. On February 19, 1942, President Franklin Roosevelt signed Executive Order 9066, authorizing military authorities to uproot ethnic Japanese living on the West Coast and confine them in isolated, heavily guarded camps. The order included citizens and non-citizens alike, and was based on deep and widespread suspicions about their identity as Americans and their loyalty to the United States. Justice Department officials actually questioned the constitutionality of such an order, and it's worth noting that there was no such directive covering Americans of German or Italian decent, whose native countries were also at war with the United States at the time.

About 120,000 West Coast Japanese Americans, two-thirds of them American citizens, were rounded up by the U.S. government and designated as evacuees. They had to leave their homes; they had to leave their communities with only as many possessions as they could carry. Many had to sell their homes and businesses quickly and at a loss. They were sent first to temporary assembly centers in California, Arizona, Oregon, and Washington State, and then, some to jails and prisons, others to military installations, and many to relocation camps, which were constructed very quickly and poorly by the War Relocation Authority.

These camps were stark; they were isolated geographically and socially. Due to a wartime shortage of critical building materials, some evacuees were forced temporarily to live in barracks without lights, laundry facilities, or adequate toilets. Mess halls designated to accommodate several hundred people handled two and three times that number for short periods of time, according to the government's own records.

The internees lived behind barbed-wire fences, watched over by military police. One of their few opportunities for self-expression was through art. Painters, artists, and craftspeople employed naturally occurring materials and scraps, including shells, buttons, fragments of wood, and discarded shutters even, to express their feelings about their confinement.

Henry Sugimoto, a Japanese-born artist who settled with his parents in Hanford, California, after World War I, grew up in California's rich, agricultural San Joaquin Valley and graduated with honors from the college-level California School of Arts and Crafts. Nevertheless, he was interned halfway across the country in 1942 under government order, first in Jerome, Arkansas, and later at the Rohwer camp, more than 20 years after arriving in America as a boy.

While in confinement, Sugimoto completed about 100 paintings. This one, called Thinking of Loved One depicts a Japanese-American mother and her newborn child. It's a beautiful, moving work, and I want to point out a few of its significant features.

The woman has just received a letter from her husband, a soldier serving with the Army's 442nd Regimental Combat Team. This infantry regiment of Japanese Americans fought in Italy and France during World War II. The irony is clear. A baby born in America, the land of the free, is comforted by its mother within sight of a watchtower. The blue-star flag on the wall signifies a fighting family member. The framed photograph depicts her husband, in uniform, fighting for their country, the United States of America. Though Japanese Americans were initially classified as enemy aliens for the purposes of military service, that changed in late 1942. Hawaiian Nisei formed the 100th Infantry Battalion, later incorporated into the 442nd. Some 25,000 Nisei served in the war effort, enduring high casualty rates and rewarded with many decorations of honor.

Among them was the late U.S. Senator from Hawaii, Daniel Ken Inouye, who at age 17, enlisted after the Pearl Harbor attack and lost his right arm in an Army assault on an enemy machine-gun nest in Italy. Inouye served with E company in the 442nd Regimental Combat Team. He was awarded the Medal of Honor and later became Hawaii's first congressman.

The system of interment ended in December 1944 with the Supreme Court ruling that claims of military necessity could not justify holding American citizens against their will. The camps were closed. Each internee received a 25 dollars payment and transportation home. In 1988, President Ronald Reagan issued a formal apology on behalf of the American people and granted each former internee a largely symbolic payment of 20,000 dollars under belated civil-liberties legislation passed by Congress and signed by the president.

A similar type of struggle for recognition and respect occupied Cesar Chavez, a Mexican-American founder and leader of the United Farm Workers union. During World War II, the United States government established the Bracero Program, extending an opportunity for Mexican guest workers to temporarily work on American farms, fields, and orchards to help alleviate agricultural labor shortages and feed America's families.

Braceros, a Spanish-language term that refers to manual laborers, were often willing to work for less money than most Americans and frequently accepted substandard working conditions. After the program ended in 1964, millions of Mexican workers continued to pass back and forth across the border illegally, responding to seasonal labor demands. This sparked a conflict with naturalized Mexicans and their American-born offspring, many of whom depended upon jobs in Texas' cotton fields and California's orchards. Aggressive border-enforcement campaigns such as "Operation Wetback" in 1954 heightened tensions.

Cesar Chavez was a labor organizer and conciliator whose methods of non-violent protest were remarkably effective, given the lack of leverage farm workers traditionally had possessed. Born near Yuma, Arizona, in March 1927, Chavez and his parents worked as migrant laborers, picking peas and lettuce in the winter; cherries and beans in the spring; corn and grapes in the summer, and cotton in the fall. After attending dozens of schools as a boy, Chavez dropped out to work in the fields and then joined the U.S. Navy in 1946, after World War II had ended.

Migrant farmworkers made the equivalent of about 90 cents an hour in the early 1960s, at a time when the federal minimum was 1.25 dollars. They paid daily rent for housing, frequently let to them by their employers, but often lacking power or plumbing. Farmworkers also had few benefits and virtually no security. State regulations governing workplace safety were often ignored.

For all that, these farmworkers did backbreaking work; they used implements like this short-handled hoe. Little more than a foot long, it meant workers had to virtually kneel down and crab walk in the hot sun as they did their work all day, dawn to dusk. Chavez' big effort was aimed at unionizing workers so they could demand and receive the minimum wage, and basic benefits, and decent treatment. He modeled his initiatives, including marches and boycotts of table grapes and lettuce, on the burgeoning Civil Rights Movement.

Chavez identified closely with the Reverend Martin Luther King Jr. Following Mahatma Gandhi's example, he also fasted in pursuit of justice. In 1972, during a 24-day fast in Arizona, Chavez adopted the Spanish-language slogan "Sí, se puede"—Yes, it can be done, or yes we can—a rallying cry for farmworkers, later adapted by the Latino civil rights and immigration advocates.

After years of struggle, Chavez gained support from consumers and other labor unions to form the United Farm Workers of America, and with it, the right to organize agricultural workers. At the Smithsonian, we have his union jacket, donated after his death in 1993 by his widow and fellow activist, Dolores Huerta. It bears the union's logo, a stylized eagle with wings in the shape of an inverted Aztec pyramid, and the colors black for struggle, red for sacrifice, white for hope—all of them symbols that resonated with Mexican Americans.

In 1975, California banned the use of the hated short-handled hoe under an administrative order that found that they were unsafe and constituted an occupational hazard. At the Smithsonian, we're proud to have this one, once belonging to Cesar Chavez, and we're hopeful that such crippling implements of labor, so incompatible with freedom, are never used again.

Whether seeking freedom and opportunity, coming in chains, fleeing persecution, or sent in exile, America's immigrants have faced struggles and have overcome them. Though we haven't always been perfect, over the long term, America does get it right and provides a home for more immigrants from more nations than any country in human history. Whether they be Cubans in Miami, Czechs in Texas, Armenians in Los Angeles, Hmong in Minneapolis, or Senegalese in New York, or hundreds of other groups, these immigrants have brought with them their dreams, talents, and determination, adding amazing vitality to our national tapestry.

User Friendly—Democratizing Technology
Lecture 11

The success of a newly developed product in a relatively free market economy depends on its functionality and good design. As you will learn in this lecture, the Singer sewing machine, the Brownie camera, and the Apple Mac are all examples. They had a transformative effect because they were easy to use and affordable. This meant that more Americans could make them part of their lives. The American economy has succeeded mainly because technological benefits have become widely available to huge portions of the population, and that has resulted in an increasingly higher standard of living and the continuity of our deeply rooted sense of democracy.

The Singer Sewing Machine

- Since prehistoric times, sewing was a time-consuming, manual task. But while seamstresses and tailors were still working by hand, thread and yarn making were industrialized with the development of the fly-shuttle loom and spinning jenny. These machines lead to the growth of the textile industry. In addition, Eli Whitney's cotton gin—and its imitators—led to a boom in cotton production. More raw materials led to more factories.

- In England, the number of steam-powered mechanical looms increased from about 5,000 in 1818 to more than 250,000 by 1850. In America, the tiny Massachusetts farm village of Lowell became a booming industrial metropolis between 1820 and 1850. The population jumped from about 250 to 33,000, because it was the perfect place for clever investors to build their water-powered textile mills.

- Thanks to these new factories, a huge amount of cloth was being produced for worldwide consumption at ever-lower prices, generating new opportunities to assemble it into finished goods. Yet high-end customers still went to tailors for custom-made items.

Early producers of ready-made items, such as men's shirts, typically farmed out hand sewing to women, who would assemble finished goods at home and get paid by the piece.

Howe Sewing Machine

- The race to mechanize sewing began in the 18th and accelerated through the mid-19th century, spurred by the increased production of fabric, the burgeoning populations in cities, and a growing demand for ready-made clothing. Cotton industry simply could not keep up.

- Starting in the 1840s, scores of patents were issued in the United States for prototype machines, all intended for factory use, not home production. The Smithsonian's collections have more than a dozen of these patent models.

- In 1846, the inventor Elias Howe patented the first two-thread machine that, like machines today, used a threaded-eye pointed needle to push one looped thread through a tiny hole in the fabric, where it caught another thread on the underside of the machine, producing a lockstitch.

- Howe's innovation was soon eclipsed by Isaac Singer's. Singer joined forces with Boston engineer Orson Phelps, who was developing a sewing machine based on Howe's. Singer improved on Phelps's design with a forward-moving shuttle that tightened stitches, the use of a friction pad to control the tension of the thread from the spool, and an adjustable arm to permit the spooled thread to be changed as needed. This allowed for more reliable and continuous stitching.

- By 1856, Singer and Co. was making more than 2,500 units per year, expanding to 13,000 in 1860. While the machine could be powered by a hand wheel, Singer added a foot treadle to free both hands to guide cloth while stitching. Singer also developed a cheaper home version.

- Mass production, not surprisingly, encouraged a division of labor between workers and managers in the garment industry and led to further labor efficiencies in packing and shipping of material and finished goods. Levels of production skyrocketed, and costs plummeted. And markets were always expanding.

- After the Civil War, immigration and domestic migration increased, cities grew even more rapidly, and the national need for manufactured clothing expanded across the continent. By the turn of the 20th century, virtually all Americans were buying ready-made clothing in shops or catalogs like those produced by Sears, Roebuck and Company.

- New York City was a center of clothing manufacture. Baltimore was big for men's suits, and Los Angeles was emerging as a center for sportswear. Apparel factories grew in size and number, as did their workforce. Manufacturers could pay low wages and impose tough conditions on workers.

- The garment industry became a magnet for new immigrant labor and for women and children. The growing industry led to calls for increased rights for workers. Reformers worried about bad factory conditions—poor light, bad air, overcrowding, and dangerous tasks.

- In 1900, the International Ladies' Garment Workers' Union was formed in New York City to protect the rights and improve the conditions of garment workers—largely women working at sewing machines in hot, dusty, fetid tenement shops.

- Through the 20th century, sweatshops continued to operate in New York's Chinatown and in other U.S. cities, although American manufacturers increasingly moved their operations to nations where labor costs were cheaper and standards were less exacting. Today, millions of workers use a variety of sewing machines in China, Vietnam, India, Bangladesh, the Philippines, Mexico, Central America, and parts of Africa to fulfill the needs of a global market.

- Meanwhile, in America, sewing machines became a product increasingly marketed for noncommercial use, mainly by women to advance their creative talents and homemaking skills through the textile arts. That trend continues today.

- Many sewing machines are now sold to immigrant women from developing countries who choose to maintain their tradition of home sewing or who have religious reasons for wanting noncommercial clothing. Sewing machines are also popular among the young, hip followers of the "maker movement," for whom handmade or hand-modified clothing is a fashion statement.

The Brownie Camera

- In its early days, taking photographs involved transporting heavy, cumbersome equipment; applying emulsions to temperamental glass plates in the dark; loading them one by one into a camera; and processing exposures with toxic chemicals. The highly technical process required a good deal of expertise and a great deal of time, making it either a professional pursuit or a very expensive hobby.

- All that changed because of a man from Rochester, New York, named George Eastman, who developed a technique that enabled the commercial production of prepared "dry coated" photographic plates. This eliminated the messy chemical step of preparing negatives. Eastman essentially separated the act of picture taking from picture making and went into business supplying these plates to a growing number of photographers.

- In 1885, Eastman introduced the first lightweight roll film pre-coated with emulsions, simplifying the photographic process even further. He made up the brand name Kodak a few years later and advertised his product vigorously. People could now take their own snapshots, and Kodak would develop the pictures.

Kodak Brownie Camera

- Eastman and his research chemist then perfected transparent roll film, which allowed a long strip of sequential negatives to be spooled onto a portable reel. This facilitated Thomas Edison's development of the motion picture camera in 1891.

- That same year, Kodak introduced its first daylight-loading camera, which allowed photographers to reload a camera without retreating to a darkroom. People could now snap even more images, which in turn increased sales of Kodak film.

- In 1895, Kodak introduced its Pocket camera and, three years later, came out with the Folding Pocket Kodak camera, the ancestor of all modern roll-film cameras. In 1900, Kodak marketed the first Brownie camera. It sold for a dollar and used Kodak film that initially sold for 15 cents per roll.

- The early Brownie camera was basically a cardboard box, coated and stamped to resemble leather, with a simple meniscus lens that took pictures on roll film. After the film had been exposed, the owner had to remove the film cartridge from the camera, wrap it in provided protective paper, and deliver it to a Kodak film developer. This was much simpler than the previous processes of either sending in the whole camera or developing the negatives on one's own.

- The camera was an immediate hit, selling more than 100,000 units in the first year. For the first time, the hobby of photography was within the financial reach of virtually everyone; vast numbers of ordinary people could now document their life experiences and share them with family, friends, and anyone. One of those ordinary people was Bernice Palmer, whose very special camera is in the collections of the Smithsonian.

- In April 1912, just months after receiving a Brownie camera, the teenage Bernice and her mother boarded the Cunard liner R.M.S. *Carpathia* in New York for a Mediterranean cruise. *Carpathia* received a distress call just after midnight on April 15 from the White Star ocean liner R.M.S. *Titanic*. The *Carpathia* sped to the scene of the sinking ship. Of the Titanic's original 2,200-plus passengers, its crew managed to rescue more than 700 survivors from the icy ocean. Equipped with her new camera, Bernice took the key pictures of the tragedy.

- Somehow, the agent for Underwood & Underwood, the major photographic news service of the times, heard that there was a camera aboard, wielded by a teenage girl. Bernice sold publication rights to her film for 10 dollars, which must have seemed like a lot, given that a roll of film cost just 25 cents at the time.

- No one knew whether her snapshots would actually turn out. But Bernice's photographs were well composed and properly exposed. Her pictures appeared in newspapers around the world and provided the best documentation of a tragedy that immediately assumed mythic proportions. Underwood returned the developed pictures to her, and later in life, Bernice donated the photographs and her Brownie camera to the Smithsonian.

The Apple Mac

- Sometime in the not-too-distant future, visitors to the Smithsonian will see the Apple Macintosh personal computer in a museum case. It will look awfully old, and they'll wonder what all the fuss was about. When it was first released in January 1984, the Macintosh was out to make history. It was intended by Apple's cofounder Steve Jobs to be revolutionary.

- The personal computer had been around for about a decade. Most historians consider the Altair 8800 to be the first of the species. This computer, first sold in 1975, had no screen and no keyboard. It was operated by a series of lights and switches, and owners had to build it themselves from a kit.

- The Altair wasn't very useful, except in one important respect: It inspired a group of Silicon Valley hobbyists known as the Homebrew Computer Club to start designing their own machines. Among that club's members were Steve Wozniak and Steve Jobs.

- These two friends formed Apple Computer in a Silicon Valley garage in 1976. Wozniak had the stronger technical knowledge, and Jobs had a stronger sense of design, entrepreneurial deal making, and marketing skill. They'd created the first Apple when Wozniak programmed a microprocessor on a motherboard and connected it to a keyboard and a screen to sell to a few hundred hobbyists.

- The two formed Apple, succeeded in raising money, and engineered technical improvements that led to the much more finished Apple II.

- While somewhat awkward, the Apple II was a completely assembled, marketable personal computer. It sold about 140,000 units in its first few years and made considerable profits. When Apple went public in December 1980, the company was capitalized at 1.8 billion dollars, making Jobs and Wozniak rich.

- Flush with cash, Apple developed two new computers using an innovative graphic user interface that grew out of internal efforts as well as a project at Xerox's Palo Alto Research Center. Jobs was convinced that the overlapping "windows" represented the future of personal computing.

- One of these computers, the Lisa, was envisioned as a premium personal computer. But it failed, being too expensive to succeed in the marketplace. The other, the Macintosh, was an easy-to-use computer for the average consumer. With a "reasonable" retail cost of about 2,500 dollars, the Macintosh was much more expensive than IBM PCs or clones, but it was much more likable.

- Jobs wanted to make a personal computer that was very different from IBM's. The IBM PC was considered unfriendly to users. The IBM PC and the clones modeled on it were largely intended for office and business use. The Macintosh was developed to be friendly, approachable, and aesthetically pleasing. It quickly acquired its nickname, the "Mac," and proved to be a critical and commercial success.

- Technically, in terms of processing speed and memory, it was not the most powerful personal computer of the time, but aficionados, designers, artists, teachers, and students loved it. Instead of the cumbersome, difficult-to-remember MS-DOS interface, which required the user to type in cryptic commands, working on the Mac was easy and highly intuitive.

- The Mac developed a cadre of loyal followers. It sold about 70,000 units in the first few months, which was good but minor compared to the sales of PCs. A lack of third-party applications initially limited what people could do with their Macs. In the next few years, versions featuring expanded memory and additional applications for design, graphics, desktop publishing, spreadsheets, and children's educational use made it very popular.

- Jobs envisioned the Mac to be more like an everyday household or personal appliance than a piece of machinery. It also had to look cool to reflect a certain lifestyle connecting the technical engineering geeks of Silicon Valley to the edgy counterculture of the Bay Area.

- While Jobs's design of the Mac did control user choice—with no plug-ins or modifications and complete hardware/software integration—it did so in a seemingly benevolent way, and the small, simple profile of the Mac, with its rainbow apple logo, belied the thought of any hidden, ulterior technology that would usurp the user's will. Jobs brilliantly positioned the Mac among designers, artists, and counterculture types as a tool for democratizing creativity, not limiting it.

- The innovations developed by Jobs and Apple for the Mac set the path for their future success. They melded advanced technology and elegantly simple design with an eye toward consumer ease of use and developed a marketing strategy that made the product cool. With this approach, Jobs made Apple one of the largest and most profitable companies in history and the leader in the digital revolution that transformed how billions of people communicate worldwide.

- The Mac also laid the foundation for other enormously popular products, such as the iPod and iTunes, the iPhone, and the iPad, all of which have found their places in the hands of American and worldwide users—and in the collections of the Smithsonian.

Featured Objects

Singer Sewing Machine

Kodak Brownie Camera

Apple Macintosh

Suggested Reading

Anderson, *Makers*.

Gustavson, *Camera*.

Norman, *The Design of Everyday Things*.

Pursell, *The Machine in America*.

User Friendly—Democratizing Technology
Lecture 11—Transcript

The American economy has long been tied to its system of political democracy. The pursuit of happiness early on became associated with utilitarian ideas of the greatest good for the greatest number. The means of achieving it was to encourage individual and private initiative in free-market commerce.

Indeed, since the advent of the industrial revolution in the 1800s, democratic governance has fostered broadening economic opportunity and increasing productivity. The economy has historically thrived with the growth of farms, factories, and businesses, high employment, and the production and purchase of consumer goods. For example, we saw in an earlier lecture how technologies, like the Conestoga wagon, enabled the United States to grow geographically, which in turn allowed us to grow economically. And then we saw how the steam locomotive helped bring new wealth from farms into cities to get goods to market in a faster and cheaper way.

The democratization of the economy has generally meant putting affordable, easy-to-use technology in the hands of vast numbers of Americans. Well-designed, affordable machines created business, as well as domestic and international markets for American goods. Perhaps the most dramatic early case of this was the sewing machine. Since prehistoric times, sewing was a time-consuming manual task. Early in the 19th century, professionals like Mary Pickersgill, who made the Star-Spangled Banner, did their work entirely by hand. But even while seamstresses and tailors were still working by hand, thread and yarn making were industrialized with the development of the fly-shuttle loom and spinning jenny. These machines led to the growth of the textile industry. Remember, too, that Eli Whitney's cotton gin—and its imitators—led to a boom in cotton production. More raw materials led to more factories.

In England, the number of steam-powered mechanical looms increased from about 5,000 in 1818 to more than 250,000 by 1850. In America, the tiny Massachusetts farm village of Lowell became a booming industrial metropolis between 1820 and 1850. The population jumped from about 250 to 33,000, because it was the perfect place for clever investors to build their water-powered textile mills.

Thanks to these new factories, a huge amount of cloth was being produced for worldwide consumption at ever-lower prices, generating new opportunities to assemble them into finished goods. Yet high-end customers still went to tailors for custom-made items. Early producers of ready-made items, such as men's shirts, typically farmed out hand sewing to women. These women would assemble finished goods at home and get paid by the piece.

The race to mechanizing sewing began in the 18th and accelerated through the mid-19th century, spurred by increased production of fabric, the burgeoning populations in cities, and a growing demand for ready-made clothing. Cottage industry simply could not keep up. Starting in the 1840s, scores of patents were issued in the U.S. for prototype machines, all intended for factory use, not home production. The Smithsonian's collections have more than a dozen of these patent models.

It's worth noting, though, that even the inventors had some doubts about the new technology. Walter Hunt, an American who invented a straight-stitching machine in 1834, said he feared that machines like his might cause the loss of jobs. And he wasn't the only one who thought that way. Just two decades earlier, in England, a group of people called the Luddites broke into textile factories and destroyed some of the early mechanical looms. The Luddites feared they would lose their jobs to these more efficient machines. New technologies are often greeted with fear and distrust, and we still use the word "Luddite" to describe a technophobe today.

In 1846, Elias Howe patented the first two-thread machine that, like machines today, used a threaded-eye pointed needle to push one looped thread through a tiny hole in the fabric, where it caught another thread on the underside of the machine, producing a lockstitch. Howe's innovation was soon eclipsed by Isaac Singer. Isaac Singer, the eighth child of poor German Jewish immigrants, joined forces with Boston engineer Orson Phelps, who was developing a sewing machine based on Howe's. Singer improved on Phelps's design with a forward-moving shuttle that tightened stitches, the use of a friction pad to control the tension of the thread from the spool, and an adjustable arm to permit the spooled thread to be changed as needed. This allowed for more reliable and continuous stitching.

Phelps produced the machines in his shop for heavy-duty commercial use, making the head, base cams, and gear wheels out of cast iron. The machine was transported in its packing crate, which then doubled as a work stand. Singer proved a very good salesman. He demonstrated that just about anyone, even the tiniest woman, could easily operate this machine and could quickly learn to sew 900 stitches per minute, more than 20 times as many as a skilled hand seamstress.

By 1856, Singer and Co. was making more than 2,500 units per year, expanding to 13,000 in 1860. While the machine could be powered by a hand wheel, Singer added a foot treadle to free both hands to guide the cloth while stitching. Singer also developed a cheaper home version. Mass production, not surprisingly, encouraged a division of labor between workers and management in the garment industry and led to further labor efficiencies in packing and shipping of material and finished goods. Levels of production skyrocketed, and costs for clothing plummeted. And markets were always expanding. Remember that Mary Pickersgill's mother had made uniforms by hand for the Continental Army during the American Revolution? Well, during the Civil War, both the Union and the Confederacy needed hundreds of thousands of uniforms and tents, which could now be made quickly and inexpensively mass-manufactured. The war provided a boon to Singer's business, and those of many others.

After the Civil War, immigration and domestic migration increased, cities grew even more rapidly, and the national need for manufactured clothing expanded across the continent. By the turn of the 20th century, virtually all Americans were buying ready-made clothing in shops or catalogs like those produced by Sears, Roebuck and Company. New York City was a center of clothing manufacture. Baltimore was big for men's suits, and Los Angeles was emerging as a center for sportswear. Apparel factories grew in size and number, as did their workforce.

Manufacturers could pay low wages and impose tough conditions on workers. In the 1880s, weekly wages for sewing machine operators in

Baltimore, Boston, and New York ranged from about 3.50 dollars to 7.00 dollars, which put them among the working poor. Working conditions were generally unsafe and hours long. "If you don't come in on Sunday, don't come in Monday" was famously posted on many sweatshop walls.

The garment industry became a magnet for new immigrant labor and for women and children. The growing industry led to calls for increased rights for workers. Reformers worried about bad factory conditions—poor light, bad air, overcrowding, and dangerous tasks. In 1900, the International Ladies' Garment Workers' Union was formed in New York City to protect the rights and improve the conditions of garment workers, largely women working at sewing machines in hot, dusty, fetid tenement shops.

Reformers, like the journalist Jacob Riis, published stories and photographs exposing the horrific living conditions of the working poor, and this prompted widespread public outcry for some kind of government regulation of the industry. Tragedies, like the 1909 Triangle factory fire, in which 148 workers died, proved that the unions' and reformers' fears were all too well founded. Still, the minimum wage and most benefits took decades to achieve.

Through the 20th century, sweatshops continued to operate in New York's Chinatown and in other U.S. cities, although American manufacturers increasingly moved their operations to nations where labor costs were cheaper and standards less exacting. Today, millions of workers use a variety of sewing machines in China, Vietnam, India, Bangladesh, the Philippines, Mexico, Central America, and parts of Africa to fulfill the needs of a global market. Some economists see this as a natural part of a developing economy, while others tend to see it as a form of abuse related to other ills, such as human trafficking and indentured and child labor.

Meanwhile, in America, sewing machines have become a product increasingly marketed for noncommercial use, mainly by women to advance their creative talents and homemaking skills through the textile arts. That trend continues today. Many sewing machines are now sold to immigrant women from developing countries who choose to maintain their tradition of home sewing or who have religious reasons for not wearing commercial clothing. Sewing machines are also popular among the young, hip followers of the maker movement, form whom homemade or handmade modified clothing is a fashion statement.

In fact, when it comes to hobbies, the do-it-yourself spirit of the early 21st century is almost universal, whether it's fashion, or cooking, or home improvement, or music, or, perhaps, above all, photography. In its early days, taking photographs involved transporting heavy, cumbersome equipment, applying emulsions to temperamental glass plates in the dark, loading them one by one into a camera, and processing exposures with toxic chemicals. The highly technical process required a good deal of expertise and a great deal of time, making it either a professional pursuit or a very expensive hobby. Now, it's as simple as a good cell phone and a steady hand.

All that changed because of a man from Rochester, New York, named George Eastman. Eastman, who developed an interest in photography as a young man, developed a technique that enabled the commercial production of prepared dry-coated photographic plates. This eliminated the messy chemical step of preparing negatives. Eastman essentially separated the act of picture taking from picture making, and he went into business supplying these plates to a growing number of photographers.

In 1885, Eastman introduced the first lightweight roll film pre-coated with emulsions, basically simplifying the photographic process even more. He made up the brand name Kodak a few years later; he thought it sounded good, and he advertised his product vigorously. He wrote his own copy. He wrote, "You press the button, we do the rest." People could now take their own snapshots, and Kodak would develop the pictures.

Eastman and his research chemist then perfected transparent roll film, which allowed a long strip of sequential negatives to be spooled onto a portable reel. This facilitated Thomas Edison's development of the motion picture camera in 1891. That same year Kodak introduced its first daylight-loading camera. Now a photographer could reload a camera without retreating to a darkroom. People could now snap even more images, which in turn increased sales of Kodak film. In 1895, Kodak introduced its pocket camera, then three years later came out with the Folding Pocket Kodak camera, the ancestor of all modern roll-film cameras. It produced a 2¼-by-3¼-inch negative, which remained the standard size for decades.

In 1900, Kodak marketed the first Brownie camera. It sold for one 1.00 and used Kodak film that initially sold for 15 cents a roll. The Brownie was named after the fun-loving fairy goblins created by Canadian writer and illustrator Palmer Cox. The name resonated with the fun and magic of picture taking. The early Brownie camera was basically a cardboard box, coated and stamped to resemble leather, with a simple meniscus lens that took pictures on roll film. After the film had been exposed, the owner had to remove the film cartridge from the camera, wrap it in provided protective paper, and deliver it to a Kodak film developer. This was much simpler than the previous processes of either sending in the whole camera or developing the negatives on one's own.

The camera was an immediate hit, selling more than 100,000 units in the first year. For the first time, the hobby of photography was in the financial reach of virtually everyone. Vast numbers of ordinary people could now document their life experience in pictures and share them with family, friends, and literally, anyone. One of those ordinary people was Bernice Palmer, whose very, very special camera is in the collections of the Smithsonian. In 1911, the teenage Bernice had been attracted to the camera by an advertising promotion—the Kodak girl—a confident young woman in a blue-and-white-striped dress, ready to go anywhere with her camera. Bernice received a Brownie either that Christmas or for her 17th birthday a month later. It came with an easy-to-read booklet with illustrations and instructions on how to take a good picture.

In April 1912, just months after receiving the camera, Bernice and her mother boarded the Cunard liner R.M.S. Carpathia in New York for a Mediterranean cruise. Carpathia received a distress call just after midnight, April 15th, from the White Star ocean liner R.M.S. Titanic. The Carpathia sped to the scene of the sinking ship. Of the Titanic's original 2,200-plus passengers, its crew managed to rescue more than 700 survivors from the icy ocean. Equipped with her new camera, it was Bernice who took the key pictures of the tragedy. Now I have here some reproductions of these pictures, made especially for this lecture from direct scans of the original.

This is Bernice and her Brownie, taken before the trip. You can see a couple of things here. First, the camera isn't small by our standards, but it still fits comfortably into a young woman's hands. It's certainly an improvement over the cumbersome, older cameras. Second, Bernice is ready to take a photo here. To operate a Brownie, you held the camera at waist height and looked down into the viewfinder. Finally, we know camera in December or January, and obviously, it's still wintertime here, but Bernice is already comfortable and confident with her camera. That's a testament to Eastman's design, and it's very fortunate for us, because here's what she captured for us.

This photo was taken on the deck of the Carpathia, just a few months later. Notice the intimacy and the informality of the shot. That's something we take for granted now, but it was rare in early 20th-century photography, especially portrait-taking, which was usually a very formal occasion. Think of all those stiff, unsmiling images of your grandparents and great-grandparents in family albums. There's something very modern about this image, very journalistic, and we are struck by the contrast between the survivors' finery, and their palpable distress. Finally, we have what in some ways is the most striking image of all. Certainly, it is the most unsettling. Here, Bernice has captured what historians believe is the iceberg that sank the Titanic. Pictures like these, taken by this amateur photographer with a consumer-grade camera, constitute an important visual record of an iconic moment in world history, and we're very fortunate to have Bernice's camera and these photographs at the Smithsonian.

Lacking the resources to feed and care for both its passengers and the Titanic's survivors, the Carpathia headed back to New York. When it arrived three days later, the ship was met by tens of thousands hankering for news of the survivors and reports of the disaster. Somehow, the agent for to Underwood & Underwood, the major photographic news service of the times, heard that there was a camera aboard, wielded by a teenage girl. Bernice sold publication rights to her film for 10 dollars, which must have seemed like a lot, given that a roll of film cost just twenty-five cents at the time.

No one really knew whether her snapshots would actually turn out. But Bernice's photographs were well composed and properly exposed, no small feat given the extraordinary shock and chaos surrounding the rescue. Her pictures appeared in newspapers around the world and provided the best documentation of a tragedy that immediately assumed mythic proportions. Underwood returned the developed pictures to her, as they'd promised, and later in life Bernice donated the photographs and her Brownie camera to the Smithsonian.

The portability and increasing popularity of the Brownie meant that, more and more often, Brownies and their owners were there to witness major world events. Even as professional photojournalism boomed, so did citizen journalism via the Brownie. The Brownie ushered in a new age of citizen eyewitnesses to history. Well designed, easy-to-use cameras have continued to evolve and proliferate, and now digital cameras on cell phones, coupled with the Internet, do more than George Eastman could have anticipated in democratizing photography.

Thinking about the juxtaposition of the historical Kodak camera with the digital photography of today puts the process of technological design in perspective. Sometime in the not-too-distant future, visitors to the Smithsonian will see this Macintosh personal computer in a museum case. It will look awfully old, and they'll wonder what all the fuss was about. When it was first released in January 1984, the Macintosh was out to make history. It was intended by Apple's cofounder Steve Jobs to be revolutionary.

The personal computer had been around for about a decade. Most historians consider the Altair 8800 to be the first of the species. This computer, first sold in 1975, had no screen, no keyboard. It was operated by a series of lights and switches, and owners had to build it themselves from a kit. The Altair wasn't very useful, except in one important respect—It inspired a group of Silicon Valley hobbyists known as the Homebrew Computer Club to start designing their own machines. Among that club's members were Steve Wozniak and Steve Jobs.

These two friends formed Apple Computer in a Silicon Valley garage in 1976. Wozniak had the stronger technical knowledge, Jobs a stronger sense of design, entrepreneurial deal making, and marketing skill. They'd created the first Apple when Wozniak programmed a microprocessor on a motherboard and connected it to a keyboard and a screen to sell to a few hundred to hobbyists. The two formed Apple and succeeded in raising money and engineered technical improvements that led to the much more finished Apple II.

While somewhat awkward, the Apple II was a completely assembled computer. It sold about 140,000 units in its first few years and made considerable profits. When Apple went public in December 1980, the company was capitalized at $1.8 billion, making Jobs and Wozniak rich. Flush with cash, Apple developed two new computers using an innovative graphic user interface that grew out of internal efforts as well as a project at Xerox's Palo Alto Research Center. Jobs was convinced that the overlapping "windows" represented the future of personal computing. One of these computers, the Lisa, was envisioned as a premium personal computer. But it failed, being too expensive to succeed in the marketplace. The other, the Macintosh, was an easy-to-use computer for the average consumer. With a somewhat reasonable retail cost of about 2,500 dollars, the Macintosh was much more expensive than IBM PCs or clones, but it was much more likable.

Jobs' wanted to make a personal computer that was very different from IBM's. The IBM PC was the product of a giant corporation that had made its fortune building large, commercial mainframe computers. It was considered unfriendly to users. The IBM PC and the clones modeled on it were largely intended for office and business use, and it showed. As one accomplished programmer said at the time, "The IBM is a machine you can respect. The Macintosh is a machine you can love."

The Macintosh was developed to be friendly, approachable, and aesthetically pleasing, one with a personality, and it quickly acquired its nickname, the "Mac." The Mac proved to be a critical and commercial success. Technically, in terms of processing speed and memory, it was not the most powerful personal computer of the time, but aficionados, designers, artists, teachers, and students loved it. Instead of the cumbersome, hard-to-remember MS-DOS interface, which required the user to type in cryptic commands, working on the Mac was easy and highly intuitive. It had icons to click on with a cute, recently developed device called a mouse. It had a finder to help you navigate, and folders where you could save your work. It had a trash can where you could drag and delete unwanted work. The system software and the programs were totally integrated, so everything just worked.

The Mac developed a cadre of loyal followers. It sold about 70,000 units in the first few months, which was good, but minor compared to the sales of PCs. A lack of third-party applications initially limited what people could do with their Macs. And in the next few years, versions featuring expanded memory and additional applications for design, graphics, desktop publishing, spreadsheets, and children's educational use made it very popular.

Jobs envisioned the Mac to be more like an everyday household or personal appliance than a piece of machinery. It also had to look cool to reflect a certain lifestyle connecting the technical engineering geeks of Silicon Valley with the edgy counterculture of the Bay Area. It had to be appealing, or, as he told engineers, "friendly." This literally meant anthropomorphizing the machine. The Lisa was short and squat and asymmetrical. The Mac was a little taller and symmetrical. Its forehead was beveled back to give a more open, cheerful appearance. It almost looked human. The screen became its eyes. The disk drive looked like a mouth, and the beveled base a chin. The specially designed roller-ball mouse allowed a full range of on-screen movement while promoting hand and arm interactivity with the machine. The Mac mirrored Jobs's own tastes and also relieved the machine of a specific personality. It was a friendly vessel. As it turned on, the Mac welcomed users with a simple and unassuming "Hello."

While Jobs's design of the Mac did control user choice with no plug-ins or modifications and complete hardware/software integration, it did so in a seemingly benevolent way, and the small, simple profile of the Mac, with its rainbow apple logo, belied the thought of any hidden, ulterior technology that would usurp the user's will. Jobs brilliantly positioned the Mac among designers, artists, and counterculture types as a tool for democratizing creativity, not limiting it.

The innovations developed by Jobs and Apple for the Mac set the path for their future success. They melded advanced technology and elegantly simple design with an eye toward consumer ease of use, and developed a marketing strategy that made the product cool. With this approach, Jobs made Apple one of the largest and most profitable companies in history and the leader in the digital revolution that transformed how billions of people now communicate worldwide. The Mac also laid the foundation for other enormously popular products, like the iPod, iTunes, the iPhone, and the iPad, all of which have found their places in the hands of American and worldwide users, and, into the collections of the Smithsonian.

And so we see, through these various innovations, a pattern in American history, economy and social life. The success of a newly developed product in a relatively free market economy depends on its functionality and good design. The Singer sewing machine, the Brownie camera, and the Apple Mac are all fine examples; they had a transformative effect because they were easy to use, and also affordable. This meant more and more Americans could make them part of their lives. By and large, the American economy has succeeded because technological benefits have become widely available to huge portions of the population, and that has resulted in an increasingly higher standard of living and the continuity of our deeply rooted sense of democracy.

Extinction and Conservation

Lecture 12

The subject of this lecture is conservation in American history, particularly the conservation of species. Specifically, this lecture will focus on several distinct and particular items in the Smithsonian's collection: a buffalo named Sandy; Tioga the eagle; Martha, a pigeon; and a pair of pandas named Hsing-Hsing and Ling-Ling. Each in its own right tells an interesting story of our relationship to the land and its bounty and how, over time, Americans have alternatively plundered and preserved species and environments as our nation developed.

Sandy the Buffalo

- In the 1880s, a Smithsonian taxidermist named William Temple Hornaday was a pioneer of realistic, lifelike, large dioramas; his work helped define modern museum taxidermy. He wanted to create at the Smithsonian's National Museum the world's first display of an entire family group of buffalo—so that people could see what this creature looked like before it became extinct.

- As part of his duties, he had conducted a census of living buffalo and found that while there might have been as many as 15 million buffalo living at the end of the Civil War, by the 1880s, they were on the very verge of extinction.

- The buffalo's ancestry goes back to the Asian steppe bison that migrated across the land bridge from Asia to North America probably hundreds of thousands of years ago. It evolved over time into the giant bison and was eventually hunted by early Native Americans. Scientists believe that the smaller American bison, or buffalo, evolved into its current form about 10,000 years ago.

- The buffalo lived in the vast American grassland prairies. Native Americans valued and revered the buffalo as a source of food, clothing, and shelter, as well as for social and ritual needs. Ancient rock drawings depict buffalo as a symbol of power, freedom, and plenty.

- By the time European explorers and settlers started to reach the plains, there were perhaps 50 million buffalo in North America, making them one of the most populous species of large mammal on the planet. While most American Indian buffalo hunts were relatively modest and controlled—as depicted in the contemporaneous paintings of John Mix Stanley and George Catlin in the Smithsonian collections—some tribes were, by the 1830s, engaged in mass exploitation. After the Civil War, buffalo killing went into high gear.

- The combination of guns, railroads, commercial activity, and war between European settlers and American Indians proved deadly to the species. There was a huge market for buffalo skins and hides in the Northeast and Europe. Buffalo leather was also well suited and highly in demand for the belts used with pulleys and steam engines in the factories of the time.

- Commercial hunters spread across the country and turned their techniques for slaughtering and processing buffalo into a highly organized business enterprise. Teams of professional hunters were accompanied by congeries of wranglers, gun loaders and cleaners, skinners, cooks, blacksmiths, guards, and teamsters with their horses and wagons.

- Given the scope of the carnage, some hunters, including Buffalo Bill Cody, spoke out in favor of protecting the bison, but President Ulysses S. Grant refused to sign legislation to that effect. The U.S. Army encouraged the excessive killing of buffalo as a way of eliminating food supplies for Indian communities. Realizing that there was a real prospect of true extinction, some ranchers in Montana, South Dakota, Oklahoma, and Texas started to preserve very small herds of surviving buffalo.

- In the spring of 1886, Hornaday and a Smithsonian team headed to Montana to collect specimens for the museum and observe their natural movement so that they could be taxidermied and displayed in natural poses. Hornaday was stunned to find no live buffalo on the plains, only thousands of skeletons bleaching in the sun.

- It took a second trip and three months of hunting that fall for Hornaday to find the specimens he needed. He brought back to Washington a calf he named Sandy, who was kept tied to a stake outside the National Museum and was a big hit with visitors. To Hornaday's devastation, Sandy died only a few weeks after his arrival in Washington from pasture bloat. Hornaday skinned and mounted the animal to add to the bison family group exhibit.

- Sandy inspired Hornaday to initiate the Smithsonian's Department of Living Animals, part of a plan to establish a breeding program to help save the buffalo. Housed in pens on the south lawn of the Smithsonian Castle, the popular living animal exhibition soon grew to 172 mammals and birds and drew many visitors.

- Hornaday advocated for a National Zoological Park, for the conservation and study of wild animals sacred to the national heritage. He wanted to preserve buffalo not only in museum exhibits, but also as a living herd in captivity to educate Americans. He was successful on both counts.

- In 1889, Congress passed legislation creating the National Zoo, and Hornaday was appointed its head. To spread his message, Hornaday published *The Extermination of the American Bison*, considered the first important book of the American conservation movement. He cofounded the National Bison Society with President Theodore Roosevelt, sent 15 of the zoo's buffalo west to seed a herd, and established National Bison Ranges in Kansas and Montana to ensure the survival of the American buffalo.

- Thanks to Hornaday's pioneering efforts, western herds were slowly built up. Today, there are perhaps 500,000 American buffalo, though only about 30,000 are in the wild in national parks.

Tioga the Eagle

- Another threatened species associated with Native American culture was the bald eagle, the only species of eagle that is unique to North America. It probably split off from the Eurasian white-tailed eagle during the Miocene age, 10 to 18 million years ago in the northern Pacific region. With a distinctive hooked yellow beak and strong talons, a wingspan of seven feet, and a normal flying speed of about 35 miles per hour, the bald eagle exudes power in the sky.

Bald Eagle

- The bald eagle is sacred to a number of American Indian tribes, considered to be a messenger between humans and divine spirits. Eagle feathers are often part of traditional regalia, like headdresses. Feathers and claws are used in traditional ceremonies.

- After the United States declared its independence, one of the Continental Congress's first acts was to commission a great seal. It took six years, three committees, and a good deal of debate. Finally, in 1782, with the American Revolutionary War coming to an end, it settled on a symbol of nationhood with the bald eagle at its center.

- Congress admired this distinctive American bird for its physical prowess and liked the parallels it suggested with the ancient Roman Republic, which also used the eagle in its symbolism. In the Great Seal of the United States, the eagle holds 13 arrows and a 13-leaf olive branch in its talons, representing the 13 original colonies.

- Since then, the bald eagle has been used on the presidential seal, as part of the logo for many federal departments and agencies, and as a design element on U.S. coins and stamps. It has become a patriotic symbol used in political campaigns and to recruit soldiers.

- Despite the visual ubiquity of its image, the bald eagle became endangered because of habitat destruction, illegal shooting, and the effects of contaminants, particularly the insecticide DDT, in its prey. Although legal protection began with the Lacey Act of 1900, followed by the Migratory Bird Treaty of 1918, and then, more specifically, by the Bald Eagle Protection Act of 1940, fewer than 1,000 bald eagles remained in the wild by 1963. Endangered species legislation in the 1960s and 1970s helped with restoration efforts.

- Hunting eagles and limiting the collection of feathers only for Native American religious practice has helped increase the eagle population to well over 10,000 and allowed them to be removed from the endangered species list. But ongoing threats remain, and these include loss of wetland habitats, illegal shooting, poisoning from lead, and the ingestion of pesticide and chemical residues.

- The Smithsonian's National Zoological Park has contributed to the conservation effort, providing a Bald Eagle Wildlife Refuge for about 500 pairs of eagles in the Chesapeake Bay region.

- Zoo scientists also study the behavior of its resident bald eagles, the oldest of which is named Tioga. This male eagle was found as a fledgling near his nest in Pennsylvania in 1998 with a badly healed fracture of his left shoulder that made him incapable of flight. Such studies contribute to our knowledge of the animal's health, diet, and interactions with a host of environmental factors—useful in the preservation of the species.

Martha the Pigeon

- It's hard to believe that the passenger pigeon was once the most common bird in the United States, numbering in the billions. Going back centuries, writers and observers noted how the flock of birds would fill the sky with a flying column stretching a mile wide or more and take hours to pass overhead.

- The spectacle of this migratory mass was one of the of the signature wonders of the New World, a metaphor for its seemingly limitless natural abundance. John James Audubon, who artfully studied and drew the birds, likened their presence to an eclipse shutting out the sun, accompanied by the thunderous noise and gale-force wind of their wings.

- Passenger pigeons spent summers in various parts of Canada and then migrated about 2,000 miles in a weeklong journey to the American South to spend the winter. As Americans cleared eastern forests for farming or timber in the 1800s, the pigeon's migratory route was forced westward, and soon the birds adapted to the deforested landscape by shifting their diet from foraged nuts and insects to grain from farmers' painstakingly cultivated fields. The birds devastated crops and endangered farmers' livelihoods.

- To protect their crops, farmers shot at passenger pigeon flocks. They promoted pigeon shooting as sport, and they sold pigeon meat to cities as a cheap food source for the poor. By 1857, people began to notice fewer passenger pigeons.

- A bill was proposed in the Ohio legislature to limit the number of passenger pigeons that could be killed, but opponents derided the idea that there was any potential threat to the species. Few people could imagine that the ravenous passenger pigeon that darkened the skies in massive numbers was truly endangered, and fewer still found the prospect of extinction unwelcome.

- Overhunting, habitat loss, and possibly infectious disease made the passenger pigeon increasingly rare by the late 19th century. The last confirmed sighting of a wild passenger pigeon was in 1900. From 1909 to 1912, the American Ornithologists' Union offered 1,500 dollars to anyone finding a nesting colony of passenger pigeons, but all efforts were futile. A few survived in captivity, but attempts to save the species by breeding them were unsuccessful.

- Martha, a passenger pigeon named after George Washington's wife, lived her whole 29-year life in the Cincinnati Zoo and was the last surviving member of the species. It is rare to know the precise date a species dies out, but in this case we do. It was September 1, 1914.

- Immediately following Martha's death, the Cincinnati Zoological Garden packed her in an enormous 300-pound block of ice and shipped her to the Smithsonian. Following her arrival in Washington, Martha's skin was mounted for display by a Smithsonian taxidermist and her internal organs were preserved as part of the fluid, or "wet," collections of the National Museum of Natural History.

- Martha's widely reported death had a sobering public impact. Americans had long held the idea that the continent's natural resources were boundless; now they realized that progress and civilization could have irreparable and undesirable consequences. The fate of the passenger pigeon helped spur the Migratory Bird Treaty and other legislation that established precedents for a host of other wildlife and habitat protection measures.

Hsing-Hsing and Ling-Ling the Pandas

- In February 1972, U.S. President Richard Nixon traveled to mainland China, ending 22 years of diplomatic isolation from the People's Republic of China—a Communist country led by Mao Zedong. By visiting China and starting to normalize the relationship, Nixon hoped to enhance the U.S. position in its Cold War struggle with the Soviet Union and stabilize possible conflicts with China in Asia.

- Nixon's eight-day visit was heavily televised. The reciprocal presentation of gifts between host and guest is quite important in Chinese culture, and in this case, the gifts needed to suitably mark the occasion that Nixon referred to as "the week that changed the world."

- The Chinese gift was two pandas that had been captured in the wild months before. The pandas were strongly desired by the Smithsonian's National Zoo; no American zoo had hosted a member of this distinctive and rare species for about two decades.

Giant Pandas, Hsing-Hsing and Ling-Ling

- In return, the National Zoo and State Department wanted to give them American bison, but the Beijing Zoo already had some. Musk oxen were settled on as a compromise. Because the National Zoo had no musk oxen, the Smithsonian purchased a pair named Milton and Matilda from the San Francisco Zoo.

- The pandas retained their Chinese names, Hsing-Hsing for the male and Ling-Ling for the female, when they arrived and took up residence at the National Zoo. They became instant celebrities.

- Pandas are challenged, not only given the reduction of their natural habitat, but also because of somewhat puzzling characteristics concerning their reproductive life. Hsing-Hsing and Ling-Ling eventually produced five cubs, but none survived more than a few days. Neither mating nor artificial insemination—nor even bringing in another, more robust suitor for Ling-Ling—succeeded in producing a viable offspring.

- Ling-Ling died from heart failure at the age of 23 in 1992. Hsing-Hsing lived several more years, to the advanced age of 28 and was euthanized in 1999.

- The Smithsonian successfully negotiated the 10-year loan of a new pair of pandas, Mei Xiang and Tian Tian, with funds from the loan fee designated for work on panda reproduction and survival at the panda research center in Chengdu, China.

- The National Zoo's premier wildlife veterinarian and reproductive scientist JoGayle Howard developed numerous advances and mentored other zoologists in the United States and in China, at Chengdu, in an effort to see the pandas thrive.

- Mei Xiang and Tian Tian did not mate successfully. Howard oversaw the artificial insemination of Mei Xiang, and in 2005, she gave birth to Tai Shan, causing "Pandamania" in Washington DC. Panda cams, webcams trained on the panda enclosures, proved very popular.

- As stipulated in the loan agreement, Tai Shan had to return to China in 2010 to enter a breeding program. Washingtonians greatly lamented his departure, but then in 2013, along with many Americans, they greeted Mei Xiang's birth of another panda cub, Bao Bao.

Featured Objects

American Buffalo

Martha the Last Passenger Pigeon

Bald Eagle

Giant Panda

Suggested Reading

Gorrow and Koppie, *Inside a Bald Eagle's Nest.*

Greenberg, *A Feathered River across the Sky.*

Rinella, *American Buffalo.*

Seidensticker and Lumpkin, *Giant Pandas.*

Extinction and Conservation
Lecture 12—Transcript

In this lecture, I want to discuss conservation in American history, particularly the conservation of species. So, I will talk about several distinct and particular items in the Smithsonian's collection. Let me introduce you to them: a buffalo named Sandy; Tioga the eagle; Martha, a pigeon; and a pair of pandas, Hsing Hsing and Ling Ling. Each in their own right tells an interesting story of our relationship to the land and its bounty, and how, over time, Americans have alternatively plundered and preserved species and environments as our nation developed. Much of what has happened historically is still important, and, still in process today, and by running the National Zoo of the Smithsonian and various wildlife conservation projects around the world, and having its scientists and historians study the impact of our species on others, we play an important role in our current sense of stewardship.

The story begins with an unlikely character, a Smithsonian taxidermist working in the 1880s by the name of William Temple Hornaday. Hornaday was a pioneer of realistic, lifelike, large dioramas. His work helped define modern museum taxidermy, and he wanted to create at the Smithsonian's National Museum the world's first display of an entire family group of buffalo so that people could see what this creature looked like before it became extinct. As part of his duties, he had conducted a census of living buffalo and found that while there might have been as many as 15 million buffalo living at the end of the Civil War, by the 1880s, they were on the very verge of extinction. This was an enormous decline in the species.

The buffalo's ancestry goes back to the Asian steppe bison that migrated across the land bridge from Asia to North America, probably hundreds of thousands of years ago. It evolved over time to the giant bison and was eventually hunted by Native Americans, who increasingly became proficient in the use of stone-pointed weapons. Scientists believe that the smaller American bison, or what we call the buffalo, evolved into its current form about 10,000 years ago.

The buffalo lived in the vast American grassland prairies. An herbivore, in the wild, the buffalo slowly roamed to different foraging sites, grazing on grass during the day. They're large animals; an adult male may weigh up to 2,000 pounds, females, a bit less. But the buffalo can be surprisingly quick and agile, able to gallop at more than 30 miles an hour, and jump up to 6 feet in the air.

Buffalos are characterized by their horns and shaggy, wooly coat, which protects them from the winter's cold, and that coat is shed in the summer. Buffalos mate in late summer; now, males compete for dominance by bellowing and head-butting other bulls. Bison cows birth and nurse single calves. They mature in about three years and have a lifespan of about 15 years in the wild. Buffalo congregate in small herds of about 20 animals, with males and females in separate herds, except, of course, when mating. Sometimes herds clustered in groups, numbering in the thousands, and it was these groups, roaming to feeding grounds and salt licks, that tamped down pathways and cleared "traces" across the continent that were later used by human beings—American Indians, settlers, and railroad builders. And they turned into trails, routes, and rail beds that eventually traversed the United States.

Natural threats against buffalo are very limited; its most dangerous predator is man. Native Americans valued and revered the buffalo as a source of food, clothing, and shelter, as well as for social and ritual needs. Ancient rock drawings depict buffalo as a symbol of power, freedom, and plenty. Plains Indians likely realized how dependent the buffalo were on grasslands, and probably managed the herds through selective and deliberate fire burns. Even before the widespread introduction of the horse by European settlers, American Indians learned to stampede herds of buffalo over cliffs for mass slaughter. Butchery was perfected so as to remove the meat and make maximum use of body parts for making tools, clothing, items for shelter, and ritual objects. Hides were often turned into leather for recording winter counts, these pictorial depictions of community events.

By the time European explorers and settlers started to reach the plains, there were perhaps fifty million buffalo in North America, making them one of the most populous species of large mammals on the planet! While most American Indian buffalo hunts were relatively modest and controlled, as depicted in the contemporaneous paintings of John Mix Stanley and George

Catlin in the Smithsonian collections, some tribes, by the 1830s, were engaged in mass exploitation. The Comanche, for example, were then killing hundreds of thousands of buffalo annually and selling their meat and skins. After the Civil War, as Hornaday documented, buffalo killing really went into high gear.

The combination of guns, railroads, commercial activity, and war between European settlers and American Indians proved deadly to the species. Horses provided greater mobility in tracking down and reaching herds, and ever-evolving guns allowed for increased killing efficiency. Railroads enabled both easier access of hunters to the herds and the mass shipment of hides and skins to consumer markets back in the East and even beyond. There was a huge market for buffalo skins and hides in the Northeast United States and in Europe. A good buffalo skin would sell for 3.00 dollars in Kansas, and a finished buffalo-hide winter coat would sell for 50.00 dollars. Buffalo leather was also well suited and in high demand for the belts used in pulleys and for steam engines in factories of the time.

Commercial hunters spread across the country and turned their techniques for slaughtering and processing buffalo into a highly organized business enterprise. Teams of professional hunters were accompanied by congeries of wranglers, and gun loaders, and cleaners, and skinners, and cooks, and blacksmiths, guards, and teamsters with their horses and wagons. A hunter could kill 100 buffalo in one session, and there were hundreds of such teams operating daily. An estimated 100,000 buffalo could be slaughtered in a single day; their hides taken, cleaned, stacked, and shipped eastward by wagon and railroad.

Given the scope of this carnage, some hunters, including Buffalo Bill Cody, spoke out in favor of protecting the bison, but President Ulysses S. Grant refused to sign legislation to that effect. The U.S. Army actually encouraged the excessive killing of buffalo as a way of eliminating food supplies for Indian communities, enabling them to starve Indians off their land and onto reservations. Realizing there was a real prospect of true extinction, some ranchers in Montana, South Dakota, Oklahoma, and Texas actually started to preserve very small herds of surviving buffalo.

In the spring of 1886 taxidermist from the Smithsonian, Hornaday, and a team headed to Montana to collect specimens for the museum to observe their natural movement so they could be taxiermied and displayed in natural poses. Hornaday, when he went west, was stunned to find no live buffalo on the plains, only thousands of skeletons bleaching in the sun. It took a second trip three months later and hunting in the fall for Hornaday to actually find the specimens he needed. The impact of killing some of the last buffalo was not lost on Hornaday, and he began to think about how to save the species.

Hornaday actually brought back to Washington a calf he named Sandy, on account of the animal's wavy, yellowish-brown hair. Sandy, who was kept tied to a stake outside the National Museum, right there in Washington, was a great hit with visitors, but to Hornaday's disappointment, Sandy died only a few weeks after his arrival in Washington from pasture bloat, a result of eating damp clover. Hornaday, again sadly, skinned and mounted the animal to add to the bison family group exhibit at the museum.

But Sandy inspired Hornaday to initiate what he called at the time the Smithsonian's Department of Living Animals, part of a plan to establish a breeding program to actually help save the buffalo. Housed in pens on the south lawn of the Smithsonian Castle, the popular living animal exhibit soon grew to 172 mammals and birds and drew many visitors. Hornaday advocated for a National Zoological Park, for the conservation and study of wild animals sacred to national heritage. He wanted to preserve buffalo not only in museum exhibits, but as a living herd in captivity to educate Americans, and, as he said, to help atone for America's extermination of the species. He was successful on both counts. The Smithsonian acquired six buffalo, the first ever to become the property of the U.S. government.

In 1889 Congress passed legislation creating the National Zoo, and Hornaday was appointed its head. Now, he left soon after that to become the head, and founding, and long-term director of the Bronx Zoo. But to spread his message, Hornaday published The Extermination of the American Bison, considered the first important book of the American conservation movement. He cofounded the National Bison Society with President Theodore Roosevelt, and he sent 15 of the zoo's buffalo west to seed a herd, and established the National Bison Ranges in Kansas and Montana to ensure the survival of the American buffalo. These efforts inspired the use of the buffalo and, as well, the American Indian, on the buffalo nickel, first minted by the U.S. government in 1913. And subsequently, numerous universities, and organizations, and even several states adopted the buffalo as a mascot or a logo for their official seal. Thanks to Hornaday's pioneering efforts, western herds were slowly built up. And today there are, perhaps, 500,000 American buffalo, though only about 30,000 are in the wild in national parks.

Hornaday's decision to bring live buffalo to the National Mall was reprised 100 years later in 1989, when Mandan and Hidatsa tribes from South Dakota participated in the Smithsonian's annual Folklife Festival. During the festival, they tanned buffalo hides, performed buffalo songs and dances, made buffalo-hide boats and buffalo regalia, all to demonstrate the importance of buffalo in their culture and herd regeneration. One of their female buffalo unexpectedly gave birth to a baby calf just after midnight on June 24th, within a stone's throw of the Washington Monument. The calf was given the Mandan name Nasca Nacasire, or Summer Calf. Indian elders, that summer, connected the calf's birth to the legislative process, then moving forward, to give birth to another Native American presence on the Mall, the National Museum of the American Indian. Both, the museum and the buffalo, would signal the resurgent vitality of America's oldest inhabitants.

Another threatened species associated with Native American culture was the bald eagle. And despite the name, the bald eagle is not really bald, but rather, has a rather distinctive smooth white feathered crown. It is the only species of eagle that is unique to North America. It probably split off from the Eurasian white-tailed eagle during the Miocene age, some ten to eighteen million years ago in the northern Pacific region. With a distinctive hooked yellow beak and strong talons, a wing span of seven feet, and a flying speed of about 35 miles an hour, the bald eagle exudes power in the sky.

Bald eagles live for about 20 years in the wild. They typically occupy habitats near water, eat fish and small mammals, and are renowned scavengers. Their fine eagle-eye vision enables them to spot and then swoop down and catch prey in their talons. They typically form monogamous pairs and construct their nests in tall trees or on cliffs; some nests occupied by successive generations of eagles might weigh more than a ton. In the late 1700s, there were about 100,000 eagles in the continental United States.

The bald eagle is sacred to a number of American Indian tribes, considered to be a messenger between humans and divine spirits. Eagle feathers are often part of traditional regalia, like headdresses. Feathers and claws are used in traditional ceremonies. Plains Indians, for example, use eagle feathers as part of a medicine fan to help cure illness. Lakota present eagle feathers to those they honor; "a feather in the cap" is an expression deriving from this usage. Other Native tribes use representations of eagles to symbolize fertility and strength in their dances and prayers like this Tlingit art.

After the United States declared its independence, one of the Continental Congress's first acts was to commission a great seal. Now, it took six years, three committees, and a good deal of debate. But finally, in 1782, with the American Revolutionary War coming to an end, it settled on a symbol of nationhood with the bald eagle at its center. Congress admired this distinctive American bird for its physical prowess and liked the parallels it suggested with the ancient Roman Republic, which also used eagle in its symbolism. In the Great Seal of the United States, the eagle holds 13 arrows and a 13-leaf olive branch in its talons, representing the 13 original colonies. Since then, and despite Benjamin Franklin's preference for the turkey, the bald eagle has been used on the presidential seal, as part of the logo for many federal departments and agencies, and as a design element on U.S. coins and stamps. It has become a patriotic symbol used in political campaigns and to recruit soldiers.

Despite the visual ubiquity of its image, however, the bald eagle became an endangered species because of habitat destruction, illegal shooting, and the effects of contaminants, particularly the insecticide DDT, in its prey. Though legal protection began with the Lacey Act of 1900, followed by the Migratory Bird Treaty of 1918, and then, more specifically, by the Bald Eagle Protection Act of 1940, fewer than 1,000 bald eagles remained in the wild by 1963. Endangered species legislation in the 1960s and 1970s helped with the restoration efforts.

Hunting eagles and limiting the collection of feathers only for Native American religious practice has helped increase the eagle population to well over 10,000, and allowed them to be removed now from the endangered species list. But ongoing threats remain and include the loss of wetland habitats, illegal shooting, poisoning from lead, and the ingesting of pesticide and chemical residues.

The Smithsonian's National Zoological Park has contributed to the conservation effort, providing a Bald Eagle Wildlife Refuge for some 500 pairs of eagles in the Chesapeake Bay region. Zoo scientists also study the behavior of its resident bald eagles, the oldest of which is named Tioga. This male eagle was found as a fledgling near his nest in Pennsylvania in 1998 with a badly healed fracture of his left shoulder that made him incapable of flight. But our studies at the zoo contribute to our knowledge of the animal's health, diet, and interactions with a host of environmental factors, and that is very useful in figuring out the preservation of the species.

Now, less majestic than the eagle, another resident of the Smithsonian fared less well. She is a passenger pigeon named Martha, and the sign under her display at the Smithsonian reads,

> MARTHA
>
> Last of her species, died at 1 p.m.,
>
> 1 September 1914, age 29,
>
> Cincinnati Zoological Garden.
>
> EXTINCT

It is hard to believe that the passenger pigeon was once the most common bird in the United States, numbering in the billions. Going back centuries, writers and observers from the French explorer Jacques Cartier in 1534, to Cotton Mather in the late 1600s, to John James Audubon in 1813 noted how the flock of birds would literally fill the sky with a flying column stretching a mile wide or more and literally taking hours to pass overhead. The spectacle of this migratory mass was one of the of the signature wonders of the New World, a metaphor for its seemingly limitless natural bounty.

Audubon, who artfully studied and drew the birds, likened their presence to an eclipse shutting out the sun, accompanied by thunderous noise and even gale-force winds from their wings. As drawn by Audubon, the passenger pigeon was 15 or 16 inches long; had a small head and neck; the tail was long and wedge-shaped; and the wings, long and pointed, powered by large breast muscles that gave the capability for prolonged and rapid flight, some 60 miles an hour.

Passenger pigeons spent summers in various parts of Canada and then migrated about 2,000 miles in a weeklong journey to the American South, where they would spend the winter. And along the way they ate beechnuts, acorns, chestnuts, seeds, berries, and insects found aplenty in large swaths of undisturbed temperate forests. Their nightly roosts massed so many birds together that they frequently broke the limbs of the trees with their weight. Their scolding and chattering as they settled down could be heard for miles.

As Americans cleared eastern forests for farming or timber in the 1800s, the pigeon's migratory route was forced westward, and soon the birds adapted to the deforested landscape by shifting their diet from foraged nuts and insects to grain from farmers' painstakingly cultivated fields. The birds devastated crops and endangered farmers' livelihoods. Their impact was huge, comparable to a prairie fire or bison stampede. One documented flock of passenger pigeons was about 125 miles long and between 6 and 8 miles wide, and consumed an estimated 6 million bushels of grain, all in one day just imagine.

To protect their crops, farmers shot at passenger pigeon flocks. They promoted pigeon shooting as sport, and they sold pigeon meat to cities as a cheap food source for the poor. By 1857, people began to notice fewer passenger pigeons. A bill was proposed in the Ohio legislature to limit the number of passenger pigeons that could be killed, but opponents derided the idea that there was any potential threat to the preservation of the species. Few people could imagine that the ravenous passenger pigeon that darkened the skies in massive numbers was truly endangered, and fewer still found the prospect of extinction unwelcome.

One of the last large nestings—and slaughters—of passenger pigeons occurred in Michigan in 1878. Some seven million birds were hunted and killed. Professional hunters used bait and traps to net and shoot the birds to sell to city markets at 50¢ a dozen. Hunters would attack nests, kill young birds, and disable older roosting ones with fumes from burning sulfur. Overhunting, habitat loss, and possibly infectious disease made the passenger pigeon increasingly rare by the late 19th century. The last confirmed sighting of a wild passenger pigeon was in 1900. Never again would man witness the overwhelming spring and fall migratory flights of this swift and graceful bird. A few survived in captivity, but attempts to save the species by breeding them were unsuccessful. The small captive flocks weakened and died.

Martha, a passenger pigeon named after George Washington's wife, who lived her whole 29-year life in the Cincinnati Zoo, was the last surviving member of the species. It's rare for us to know the precise day and time when a species dies out from this planet, but in this case we do. It was September 1, 1914. On that date, passenger pigeons went from billions to zero. Immediately following Martha's death, the Cincinnati Zoological Garden packed her in an enormous 300-pound block of ice and shipped her to the Smithsonian. Following her arrival in Washington, Martha's skin was mounted for display by a Smithsonian taxidermist, and her internal organs preserved as part of the fluid, or what we affectionally at the Smithsonian call the "wet," collections at the National Museum of Natural History.

Martha's widely reported death had a sobering public impact. Americans had long held the idea that the continent's natural resources were boundless; now they realized that progress and civilization could have irreparable and undesirable consequences. The fate of the passenger pigeon helped spur the Migratory Bird Treaty and other legislation that established precedents for a host of other wildlife and habitat protection measures. Though that effort helped save the eagle, it was too late for Martha, and her display in National Museum of Natural History has helped remind millions of the fragility of nature's creatures, the relationship between habitat and humanity, and our role in species preservation and demise.

That point was brought home once again in the 1970s with one of the Smithsonian's most dramatic acquisitions, Ling-Ling and Hsing-Hsing, the pandas from China. It started with political diplomacy. In February 1972, U.S. President Richard Nixon traveled to mainland China, ending 22 years of diplomatic isolation from the People's Republic of China, a Communist country led by Mao Zedong. The United States had long recognized the Republic of China on the offshore island of Taiwan and opposed to the Communists. By visiting China and starting to normalize the relationship, Nixon hoped to enhance the U.S. position in its Cold War struggle with the Soviet Union and stabilize possible conflicts with China in Asia.

Nixon's eight-day visit was heavily televised. He and his wife, Pat, visited the Forbidden City, the Ming Tombs, the Great Wall, and were guests at a state banquet where they were served such exotic fare as thousand-year-old eggs and tiny songbirds en brochette. The reciprocal presentation of gifts between host and guest is quite important in Chinese culture, and in this case, the gifts needed to suitably mark the occasion that Nixon referred to as "the week that changed the world." The Chinese gift: two pandas that had been captured in the wild months before. The pandas were strongly desired by the Smithsonian's National Zoo; no American zoo had hosted a member of this distinctive and rare species for some two decades. It was a wonderful goodwill gesture.

What did Nixon give the Chinese in return? Well, that occasioned considerable debate prior to the trip. American bald eagles were thought by the U.S. Department of State to be inappropriate because no one at that time was quite sure exactly how friendly the relationship between the two countries would be. Mountain lions were thought of as a gift, but they were a killer, and they were ruled out, as were grizzly bears, because, well, grizzly bears might be taken to symbolize the Soviet Union. The U.S. thought about mountain sheep, goats, antelope, all deemed a bit too delicate for the trip. American elk and deer were not sufficiently different from Chinese elk and deer to merit a gift. The National Zoo and State Department settled on the American bison, the buffalo. But the Beijing Zoo already had some. So musk ox were settled on as a compromise. As the National Zoo had no musk oxen, the Smithsonian purchased a pair from the San Francisco Zoo. Named Milton and Matilda, they were given to the Chinese government. I think we got the better of the deal.

The pandas retained their Chinese names, Hsing-Hsing for the male and Ling-Ling for the female, and when they arrived to the United States they were greeted by Pat Nixon and took up residence at the National Zoo. They became instant celebrities, thought to be especially adorable given their large, oversized heads and their black-and-white coloration. And though they look like soft, plush stuffed animals, they are really anything but. I've held a panda at the Zoo. They are bears; they have gristly, stiff fur, and they're immensely strong, with claws the size of my fingers.

Ling-Ling died from heart failure at the age of 23 in 1992, and Hsing-Hsing lived several more years to the advanced age of 28 and was euthanized in 1999. The Smithsonian successfully negotiated the 10-year loan of a new pair of pandas, Mei Xiang and Tian Tian, with funds from the loan fee designated for work on panda reproduction and survival at the panda research center in Chengdu, China. The National Zoo's premier wildlife veterinarian and reproductive scientist JoGayle Howard developed numerous advances and mentored other zoologists in the United States and in China, at Chengdu, in an effort to see the pandas thrive.

These two did not mate successfully, and so Howard oversaw the artificial insemination of Mei Xiang, who in 2005 gave birth to Tai Shan, causing what we called Pandamania in Washington DC. Panda cams, that is, webcams trained on the panda enclosures, proved very popular. As stipulated in the loan agreement, Tai Shan had to return to China in 2010 to enter a breeding program, and Washingtonians greatly lamented his departure, but then, 2013 greeted Mei Xiang's birth of another panda cub, the adorable Bao Bao.

Now, politics aside, the presence of the pandas at the National Zoo has made it one of the leading centers for giant panda biology and conservation. This is essential, as the giant pandas are an endangered species; only about 1,600 are estimated to live in the wild, while just over 300 live in captivity in zoos and breeding centers around the world. Additionally, tens of millions, maybe even hundreds of millions of people have become aware of pandas and the challenges they face as a result of visiting the zoo, whether in person or through the Pandacam. The National Zoo at the Smithsonian sees their pandas now as ambassadors for conservation. While this is a different diplomatic role than the one foreseen by President Nixon, it is certainly a most worthwhile one.

Kitty Hawk to Tranquility—Innovation and Flight

Lecture 13

In this lecture, you will learn about two seminal inventions relating to air and space travel that capture the spirit of innovation in our nation. The Wright brothers' Flyer demonstrated the possibility of air travel and spurred the airline, defense, and aerospace industries. If anything could be more astonishing than the Wrights' achievement, it was the moment Neil Armstrong stepped onto the surface of the Moon. His space suit tells a remarkable tale of the power and promise of American innovation.

The Wright Brothers' Flyer

- Since 1887, the secretary of the Smithsonian, Samuel Langley, had been experimenting with aeronautical models and gliders. In 1896, working in a shed located behind the Smithsonian Castle, he developed two unpiloted heavier-than-air steam-powered flying machines. They were launched from a catapult on a houseboat in the Potomac River and flew about three-quarters of a mile. Langley later received funds from the War Department to develop a piloted version.

- Wilbur and Orville Wright were two brothers operating a bicycle store in Dayton, Ohio. They studied Langley's research and the reports of others, experimented with hang gliders, and posited that a successful airplane would feature three systems: a set of lifting surfaces, or wings; a method of balancing and controlling the aircraft; and a means of propulsion.

- They first concentrated on how to maintain balance and control because they thought that that was the toughest problem. Based on their experience, they realized that, like the bicycle, a flying machine would be fundamentally unstable as it traveled through air, yet could, like a bicycle, be controlled.

- The Wrights realized that if the wing on one side of a craft met the oncoming flow of air at a greater angle than the opposite wing, it

Wright Flyer

would generate more lift on that side, causing the wing to rise and the aircraft to bank. If pilots could manipulate the wings using this principle, they could maintain balance and turn the aircraft as well.

- The brothers considered but rejected using a system of gears and pivoting shafts to change the angles of the wings because it would be too heavy and complex. Instead, they came up with the idea of twisting, or warping, the wing structure in controlled ways using interconnected wire cables.

- In building their first experimental aircraft in 1899, a kite with a five-foot wingspan, the Wrights combined their wing-warping innovation with braced biplane wings inspired by the 1896 glider made by aviation pioneers Octave Chanute and Augustus Herring. That glider used steel wires crisscrossed between vertical wooden struts to support the upper and lower wings. Wilbur flew the test kite, and the wing-warping controls worked well.

- The brothers next turned their attention to testing the curve of the wing profile, the wing area necessary to lift a pilot, and the type of materials best suited to construct a glider. They needed wide-open spaces with strong, steady winds; they settled on Kitty Hawk, North Carolina. In 1900, they built a glider and repeatedly tested it by flying it as a kite and recording and analyzing the results. The glider produced less lift than predicted.

- To increase lift, they increased the wing size to a 22-foot span and changed its curvature—also known as the airfoil. They also changed the fabric covering the wing, from a French cotton sateen to an unbleached cotton muslin. For the first time, the brothers could make real flights, and these revealed serious control problems.

- They suspected that the information used to compute lift and drag might be wrong. During the fall of 1901, they built their own primitive wind tunnel for testing the aerodynamics of different wing shapes. They increased lift efficiency with a thinner and longer wing and an improved airfoil for a new glider.

- Testing their third glider at Kitty Hawk in 1902, they decided on a movable rudder and integrated its controls with the wing-warping controls for better handling. The key here was a wooden hip harness or cradle that enabled the pilot to move the wing-warping cables by jutting his hips this way or that. The brothers made somewhere between 700 and 1,000 glides; flights of 500 feet were common.

- Now they could add a propulsion system. They designed a single 12-horsepower gasoline-powered internal combustion engine to turn two propellers rotating in opposite directions behind the wings. Wind-tunnel tests led them to further increase wing area to get the lift to carry the added weight of the engine, the two propellers, and structural reinforcement. The wind-tunnel data were also crucial to the design of the very efficient propellers.

- The Wrights then returned to Kitty Hawk in 1903 with what they simply called the Flyer. Meanwhile, back along the Potomac,

Langley thought he was on the verge of manned flight. But when he launched what he called the aerodrome on October 7, 1903, the craft plunged directly into the river. He tried again on December 8. This time, the craft broke apart upon launch. Langley was ridiculed in the newspapers and excoriated in Congress.

- Six days later, on December 14, the Wrights were finally ready. They tossed a coin to see who would make the first attempt. Wilbur won and climbed into the pilot's position. The Flyer powered down 40 feet of rail reached about 20 miles per hour, lurched up, stalled, and smashed into the sand after a three-second flight. But Wilbur was confident.

- The plane was repaired and readied for the next try on December 17. With Orville at the controls this time, the Flyer darted up, sailed slowly over the sand, and came to rest 12 seconds later, about 120 feet from where it had taken off. A man had flown.

- The Wright brothers made three more flights that day. Wilbur flew 175 feet; Orville then covered more than 200 feet in 15 seconds. Then, with Wilbur at the controls, the Flyer flew 852 feet in 59 seconds, clearly demonstrating that the plane was capable of sustained controlled flight. Just after the fourth flight, a gust of wind overturned the airplane and sent it tumbling across the sand. Severely damaged, the 1903 Flyer never flew again.

- The Wrights tested two more machines in an Ohio pasture in 1904 and 1905. By October 1905, they had transformed the experimental success of 1903 into the reality of a practical airplane capable of remaining aloft under the full control of the pilot for extended periods of time.

- Before revealing their triumph to the public, however, the brothers wanted to secure a patent and contracts for the sale of their invention. Their patent was for the system of controls—not the airplane. Finally, in the summer of 1908, Wilbur flew in public for the first time in France while Orville flew for the U.S. Army at Fort Myer in Virginia.

- In 1910, a Smithsonian curator noted that visitors to the U.S. National Museum wanted to see the famous Wright Flyer. Smithsonian Secretary Charles Walcott wrote to Wilbur asking for a model and an actual aircraft. The Wrights were receptive but noted that they didn't have a craft in adequate condition for exhibit.

- Wilbur Wright died in 1912. In 1914, Smithsonian Secretary Walcott was reassessing the historical role of Langley's Aerodrome, largely to bolster his predecessor's legacy. Walcott paid another aviation engineer, Glenn H. Curtiss, to rebuild and test the Aerodrome.

- Curtiss had just lost a lawsuit with the Wrights' company for violating the brothers' wing-warping patent. Curtiss rebuilt Langley's old craft, incorporating a great many fundamental changes, after which the craft made several short, straight-line flights. Langley's plane was then restored to its failed 1903 configuration and placed on display in the museum with a label identifying it as the "first man-carrying aeroplane in the history of the world capable of sustained free flight."

- This declaration understandably angered Orville Wright. He refused to donate the Kitty Hawk Flyer to the Smithsonian until the Institution admitted that the 1914 test of the Curtis-refurbished Langley craft did not prove that it had been capable of flight in 1903. Walcott refused to alter his position.

- Over the next decade, Orville exhibited the restored Flyer at the Massachusetts Institute of Technology and at aeronautical and automotive expositions in New York and Dayton while the controversy with the Smithsonian festered.

- Orville genuinely hoped that the airplane would one day go to the U.S. National Museum, but the Smithsonian refused to change the label for the Langley Aerodrome. So, Orville shipped the Flyer to the London Science Museum in 1928, and he altered his will to ensure that it would remain there permanently if the Smithsonian did not change course.

- In 1934, Charles Lindbergh wrote to Walcott's successor, Smithsonian Secretary Charles G. Abbot, offering to mediate the dispute with Orville Wright. Abbot met with Lindbergh and Wright, but to no avail. In 1942, fearing he'd lose the Wright Flyer, Abbot finally agreed to publish a full account of the alterations made to Langley's plane and remove the contested aerodrome label. This was enough for Orville.

- The Flyer came back to Washington after World War II and after Orville Wright passed away in 1948. It was exhibited in the Arts and Industries Building and then transferred to the National Air and Space Museum when it opened in 1976. It remains there today as one of the Smithsonian's most popular and beloved displays.

Neil Armstrong's Space Suit

- On July 21, 1969 astronaut Neil Armstrong declared, "One small step for [a] man, one giant leap for mankind," as he stepped onto the Moon's surface. In a heart-stopping moment televised live to 600 million people on Earth, Armstrong and his lunar module pilot, Buzz Aldrin, fulfilled the historic pledge made by President John F. Kennedy for the United States to land a man on the Moon. The third member of the team, Michael Collins, orbited the Moon from their lunar module.

- The Moon voyage was a scientific and technological triumph. Among the numerous inventions that made their mission possible—from rockets to computers—was the space suit. The Moon has only a negligible atmosphere, with no air for humans to breathe. Its gravity is just one-sixth of Earth's, and its temperature ranges are extreme—above the boiling point of water in the sun and approaching absolute zero in the shade.

- Everything Armstrong and Aldrin did on the Moon—including collecting about 47 pounds of rock and lunar soil samples and planting an American flag on the surface—depended on their space suits and their portable life-support systems, which essentially provided the microenvironments they needed to survive.

- The suits insulated them from extreme temperatures, provided protection from environmental hazards and cosmic rays, enabled them to breathe, and allowed them to move about and do their work. The space suits hosted the communications equipment allowing them to talk with each other, with Collins in the spacecraft *Columbia*, and with Mission Control on Earth. The suits also enabled Mission Control to monitor the bodily functions of the astronauts.

- The Mercury astronauts of the early 1960s had basically worn modified high-altitude air flight suits done up in silver to give them a futuristic appearance. But the Mercury astronauts had been stationary, strapped into their seats. Something dramatically more functional was needed to walk and work on the Moon. Engineers had envisioned a hard suit—a shell made out of fiberglass, aluminum, and plastic. NASA found that they weren't flexible enough for movement or to integrate pressurized life-support systems.

- So, in 1965 NASA held a competition to design the new suit. Participants included Hamilton Standard, B. F. Goodrich, the David Clark Company, and the International Latex Corporation (which is known by another of its brand names—Platex, the designer and manufacturers of bras and girdles). Ultimately, International Latex came up with the winning concept. The company developed a soft suit composed of 26 layers of synthetic materials that could withstand pressurization, protect the astronauts, retard fire, and also provide the flexibility needed for the mission.

- Armstrong's suit weighed about 56 pounds by itself, but 189 pounds when combined with life-support systems. It had a liquid-circulating, temperature-modulating undergarment closest to the skin. The suits were fitted with rubber and neoprene to allow

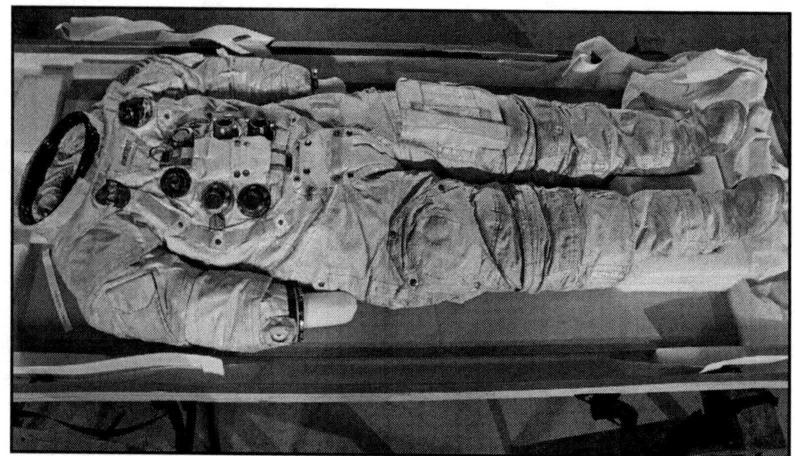

Apollo Space Suit

flexibility in arm, knee, and hip joints, with a system of nylon tunneling and steel cables to prevent ballooning from pressurization. Two sets of zippers held the suit closed, the outer one running from the back of the neck down to the crotch and up the front and covered by a flap.

- The torso of the suit included two sets of connectors for life-support hoses. The pressure bubble helmet connected to the suit with a neck ring and had a comfort pad at the back that linked it to the airflow system. It was made of clear polycarbonate, giving the astronauts a wide field of vision; they could move their heads but not turn the helmet itself.

- On the Moon's surface, the astronauts donned an "overhelmet," which had two visors, an outer one for protection from micrometeorites and ultraviolet light and a 24-karat-gold-coated one that reduced the light entering the helmet to prevent overheating. Their boots, which left the footprints on the lunar surface, also had layered synthetic materials. The space suits had pockets for storage and a "bio-belt" to monitor the astronauts' vital signs.

- The Latex corporation hand-tailored and -crafted the whole suit to each individual astronaut. Although there were minor complaints, the space suits worked exceedingly well. Both Armstrong and Aldrin loped hundreds of yards around their Moon base in the low gravity with no problem.

- After Aldrin and Armstrong returned to the lander, they jettisoned some of their unneeded equipment, blasted off from the Moon's surface, and reunited with Collins for the journey back to Earth. Their module splashed into the Pacific Ocean near Johnston Atoll, about 860 miles west of Hawaii, and was safely recovered by a U.S. Navy ship. The space suits and other materials were dry-cleaned upon their return amid fears that the lunar dirt and dust could possibly contain unknown bacteria and viruses that could have disastrous effects on Earth.

- Since being accessed into the collections of the Smithsonian's National Air and Space Museum, Armstrong's and Aldrin's space suits have required ongoing conservation treatment. Their exposure to lunar materials, and the suit materials themselves, are causing rapid decay. Because of their fragile state, the suits must be kept in strict climate-controlled environments and only shown on special occasions. Armstrong's suit was taken off exhibition in 2006 so that it could receive more intensive care.

Featured Objects

Wright Flyer

Apollo Space Suit

Suggested Reading

De Monchaux, *Spacesuit.*

Goldstone, *Birdmen.*

Kitty Hawk to Tranquility—Innovation and Flight
Lecture 13—Transcript

The United States has long been characterized by the spirit of creativity, invention, and innovation. Benjamin Franklin perhaps best exemplified this spirit during the independence era. He demonstrated that lighting is electricity and charted the Gulf Stream. He came up with useful inventions—the lightning rod; bifocals; and even a musical instrument, the glass armonica. He created a new, widely used consumer product, Poor Richard's Almanack, and became wealthy as its publisher. He also established the country's first postal system, a public library, a volunteer fire department, a college, a hospital, and America's most prominent scholarly and scientific society of the time, the Philosophical Society of America.

Franklin was not alone in developing ways to make life better. The nation's first leaders constantly thought of ways of improving agricultural production. George Washington tested improved plowing methods at his plantation at Mount Vernon. His compatriot, Thomas Jefferson, even invented a plow to make turning the soil more efficient at his hilly Monticello estate. As the nation expanded westward, new lands were opened to settlement and cultivation. But the ground was harder and the soil stickier than back East. The more traditional wooden and iron plows literally couldn't cut it. John Deere came up with the idea of using steel instead of iron for his plow. He also experimented with the shape of its moldboard, finding that a concave parallelogram with a specific contour worked best in turning and dumping the soil. He transformed his insight into a product and a business, selling a few hundred plows a year locally in the early 1840s and tens of thousands in the 1850s. The John Deere Company is now a global giant approaching 40 billion dollars in annual sales.

Inventions teach us a lot about history. They often reveal the opportunities and the problems of the time. For example, we saw how the invention of the cotton gin allowed the widespread growing of cotton, which led to the construction of more mills and the production of more cloth. This led to the invention of the sewing machine, the massive growth of the American clothing industry, and to many jobs, massive immigration, seminal unions, and global competition.

Sometimes an invention is not an object, but a process. Andrew Carnegie's innovation was the integration of the steel industry, as he adeptly connected his manufacturing enterprise to the supply chain of raw materials and the distribution of the final product. He owned steel from beginning to end, and thus could achieve greater efficiencies and make more money than his competitors.

Thomas Edison is perhaps America's most famous inventor, but his success was due as much to his business acumen as his scientific skill. He had many competitors, all trying to develop the best way to light the world. Edison won not only because he determined the best filament to use in a light bulb, but also because he was a great showman, lighting up Menlo Park, New Jersey for New Years Eve in 1879; strongly defending his patent rights; and displaying a remarkable taste for business that won him the public utility contract to light lower Manhattan. At the Smithsonian we have Edison's light bulbs and Carnegie's steel, along with the Model T automobile, the Bakelizer plastic maker, Jonas Salk's polio vaccine, the ENIAC computer, and the Apple Macintosh, all inventions that have changed our lives and our world, as we'll see in some future lectures.

For me, two seminal inventions relating to air and space travel really capture the spirit of innovation in our nation. The first is the invention of Wilbur and Orville Wright, two brothers operating a bicycle store in Dayton, Ohio. Their invention demonstrated the possibility of air travel and spurred the airline, defense, and aerospace industries. Their case strongly illustrates the importance of the experimental process in invention, how patents are tied to business enterprise, and how historical credit for an innovation may be quite contentious.

On May 30, 1899, Wilbur sent a letter to the Smithsonian:

> Dear Sirs: I am an enthusiast, but not a crank in the sense that I have some pet theories as to the proper construction of a flying machine. I wish to avail myself of all that is already known and then if possible add my mite to help on the future worker who will attain final success.

The Smithsonian sent the Wright brothers the material they requested. Indeed, at that time, the secretary of the Smithsonian, Samuel Langley, was deeply involved in his own aeronautical experiments. Langley was a brilliant, self-taught astronomer and physicist. He'd been experimenting with models and gliders since 1887. In 1896, working in a shed located behind the Smithsonian Castle in Washington DC, he developed two unpiloted, heavier-than-air, steam-powered flying machines. They were launched from a catapult on a houseboat in the Potomac River and flew about three-quarters of a mile. Langley later received funds from the War Department to develop a piloted version.

The Wrights studied Langley's research and the reports of others, experimented with hang gliders, and posited that a successful airplane would feature three systems: one, a set of lifting surfaces, or wings; two, a method of balancing and controlling the aircraft; and three, a means of propulsion. They first concentrated on how to maintain balance and control, because they thought that was the toughest problem. Based on their experience, they realized that, like a bicycle, a flying machine would be fundamentally unstable as it traveled through air, yet, it could, like a bicycle, be controlled.

The Wrights realized that the wing on one side of a craft met the oncoming flow of air at a greater angle than the opposite wing, then it would generate more lift on that side, causing the wing to rise and the aircraft to bank. If pilots could manipulate the wings using this principle, they could maintain balance and turn the aircraft as well. The brothers considered but rejected using a system of gears and pivoting shafts to change the angles of the wings because it would be too heavy and too complex. Instead, they came up with the idea of twisting, or warping, the wing structure in controlled ways using interconnected wire cables.

In building their first experimental aircraft in 1899, a kite with a five-foot wingspan, the Wrights combined their wing-warping innovation with braced biplane wings inspired by the 1896 glider made by aviation pioneers Octave Chanute and Augustus Herring. That glider used steel wires crisscrossed between vertical wooden struts to support the upper and lower wings. Wilbur flew the test kite and the wing-warping controls worked well.

The brothers next turned their attention to testing the curve of the wing profile, the wing area necessary to lift a pilot, and the type of materials best suited to construct a glider. They needed wide-open spaces with strong, steady winds; they settled on Kitty Hawk, North Carolina. In 1900, they built a glider for about 15 dollars, which was cheaper than the cost of a bicycle at the time. They repeatedly tested it, flying it as a kite, and recording and analyzing the results. The glider was something of a disappointment, though, producing less lift than predicted. To increase the lift, they increased the wing size to a 22-foot span and changed its curvature, also known as the airfoil. They also changed the fabric covering the wing from a French cotton sateen to an unbleached cotton muslin. For the first time, the brothers could make real flights and these revealed very serious control problems.

They suspected that the information they used to compute lift and drag might be wrong, and so during the fall of 1901, they built their own primitive wind tunnel for testing the aerodynamics of different wing shapes. They increased lift efficiency with a thinner and longer wing and an improved airfoil for a new glider. Testing their third glider at Kitty Hawk in 1902, they decided on a movable rudder and integrated its controls with the wing-warping controls for better handling. The key here was a wooden hip harness, or a cradle, that enabled the pilot to move the wing-warping cables by jutting his hips this way or that. The brothers made somewhere between 700 and 1,000 glides; flights of 500 feet were common.

Now they could add a propulsion system. They designed a single 12-horsepower, gasoline-powered internal combustion engine to turn two propellers rotating in opposite directions behind the wings. Wind-tunnel tests led them to further increase wing area to get the lift to carry the added weight of the engine, the two propellers, and all the structural reinforcement. The wind-tunnel data were also crucial to the design of the very efficient propellers.

The Wrights then returned to Kitty Hawk in 1903 with what they simply called the Flyer. Meanwhile, back along the Potomac, Langley thought he was on the verge of manned flight. But when he launched what he called the Aerodrome on October 7, 1903, the craft plunged directly into the river. He tried again on December 8th. This time the craft broke apart upon launch. Langley was ridiculed in the newspapers and excoriated in Congress. Six days later, on December 14th, the Wrights were finally ready. They tossed a coin to see who would make the first attempt. Wilbur won. He climbed into the pilot's position. The Flyer powered down 40 feet of rail; it was almost like a skateboard on a track, and it reached 20 miles an hour, and when it did, it lurched up, and it stalled, and it smashed into the sand, after a flight of three seconds.

But Wilbur Wright was confident. The plane was repaired, and it was readied for the next try on December 17th. With Orville at the controls this time, the flyer darted up and sailed slowly over the sand and came to rest with a thud 12 seconds later, about 120 feet from where it had taken off. A man had flown.

The Wright brothers made three more flights that day. Wilbur flew 175 feet; Orville then covered more than 200 feet in 15 seconds. And then, with Wilbur at the controls, the flyer flew 852 feet in 59 seconds, clearly demonstrating that the plane was capable of sustained controlled flight. Just after the fourth flight, a gust of wind overturned the airplane and sent it tumbling across the sand. Severely damaged, the 1903 Flyer never flew again.

The Wrights tested two more machines in an Ohio pasture in 1904 and 1905. By October 1905 they had transformed the experimental success of 1903 into the reality of a practical airplane capable of remaining aloft under the full control of the pilot for extended periods of time. Now, before revealing their triumph to the public, however, the brothers wanted to secure a patent and contracts for the sale of their invention. Their patent was for the system of controls, not the airplane. And finally, in the summer of 1908, Wilbur flew in public for the first time in France, while Orville flew for the U.S. Army at Fort Myer in Virginia.

In 1910, a Smithsonian curator noted that visitors to the United States National Museum wanted to see this famous Wright Flyer. The Smithsonian secretary at the time was Charles Walcott, a distinguished geologist. He wrote to Wilbur asking for a model and an actual aircraft. The Wrights were receptive but noted that they didn't have a craft in an adequate condition for an exhibit. Wilbur Wright died in 1912. In 1914, Smithsonian Secretary Walcott was reassessing the historical role of Langley's Aerodrome, largely to bolster his predecessor's legacy. Walcott paid another aviation engineer, Glenn Curtiss, to rebuild and test Langley's Aerodrome. Curtiss had just lost a lawsuit with the Wrights' company for violating the brothers' wing-warping patent. Curtiss rebuilt Langley's old craft incorporating a great many fundamental changes, after which the craft did make several short, straight-line flights. Langley's plane was then restored to its failed 1903 configuration and placed on display in the museum with a label identifying it as, "the first man-carrying aeroplane in the history of the world capable of sustained free flight."

Well this declaration understandably angered Orville Wright. He refused to donate the Kitty Hawk Flyer to the Smithsonian until the Institution admitted that the 1914 test of the Curtis-refurbished Langley craft did not prove that it had actually been capable of flight all the way back in 1903. Walcott refused to alter his position, and so over the next decade, Orville exhibited the restored Flyer at the Massachusetts Institute of Technology and at aeronautical and automotive expositions in New York and in Dayton, while the controversy with the Smithsonian festered.

Orville genuinely hoped that the airplane would one day go to the United States National Museum, but the Smithsonian dug in its heels at the time and refused to change the label for the Langley Aerodrome. So Orville shipped the Flyer to London, to the science museum in 1928, and he altered his will to ensure that it would remain there, at the London Science Museum, permanently if the Smithsonian did not change course. In 1934, Charles Lindbergh wrote to Walcott's successor, Smithsonian Secretary Charles Abbot, offering to mediate the dispute with Orville Wright. Abbot met with Lindbergh and with Wright, but to no avail. The London Science Museum took very good care of the plane, and during the London Blitz in World War II, the Flyer was even evacuated with other important collections to a cave outside the city.

In 1942, fearing he'd lose the Wright Flyer forever, Abbot finally agreed to publish a full account of the alterations made to Langley's plane and remove the contested Aerodrome label. This was enough for Orville. The Flyer came back to Washington after the war and after Orville Wright had passed away in 1948. It was exhibited in the Arts and Industries Building and then transferred to the National Air and Space Museum when it opened to the public in 1976. It remains there today as one of the Smithsonian's most popular and beloved displays. People generally marvel at seeming simplicity of this rough-hewn machine that initiated the age of flight but are also typically unaware of its contentious history.

If anything could be more astonishing than the Wrights' achievement, it was that moment on July 21, 1969 that astronaut Neil Armstrong declared, "One small step for [a] man, one giant leap for mankind," as he stepped onto the Moon's surface. In a heart-stopping moment televised to some 600 million people back on Earth, Armstrong and his lunar module pilot, "Buzz" Aldrin, fulfilled the historic pledge made by President John F. Kennedy for the United States to land a man on the Moon. Armstrong and Aldrin descended to the Moon's soft, powdery surface—"magnificent desolation," as Aldrin described it—while a third member of the team, Michael Collins, orbited the moon from their lunar module.

The Moon voyage was a scientific and technological triumph. The three astronauts on the Apollo 11 mission were propelled into space atop a powerful Saturn V rocket that blasted off from Kennedy Space Center in Florida. Saturn V reached Earth's orbit with the help of three rocket stage, sections with their own engines and fuel supply, the first two of which were jettisoned after use. After orbiting Earth, the rocket's third stage reignited, sending the mission's payload toward the Moon.

Three days later, the spacecraft, called Columbia, was orbiting the Moon. The spacecraft itself consisted of three modules, or component vehicles, that attached and separated from each other. The service module provided the power, propulsion, water, oxygen, and other support. And the lunar module, called Eagle when in flight, would descend to the Moon, and its top portion would bring the astronauts back up, while its lower portion, the lunar lander would remain on the Moon. The command module housed the astronauts and computer controls and life-support systems; it was the only portion of the craft that would actually return to Earth.

The lunar module with Armstrong and Aldrin aboard separated from the rest of the spacecraft and fired up its descent engines to land on the Moon's surface, aiming for a relatively flat region named the Sea of Tranquility. About two hours later, Eagle touched down in a boulder-strewn area. The astronauts secured the lander, calling their new location Tranquility Base. Scheduled to sleep but finding it impossible to do so given their excitement, they began their preparations to leave the craft.

Opening the hatch, Armstrong deployed the camera that would capture his step on the moon, and then he descended the ladder. Aldrin followed. They relocated the camera, setting it on a tripod, filmed the surrounding area, and went to work over the next two hours. They took pictures of the lunar module so that its status could be assessed and with a hammer, scoops, and tongs, collected about 47 pounds of rock and lunar soil samples for later study back on Earth. The astronauts deployed scientific equipment and took a congratulatory radio call from President Richard M. Nixon. They planted an American flag on the surface and left behind a memorial bag with a silicon disk containing goodwill statements from American presidents and other world leaders, as well as a golden olive branch as a symbol of peace. They also left a plaque with the inscription, HERE MEN FROM THE PLANET EARTH FIRST SET FOOT UPON THE MOON JULY 1969, A.D. WE CAME IN PEACE FOR ALL MANKIND.

Among the numerous inventions from rockets to the computers that made their mission possible was the space suit. The moon has only a negligible atmosphere, with no air for humans to breathe. Its gravity is just one-sixth of Earth's, and its temperature ranges are extreme, above the boiling point of water in the sun, approaching absolute zero in the shade. Everything Armstrong and Aldrin did on the moon depended on their space suits and their portable life-support systems, which essentially provided the microenvironments they needed to survive; the suits insulated them from extreme temperatures, provided protection from environmental hazards and cosmic rays, enabled them to breathe, allowed them to move about and do their work. The space suits hosted the communications equipment allowing them to talk with each other, with Collins in Columbia overhead, with Mission Control back on Earth. The suits also enabled Mission Control to monitor the body functions of the astronauts so they could head off or deal with stresses and other dangers.

So, how did these space suits, so crucial to the Apollo mission, come to be? Well, it's an interesting and instructive story of innovation. The Mercury astronauts of the early 1960s had basically worn modified high-altitude flight suits done up in silver to give them a futuristic appearance. But the Mercury astronauts had been stationary, strapped into their seats. Something dramatically more functional was needed to walk and work on the moon. Engineers had envisioned a hard suit, a shell made out of fiberglass, aluminum, and plastic. NASA found they weren't flexible enough for movement or to integrate pressurized life-support systems.

So in 1965, they held a competition to design the new suit. Participants included Hamilton Standard, BF Goodrich, the David Clark Company, and the International Latex Corporation. International Latex was not a newcomer to the field; it had been fabricating high-altitude pressure suits for the Air Force since the 1950s and had worked on space suits with Hamilton Standard in the early 60s. But most people know International Latex by another brand name—Platex—the designer and manufacturer of bras and girdles. And ultimately, it was International Latex which came up with the winning concept. As one writer opined, and I paraphrase, Neil Armstong took a giant step for mankind, and an even a larger step for ladies underwear.

ILC engineers and textile designers won because they knew a lot about flexibility, and layering, and movement. The company developed a soft suit composed of some 26 layers of synthetic materials that could withstand pressurization, protect the astronauts, retard fire, and also provide the flexibility needed for the mission. Armstrong's suit weighed about 56 pounds by itself but 189 pounds when combined with life-support systems. It had a liquid-circulating, temperature-modulating undergarment closest to the skin. That was fitted with rubber and neoprene to allow flexibility in arm, knee, and hip joints, with a system of nylon tunneling and steel cables to prevent ballooning from pressurization. Two sets of zippers held the suit closed; the outer one running from the back of the neck down to the crotch, and up the front, covered by a flap.

The torso of the suit included two sets of connectors for life-support hoses—blue for the good air, red for the bad. The pressure bubble helmet connected to the suit with a neck ring and had a comfort pad in the back that linked it to the airflow system. It was made of clear polycarbonate, giving the astronauts a wide field of vision; they could move their heads but not turn the helmet itself.

On the moon's surface, the astronauts donned an overhelmet, which had two visors, an outer one for protection from micrometeorites and ultraviolet light, and a 24-karat-gold-coated one that reduced the light entering the helmet to prevent overheating. Their boots, which left the footprints on the lunar surface, also had layered synthetic materials. The space suits had pockets for storage and a bio-belt to monitor the astronauts' vital signs.

Here we have one of the gloves worn by lunar module pilot William Anders during the very first lunar orbit mission, known as Apollo 8. Although this glove was never worn on the surface of the moon, it was made to the same rigorous standards. These gloves were custom made to fit each astronaut, to ensure their fit and functionality. They were constructed from layers of AL-7 fireproof thermal insulation to provide protection. Later versions of the glove added a silvery Chromel R fabric to resist tearing. The gloves, as you can see, were attached to the arm of the suit by aluminum connection rings—red for the right hand, blue for the left.

The Latex corporation hand tailored and crafted the whole suit to each individual astronaut. Though there were minor complaints, the space suits worked exceedingly well. Both Armstrong and Aldrin loped hundreds of yards around their Moon base in the low gravity with no problem. They had no difficulty setting up equipment, wielding a geological hammer, manipulating a camera, and using other tools. After Aldrin and Armstrong returned to the lander, they jettisoned some of the unneeded equipment, rested for several hours, blasted off from the Moon's surface, and reunited with Collins for the journey back to Earth. Their module splashed into the Pacific Ocean near Johnston Atoll, about 860 miles west of Hawaii and was safely recovered by a U.S. Navy ship.

The space suits and other materials were dry-cleaned upon their return amid fears that the lunar dirt and dust could possibly contain unknown bacteria and viruses that could have disastrous effects back here on Earth. Since being accessed into the collections of the Smithsonian's National Air and

Space Museum, Armstrong and Aldrin's space suits have required ongoing conservation treatment. Their exposure to lunar materials, and the suit materials themselves, are causing rapid decay. Because of their fragile state, the suits, including Armstrong's glove and various apparati, must be kept in strict climate-controlled environments and only shown on special occasions.

Armstrong's suit was taken off exhibition in 2006 so that it could receive more intensive care. Ironically, space suits designed to survive the extremities of the Moon for a short period of time are having a hard time surviving for a long period of time in a museum back here on Earth. That said, like the Wright Flyer, and so many of the marvelous machines in the Smithsonian's collection, they nonetheless tell a remarkable tale of the power and the promise of American innovation.

Cold War—Red Badges, Bombs, and the Berlin Wall
Lecture 14

As you will learn in this lecture, the overwhelming American foreign policy and defense issue during the latter half of the 20th century was the Cold War with the Soviet Union. That conflict—part ideological, part practical—permeated American life. It underlies the building of U.S. defense industries, the space race, support for higher education, and even the pursuit of sporting victories at the Olympics. While the relationship between these two superpowers never evolved into open warfare, proxy wars emerged in such places as Korea, Vietnam, the Congo, Afghanistan, and the Middle East, where the two countries' interests were opposed.

Red Badges

- One reason that the Cold War stayed cold is that the United States and the Soviet Union each possessed enough nuclear bombs to devastate the world several times over. Had the Cold War overheated, it might have ended in a worldwide nuclear conflagration.

- Historians date the Cold War from the end of World War II in 1945 to the period between the fall of the Berlin Wall in 1989 and the Soviet Union two years later. The tension had its roots in the Russian revolutions of 1917. Members of the Russian Imperial parliament deposed the tsar, or monarch, in February 1917. Then, in October, the communist Bolsheviks, or "Reds," backed by factory committees and workers' councils, pitted themselves against the military, civil servants, professionals, and peasants—the "Whites"—for control.

- The Reds won. Communist rulers and councils took charge of a new Russian Socialist Federative Soviet Republic, which evolved into the Union of Soviet Socialist Republics (USSR). The Soviet Union embraced the revolutionary political and social philosophy of German philosopher Karl Marx. It formed a single-party government that valued state control of enterprise of property and most everything else. It did not protect individuals' rights and liberties, and it lacked democratic processes.

- The Soviet government was decidedly anticapitalist, discouraging a free-market economy. Although it provided a range of educational, health-care, and housing services, it was often heavy handed, coercing workers and citizens through its police and the threat of military force.

- The U.S. government saw Soviet Communism as antithetical to American life and supported the "White Russians" over the "Red Russians." Nonetheless, some Americans, particularly immigrants from Europe, were comfortable with socialist ideas. During the Great Depression, more and more Americans came to flirt with communism as a vehicle of workers' rights. Much of this support was found within the fledgling labor-union movement.

- A particularly good example is coal mining, which was a tough, brutal, and risky business. Mine owners could make high profits, especially if they skimped on safety or paid low wages. In the United States and abroad, some miners and early unions thought it better for governments, rather than private owners, to operate those mines. The United Mine Workers of America became a battlefield for such competing interests and symbolic of the struggle between the United States and the Soviet Union.

- Delegates to labor conferences wore badges to identify themselves and their industries. Union leaders who supported socialist causes sometimes demonstrated their sympathies with badges that featured red ribbons, red lettering, and red backgrounds.

- Union boss John L. Lewis's badge was different, and so were his views. Lewis allied himself with the GOP through the 1920s. As the Depression deepened, he became a strong supporter of Democratic President Franklin Delano Roosevelt, whose New Deal Program to regulate the nation's economy and restore national prosperity was sometimes deemed "pink"—putting the United States on the road to "red" communism.

- At the Smithsonian is Lewis's union badge from the United Mine Workers' 1936 national convention in Washington DC—which he presided over. It speaks to the era and the heightened awareness about two competing systems of political beliefs. The badge displays a red, white, and blue ribbon; the American eagle; and the Capitol building. Lewis was signaling that unionism was part and parcel of American life.

Bombs

- By the late 1930s, the greatest threat to the United States came not from the Soviet Union but from Germany, Adolf Hitler, and the Nazis. American physicist Albert Einstein heard from European colleagues in 1939 that Germany's experiments with uranium were advancing toward unleashing a massive nuclear chain reaction. It could become the basis for a weapon more powerful than any previously known to man.

- Einstein wrote to President Roosevelt, imploring him to "speed up" experimental work on nuclear fission in the United States. The result was the Manhattan Project, the program that produced the world's first atomic bomb.

- In August 1939, the same month Einstein wrote to FDR, the Soviet Union signed a mutual nonaggression pact with Germany called the Molotov-Ribbentropt Pact. It divided eastern Europe into Soviet and Nazi "spheres of influence." Germany broke the agreement a few days later, invading Poland on September 1. The Soviet Union itself invaded Poland on September 17. But the agreement technically remained in force until the Nazis attacked the Soviets in June 1941.

- The Soviet Union and the United States became war allies after Japan's bombing of Pearl Harbor on December 7, 1941, drew the United States into the global conflict. Together, they stood against the Axis powers, led by Germany and Japan. FDR, Joseph Stalin, and Winston Churchill coordinated military strategy between the Eastern Front, reaching into the Soviet Union, and the Western Front, which encompassed Britain, France, and the Low Countries.

- The war drove the United States to ramp up the development of its atomic bomb. Scientists at Los Alamos, New Mexico, developed two types of bombs under nuclear physicist Robert Oppenheimer. One was a gun-fission explosive made with uranium-235, a rare isotope extracted at a top-secret government installation in Oak Ridge, Tennessee.

- The other was an implosion-type device made with plutonium-239, a synthetic element produced at nuclear reactors in remote, isolated Hanford, Washington. The Smithsonian has a sample of that early plutonium.

- The Allied invasion of Europe under U.S. General Dwight Eisenhower proved successful. So, too, was the progress of the Red Army on the Eastern Front—despite a huge death and casualty count. By April 1945, Soviet troops surrounded the German capital of Berlin and were bombing it to ruin. A month later, Hitler was dead, and the war in Europe ended.

- The Soviets, while occupying the eastern zone of Berlin, turned over three sections of the city to France, the United Kingdom, and the United States, as called for by the diplomatic London Protocol of 1944. It was to be a temporary arrangement until the country could be reconstituted and reunified. That took decades. Meanwhile, the U.S. war effort turned to the Pacific.

- On July 16, 1945, American scientists tested the plutonium version of the atomic bomb at Trinity Site near Alamogordo, New Mexico. In a blinding flash, the unit detonated, demonstrating extraordinary destructive power.

- A second bomb already had been secretly dispatched to the Pacific for use in an upcoming attack on the Japanese city of Hiroshima. U.S. Army Air Forces Colonel Paul Tibbets commanded the newly formed 509th Composite Group, trained for atomic warfare and shrouded in secrecy. The unit consisted of more than 200 officers and 1,500 enlisted men whose work revolved around 15 modified B-29 bombers that were especially equipped to drop a nuclear bomb.

- The B-29s were flown to the Mariana Islands—then controlled by the United States—in July 1945. North Field, on the island of Tinian, became the base for the 509th Composite Group and for launching the upcoming raids on Japan.

- The ultimate decision rested with Harry S Truman, who became president in April 1945 upon the death of Franklin Roosevelt. Even though Germany had surrendered, the Japanese military leadership fought on. U.S. military leaders were planning for a land invasion of Japan that might stretch into 1946 and beyond. They were convinced that the assault would lead to hundreds of thousands of U.S. casualties. A nuclear bomb would inflict unprecedented destruction yet might render an invasion unnecessary.

- Impressed by the Trinity test at Alomogordo, New Mexico, Truman was ready to proceed. On July 26, 1945, Churchill and Chinese leader Chang Kai-shek joined Truman in issuing the Potsdam Declaration, calling for Japan to offer unconditional surrender or face "prompt and utter destruction." Japan's leaders rejected the declaration.

- When Truman gave the go-ahead, Tibbets decided to pilot the mission himself. He named the B-29 Superfortress he would fly after his mother: *Enola Gay*. The bomb, designated "Little Boy"—the uranium version not previously tested—was loaded on August 5. Its target, Hiroshima, was a port city and military center surrounded by hills that would magnify the blast's effects.

Enola Gay

- Approximately 8,000 people were killed as a direct result of the blast. As many as 55,000 more died in coming months due to related injuries and radiation sickness.

- A few days later, with no Japanese surrender forthcoming, the U.S. B-29 bomber *Bockscar* dropped a plutonium bomb, the "Fat Man," on Nagasaki. The devastation and casualties from this August 9 attack were again horrendous.

- On August 15, in a radio address to the nation, Japanese Emperor Hirohito announced the country's surrender. The war was over. The nuclear age had begun. Today, the *Enola Gay* is on display at the Smithsonian.

The Berlin Wall

- After the war, historical tensions between the Soviet Union and the West—primarily the United States, Britain, and France—resurfaced and hardened. The Soviet army installed communist governments in eastern European countries it now controlled, producing a geopolitical fault line between the former allies.

- Berlin became the focal point. When the United States, France, and Britain devised plans to unite their occupation zones in West Berlin in 1948 to better integrate it with the rest of western Germany, the Soviets reacted with the Berlin blockade, cutting off all road corridors to the city.

- Realizing that this amounted to a siege of the two million inhabitants in the western part of the city, the Western Allies countered with the Berlin airlift, a massive, expensive, and complex lifeline to the local population. The air bridge, as Berliners called it, continued for 11 months, until May 1949 when the Soviets relented, once again allowing trucks and vehicles to pass into Berlin.

- During the Cold War, the possibility of nuclear confrontation between the two superpowers loomed large in the public imagination. When the Soviets successfully detonated their first nuclear weapon on August 29, 1949, in present-day Kazakhstan, it was widely interpreted as a warning that the United States was now vulnerable to nuclear attack.

- Governments in the United States and Europe began to designate reinforced underground bunkers as safe retreats for high-ranking officials in the event of nuclear attack. In the civilian sector, existing public buildings with sturdy basements were designated as fallout shelters.

- The U.S. Federal Civilian Defense Administration distributed information broadly on how to survive a nuclear attack. Instructive films were distributed to schools, where children practiced federally mandated—and, in actuality, pointless—"duck and cover" drills. The government also published plans for how people could build their own fallout shelters, endorsing the idea that Americans could survive nuclear war one family at a time.

- The fallout shelter illustrates a pervasive fear of nuclear attack and its aftermath at the height of the Cold War between the United States and the Soviet Union. Shelters, such as one at the Smithsonian that was installed in 1955 in Fort Wayne, Indiana, were equipped with generators for power and filtered-air ventilation.

- Tensions between the Soviet Union and the West escalated around the world and continued to fuel fears of nuclear war into the 1960s. Nowhere were they felt as directly nor so acutely as in Berlin. Thousands of German citizens fled through politically repressed and economically depressed eastern Berlin to seek work, wages, and a better quality of life in the democratically oriented and more prosperous western sector of the city.

- On the evening of August 13, 1961, as most residents slept, the embattled East German government began to close the border between the two halves of the city. Troops installed barbed-wire fences, with concrete blocks to follow. In a few months' time, a wall 12 feet high and 103 miles long imprisoned East Berliners.

- Official checkpoints regulated travel between East and West, replete with armed military officials and guard dogs. West Berliners were initially kept away from the wall by West German police and by U.S. military support troops, so as not to provoke an armed response.

- Berlin wasn't the only hot spot in the Cold War. In October 1962, the Soviets clandestinely installed ballistic missiles in Cuba, 90 miles from Florida. President John F. Kennedy launched an embargo to prevent the Soviet navy and merchant ships from resupplying the island nation. A dangerous military confrontation was at hand that could escalate into a nuclear exchange.

- In its aftermath, the crisis was interpreted as demonstrating the concept of mutually assured destruction, the idea that neither the United States nor Russia would launch a nuclear attack knowing the other could retaliate in kind. Nonetheless, Cold War conflict and tensions continued.

- As a symbol of the Cold War, the wall grimly persisted for decades. Over time, West Berliners painted their side in bright colors,

Fallout Shelter

taunting the Communists with graffiti messages of freedom, both poignant and irreverent. Easterners, though allowed to cross in theory, were rarely permitted to do so, for fear they would defect.

- In 1987, U.S. President Ronald Reagan stood at the Berlin Wall to deliver a direct challenge to the Soviet Union and its leader, Mikhail Gorbachev: "Mr. Gorbachev, tear down this wall!" Gorbachev did not tear down the wall, but holes in the Iron Curtain were opening in Hungary and Poland. And East Germany was a failing state.

- On November 9, 1989, unexpected news spread throughout Berlin: There would no longer be travel restrictions between East and West. It turns out that a minor official had spoken in error, but it was too late. Berliners on both sides of the wall joyfully began to dismantle it in a celebration of freedom. Government authorities did nothing to stop them.

- A chunk of the Berlin Wall came to the Smithsonian from John F. W. Rogers, who served in the Reagan White House and accompanied the president to Berlin. He had seen the wall and couldn't ever imagine it coming down. When it did, Rogers returned to Berlin to see for himself. He and his friends encountered a German with a hammer and chisel, removing chunks of the Wall. The man offered the Americans his tools so that they could join in the demolition. Rogers then did what he thought would never be possible—he helped dismantle this barrier to freedom and foremost symbol of the Cold War.

Featured Objects

John L. Lewis's Labor Union Medal

Enola Gay

Fallout Shelter

Berlin Wall

Suggested Reading

Rose, *One Nation Underground.*

Taylor, *The Berlin Wall.*

Walker, *Prompt and Utter Destruction.*

Cold War—Red Badges, Bombs, and the Berlin Wall
Lecture 14—Transcript

The overwhelming American foreign policy and defense issue during the latter half of the 20th century was the Cold War with the Soviet Union. That conflict, part ideological, part practical, permeated American life. It underlies the building of U.S. defense industries, the space race, support for higher education, and even the pursuit of sporting victories at the Olympics. While the relationship between those two superpowers never evolved into open warfare, proxy wars emerged in such places as Korea, Vietnam, the Congo, Afghanistan, Middle East, where the two countries' opposed interests clashed. The Cuban Missile Crisis of 1962 was as close as we've ever come to a hot conflict.

One reason this Cold War stayed cold is that the United States and the Soviet Union each possessed enough nuclear weapons to devastate the world several times over. Had the Cold War over-heated, it might have ended in a world-wide nuclear conflagration. Historians date the Cold War from the end of World War II in 1945 to the period between the fall of the Berlin Wall in 1989 and the Soviet Union two years later.

The tension had its roots in the Russian revolutions of 1917. Members of the Russian Imperial parliament deposed the tsar, or monarch, in February 1917. Then in October, the communist Bolsheviks, or Reds, as they were called, backed by factory workers and worker councils, pitted themselves against the military, civil servants, professionals and peasants; they were called the Whites. The Reds won. Communist rulers and councils took charge of a new Russian Socialist Federative Soviet Republic, which evolved into the Union of Soviet Socialist Republics, or the U.S.S.R. The Soviet Union embraced the revolutionary political and social philosophy of German philosopher Karl Marx. It formed a single-party government that valued state control of enterprise, control of property, and most everything else. It did not protect individuals rights and liberties, and it lacked democratic processes. The Soviet government was decidedly anti-capitalist, discouraging a free-market economy. Though it provided a range of educational, health, and housing services, it was often heavy handed, coercing workers and citizens through its police and the threat of military force.

The U.S. government saw Soviet Communism as antithetical to American life and supported the White Russians over the Red Russians. Nonetheless, some Americans, particularly immigrants from Europe, were more comfortable with socialist ideas. During the Great Depression, more and more Americans came to flirt with communism as a vehicle of workers' rights. Much of this support was found within the fledgling labor-union movement.

Coal miners were a particularly good example. Coal mining was a tough, brutal, risky business, but vital to an industrialized economy. Mine owners could make high profits, especially if they skimped on safety, or paid low wages. In the United States and abroad, some miners and early unions thought it better for governments, rather than private owners, to operate those mines. The United Mine Workers of America became such a battlefield for competing interests and symbolic of the struggle between the United States and the Soviet Union. You can see all of this if you look closely at a badge that union boss John L. Lewis wore to the United Mine Workers' 1936 national convention in Washington, DC; convened in the nation's capital, it promoted the union's closeness to American democracy.

Labor unions all over the world had been issuing commemorative badges since the 1830s. Some were cast for special events, such as an important work project, or a strike, or a funeral. Delegates to labor conferences wore the badges to identify themselves and their industries. Union leaders who supported socialist causes sometimes demonstrated their sympathies with badges that featured red ribbons, red lettering, and red backgrounds. Some featured engravings of the world's continents, indicating a class-oriented struggle, or a handshake, symbolizing workers' solidarity.

Lewis's badge was different and so were his views. Born into a Republican household, Lewis allied himself with the GOP through the 1920s even though some of his closest advisers had Marxist leanings. As the Depression deepened, he became a strong supporter of Democratic President Franklin Delano Roosevelt, whose New Deal Program to regulate the nation's economy and restore national prosperity was sometimes deemed "pink," putting the U.S. on the road to red communism. Lewis, like Roosevelt, sought to clothe New Deal progressivism in traditional American concepts of fairness. And we have at the Smithsonian Lewis's union badge from that

1936 convention, which he presided over. It really speaks to the era and the heightened awareness about two competing systems of political beliefs. Note the red, white, and blue ribbon, the American eagle, and the Capitol building. Lewis was very clearly signaling that unionism was part and parcel of American life.

By the late 1930s, the greatest threat to the United States came not from the Soviet Union, but from Germany, Adolf Hitler, and the Nazis. American physicist Albert Einstein heard from European colleagues in 1939 that Germany's experiments with uranium were advancing toward unleashing a massive chain reaction. It could become the basis for a weapon more powerful than anything known to mankind. Einstein wrote to President Roosevelt imploring him to "speed up" experimental work on nuclear fission in the United States. The result was the Manhattan Project, the program that produced the world's first atomic bomb.

In August 1939, the same month Einstein wrote FDR, the Soviet Union signed a mutual non-aggression pact with Germany, called the Molotov-Ribbentropt Pact. It divided Eastern Europe into Soviet and Nazi spheres of influence. Germany broke the agreement a few days later, invading Poland on September 1. The Soviet Union, itself, invaded Poland on September 17. But the agreement, technically, remained in force until the Nazis attacked the Soviets in June 1941.

The Soviet Union and the United States became war allies after Japan's bombing of Pearl Harbor on December 7, 1941, and that drew the United States into global conflict. Together—the United States and the Soviet Union—stood against the Axis powers led by Germany and Japan. Roosevelt; Stalin; and Britain's leader, Winston Churchill, coordinated military strategy between the Eastern front, reaching into the Soviet Union, and the Western front, which encompassed Britain, France, and the Low Countries .

The war drove the United States to ramp up the development of its atomic bomb. Scientists at Los Alamos, New Mexico, developed two types of bomb under nuclear physicist Robert Oppenheimer. One was a gun-fission explosive made with uranium-235, a rare isotope extracted at a top-secret government installation in Oak Ridge, Tennessee, a town that did not appear on any public map at the time. The other was an implosion-type device made with plutonium-239, a synthetic element produced at nuclear reactors in remote, and isolated, Hanford, Washington. We have a sample of that early plutonium at the Smithsonian. It came to us as it was stored, in a cigar box. But it is perfectly safe.

Many assumed the first atomic bomb would be used against Germany. But that proved unnecessary. The Allied invasion of Europe under U.S. General Dwight Eisenhower proved successful. So, too, was the progress of the Red Army on the Eastern front, despite a huge death and casualty count. By April 1945, Soviet troops surrounded the German capital, of Berlin, and were bombing it to ruin. A month later, Hitler was dead and the war in Europe ended.

The Soviets, while occupying the eastern zone of Berlin, turned over three sections of the city to France, the United Kingdom, and the United States, as called for by the diplomatic London Protocol of 1944. It was to be a temporary arrangement until the country could be reconstituted and reunified. It took decades. Meanwhile, the United States pursued the war in the Pacific.

On July 16, 1945, American scientists tested the plutonium version of the atomic bomb at Trinity Site near Alamogordo, New Mexico. To quote Brigadier General Thomas Farrell, who witnessed the experiment, "We were reaching into the unknown and we did not know what might come of it," In a blinding flash, the unit detonated, demonstrating extraordinary destructive power. A second bomb already had been secretly dispatched to the Pacific for use in an upcoming attack on the Japanese city of Hiroshima. U.S. Army Air Force Colonel Paul Tibbets commanded the newly formed 509th Composite Group, trained for atomic warfare and shrouded in secrecy. It had begun developing a plan to deliver atomic payloads the previous December. The unit consisted of more than 200 officers and some 1,500 enlisted men whose work revolved around 15 modified B-29 bombers.

The B-29s were manufactured by the Glenn Martin Company in Bellevue, Nebraska and especially equipped to drop a nuclear bomb. Among the modifications were a bomb bay with pneumatic doors, special propellers, modified engine, and, placing pilot and crew at heightened risk, the elimination of protective armor and gun turrets, to reduce the weight of the aircraft. The B-29s were flown to the Mariana Islands, then controlled by the United Sates; that happened in July 1945. North Field, on the island of Tinian, became the base for the 509th and for launching the upcoming raids on Japan. But the ultimate decision rested with Harry S. Truman, who had become president in April 1945 upon the death of Franklin Roosevelt.

Even though Germany had surrendered, the Japanese military leadership had fought on. The war in the Pacific was brutal, with 100,000 U.S. military personnel dead. U.S. military leaders were planning for a land invasion of Japan that might stretch into 1946, or even beyond. And they were convinced the assault would lead to hundreds of thousands of U.S. casualties, indeed, they'd ordered 500,000 Purple Heart medals, anticipating mass casualties. They also sought alternatives. One was to use poisonous gas. A massive B-29 fire-bombing campaign had devastated Japanese cities but not forced the Japanese to surrender. A nuclear bomb would inflict unprecedented destruction, yet might render an invasion and all those casualties unnecessary.

Impressed by the Trinity test at Alomogordo, Truman was ready to proceed. On July 26, 1945, Churchill and Chang Kai-shek joined Truman in issuing the Potsdam Declaration, calling for Japan to offer unconditional surrender or face "prompt and utter destruction." Allied forces broadcast the key points to Japan and even dropped flyers alerting the civilian population, but Japan's leaders rejected the declaration and were determined to fight on.

When Truman gave the go-ahead, Tibbets decided to pilot the mission himself. He named the B-29 Superfortress he would fly after his mother, Enola Gay. Her name was painted on its nose. The bomb, designated Little Boy—the uranium version not previously tested—was loaded on August 5. Its target, Hiroshima, was a port city and military center surrounded by hills that would magnify the blast's effects. The *Enola Gay* had a crew of 12, but only three men—Tibbets, the weaponeer, and the bombardier—were aware of the nature of the mission before takeoff. The Superfortress left Tinian at 2:45 a.m. Two other B-29s—the *Necessary Evil*, carrying scientific observers and cameras, and the *Great Artiste*, with instruments to record blast measurements—departed separately. The three planes rendezvoused over Iwo Jima and set their course for Hiroshima.

The atomic explosive was armed in the air. Though Japanese radar detected the approach of American planes, the Japanese failed to intercept them with either fighters or antiaircraft batteries, assuming that the enemy's small formation would inflict only limited damage. An American reconnaissance aircraft, the Straight Flush, reported clear skies. The *Enola Gay* arrived at 8:09 a.m., flying at about 32,000 feet. Six minutes later the *Enola Gay* dropped its payload.

The bomb exploded at its predetermined altitude 1,900 feet above the city. Because of crosswinds, it missed the bridge, exploding with the force of about 12,500 tons of TNT over the Shima Surgical Clinic. A mushroom cloud rose into the sky. And much of the city was leveled. Approximately 80,000 people were killed as a direct result of the blast, and as many as 55,000 more died in the coming months due to related injuries and radiation sickness.

The *Enola Gay* crew was both awed and cheered as they surveyed the damage and returned to base. A few days later, with no Japanese surrender forthcoming, the U.S. B-29 bomber Bockscar dropped a plutonium bomb, called the Fat Man, on Nagasaki. The devastation and casualties from this August 9 attack were again horrendous. The message was clear: The United States had the ability and will to unleash multiple atomic attacks on Japan. August 15, in a radio address to the nation, Japanese Emperor Hirohito announced the country's surrender. The war was over, but the nuclear age had begun.

Today, the *Enola Gay* is on display at the Smithsonian. After the war, historical tensions between the Soviet Union and the West, primarily the U.S., Britain, and France, resurfaced and hardened. The Soviet army installed communist governments in Eastern European countries it now controlled, producing a geo-political fault line between the former allies. Speaking in Fulton, Missouri, in March 1946, Winston Churchill provided a graphic image of this division to the American public. He said, "From Stettin in the Baltic to Trieste in the Adriatic, an iron curtain has descended across the Continent," he said. Berlin became the focal point. When the United States, France, and Britain devised plans to unite their occupation zones in western Berlin in 1948 to better integrate it with the rest of western Germany, the Soviets reacted with the Berlin Blockade, cutting off all road corridors to the city.

Realizing that this amounted to a siege of two million inhabitants in the western part of the city, the Western allies countered with the Berlin Airlift, a massive, expensive, and complex lifeline to the local population. The air bridge, as Berliners called it, continued for 11 months until May 1949 when the Soviets finally relented, again, allowing trucks and vehicles to pass into Berlin.

During the cold war, the possibility of nuclear confrontation between the two superpowers loomed large in the public imagination to an extent that is today very difficult for us to imagine. When the Soviets successfully detonated their first nuclear weapon on August 29, 1949 in present-day Kazakhstan, it was widely interpreted as a warning that the United States itself was now vulnerable to nuclear attack. Further driving American fears was growing awareness of the terrible aftereffects of radiation exposure. Popular culture responded with such artifacts as the 1954 film Godzilla, featuring a monster born from the effects of the nuclear warfare in Japan.

Just as emphatically, governments in the United States and Europe began to designate reinforced underground bunkers as safe retreats for high-ranking officials in the event of nuclear attack. The luxury Greenbrier Resort in White Sulphur Springs, West Virginia, 248 miles from Washington, DC, was outfitted with an elaborate underground facility capable of housing high-ranking federal officials for up to several months at a time. In the civilian sector, existing public buildings with sturdy basements were designated as fallout shelters.

The U.S. Federal Civil Defense Administration distributed information broadly on how to survive a nuclear attack. Instructive films were distributed to schools, where children practiced federally mandated, and in actuality, pointless duck-and-cover drills. The government also published plans for how people could build their own fallout shelters, endorsing the idea that Americans could survive nuclear war, one family at a time.

In the Midwest, a tradition of residential storm cellars already existed to shelter families from tornadoes. In other parts of the country, people latched on to this idea, updating their own basements with heavy concrete or lead lining to protect against radiation and stocking the shelves with supplies, including a recommended seven gallons of water per person, that's half a gallon per day; non-perishable food; receptacles for human waste; a first-aid kit; a flashlight; and a battery-operated radio for news of the outside world. The FCDA also recommended storing board games, books, and magazines to help pass the time until it was safe to emerge from one's basement.

The fallout shelter illustrates a pervasive fear of nuclear attack and its aftermath at the height of the cold war between the United States and the Soviet Union. Shelters, such as this one at the Smithsonian, were equipped with generators for power and filtered-air ventilation. Their decorations tended to be, well, quite spartan, reflecting a very grim, survivalist aesthetic. This particular unit, a freestanding, double-hulled steel structure, was installed in 1955 beneath the front yard of Mr. and Mrs. Murland Anderson of Fort Wayne, Indiana. Local residents were concerned they might become targets due to the large number of military industrial sites in the Fort Wayne region. They, like thousands of other American families, went to extremes to protect themselves from a potential nuclear catastrophe.

Tensions between the Soviet Union and the West escalated around the world and continued to fuel fears of nuclear war into the 1960s. Nowhere were they felt as directly nor so acutely as in Berlin. Thousands of German citizens fled through politically repressed and economically depressed eastern Berlin to seek work, wages, and better quality of life in the democratically oriented and more prosperous western sector of the city.

On the evening of August 13, 1961, as most residents of Berlin slept, the embattled East German government began to close the border between the two halves of the city. Troops installed barbed-wire fences with concrete blocks to follow. In a few months' time, a wall 12 feet high and 103 miles long imprisoned East Berliners. The government called this barrier the anti-fascist protection wall, implying that its purpose was to protect citizens from the pernicious and dangerous influences of the West. However, everyone knew its real purpose.

Official checkpoints regulated travel between East and West, replete with armed military officials and guard dogs. West Berliners were initially kept away from the wall by West German police and by U.S. military troops, so as not to provoke an armed response from the East Germans.

Berlin wasn't the only hot spot, however, in the Cold War. In October 1962, the Soviets clandestinely installed ballistic missiles in Cuba, 90 miles from Florida. President John F. Kennedy launched an embargo to prevent the Soviet navy and merchant ships from resupplying the island nation. A dangerous military confrontation was at hand that could escalate into a possible nuclear exchange. I was a young teenager during the Cuban Missile Crisis, and I remember thinking that I would have 19 minutes to retrieve my younger brother in elementary school, hurry home, and hide in a nearby community basement fallout shelter in the event of a nuclear attack.

In its aftermath, the crisis was interpreted as demonstrating the concept of mutually assured destruction, the idea that neither the United States nor Russia would actually launch a nuclear attack knowing that the other would retaliate in kind. And whether because of an increased public sense of futility or through extended exposure to the concept of nuclear annihilation, nuclear fallout shelters became somewhat passé. A number of films, novels, and television programs satirized America's bunker mentality and the futility of public safety efforts, along with Cold War stereotypes.

Nonetheless, Cold War conflict and tensions continued. U.S. President John F. Kennedy visited West Berlin. The president declared:

> Freedom has many difficulties and democracy is not perfect . . . but we never had to put up a wall to keep our people in. All free men, wherever they may live, are citizens of Berlin, and therefore, as a free man, I take pride in the words, "Ich bin ein Berliner."

As a symbol of the Cold War, the wall grimly persisted for decades. Over time, West Berliners painted their side in bright colors, taunting the Communists with graffiti images of freedom, both poignant and irreverent. Easterners, though allowed to cross in theory, were rarely permitted to do so for fear they would defect. In the decades following its construction, about

5,000 people escaped over the wall or under it, through tunnels that were far more effective than above-ground gambits. Officially, 136 people were killed trying to cross the wall. The actual number could be several times greater. Hundreds more were seriously injured, mainly, when the sandy soil beneath the wall caused the makeshift tunnels to collapse.

In 1987, United States President Ronald Reagan stood at the Berlin Wall to deliver a direct challenge to the Soviet Union and its leader, Mikhail Gorbachev:

> There is one sign the Soviets can make that would be unmistakable, that would advance dramatically the cause of freedom and peace. General Secretary Gorbachev, if you seek peace, if you seek prosperity for the Soviet Union and Eastern Europe, if you seek liberalization: Come here to this gate! Mr. Gorbachev, open this gate! Mr. Gorbachev, tear down this wall!

Gorbachev did not tear down the wall, but holes in the Iron Curtain were opening in Hungary and Poland. And in East Germany, it was turning into a failing state.

On November 9, 1989, unexpected news spread throughout Berlin; there would no longer be travel restrictions between East and the West. It turns out that a minor official had spoken in error, but it was too late. Berliners on both sides of the wall joyfully began to dismantle it in a celebration of freedom. Government authorities did nothing to stop them.

This chunk of the Berlin Wall came to the Smithsonian from John Rogers, who served in the Reagan White House and accompanied the president to Berlin. He'd seen the wall, and he couldn't ever imagine it coming down. When it did, Rogers returned to Berlin to see for himself. He and his friends encountered a German with a hammer and chisel, removing chunks of the Wall. The man offered the Americans his tools so they, too, could join in the demolition. Having left government work by this time, Rogers then did what he thought he would never be able to do —he personally helped dismantle this barrier to freedom and foremost symbol of the Cold War. Now, the Smithsonian typically likes its treasures in one piece. This one has special meaning precisely because it's broken.

National Tragedy—*Maine*, Pearl Harbor, 9/11
Lecture 15

Sadly, the Smithsonian's collections include items that bear witness to our most devastating national tragedies—tragedies that not only involved tremendous loss of human life, but also drove America into war. In this lecture, you will learn the stories behind a bugle from the USS *Maine*, hand stamps from the USS *Oklahoma*, and several objects from the September 11 attacks. These artifacts help us understand the American experience on both a geopolitical and a personal scale. They are ordinary, mundane objects that have extraordinary significance.

Maine

- The United States had long expressed an interest in Cuba, which had been under Spanish control since the time of Christopher Columbus. Indeed, after the Mexican-American War in the 1840s, the United States sought to buy Cuba from Spain, but was rebuffed. Some Southerners envisioned a Cuba that would be aligned with pro-slave states. Others saw it as a way station for freed slaves being repatriated to Liberia.

- Meanwhile, the Cubans themselves had begun to resist Spanish rule. Rebel forces fought a 10-year war, from 1868 to 1878, before being suppressed by Spanish authorities. Then, in 1891, Cuban independence leader José Martí established a U.S. headquarters for the revolutionary movement.

- In 1895, Martí led an armed force into Cuba, but once more, the rebels were unsuccessful. Even so, and even though Martí was killed in the conflict, the rebels continued to pursue their goal through a series of guerrilla actions.

- As these events were unfolding, various U.S. interests debated policies toward Cuba. During his second term in the 1890s, President Grover Cleveland estimated U.S. commercial investment in Cuba at about 100 million dollars—largely in sugar plantations, mining, and railroads. This was, Cleveland recognized, a crucial investment that had to be protected.

- In addition, during the second half of the 19th century, the United States was fast becoming the leading manufacturing nation in the world. The country needed markets for its steel, oil, cotton, and manufactured products. To American businesses, this meant new markets beyond our borders.

- Establishing footholds or even control over the Philippines, Panama, Cuba, and other places would give the United States commercial markets, military bases, canals, and facilities so that it could take its place as one of the greatest and most powerful nations in the world. With that grand goal in mind, Roosevelt was practically spoiling for a fight with the Spanish over Cuba.

- Of course, there were many Americans, including many businessmen, who opposed American military intervention in Cuba. For them, stability in Cuba was more important than victory over Spain. So, when William McKinley became president in 1897, he inherited a complex diplomatic situation.

- This complexity is reflected in the fact that the McKinley administration was negotiating with Spain about Cuba's future even as the United States built up its naval presence in the Caribbean to show the flag and pressure the Spanish. The situation only got thornier when a pro-Spanish riot broke out in Cuba's capital city of Havana in January 1898.

- In response to the riot, McKinley sent the battleship *Maine* into Havana harbor, an action he thought necessary to protect American interests there. But because America took this step without informing Spanish authorities first, it was viewed as a provocation.

- On the night of February 15, 1898, the battleship USS *Maine* blew up in the harbor of Havana, Cuba, killing 266 American sailors.

What actually caused the explosion and sent the ship to its watery grave is still a mystery. But the destruction of the *Maine* outraged the American people and ultimately propelled the nation into the Spanish-American War.

- The U.S. Navy conducted an investigation and concluded that the ship's stock of ammunition had been set afire by an external mine. Subsequent investigations, including one conducted in 1976, have failed to find evidence in support of this conclusion.

- Newspapers quickly blamed the Spanish for sinking the *Maine* and called for war. "Remember the *Maine*, to hell with Spain," they proclaimed. "Remember the *Maine*" soon appeared on a variety of souvenirs. It was the rallying cry of the war.

- In the weeks after the tragedy, the business community increasingly saw military action as the only viable course. President McKinley agreed, and in April, he issued an ultimatum to Spain: Either give up your colony—to the United States, not to the rebels—or face war. Spain's response was to declare war on the United States on April 24.

- The Spanish-American War did not last long—about four months. The U.S. Navy was far superior, and the Spanish military forces had been weakened by internal rebellion in Cuba and an independence movement in the Philippines. By December, the parties had signed the Treaty of Paris.

- Spain relinquished its sovereignty over Cuba, ceding temporary control of the island to the United States. It also gave up its colonies of Puerto Rico, Guam, and the Philippines to the United States. Whatever its cause, the destruction of the *Maine* had played its part in creating a new geopolitical order.

- On a smaller scale, the aftermath of the explosion was a story of recovery and salvage. In 1899, the U.S. Navy retrieved some of the human remains and other items from the *Maine*. The Smithsonian

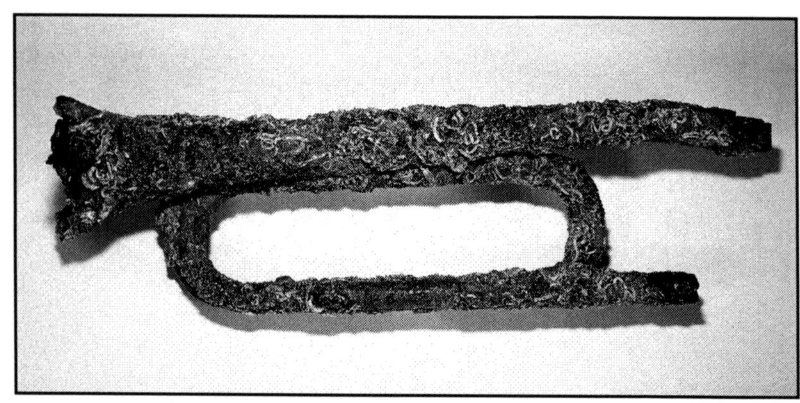

Bugle from *Maine*

sought and received the ship's steering wheel and prominently displayed it in the National Museum.

- But it wasn't until 1910 that Congress provided funds for a complete salvage operation. In March 16, 1912, the ship's intact wreckage was floated out to sea and—amid somber, patriotic ceremony—sunk. The human remains were buried at Arlington National Cemetery, and the ship's mast was installed there as a memorial.

- Other artifacts from the ship—anchors, bells, life preservers, guns—were distributed to the Naval Academy, Naval Yards, parks, courthouses, and museums. The bugle played by marine fifer C. H. Newton mere minutes before his death in the explosion came to the Smithsonian. It serves as a reminder of a crucial moment in world history, a moment that marked the end of the Spanish empire and a new era of American expansionism.

Pearl Harbor

- On December 7, 1941, the Imperial Japanese Navy launched a surprise attack against the U.S. naval base at Pearl Harbor, Hawaii. More than 350 Japanese planes, launched from aircraft carriers, descended on the base. And the result was devastation: more than

2,400 Americans killed and almost 1,200 wounded, and almost 200 U.S. aircraft destroyed. In a little less than two hours, the Japanese had immobilized the entire U.S. Pacific Fleet.

- One of the battleships that sank that day was the USS *Oklahoma*. Commissioned in May 1916, the *Oklahoma* had protected World War I convoys across the Atlantic Ocean. It had escorted President Woodrow Wilson to peace negotiations in France in 1919. And it had helped rescue refugees fleeing the Spanish Civil War. Since 1937, the battleship had been based at Pearl Harbor for patrols and exercises.

- Like all naval ships, the *Oklahoma* was equipped to offer postal services. Of course, this was important for military communications, but it also gave the crew a vital link to family and friends back home. For sailors on the *Oklahoma*, outgoing letters were stamped by hand in the shipboard post office.

- Such hand stamps indicated the date and general time a letter or parcel was mailed and if any special services were required, such as registered or special delivery. They showed the originating post office—in this case, in capital letters, "U.S.S. OKLAHOMA." The Smithsonian holds two hand stamps that were salvaged from the *Oklahoma*.

- The postal clerks last stamped the mail on Saturday, December 6, 1941. They used the two hand stamps that are now in the Smithsonian, both of which indicate the date. Navy postal clerks on *Oklahoma* did not have the chance to change the date on the hand stamps before the attack on Pearl Harbor began early Sunday morning.

- Moored in Battleship Row, *Oklahoma* was hit on its port side by three torpedoes at the outset of the attack. It had already begun to capsize when it was hit by more torpedoes, reportedly nine in all. Within minutes, *Oklahoma* rolled over on its side, its keel exposed. Hundreds were trapped inside and in danger of being drowned or killed.

- By around 10 am, the attack was over. The surviving sailors took small boats out into the harbor to search the wreckage. As they passed the *Oklahoma*, they heard the sound of tapping coming from inside the hull. After a two-day rescue attempt, 32 trapped seamen were freed through holes cut into the bottom of the ship. They were among the fortunate. Of the more than 2,100 men serving on the *Oklahoma*, 429 were listed as killed or missing.

- As for the *Oklahoma* itself, the ship lay in the harbor, inoperable and severely damaged. About seven months after the attack on Pearl Harbor, the Navy began complex salvage operations. It took almost a year to right the ship. Navy teams removed human remains as well as other items. Then, the ship was towed to dry dock, where guns, machinery, and ammunition were salvaged.

- Although the hull was repaired, initial plans to reuse the ship were canceled, and it was decommissioned in 1944. While being towed across the Pacific to a San Francisco scrap yard in 1947, *Oklahoma* started taking on water and sank.

- The hand stamps survived the attack on Pearl Harbor. Recovered by the Navy, they were subsequently turned over to the Post Office Department, which transferred them to the Smithsonian in the mid-1960s.

- On their last day of regular use, clerks stamped mail that made its way back home. Some of these letters were the last communication that families would ever receive from their loved ones, a powerful reminder of the role that mail played during wartime.

USS *Oklahoma* duplex handstamp

9/11

- On September 11, 2001, nearly 3,000 people died in terrorist attacks, as hijackers working under the auspices of al Qaeda took control of four commercial jets. One of these jets, American Airlines Flight 11, crashed into the North Tower of the World Trade Center. A few minutes later, the hijackers flew United Airlines Flight 175 into the South Tower. Then, American Airlines Flight 77 slammed into the Pentagon outside Washington DC. The fourth airliner, United Airlines Flight 93, crashed to the ground near Shanksville, Pennsylvania.

- The results were horrific. All the passengers and crew members on the airplanes perished. At the World Trade Center, thousands made their way down the stairs and survived; however, hundreds were trapped in the buildings' upper floors. About 200 people jumped or fell to their deaths to avoid fires caused by the crash; most of the victims died as the towers collapsed. As with the sinking of the *Maine* and the attack on Pearl Harbor, the events of 9/11 drove America to war.

- Extraordinary courage was displayed by ordinary Americans on that day. On Flight 93, passengers rushed the cabin to fight for control of the plane. Their bravery succeeded in derailing the terrorists' plan to crash the plane into either the U.S. Capitol or the White House.

- At the Pentagon, civilians and military personnel courageously pulled their coworkers away from the flames of the jet that had crashed through the building's outer wall.

- In New York, members of the police and fire departments rushed to the scene in lower Manhattan. Hundreds entered the World Trade Center towers and climbed the stairs to rescue survivors, while others treated victims on the ground. More than 400 first responders became victims themselves when the buildings collapsed.

- In the months that followed these tragic losses, the Smithsonian assumed the responsibility of collecting and preserving artifacts so that future generations will have a concrete record of what America went through on September 11, 2001.

- One of these items is a remnant of the World Trade Center's external sheathing. Apart from their sheer size, one of the most arresting qualities of the 110-story Twin Towers was their gleaming exterior. Brilliant white at midday, the buildings took on a golden sheen at sunrise and sunset. This was the effect of the highly reflective aluminum alloy sheathing, which magnified the towers' soaring appearance and enhanced their stature as New York City landmarks.

- Another poignant item is the crash-scarred logbook of Lorraine Bay, a 37-year veteran flight attendant and one of the seven crew members who perished on United Flight 93.

- Another moving artifact is the crumpled door of a pumper engine from the New York City Fire Department's Squad Company 1, an elite group charged with responding quickly to emergency situations. Twelve firefighters from Company 1 lost their lives trying to rescue trapped office workers from the South Tower.

- Another artifact is held at the Smithsonian's Postal Museum. Cognizant of the story of the USS *Oklahoma*, museum curators were able to recover a hand stamp from New York's Church Street post office, which serviced the World Trade Center. It bears the date of the attack, "Sep 11, 2001."

- Another item was acquired a few months after the attacks. In 1989, the Public Art Fund of New York City funded the installation of Roy Lichtenstein's sculpture *Modern Head* in Battery Park City, one block from the World Trade Center. This 31-foot sculpture survived the attacks with only surface scratches and was temporarily used by the FBI as a message board during its investigations. It was removed a few months later and subsequently was donated to the Smithsonian, where it is now installed outside the Smithsonian American Art Museum in Washington DC.

- One year after the terrorists struck, many of the objects collected by the Smithsonian were displayed in an exhibition entitled *September 11: Bearing Witness to History*. The conservators even coated a column fragment from the World Trade Center in wax so that people could touch it, which tens of thousands did.

- A decade later, the Smithsonian opened a temporary special exhibit, placing a small number of September 11 objects on tables with simple cloth coverings. The artifacts were not in cases and were directly accessible. Experts stood by to talk or answer questions; however, visitors were largely left to experience the articles on their own.

- One of these special objects is a crowbar that belonged to Lt. Kevin Pfeifer from the Engine Company 33. He used it to help save others, directing them out of the North Tower. But that day it could not save Pfeifer, who perished when the tower came down. It is a simple object, but it is part of a big story that in some way has affected every American.

Featured Objects

Bugle from *Maine*

Postal Hand Stamps from *Oklahoma*

NYFD Crowbar from 9/11

Suggested Reading

Berner, *The Spanish-American War*.

Greenwald and Chanin, eds., *The Stories They Tell.*

Prange, *At Dawn We Slept*.

National Tragedy—*Maine*, Pearl Harbor, 9/11

Lecture 15—Transcript

Sadly, the Smithsonian collections include items that bear witness to our most devastating national tragedies, tragedies that not only involved tremendous loss of human life but also drove America into war. Among the more dramatic of these artifacts is the bugle from the USS *Maine*.

On the night February 15, 1898, the battleship *Maine* blew up in the harbor of Havana, Cuba, killing 266 American sailors. What actually caused the explosion and sent the ship to its watery grave is still a mystery, but the destruction of the *Maine* outraged the American people and ultimately propelled the nation into the Spanish-American War. Thus, this bugle, that was recovered from the wreckage of the *Maine*, is a reminder of a crucial moment in world history, a moment that marked the end of the Spanish empire and a new era of American expansion.

To understand the significance of that February night in 1898, we need to understand what was going on in Cuba at the time and what the *Maine* was doing in Havana harbor in the first place. The United States had long expressed an interest in Cuba, which had been under Spanish control since the time of Christopher Columbus. Indeed, after the Mexican-American War in the 1840s, the U.S. sought to buy Cuba from Spain but was rebuffed. Some Southerners envisioned a Cuba that would be aligned with the pro-slave states; others saw it as a way station for freed slaves being repatriated to Liberia.

Meanwhile, the Cubans themselves had begun to resist Spanish rule. Rebel forces fought a ten-year war, from 1868 to 1878, before being suppressed by Spanish authorities. Then, in 1891, Cuban independence leader José Martí established a U.S. headquarters for the revolutionary movement. Traveling across America, Martí gave speeches designed to rally popular sentiment around the cause of Cuban independence. In 1895, Martí led an armed force into Cuba, but once more the rebels were unsuccessful. Even so, and even though Martí was killed in the conflict, the rebels continued to pursue their goal through a series of guerrilla actions.

Now, as these events were unfolding, various U.S. interests debated policies toward Cuba. During his second term in the 1890s, President Grover Cleveland estimated U.S. commercial investment in Cuba at about $100 million, largely in sugar plantations, mining, and railroads. This was, Cleveland recognized, a crucial investment that had to be protected. We have to realize as well that during the second half of the 19th century, the United States was fast becoming the leading manufacturing nation in the world. The country needed markets for its steel, oil, cotton, and manufactured products. And to American businesses this meant new markets beyond our borders, markets in China, and in Japan, and of course, in Cuba; all of these were viewed by American business as tremendous economic opportunities.

Others saw additional geopolitical dimensions to American expansion. Some, like Assistant Navy Secretary Theodore Roosevelt, saw a world being carved up by European imperial powers. They were convinced that it was the United States' manifest destiny to acquire control over territory and colonies beyond its continental boundaries.

Establishing footholds or even control over the Philippines, Panama, Cuba, and other places would give the United States commercial markets, military bases, canals, and facilities so that it could take its place as one of the greatest and most powerful nations in the world. With that grand goal in mind, Roosevelt was practically spoiling for a fight with the Spanish over Cuba. And he wasn't alone. For example, publishers William Randolph Hearst and Joseph Pulitzer used their newspapers, the New York Journal and the New York World, to fuel outrage against the Spanish. Articles in the papers extolled the Cuban freedom fighters and condemned the Spanish excesses against them. And much of this reporting included an undertone of anti-Catholic rhetoric implying that the Vatican was acting through Spain. Hearst and Pulitzer were also rivals in the world of sensationalist, profit-driven yellow journalism. News of the revolution sold papers, and it drove them to dramatic, hyperbolic, and sometimes inaccurate coverage of the events.

Of course, there were many Americans, including many businessmen, who opposed American military intervention in Cuba. For them, stability in Cuba was more important than victory over Spain. So when William McKinley became president in 1897, he inherited a very complex diplomatic situation. This complexity is reflected in the fact that the McKinley administration was actually negotiating with Spain about Cuba's future even as the U.S. built up its naval presence in the Caribbean to show the flag and pressure the Spanish.

The situation only got thornier when a pro-Spanish riot broke out in Cuba's capital city of Havana in January 1898. In response to that riot, McKinley sent the battleship *Maine* into Havana harbor, an action he thought necessary to protect American interests there. But because America took this step without informing Spanish authorities first, it was viewed as a provocation.

And so we came to the night of February 15, 1898. Things were quiet aboard the *Maine*. In his cabin, the ship's captain, Charles Dwight Sigsbee, was writing a letter to his wife. Then a bugle sounded, and well I'll let Captain Sigsbee describe it for us. He wrote,

"At taps … ten minutes after nine o'clock, I laid down my pen to listen to the notes of the bugle, which were singularly beautiful in the oppressive stillness of the night. The marine bugler, Newton, who was rather given to fanciful effects, was evidently doing his best … I was enclosing my letter in its envelope when the explosion came. It was a bursting, rending, and crashing roar of immense volume, largely metallic in character. It was followed by heavy, ominous, metallic sounds. There was a trembling and lurching motion of the vessel, a list to port. The electric lights went out. Then there was intense blackness and smoke." Of the 354-man crew, only 88, including the captain, survived. The ship was devastated and sank into the harbor. Hearst and Pulitzer quickly blamed the Spanish for sinking the *Maine*, and they called for war. "Remember the Maine, to hell with Spain," they proclaimed. "Remember the Maine" soon appeared on a variety of souvenirs. It was the rallying cry of the war.

The U.S. Navy conducted an investigation and concluded that the ship's stock of ammunition had been set afire by an external mine. Subsequent investigations, including one that was conducted in 1976, failed to find evidence in support of this conclusion. But, in the weeks after the tragedy, the business community increasingly saw military action as the only viable course. President McKinley agreed, and in April he issued an ultimatum to

Spain: Either give up your colony to the United States—not the rebels—or face war.

Spain's response was to declare war on the United States on April 24. The Spanish-American War did not last long, just about four months. The U.S. Navy was far superior, and the Spanish military forces had been weakened by internal rebellion in Cuba and an independence movement in the Philippines. By December, the parties had signed the Treaty of Paris. Spain relinquished its sovereignty over Cuba, ceding temporary control of the island to the United States. It also gave up its colonies of Puerto Rico, Guam, and the Philippines to the United States.

Whatever its cause, the destruction of the *Maine* had played its part in creating a new geopolitical order. On a smaller scale, the aftermath of the explosion was a story of recovery and salvage. In 1899, the U.S. Navy retrieved some of the human remains and other items from the *Maine*. The Smithsonian sought and received the ship's steering wheel. The damaged wheel was regarded as a patriotic treasure and was prominently displayed in the National Museum.

But it wasn't until 1910 that Congress provided funds for a complete salvage operation. The Army Corps of Engineers refloated the hull of the *Maine*, removed the remains of about seventy individuals, and retrieved dozens of items from the ship and the harbor floor. On March 16, 1912, the ship's intact wreckage was floated out to sea and amid somber, patriotic ceremony, it was sunk.

The human remains were buried at Arlington National Cemetery, and the ship's mast was installed there as a memorial. Other artifacts from the ship—anchors, bells, life preservers, guns—were distributed to the Naval Academy, Navy yards, parks, courthouses, and museums across the United States. And this bugle, possibly the one heard by Captain Sigsbee, the one played by marine fifer C. H. Newton mere minutes before his death in the explosion, the one now encrusted with shell, coral, and other marine detritus, this bugle came to the Smithsonian.

As we've seen, the events of February 15, 1898, galvanized public opinion into a general outcry for war. The same is true of another fateful day in American history—December 7, 1941. At 7:48 that morning, local time, the Imperial Japanese Navy launched a surprise attack against the U.S. naval base at Pearl Harbor, Hawaii. More than 350 Japanese planes, launched from aircraft carriers, descended on the base. And the result was devastation. More than 2,400 Americans killed and almost 1,200 wounded; almost 200 U.S. aircraft destroyed. Photographs and newsreel footage showed some of the 19 Navy ships sunk, damaged, engulfed in flames, with the sky blackened in smoke. In a little less than two hours, the Japanese had immobilized the entire U.S. Pacific Fleet.

One of the battleships that sank that day was the USS *Oklahoma.* Commissioned in May 1916, *Oklahoma* had protected World War I convoys across the Atlantic Ocean. It had escorted President Woodrow Wilson to peace negotiations in France in 1919. And it had helped rescue refugees fleeing the Spanish Civil War. Since 1937, the battleship had been based at Pearl Harbor for patrols and exercises. Like all naval ships, Oklahoma was equipped to offer postal services. Of course, this was important for military communications. But it also gave the crew a vital link to family and friends back home.

In today's era of e-mails, cell phones, tweeting, and the like, it's easy to forget how important the postal service used to be. Mail wasn't just a way of conveying information; its real power lay in its uniquely tangible nature. The recognizable handwriting of a parent, the perfumed scent of a wife or girlfriend, a familiar sketch from a friend, all of this brought servicemen and women momentarily closer to the life and people they cared about most. In the same way, sending a letter out through the ship's post office was a way for sailors to reassure their loved ones in a uniquely personal and palpable way.

For sailors on the *Oklahoma*, outgoing letters were stamped by hand in the shipboard post office. Such hand stamps indicated the date and the general time a letter or parcel was mailed and if any special services were required, such as registered or special delivery. They showed the originating post office, in this case, in capital letters, "U.S.S. OKLAHOMA." The

Smithsonian has two hand stamps that were salvaged from *Oklahoma*. Now, if you were thinking about what to collect from an attack of the size and scope and significance of Pearl Harbor, postal hand stamps might not be the first things that come to mind. But when you understand their story, they show how ordinary, mundane objects can take on extraordinary significance.

Navy postal clerks on *Oklahoma* had last stamped the mail on Saturday, December 6, 1941. They used these two hand stamps, both of which indicate the date. The duplex hand stamp was used as a cancellation stamp for all types of outgoing mail. Occasionally, the registered-mail hand stamp would have been used for special parcels, but mainly it was used for official navy mail. Mail stamped "REGISTERED" was recorded and secured and included military documents classified as secret.

The postal clerks did not have the chance to change the date on the hand stamps before the attack on Pearl Harbor began early Sunday morning. Moored in Battleship Row, *Oklahoma* was hit on its port side by three torpedoes at the outset of the attack. It had already begun to capsize when it was hit by more torpedoes, reportedly nine in all. Within minutes, *Oklahoma* rolled over on its side, its keel exposed. Hundreds were trapped inside and in danger of being drowned or killed.

By around 10:00 am the attack was over. The surviving sailors took small boats out into the harbor to search the wreckage. As they passed the *Oklahoma*, they heard the sound of tapping coming from within the hull. After a two-day rescue attempt, thirty-two trapped seamen were freed through holes cut into the bottom of the ship. They were among the fortunate. All told, of the 2,100 men serving on *Oklahoma*, 429 were listed as killed or missing. As for the *Oklahoma* itself, the ship lay in the harbor, inoperable and severely damaged. And of course, the usual work of the shipboard post office, the changing of the dies in the hand stamps, the processing of the mail, that all ceased forever.

Some seven months after the attack on Pearl Harbor, the Navy began complex salvage operations; 21 derricks were used to run steel cables from the *Oklahoma* to hydraulic winching machines on the shore. It took almost a year to right the ship. Navy teams removed human remains as well as other items. Then the ship was towed to dry dock, where guns, machinery, and ammunition were salvaged. Though the hull was repaired, initial plans to reuse the ship were canceled, and it was decommissioned in 1944. Finally, while being towed across the Pacific to a San Francisco scrap yard in 1947, *Oklahoma* started taking on water and sank.

The hand stamps survived the attack on Pearl Harbor. Recovered by the Navy, they were subsequently turned over to the Post Office Department, which transferred them to the Smithsonian in the mid-1960s. These simple tools tell a poignant story. On their last day of regular use, clerks stamped mail that made its way back home. Some of those letters were the last communication that families would ever receive from their loved ones, a powerful reminder of the role that the mail played during wartime.

So far today we've looked at artifacts salvaged from two ships, and we've seen how these artifacts help us understand the American experience on both a geopolitical and personal scale. Next I want to talk about a group of objects that connect global anxiety and individual courage in a uniquely powerful way. Since 1941, the attack on Pearl Harbor had stood as the biggest loss of American life ever perpetrated by an enemy on U.S. soil. On September 11, 2001 that changed. On that day, nearly 3,000 people died in terrorist attacks, as hijackers working under the auspices of Al Qaida took control of four commercial jets. One of these jets, American Airlines Flight 11, crashed into the North Tower of the World Trade Center. A few minutes later, the hijackers flew United Airlines Flight 175 into the South Tower. Then American Airlines Flight 77 slammed into the Pentagon outside Washington DC. And a fourth airliner, United Airlines Flight 93, crashed to the ground near Shanksville, Pennsylvania.

The results were horrific. All the passengers and crew members on the airplanes perished. At the World Trade Center, thousands made their way down the stairs and survived; however, hundreds were trapped in the buildings' upper floors. Some two hundred people jumped or fell to their deaths to avoid fires caused by the crash; most of the victims died as the towers collapsed.

Of course there were geopolitical results too. As with the sinking of the *Maine* and the attack on Pearl Harbor, the events of 9/11 drove America to war. And yet, if we only focus on the tragedy, we forget the extraordinary courage displayed by ordinary Americans on that day. On Flight 93, passengers rushed the cabin to fight for control of the plane. Their bravery succeeded in derailing the terrorists' plan to crash the plane into either the U.S. Capitol or the White House. At the Pentagon, civilians and military personnel courageously pulled their coworkers away from the flames of the jet that had crashed through the building's outer wall. In New York, members of the police and fire departments rushed to the scene in lower Manhattan. Hundreds entered the World Trade Center towers and climbed the stairs to rescue survivors, while others treated victims on the ground. More than 400 first responders became victims themselves when the buildings collapsed.

In the months that followed these tragic losses, the Smithsonian assumed the responsibility of collecting and preserving artifacts, so that future generations will have a concrete record of what America went through on September 11, 2001. This was no easy task, and it was unlike any other assignment the curators at the Smithsonian had ever faced. I'll let my colleague Peter Liebhold, a curator at the National Museum of American History, tell you about his experience and that of his fellow curator David Shayt:

[Video start.]

Liebhold: It was actually a pretty horrific kind of experience. We would climb into the containers, and David would work one side of the pile, and I would climb over the top and work the back of the pile, looking through it. Sort of, I guess in a cold kind of medical way, except that it was haunting because it was dark and smelled like jet fuel, and quite frankly, you had no idea what you might find, so it was pretty scary. But we got through it, and I think that we were able to recover some important pieces.

[Video end.]

Kurin: It was obviously a difficult task for Peter and David, and for all of us at the Smithsonian. Many of us, like many of you watching, were personally affected by the events of that day. Each of the items collected by Liebhold and his team tells an incredible story. One of these items is a remnant of the World Trade Center's external sheathing. Apart from their sheer size, one of the most arresting qualities of the 110-story Twin Towers was their gleaming exterior. Brilliant white at mid-day, the buildings took on a golden sheen at sunrise and sunset. It was the effect of the highly reflective aluminum alloy sheathing, which magnified the towers' soaring appearance and enhanced their stature as New York City landmarks. Now these beautiful buildings are gone.

Another item that touched me deeply is the crash-scarred logbook of Lorraine Bay, a 37-year veteran flight attendant, one of the seven crew members who perished on United Flight 93. Such an ordinary object. But because it is so ordinary, the logbook has the same kind of poignancy that Captain Sigsbee's account of the bugle sounding taps, or the hand stamps dated December 6, 1941.

The logbook also has a personal meaning for me. A bit earlier that morning, on September 11, my sister-in-law Claire was at Dulles airport picking up my nephew, who had just arrived on a red-eye flight from Los Angeles. A flight attendant for American Airlines herself, Claire met with her friends staffing the crew of Flight 77, which was preparing for the return flight for Los Angeles. Claire had worked with them for many years, and they spent some time catching up before hugging goodbye. She expected to see them again, but that never happened. At 9:37 a.m., the hijackers crashed Flight 77 into the Pentagon.

Another moving artifact is the crumpled door of a pumper engine from the New York City Fire Department's Squad Company 1. This is an elite group charged with responding quickly to emergency situations. The call for help went out just as the firehouse shift was changing. The squad raced across the Brooklyn Bridge to the World Trade Center. Twelve firefighters from Company 1 lost their lives trying to rescue trapped office workers from the South Tower.

And one more artifact, this one held at the Smithsonian's Postal Museum. Cognizant of the story of the USS *Oklahoma*, museum curators were able to recover a hand stamp from New York's Church Street post office, which serviced the World Trade Center. It bears the date of the attack, "Sep 11, 2001."

The last item I want to show you was acquired a few months after the attacks. In 1989, the Public Art Fund of New York City funded the installation of Roy Lichtenstein's sculpture—Modern Head—in Battery Park City, one block from the World Trade Center. This 31-foot sculpture survived the attacks with only surface scratches and was temporarily used by the FBI as a message board during its investigations. It was removed a few months later and subsequently donated to the Smithsonian, where it is now installed outside the Smithsonian American Art Museum in Washington, DC. It reminds me of how much the meaning of an object can change. This sculpture, originally a commentary on the diminution of humanity, now offers a message about its endurance.

One year after the terrorists struck, many of the objects collected by the Smithsonian were displayed in an exhibition entitled September 11: Bearing Witness to History. As visitors paused to learn the stories of these artifacts, the gallery was eerily and respectfully quiet. History was not some vaguely remembered collection of impersonal facts; it was shockingly close and connected to us all. The conservators even coated a column fragment from the World Trade Center in wax so people could touch it, which tens of thousands did.

A decade later, we opened a temporary special exhibit, placing a small number of September 11 artifacts on tables with simple cloth coverings. The artifacts were not in cases and were directly accessible. Visitors stood in long lines and spoke in hushed tones as they approached each object. Our experts stood by to talk or answer questions; however, visitors were largely left to experience the articles on their own. Lets do that now. This is a fireman's crowbar. It belonged to Lt. Kevin Pfeifer from the Engine Company 33. He used it to help save others, and in the World Trade Center, he directed many people out of the North Tower. But that day, this crow bar could not save Pfeifer; he perished when the tower came down. Simple object, but part of a big story that in some way has affected every American.

Like the bugle from the USS *Maine*, the hand stamp from the *Oklahoma*, each of these objects bears witness to a pivotal moment in our history, to events that dramatically shaped the course we've taken as a nation. And when you're in intimate proximity to one of these objects, as I am now, you have a link to that sweeping story. History is not distant; it's not a stranger. Rather, you feel a deep emotional connection with the past, with the person who held this, used it, died with it, even if you didn't know him or her.

When the Smithsonian had that special exhibit with the objects from 9/11, I think almost every visitor experienced such a moment of connection. One teenager who had been only a few years old at the time of the attacks, said something like, "I knew it was a bad thing that happened, but I guess I was much too young to really feel it. Now I do." Nothing speaks more to the museum experience than that.

For the Greater Good—Public Health

Lecture 16

Knowledge, invention, experimentation, and social will and support all have played a historic role in America—especially in the 20th and 21st centuries. Individual and group efforts have helped conquer diseases and improve the quality of life for millions. It is a role that has helped not only Americans, but also has benefited those around the world. In this lecture, you will learn how grassroots efforts, social activism, and the care and determination of the American people helped fund a cure for polio, led to birth control for women, and reversed the bias against those with AIDS.

Polio

- *Poliomyelitis*, commonly known as polio, was one of the world's most feared diseases in the first half of the 20th century. Although more people died of other maladies, polio's subtle symptoms—a mild sore throat, a runny nose—made everyone suspicious of the slightest sniffle. The onset belied the swift and dramatic physical effects of the disease. Within a few days, victims could lose the ability to walk or even breathe.

- Although between 1949 and 1954 35 percent of those who contracted polio were adults, the disease was mostly associated with children and teens. Thus, polio was also known as infantile paralysis. With children so vulnerable and polio on the rise, families were desperate to protect their loved ones and strapped to pay for expensive treatments. In addition, there was the cost of rehabilitation and long-term care.

- Throughout America, the sense of despair combined with the expectation that science had the power to prevent or cure polio gave powerful momentum to the push to develop a polio vaccine. For Americans, the fact that President Franklin D. Roosevelt had contracted polio in 1921 made him a symbol of survival. Roosevelt created the Warm Springs Foundation in Alabama and established the first hospital in the country to focus on polio victims. He began a modest effort to raise funds for the foundation.

- But once he was elected president, he had more opportunities to raise funds for the cause. A political supporter, Henry Doherty, donated 25,000 dollars in 1934 to set up a series of "birthday balls" to raise funds. That year, there were 600 "birthday balls" throughout America, and a million dollars was raised for the Warm Springs Foundation. This success encouraged Roosevelt and Basil O'Connor, who ran the foundation, to organize a national effort against polio.

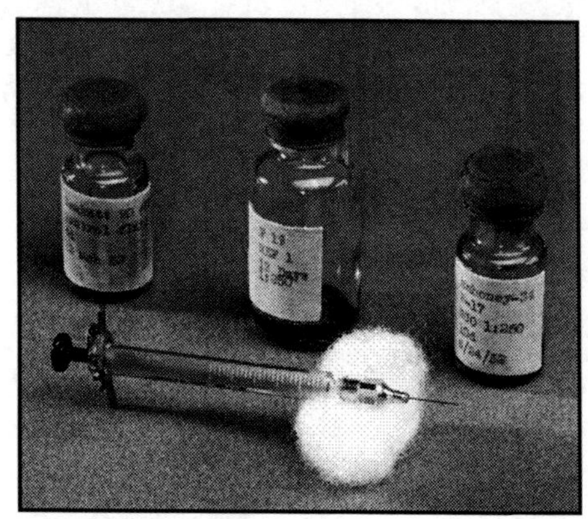

Salk Polio Vaccine

- The National Foundation for Infantile Paralysis was announced on January 3, 1938. Later that year, Eddie Cantor, a vaudeville star, organized a radio broadcast across the country to promote the fund-raising. He played off "The March of Time" newsreels by calling for Americans to donate whatever they could. Just ten cents, he said, from every child, would create "a march of dimes to reach all the way to the White House." Within weeks, nearly 2,680,000 dimes and thousands of dollars had been sent to the White House to aid in the fight against polio.

- By 1952, however, more than 50,000 new polio cases were reported in the United States, and fear gripped the American public. Public swimming pools and summer camps were closed. Families were encouraged to keep children indoors and isolated to contain the disease. Children who suffered from the effects of polio often required braces, crutches, oxygen tanks, or wheelchairs for life. The need for a cure touched the hearts of Americans.

- And Americans responded. The March of Dimes grassroots fund-raising campaign so successfully tapped America's spirit of volunteerism and the desire of neighbor to help neighbor that the effort significantly influenced how all charities approached fund-raising. Asking for small donations—just that dime—from millions of individuals empowered the givers and fostered activism.

- This, in turn, gave everyone a sense of both urgency and ownership in the efforts to find a vaccine. Eventually, the fund-raising campaigns collected hundreds of millions of dollars that made all the difference in enabling research, providing equipment and supplies, and supporting clinical trials.

- Leading the research efforts were Jonas Salk and Albert Sabin. Salk developed an injectable vaccine, while Sabin concentrated on an oral vaccine. Salk used cultures of monkey kidney tissue to produce vaccines of several experimental types. He deduced that an inactivated, or killed—rather than a weakened and living—virus was best for a safe and effective vaccine.

- The poliovirus exists in hundreds of different strains, all of which could be categorized into three major types: Mahoney, Saukett, and MEF-1. After Salk had tested the vaccine on tens of thousands of rhesus monkeys, he tested it on humans on July 2, 1952. The syringe and vials from the three strains of the virus Salk used for testing are part of the collections of the National Museum of American History.

- Between May 1953 and March 1954, Salk inoculated more than 5,000 people, including himself, his wife, and his three sons. The vaccine, which included all three strains of dead virus, was finally ready for the most elaborate field trial in history. Twenty thousand physicians and health workers, tens of thousands of school personnel, and hundreds of thousands of volunteers cooperated with the trials. Through the March of Dimes, more than 100 million people funded the program, and numerous companies donated supplies.

- On April 12, 1955, 10 years after Roosevelt's death, the results were announced by the University of Michigan: The vaccine was 80 to 90 percent effective. The nation was overjoyed, and Salk became a national and international hero. Millions would be saved from contracting the disease.

- The Smithsonian organized an exhibition on polio in 1958. It featured 12 vials containing residues of the various vaccines used in Salk's trials and 6 flasks that Dr. John F. Enders used to grow the virus in cultures of human tissue. A very small item was included as well: A Roosevelt dime signified the hundreds of millions of dollars the American people had given since 1938.

The Pill

- Oral contraception, or the birth control pill, represents a long quest—part scientific, part political—to realize a dream held by many women throughout history to gain control over the means of reproduction.

- The Smithsonian has two plastic vials of Enovid from the 1950s. These were among the first birth control pills developed by a pharmaceutical company and approved by the U.S. government. They were used in clinical trials to establish the efficacy of oral contraception.

- The idea of a "miracle pill," an inexpensive, easily taken oral contraceptive, was a dream of nurse and women's rights advocate Margaret Sanger. She coined the term "birth control" in 1914. Sanger and others faced prosecution under the so-called Comstock laws. The federal Comstock Act of 1873, and similar laws in several dozen states, made it illegal to sell or distribute any drug or device that could terminate or prevent a pregnancy. Despite facing arrest, Sanger and others persisted in efforts to offer women safe and effective means of birth control.

- Regardless of the laws, many Americans practiced various means of birth control. In 1936, a Supreme Court decision made it legal for doctors to mail contraceptives and birth control literature across state lines. By the early 1950s, in addition to abstinence, the Catholic Church sanctioned the rhythm method—avoiding intercourse during the most fertile days of the menstrual cycle—as a natural means of birth control.

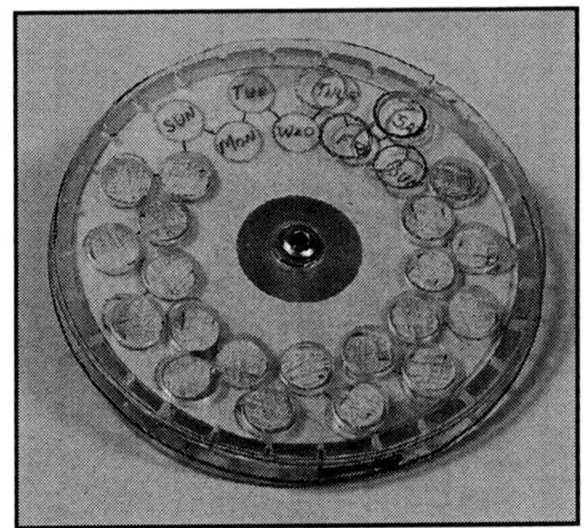

The Pill

- Sanger continued to hope for a miracle pill into her 70s. Eventually, the heiress and scientist Katharine McCormick provided critical funding. Research by doctors such as Gregory Pincus and John Rock in the 1950s led to the use of the hormone progesterone along with estrogen as an oral contraceptive. The hormones suppressed ovulation, so fertilization couldn't occur.

- They took the drug to G. D. Searle, a pharmaceutical company whose chief chemist, Frank Colton, had developed a synthetic form of progesterone. Searle called the product Enovid, and it was first prescribed and sold for treating menstrual disorders.

- In May 1960, the U.S. Food and Drug Administration approved Searle's request to manufacture and sell Enovid as the first birth control pill. Soon after approval, hundreds of thousands of women went on "the pill."

- The pill could be taken easily and was both relatively safe and effective. It was hailed by many women as providing a measure of freedom and security with regard to their reproductive choices.

But opponents worried that the pill could herald a new sexual revolution, leading to promiscuity and moral decline. Others thought that it might reduce population growth.

- The pill's developers had expected a strong backlash, but beyond some heated rhetoric, it was relatively mild. President Eisenhower had publicly stated that birth control was none of the government's business. Within a few years, more than two million women had a prescription for the pill. The market—and, more importantly, women—had spoken.

- But a challenge remained. The pill's effectiveness depended on following a rigorous schedule—taking it for 21 days, followed by 7 days off. It was easy to mess up the schedule, especially because the pill was packaged in the usual plastic vials.

- In 1962, David Wagner, an engineer in Illinois, created a container that would track the days but keep the pills safe. He made a prototype out of common materials: plastic, paper, transparent tape, a snap fastener from a toy, and thin mock pills made from sawing up a wooden dowel stick. Two years later, he was awarded the patent for the first oral contraceptive pill dispenser. Many other versions have followed this basic "dial pack" design.

The AIDS Memorial Quilt

- In June 1981, the Centers for Disease Control identified five reported cases of a similar flu-like syndrome and a specific type of deadly pneumonia usually found in people with suppressed immune systems. What was striking was that all five subjects were previously healthy young men, and all were homosexual.

- By the end of the year, 159 cases of this "new disease" were recorded. It was nicknamed "gay cancer" or "the gay plague." Medical researchers now think that acquired immune deficiency syndrome (AIDS) originated in the early 20th century and was transferred from infected chimpanzees to people by way of tainted meat consumption in sub-Saharan Africa.

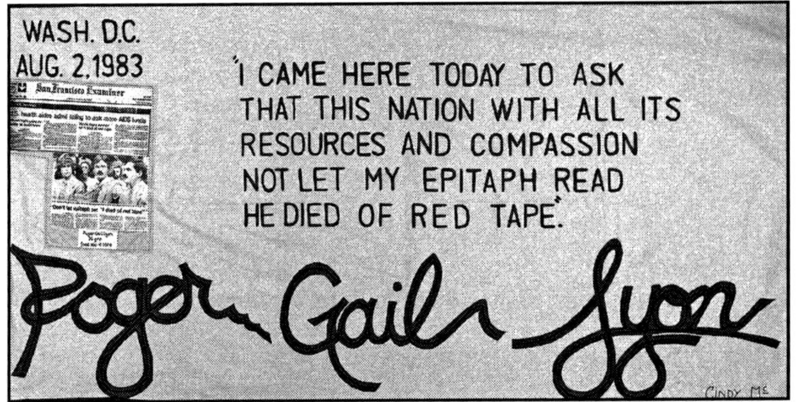

AIDS Quilt Panel

- By 1983, researchers identified the human immunodeficiency virus—HIV—that caused AIDS, and about 33 countries reported cases in their populations. But even though by year's end more than 2,000 people in the United States had died of the disease, including women, heterosexual men, and infants, the illness was still associated with gay men, so funding efforts were hampered.

- In 1985, an Indiana public school district denied admission to Ryan White. At the time, he was 13 years old. He had contracted AIDS as a result of blood transfusions he received to treat hemophilia. His family's battle to allow him to attend school drew widespread press attention to victims of the disease and tapped into pervasive fears that AIDS could be transmitted by casual contact.

- Soon after, Rock Hudson, a popular Hollywood romantic leading man of the 1950s and 1960s, issued a press release acknowledging that he was suffering from AIDS and was gay. For the first time, many Americans identified AIDS with a beloved public figure.

- Hudson's friend Elizabeth Taylor was among the first major celebrities to advocate for funding for AIDS research and public awareness of the disease. Other celebrities came forward, and the tide of public opinion turned. People began to encourage congressional support for research and stronger public appreciation for the concerns of the gay community.

- In 1983, activist Roger Gail Lyon participated in an AIDS vigil in San Francisco that echoed the theme from his appeal to Congress for funding to combat the growing epidemic: "People Are Dying; Cut the Red Tape." Lyon and another AIDS sufferer unrolled a red scroll with the names of the 118 San Francisco Bay–area residents who had died of the disease.

- For the 1985 vigil, Cleve Jones, one of the organizers, asked fellow marchers to inscribe the names of their departed friends and loved ones on the placards they carried. At the end of the march, they taped the placards to the walls of the San Francisco Federal Building. This graphic patchwork memorial inspired the idea of a massive AIDS quilt.

- Jones and friends took up the cause of making quilt panels. Actor Marvin Feldman, a friend of Cleve's who had recently died, was the first to have a panel made for him. Cindy McMullin made three panels in Lyon's honor, including the one that hangs in the Smithsonian. McMullin became an early volunteer with the NAMES Project Foundation, as the quilt organizers' group was formally called.

- The group began to accumulate hundreds of quilt panels for eventual public display. Each panel captured a personal story in different ways. Many were sewn in cotton with conventional materials, but others incorporated Barbie dolls, car keys, bubble wrap, Legos, tennis shoes, credit cards, and even a Sony Walkman.

- The quilt was displayed for the first time on the National Mall in Washington DC on October 11, 1987. By then, about 40,000 Americans had died of AIDS. The quilt included 1,920 panels. It was displayed again in 1988 and then in 1989. By then, it was five times its original size.

- The full quilt extends for 1.3 million square feet and weighs more than 54 tons. It is made up of about 48,000 separate panels that incorporate and memorialize about 93,000 people—all victims of AIDS.

- Each panel is a testament to a life lost too early. Fortunately, the AIDS quilt played a major role in removing the shame from the disease. It conveyed to the broader public the humanity of those who had been afflicted and died—it was a new generation's March of Dimes.

- In the decades since, millions of people around the world have died of AIDS. Research and treatment have progressed to the point where a diagnosis is no longer an automatic death sentence. However, while treatment can drastically reduce transmission, there is still no vaccine or cure.

- But there are new advances that hold considerable promise, one of which involves DNA research and the use of a technology embodied in another innovative machine in the Smithsonian's collection: the PCR (polymerase chain reaction) machine.

- The machine uses thermal cycling to accelerate the replication of small DNA samples, amplifying minute quantities of genetic material into larger samples that can be detected, allowing for easier diagnosis of diseases and easier evaluation of the progress of potential cures. Researchers can also now fragment DNA into isolated segments and use PCR to amplify them so that they can be used in genetic manipulation—altering cells to be able to fend off the AIDS virus, for example.

Featured Objects

Salk Polio Vaccine

The Pill

AIDS Quilt Panel

Suggested Reading

Jones and Dawson, *Stitching a Revolution.*

Kluger, *Splendid Solution.*

May, *America and the Pill.*

For the Greater Good—Public Health

Lecture 16—Transcript

In 1938, the Great New England Hurricane slammed into Long Island and southern New England, killing more than 600 people and leaving some 63,000 people homeless. In 1938 unemployment was around 19 percent, and that same year Orson Wells broadcast his famous dramatization of War of the Worlds, a tale of alien invasion and mass destruction. And a polio epidemic was killing up to a half a million people a year, many of those Americans, many of them children. It was a time of fear and worry.

In 1938, 10 cents could buy you a gallon of gas, a loaf of bread, a can of Lipton's noodle soup, and nearly a pound of hamburger. It could also buy hope for those with polio. Today we are going to look at how grass-roots efforts, social activism, and the care and determination of the American people helped fund a cure for polio, led to birth control for women, and reversed the bias against those with AIDS.

From the beginning, issues of health and disease have played a role in the history of America. The first colonists unwittingly spread diseases to native communities through personal contact and gifts, such as blankets. Without immunity, large numbers of American Indians died. Epidemics, like yellow fever and cholera, wiped out thousands of natives. Smallpox, in particular, devastated native populations in the Americas. Some estimates put the number of people who died from European diseases as high as 20 million.

By the late 19th century, American cities were expanding, attracting immigrants from Europe and rural populations looking for work. Those new urban areas grew so fast in this country that they didn't have things that we now take for granted, such as clean water and sewage. Soon, the crowded, unhealthy conditions led to a variety of epidemics.

Outbreaks of such diseases as tuberculosis, typhus, and cholera could be attributed to unsanitary living conditions often associated with poverty. Still other outbreaks resulted from great increases in worldwide travel and mobility. For example, the 1918 influenza epidemic resulted from the movement of a virus across the planet, helped along by World War I, of course. Between 20 to 40 million people died worldwide; that was more in a single year than in the worst four worst years of the Bubonic Plague. In America alone, some 675,000 people died—five to six times as many as had died in the war.

But perhaps, the most terrifying of all was a disease that struck mostly in the summer. It hit families of all income levels and all geographic regions. It swept through the country in pandemics that grew worse every year. Inspectors were positioned at railroad stations and boat landings to check health certificates. Businesses closed. People crossed the road rather than walk past hospitals. Sheriffs patrolled the roads with shotguns, turning back all cars with children younger than 16. The disease that occasioned all this, was polio.

Poliomyelitis, or polio for short, was one of the world's most feared diseases in the first half of the 20th century. It wasn't a new disease, though. An Egyptian stele from around 1300 B.C. shows a priest with a withered leg that matches the effect of polio. Although more people died of other maladies, polio's subtle symptoms—a mild sore throat, a runny nose—made everyone suspicious of the slightest sniffle. The onset belied the swift and dramatic physical effects of the disease. Within a few days, victims could lose the ability to walk or even to breathe. Although between 1949 and 1954, 35 percent of those who contracted polio were adults, the disease was mostly associated with children and teens. Thus, polio was also known as "infantile paralysis."

With children so vulnerable and polio on the rise, families were desperate to protect their loved ones and strapped to pay for the expensive treatments like the iron lung. This coffin-like device compressed and inflated the lungs, and without it, many children would have stopped breathing. Then, there was the cost of rehabilitation and long-term care. Throughout America, the sense of despair combined with the expectation that science had the power to prevent or cure polio, well, it gave powerful momentum in the country to push to develop a polio vaccine.

For Americans, the fact that Franklin D. Roosevelt, the President of the United States, had contracted polio previously in 1921 made him a symbol of survival. Roosevelt created the Warm Springs Foundation in Alabama and established the first hospital in the country to focus on polio victims. He began a modest effort to raise funds for the foundation. But once he was elected president, he had more opportunities to raise funds for the cause. A political supporter, Henry Doherty, donated $25,000 in 1934 to set up a series of birthday balls to raise funds for his favorite cause. That year there were 600 birthday balls throughout America and a million dollars were raised for the Warm Springs Foundation. The slogan, "Dance so others may walk," soon became aligned with the fight against polio.

This success encouraged Roosevelt and Basil O'Connor, who ran the foundation, to organize a national effort against polio. The National Foundation for Infantile Paralysis, or NFIP, was announced on January 3, 1938. Later that year, Eddie Cantor, a vaudeville star, organized a radio broadcast across the country to promote the fundraising. He played off of the March of Time newsreels by calling for Americans to donate whatever they could. Just ten cents, he said, from every child, would create "a march of dimes to reach all the way to the White House."

Within weeks, in this cash-strapped nation, nearly 2,680,000 dimes and thousands and thousands of dollars had been sent to the White House to aid in the fight against polio.

By 1952, however, more than 50,000 new polio cases were reported in the United States, and fear gripped the American public. Public swimming pools and summer camps were closed. Families were encouraged to keep children indoors and isolated to contain the disease. Sometimes children and parents were quarantined separately, resulting in further isolation and more dread of the disease. Children who suffered from the effects of polio often required braces, crutches, oxygen tanks, or wheelchairs for life. They were often excluded from conventional schools and extracurricular activities. The need for a cure touched the hearts of Americans everywhere.

And Americans responded. The March of Dimes grassroots fund-raising campaign so successfully tapped America's spirit of volunteerism and the desire of neighbor to help neighbor, so much so that the effect significantly influenced how all charities approached fund-raising. Asking for small donations—just that dime—from millions of individuals empowered the givers and fostered a great sense of activism.

This in turn gave everyone a sense of both urgency and ownership in the effort to find a vaccine. Eventually, the fund-raising campaigns collected hundreds of millions of dollars that made all the difference in enabling research, providing equipment and supplies, and supporting clinical trials. Leading the research efforts were Jonas Salk and Albert Sabin. Salk developed an injectable vaccine, while Sabin concentrated on an oral vaccine. We're going to focus, for a moment, on Salk's efforts.

Jonas Salk was born in 1914 in New York City to Jewish-Russian immigrant parents with little formal education themselves, but he was a star student, and after attending New York University Medical School, he went into virology. He devoted himself to research, first on influenza, and then on polio at the University of Pittsburgh. Salk used cultures of monkey kidney tissue to produce vaccines of several experimental types. He deduced that an inactivated, or killed, rather than a weakened and living, virus was best for a safe and effective vaccine.

The polio virus exists in hundreds of different strains, of which could be categorized into three basic major types—MEF-1, Mahoney, Saukett. After Salk had tested the vaccine on tens of thousands of rhesus monkeys, he tested it on humans on July 2, 1952. Using a hypodermic syringe, he inoculated children at the D. T. Watson Home for Crippled Children near Pittsburgh. These children had already contracted the Mahoney strain of polio, so Salk's test was designed to prove that his vaccine would do no harm. He also hoped it would create a higher level of immunity than a natural infection. The syringe and the vials from the three strains of the virus Salk used for testing, which you can see here, are part of the collections of the National Museum of American History. Next, Salk tested his vaccine on residents of the Polk State School for the Feeble-Minded of Western Pennsylvania. He also tested the vaccine on himself, his wife, and three sons, plus members of his laboratory staff. Between May 1953 and March 1954, Salk inoculated more than 5,000 people.

The vaccine, which included all three strains of dead virus, was finally ready for the most elaborate field trial in history. Some 1.8 million schoolchildren participated. Of those, only about one-fourth were inoculated. It was a double-blind trial, meaning neither the subjects nor the researchers knew who was getting the real vaccine. Twenty thousand physicians and health workers, tens of thousands of school personnel, and hundreds of thousands of volunteers cooperated with the trial. Through the March of Dimes, more than 100 million people—100 million people—funded the program, and numerous companies donated supplies.

On April 12, 1955, 10 years after Roosevelt's death, the results were announced by the University of Michigan. The vaccine was 80 to 90 percent effective. It worked! The nation was overjoyed, and Salk, literally, became a national and international hero. Millions would be saved from contracting the dreaded disease.

The Smithsonian organized an exhibition on polio in 1958. It was opened by and 11-year-old child named Randy Kerr, He received the first inoculation in the 1954 field trial. The exhibit featured 12 vials containing residues of the various vaccines used in Salk's trials, and six flasks that Salk's predecessor, John F. Enders, had used to grow virus in cultures in human tissue. Also, in the exhibit, were IBM punch cards that were used to record essential information about the children taking part in the trials. A very small item was included in the exhibit as well. Can you guess what it was? Well, it was a Roosevelt dime, and it signified the hundreds of millions of dollars the American people had given since 1938.

The Smithsonian's collections also document other elements of medical research in America. Among these are the "the pill" and its dispensers. These too had a tremendous social impact upon our nation. Oral contraception, or birth control pills, represent a long quest—part scientific, part political—to realize a dream held by many Americans and women throughout history to gain control over the means of reproduction.

The Smithsonian has two plastic vials of Enovid from the 1950s. These were among the first birth control pills developed by a pharmaceutical company and approved by the United States Government. They were used in clinical trials to establish the efficacy of oral contraception. The idea of a miracle pill, an inexpensive, easily taken oral contraceptive, was a dream of nurse and women's rights advocate, Margaret Sanger. She's the one that coined the term "birth control" in 1914. Sanger and others faced prosecution under the so-called Comstock laws. The federal Comstock Act of 1873, and similar laws in several dozen states, made it illegal to sell or distribute any drug or device that could terminate or prevent a pregnancy. Even books, pamphlets, or advertisements that advocated such were illegal. Despite facing arrest, Sanger and others persisted in their efforts to offer women safe and effective means of birth control so they could control the size of their families.

Regardless of the laws, many Americans practiced various means of birth control. In 1936, a Supreme Court decision made it legal for doctors to mail contraceptives and birth-control literature across state lines. Sales of condoms, diaphragms, cervical caps, and other devices, and instructional literature, generated hundreds of millions of dollars. By the early 1950s, in addition to abstinence, the Catholic Church sanctioned the rhythm method as a natural means of birth control. On the rhythm method, you simply avoided intercourse during the most fertile days of the menstrual cycle.

Sanger continued to hope for a miracle pill well into her seventies. Eventually, the heiress and scientist Katharine McCormick provided critical funding. Research by doctors, such as Gregory Pincus and John Rock in the 1950s, led to the use of the hormone progesterone, along with estrogen as an oral contraceptive. The hormones suppressed ovulation, so fertilization could not occur. They took the drug to G. D. Searle, a pharmaceutical company whose chief chemist, Frank Colton, had developed a synthetic form of progesterone. Searle called the product Enovid, and it was first prescribed and sold for treating menstrual disorders.

In May 1960, the U.S. Food and Drug Administration approved Searle's request to manufacture and sell Enovid as the first birth control pill. Soon after approval, hundreds of thousands of women went on "the pill." The pill could be taken easily and was both relatively safe and effective. It was hailed by many women as providing a measure of freedom and security with regard to their reproductive choices. But opponents worried that the pill could herald a new sexual revolution, leading to promiscuity and moral decline. Others thought it might reduce population growth.

The Catholic Church, among others, opposed human intervention in the "natural" state of affairs. But John Rock, one of the key scientists, was a Catholic. He argued that because the pill mimicked a woman's natural cycle, it was, therefore, an extension of the rhythm method. Thus it didn't really violate the Catholic Church's prohibition of birth control. Many women felt his argument justified their right to decide for themselves, even if the Church didn't agree.

The pill's developers had expected a strong backlash, but beyond some heated rhetoric, it was relatively mild. President Eisenhower publicly stated that birth control was none of the government's business, and within a few years, more than two million women had a prescription for the pill. The market, and, more importantly women, had spoken.

But a challenge remained. The pill's effectiveness depended on following a rigorous schedule—taking it for 20 days, followed by 5 days off. It was easy to mess up the schedule, especially since the pill was packaged in the usual plastic vials. In 1962, David Wagner, an engineer in Illinois, wanted to find an easy way for his wife to take the medication after she gave birth to their fourth child. His first solution was a piece of paper with the calendar marked out and a pill placed on each date. He wrote that "this lasted until the paper and pills were knocked to the floor" by their many children. It just simply didn't work.

Wagner next tried to create a container that would track the days but keep the pills safe. He made a prototype out of common materials—plastic, paper, transparent tape, a snap fastener from a toy, and thin mock pills made from sawing up a dowel stick. We have a drawing of his plans. Here it is. The snap fastener holds three round plastic plates. The bottom plate has the day-of-the-week pattern. The middle plate holds pills and rotates to match the day pill taking begins. A single hole in the top plate moves over the pill to dispense it, revealing the day of the week as a reminder that the pill was taken.

The dispenser was designed to be about the same size as a makeup compact, so that women could easily carry it discreetly in their purses. Two years later, Wagner was awarded the patent for the first oral contraceptive pill dispenser. Many other versions have followed this basic dial pack design, like the one we have here.

The pill gave women a larger degree of control over their lives. It gave them a choice in timing their education, their career, and motherhood. The resulting cultural shifts gave rise to the women's movement of the 1960s and 1970s. Ultimately, it enabled women to attain high levels of educational and career achievement, and to occupy positions of power in the civic and political life of the nation.

The pill is a small item in the Smithsonian's collection with a much larger story for our society. And we also have another small item, a three foot by six foot cloth panel of the AIDS Memorial Quilt. This, likewise, tis part of a much larger story, that of modern disease and our nation's struggle to come to grips with it. The full quilt extends for 1.3 million square feet and weighs more than 54 tons. It's made up of some 48,000 separate panels that incorporate and memorialize some 93,000 people, all victims of AIDS—acquired immune deficiency syndrome.

The panel at the Smithsonian honors activist Roger Gail Lyon, who died of AIDS in 1984. Shortly after being diagnosed, Lyon appealed to Congress for funding to combat the growing epidemic. He said, "This is not a political issue. This is a health issue. This is not a gay issue. This is a human issue. And I do not intend to be defeated by it. I came here today," he said, "to ask that this nation, with all its resources and compassion, not let my epitaph read 'he died of red tape.'" It is the last section of that quote that is embellished on the panel.

The issue of red tape concerned the very recognition of the disease and government action—or lack thereof—to treat it. In June 1981, the Centers for Disease Control identified five reported cases of a similar flu-like syndrome and a specific type of deadly pneumonia usually found in people with suppressed immune systems. What was striking was that all five subjects were previously healthy young men and all were homosexual.

By the end of the year, 159 cases of this "new disease" were recorded. It was nicknamed "gay cancer" or "the gay plague." Medical researchers now think that AIDS originated in the early 20th century and was transferred from infected chimpanzees to people by way of tainted meat consumption in sub-Saharan Africa. By 1983, researchers identified the human immunodeficiency virus—HIV—that caused AIDS, and around 33 countries reported cases in their population.

Gay activists publicly criticized the U.S. Federal Government's response to the spread of the disease as disproportionally small when compared to the funding spent on other health crises. But even though by year's end more than 2,000 people in the United States had died of the disease, including women, heterosexual men, and infants, the illness was still associated with gay men, so funding efforts were hampered. Then, in 1985, an Indiana public school district denied admission to Ryan White. At the time he was just 13 years old. He'd contracted AIDS as a result of blood transfusions he received to treat hemophilia. His family's battle to allow him to attend school drew widespread press attention to victims of the disease and tapped into the pervasive fears that AIDS could be transmitted by casual contact.

Soon after the Ryan White case, Rock Hudson, a popular romantic leading man of the 1950s and 1960s, issued a press release acknowledging that he, too, was suffering from AIDS and was gay. For the first time, many Americans identified AIDS with a beloved public figure. Hudson's friend, Elizabeth Taylor, was among the first major celebrities to advocate for funding for AIDS research and public awareness of the disease. Other celebrities came forward, and the tide of public opinion turned. People began to encourage congressional support for research and stronger appreciation for the concerns of the gay community.

In 1983, Roger Lyon participated in an AIDS vigil in San Francisco that echoed the theme from his appeal to Congress. The theme was "People Are Dying; Cut the Red Tape. Do Something." Lyon and another AIDS sufferer unrolled a red scroll with the names of the 118 San Francisco Bay Area residents who had died of the disease.

For the 1985 vigil, Cleve Jones, one of the organizers, asked fellow marchers to inscribe the names of their departed friends and loved ones on the placards they carried. At the end of the march, they taped the placards to the walls of the San Francisco Federal Building. This graphic patchwork, this memorial to their friends and loved ones, inspired the idea of a massive AIDS quilt.

Jones and friends took up the cause of making quilt panels. Actor Marvin Feldman, a friend of Cleve's who had recently died, was the first to have a panel made for him. Cindy McMullin made three panels in Lyon's honor, including the one that hangs in the Smithsonian. Her panels incorporate a variety of media, including newsprint from the San Francisco Examiner's account of his testimony. Her and other panels incorporate get-well cards that had been made for Lyon by fifth graders in a Catholic school he visited shortly before his death. McMullin became an early volunteer with the NAMES Project Foundation, as the quilt organizers' group was formally called. The group began to accumulate hundreds of quilt panels for eventual public display. Each panel captured a personal story in a different way. Many were sewn in cotton with conventional materials, but others incorporated Barbie dolls, and car keys, and bubble wrap, Legos, tennis shoes, credit cards, and even a Sony Walkman. Taken individually, each panel pointed to a life lost and to the pain of close friends and family. Taken together, they served as a call for compassion, understanding, and action.

The quilt was displayed for the first time on the National Mall in Washington, DC on October 11, 1987. By then, some 40,000 Americans had died of AIDS. The quilt included 1,920 panels. It was displayed again in 1988, and then 1989. And by then, it was five times its original size. Each panel is a testament to a life lost too early. Fortunately, the AIDS quilt played a major role in removing the shame from the disease. It conveyed to the broader public the humanity of those who had been afflicted and died; it was a new generation's March of Dimes.

In the decades since, millions of people around the world have died of AIDS. Research and treatment have now, though, progressed to a point where a diagnosis is no longer an automatic death sentence. However, while treatment can drastically reduce transmission, there is still no vaccine or cure. But there are new advances that hold considerable promise, one of which involves

DNA research and the use of a technology embodied in another innovative machine in the Smithsonian's collection—the PCR machine. PCR stands for polymerase chain reaction.

The machine uses thermal cycling to accelerate the replication of small DNA samples, amplifying minute quantities of genetic material into larger samples that can be detected, allowing for easier diagnosis of diseases and the easier evaluation of the progress of potential cures. Researchers can now fragment DNA into isolated segments and use PCR to amplify them so they can be used in genetic manipulation, altering cells to be able to fend off the AIDS virus, for example. This just illustrates how far we've come since Salk and Sabin tested vaccines on themselves and their families

Knowledge, invention, experimentation, social will and support, all have played a historic role in America, especially in the 20th and so far in the 21st century. Individual and group efforts have helped conquer diseases and improve the quality of life for millions. It is a role that has helped not only Americans, but benefited those around the world.

Women Making History

Lecture 17

Today, women occupy positions as key public officials; respected civic and cultural leaders; esteemed scientists; heads of corporations, foundations, and universities; and renowned figures in sports and the arts. Although many would argue there is still room for growth and accomplishment, progress over the course of American history has been appreciable. When measuring that progress, few milestones seem more important than the passage of the Nineteenth Amendment to the U.S. Constitution, the amendment giving all adult women the right to vote. In this lecture, you will be introduced to only a few of the remarkable women who have left their mark on American history, including Helen Keller, Amelia Earhart, and Julia Child.

The Nineteenth Amendment

- Only men were allowed to vote on the Mayflower compact. Later, each colony had made its own rules about who could vote, and this practice continued as colonies became states. Voting requirements generally called for a certain age of maturity (generally 21) and ownership of property, and so on. Younger adults, Indians, African Americans, and women were typically disqualified.

- Although women could not vote, they were not absent from American political life. The 19th century was notable for a series of social and political reform movements, including the First and Second Great Awakenings, the temperance movement, and the abolitionist movement, many of which were driven by women.

- Two leading figures among the abolitionist movement were Elizabeth Cady Stanton and Lucretia Mott. The pair met in 1840 at the World Anti-Slavery Convention, when they were both refused admittance because of their sex. Outraged, the two quickly became allies in both the abolition movement and the women's rights movement.

- In 1848, they organized a women's rights convention at Seneca Falls, New York. There, Elizabeth Cady Stanton delivered a Declaration of Sentiments, a list of grievances and demands modeled on the Declaration of Independence. This list included the demand for women's suffrage.

- But throughout the 1850s, the slavery question overwhelmed all other political concerns in the United States. And, by 1865, the abolitionists had won. Soon thereafter, the Thirteenth Amendment ended slavery. The Fourteenth Amendment confirmed the former slaves' rights of citizenship.

- The Fifteenth Amendment stated that the right to vote could not be denied based on "race, color, or previous condition of servitude." However, the federal government and the individual states still had the right to deny people the right to vote on the basis of gender.

- The Fifteenth Amendment split the women's suffrage movement. Some of its leaders refused to endorse the amendment because it did not give women the vote. Others, including long-term women's rights ally Frederick Douglass, argued that if black men were enfranchised, their support would help women achieve their goal.

- In 1887, the movement overcame internal disagreements over strategy, forming the National American Woman Suffrage Association (NAWSA), led by Susan B. Anthony. Efforts at the state level produced results, particularly in the Rockies and the West, with Wyoming, Colorado, Utah, and Idaho all granting women's suffrage in state elections before 1900. In the following decades, Washington state, California, Arizona, Kansas, Oregon, Montana, Nevada, and New York all followed suit.

- Labor unionists, temperance advocates, education reformers, and even physical fitness advocates allied themselves with the suffragists. The concept of the "new woman"—as an intelligent, independent, accomplished, and capable individual—became a staple of literature.

- Carrie Chapman Catt succeeded Anthony as NAWSA's president in 1900. Catt adopted a strategy based on logic, persuasion, and compromise—essentially, a slow and steady path toward the goal. This was precisely the opposite of the strategy adopted by Alice Paul, who guided the women's movement toward more aggressive tactics and toward federal-level efforts.

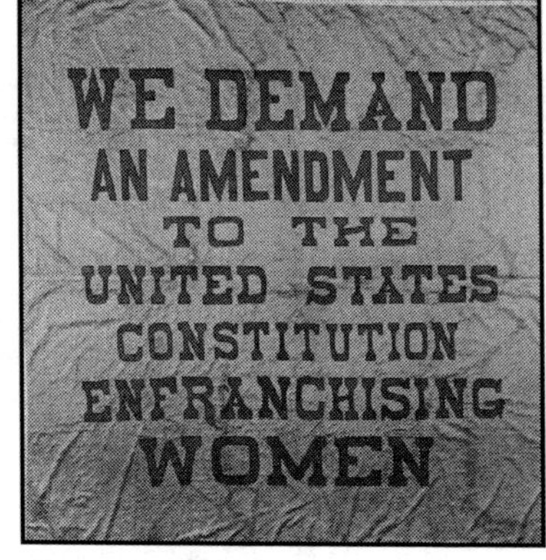

Women's Suffrage Banner

- Paul decided to put direct pressure on the newly elected Woodrow Wilson, who opposed a constitutional amendment granting women the right to vote. During his inauguration, on March 3, 1913, the suffragists marched on the White House. It was the first of many such marches.

- Banners were used at many suffrage marches, demonstrations, and vigils, and one such banner is at the National Museum of American History. The Great Demand banner, as it came to be called, declares in bold words and style the determination of the women who made and carried it to achieve their great demand—the right to vote and, hence, full civic participation in American democracy.

- Currently, there are two banners of this type known to exist, one at the Sewall-Belmont House in Washington DC and the other at the Smithsonian. Their similarities indicate that there was probably a guide or template for their creation.

- On Sunday, March 4, 1917, the day of Wilson's second inaugural, the suffragists organized a demonstration to "encircle the President's Mansion with a chain of purple, white, and gold." In spite of a cold, drenching rain, more than 1,000 women stood before the White House holding banners and signs in a silent vigil to demand a women's suffrage amendment. Meanwhile, a mile or so away, Jeannette Rankin of Montana took her seat in the House of Representatives as the first woman to be elected to the U.S. Congress.

- Paul continued the picketing after the inauguration. While Wilson might have been somewhat amused at first, his attitude changed with the picketers' persistence. The silent sentinels, as the women called themselves, were increasingly seen as an embarrassment to the administration.

- On April 2, Wilson told Congress that war against Germany was necessary that the world "be made safe for democracy." The picketers' banners pointed out the hypocrisy of fighting for democracy and freedom in Europe while denying it to women at home.

- In June 1917, the District of Columbia police began arresting picketers for obstructing sidewalk traffic. The arrested women were sent to the Occoquan Workhouse in northern Virginia. In August, scuffles broke out at the gates of the White House as angry spectators assaulted suffragists while city police stood by.

- The picketing continued. On October 20, Alice Paul was arrested and sentenced to seven months in jail. She and her companions were held in solitary confinement and denied counsel. Paul went on a hunger strike and was violently force-fed. Authorities confined her to a psychiatric ward in an effort to discredit her.

- On November 14, 30 women in Occoquan were beaten, threatened, and mistreated in what came to be known as the Night of Terror. The subsequent storm of critical publicity was such that the administration itself soon called for the release of all suffragist prisoners.

- Paul had commemorative pins made for the women who went to prison for the cause. In December 1917, at a meeting in their honor, the picketers who had been jailed were presented with small silver pins in the shape of prison doors with heart-shaped locks. The National Museum of American History now holds three of these "Jailed for Freedom" pins, including the one that belonged to Alice Paul.

- Meanwhile, Carrie Chapman Catt, who distanced herself from Paul's picketing, appealed to Wilson to support a congressional vote on the women's suffrage amendment, and he did. The Senate rejected the amendment by two votes in 1918, but the following year finally passed the Nineteenth Amendment, which stated that the right to vote could not be denied based on sex. It was ratified in 1920.

Helen Keller

- Helen Keller, one of the most admired women of her time, was an advocate for a number of causes. She strongly supported the formation of labor unions, became a member of the Socialist Party, and joined the radical Industrial Workers of the World, better known as the Wobblies. She was a friend of birth control advocate Margaret Sanger. She believed strongly in justice for African Americans and supported the National Association for the Advancement of Colored People. She was also a founding member of the American Civil Liberties Union.

- Whatever one might think of Keller's politics, she gained widespread respect for her personal achievements in overcoming her physical disabilities. She lost both her sight and her hearing at 19 months old, when she suffered so-called "brain fever"—either scarlet fever or meningitis.

Helen Keller's Pocket Watch

- Helen grew up a sheltered and difficult child—always throwing tantrums, smashing things, kicking, biting, and scratching. Her parents felt pressure to give up on the prospect of Helen having anything like a fulfilling life. Then, one day, her mother read an article about Laura Bridgman, another deaf and blind girl who learned to write and communicate through sign language.

- A physician put Helen's mother in touch with Alexander Graham Bell, who had developed new technologies for teaching the deaf. Bell suggested the Perkins School for the Blind, where Bridgman had studied. The school's director suggested a tutor named Anne Sullivan, who herself was vision impaired and was a former Perkins student.

- Sullivan moved into a small cottage on the family property to live with Helen. Sullivan's early attempts at finger spelling—signing words into Helen's palm—were a failure. Then, one day, Sullivan spelled out "w-a-t-e-r" as she ran pump water over Keller's hand. Helen had a breakthrough moment and spelled the word back to Sullivan.

- That opened the floodgates for Helen, who became a quick and obsessive learner. Within the year, Keller and Sullivan relocated to Boston to attend the Perkins School. Keller learned to read Braille, use a typewriter, and lip-read. With Sullivan always at her side, Keller eventually gained entrance to Radcliffe College and, in 1904, became the first deaf and blind person to receive a college degree in the United States.

- It was during Keller's school years that she and Sullivan traveled to Washington DC and received a watch that now is in the National Museum of American History. It was a gift from John Hitz, a former Swiss diplomat, who was serving as the superintendent of Alexander Graham Bell's Volta Bureau. Called a touch watch, the device was designed to enable a person to tell the time by feeling the watch instead of looking at it.

- Keller learned to speak and become a popular lecturer, as well as the prolific author of more than a dozen books. Until her death in 1968, she traveled the world as an advocate for those with disabilities, raising public consciousness as well as funds.

Amelia Earhart

- Amelia Earhart is the most famous female pilot in American history, but she was not America's first female pilot. The National Air and Space Museum accords that honor to Bessica Raiche, who made the first accredited solo flight by a woman in the United States on September 16, 1910. Hundreds of women were involved in the pioneering days of flight as pilots, engineers, and even barnstorming stuntwomen.

- Amelia Earhart took her first flight as a passenger in California in December 1920. Her first flight instructor was a woman, Mary Neta Snook, who gave her lessons in a Curtiss Jenny. Earhart purchased a plane and began flying in competitions with other women pilots. Thanks to publisher George Putnam, she flew across the Atlantic as a passenger in 1928.

- Putnam became her manager and companion and, a few years later, her husband. He promoted her heavily in the 1929 Women's Air Derby, the first all-female "transcontinental" (from Santa Monica, California, to Cleveland, Ohio), which proved a media sensation. She finished third. That same year, she helped found the Women Pilots Association.

- Charles Lindbergh had become America's hero in his solo flight across the Atlantic. Earhart was determined to replicate that flight and become the nation's flying heroine. In 1930, she bought a Vega 5B—now in the National Air and Space Museum—and called it her Little Red Bus. The Vega was sturdy, roomy, streamlined, and fast; it was the first plane designed by the new Lockheed company.

- On May 20 and 21, 1932, Earhart, took off alone from Harbour Grace, Newfoundland, Canada, in the Vega heading for France.

She fought fatigue, a leaky fuel tank, and a cracked manifold that spewed flames out the side of the engine cowling. Ice formed on the Vega's wings and caused a sudden 3,000-foot descent to just above the waves. Realizing she was on a course far north of France, she landed in a farmer's field in Northern Ireland.

- Later in 1932, Earhart made the first solo nonstop flight by a woman across the United States—also in the Vega. She flew 2,447 miles from Los Angeles to Newark, New Jersey, establishing a women's record of 19 hours and 5 minutes.

- In 1937, Earhart set her sights on an around-the-world flight. On May 20, 1937, she took off from Oakland, California, in a new twin-engine Lockheed 10E Electra. This time, she brought a navigator, Fred Noonan. By June 29, they had flown across Africa, the Middle East, South Asia, and Australia to a landing in New Guinea.

- On July 2, they took off for tiny Howland Island for refueling. A U.S. Coast Guard cutter heard Earhart's radio transmissions as she approached the area, but the plane never arrived. Despite a massive search, the plane was never found, and Earhart and Noonan were declared lost at sea.

- The Smithsonian has a number of items associated with Earhart in addition to the Vega, including her flight coat, goggles, flying helmet, and the trophy (in the National Air and Space Museum) that Earhart would have won had she completed her around-the-world flight.

Julia Child

- For much of American history, cooking for one's family was regarded as women's work and largely a utilitarian pursuit. Truly exceptional cooking, like classical French cuisine, had largely been viewed as the purview of the professional chef. Julia Child changed that. By using her own kitchen as a classroom and turning food preparation into charming and entertaining televised performances, she demystified haute cuisine.

Julia Child's Kitchen

- Her 700-plus-page book, coauthored with Simone Beck and Louise Bertholle, was published as *Mastering the Art of French Cooking* in 1961. A surprising and whopping success, it sold more than 100,000 copies in its first year. Moving to Cambridge, Massachusetts, Julia appeared on an educational television program in the Boston area. This led to an 11-year run as *The French Chef*, produced by WGBH-TV.

- Julia Child's book and television program was successful for several reasons. First, the time was right: Jackie Kennedy, of French background and elegant taste, was in the White House. Maybe Child's cooking provided a broadly accessible pathway for women to identify with First Lady and President Kennedy.

- Alternatively, maybe Julia had turned the kitchen into a place for intelligence, talent, and mastery, a domestic setting where many women, denied a skilled job in the workforce, could nonetheless seek personal growth and fulfillment. Or maybe the exploration of French cuisine represented the hankering for adventurous new experiences and signaled the cultural turn of the 1960s away from the conventional and toward the foreign and exotic. Julia was also, quite simply, an excellent teacher.

- For several of the later shows, Julia welcomed her viewers into her Cambridge home kitchen. Indeed, it became the historical artifact of Julia Child's life's work.

- In 2001, Julia was planning to leave Cambridge for a retirement home in Santa Barbara, California. In 2002, the kitchen was meticulously taken apart, transported, and then reconstituted in the Smithsonian's American History museum. The kitchen has now become a popular pilgrimage stop for foodies, a reminder of how a talented woman stirred delight and creativity in American culture.

Featured Objects

Women's Suffrage Banner

Helen Keller's Pocket Watch

Amelia Earhart's Flight Gear and Trophy

Julia Child's Kitchen

Suggested Reading

Barr, *Provence.*

Keller, *The Story of My Life.*

Rich, *Amelia Earhart.*

Walton, *A Woman's Crusade.*

Women Making History

Lecture 17—Transcript

Today we find women occupying positions as key public officials; as respected civic and cultural leaders; esteemed scientists; heads of corporations, foundations and universities; renowned figures in sports and the arts. Although many would argue there is still room for growth and accomplishment, progress over the course of American history has been appreciable.

When measuring that progress, few milestones seem more important than the passage of the 19th amendment to the U.S. Constitution, the amendment giving all adult women the right to vote. Recall from a previous lecture that only men were allowed to vote on the Mayflower compact. Later, each colony made its own rules about who could vote, and this practice continued as colonies became states. Voting requirements generally called for a certain age of maturity, generally 21, and ownership of property, and so on. Younger adults, American Indians, African Americans, and women were typically disqualified.

Though women could not vote, they were not absent from American political life. The 19th century was notable for a series of social and political reform movements, many of which were driven by women. You're likely familiar with some of these movements. In an earlier lecture, I mentioned the First and Second Great Awakenings, which gave rise to a number of American religious movements. The Shaker community arose out of this movement. It was not only a religion but a utopian social community, and it had several women leaders, such as Ann Lee and Lucy Wright. The temperance movement—the movement to ban alcohol—also emerged from the Second Great Awakening. One of its most famous leaders was a woman named Carry Nation. A formidable figure, she was famous for singing hymns while attacking bar rooms with a hatchet!

But foremost among the early American reform movements was the abolitionist movement. Thousands of women joined the fight to abolish slavery. They wrote for the abolitionist press. They distributed pamphlets and circulated petitions. They spoke at rallies, a radical act that was often condemned by the clergy of the day. Two leading figures among the abolitionist movement were Elizabeth Cady Stanton and Lucretia Mott. The pair met in 1840 at the World Anti-Slavery Convention, when they were both refused admittance because of their gender. Outraged, the two quickly became allies in both the abolitionist movement and the women's rights movement. In 1848, they organized a women's rights convention at Seneca Falls, New York. There, Elizabeth Cady Stanton delivered a Declaration of Sentiments, a list of grievances and demands modeled on the Declaration of Independence. This list included the demand for women's suffrage.

But throughout the 1850s, the slavery question overwhelmed all other political concerns in the United States. And by 1865, of course, the abolitionists had won. Soon thereafter, the 13th amendment ended slavery. The 14th amendment confirmed the former slaves' rights of citizenship. And the 15th amendment said this: "[The] right of citizens of the United States to vote shall not be denied or abridged by the United States or by any state on account of race, color, or previous condition of servitude." Notice what it doesn't say. The federal government and the individual states still had the right to deny people the right to vote on the basis of gender.

The 15th Amendment split the women's suffrage movement. Some of its leaders refused to endorse the amendment because it did not give women the vote. Others, including long-time women's rights ally Frederick Douglass, argued that if black men were enfranchised, their support would help women achieve their goal. In 1887, the movement overcame internal disagreements over strategy, forming the National American Woman Suffrage Association, NAWSA, led by Susan B. Anthony. Efforts at the state level produced results, particularly in the Rockies and the West, with Wyoming, Colorado, Utah, and Idaho all granting women's suffrage in state elections before 1900. In the following decades, Washington state, California, Arizona, Kansas, Oregon, Montana, Nevada, and New York all followed suit.

Labor unions, temperance advocates, education reformers, and even physical fitness advocates allied themselves with the suffragists. The concept of the new woman as an intelligent, independent, accomplished, and capable individual became a staple of literature. Carrie Chapman Catt succeeded Anthony as NAWSA's president in 1900. A former school superintendent, she had spent some time in law school and was a skilled organizer and negotiator. In fact, before marrying her second husband, George Catt, in 1890, she negotiated a prenuptial agreement that guaranteed her four months of every year to devote to the cause of women's suffrage. Catt adopted a strategy based on logic, persuasion, and compromise, essentially, a slow and steady path toward the goal.

This was precisely the opposite of the strategy adopted by Alice Paul. Paul was a Quaker graduate of Swarthmore College, where she studied biology. She went to Great Britain in 1907 while working toward her Ph.D. in Social Work. There she encountered the militant tactics of the British suffrage movement. British suffragists heckled politicians; they smashed windows; they went on hunger strikes; they deliberately got arrested to get their cause in the newspapers. While living in Britain, Paul was arrested for these activities on several occasions.

When she returned to the United States, she guided the women's movement toward more aggressive tactics and toward federal-level efforts. Paul decided to put direct pressure on the newly elected Woodrow Wilson, who opposed a constitutional amendment guaranteeing women the right to vote. During his inauguration, on March 3, 1913, the suffragists marched on the White House. It was the first of many such marches. Banners like, this one at the National Museum of American History, were used at many suffrage marches, demonstrations, and vigils. The Great Demand banner, as it came to be called, declares in bold words and style the determination of the women who made it and carried it to achieve their great demand, the right to vote, and hence, full civic participation in American democracy.

Archival photographs show a sign that matches the wording and style of the Smithsonian banner; their similarities indicate that there was probably a guide or template for their creation.

On Sunday, March 4, 1917, the day of Wilson's second inaugural, the suffragists organized a demonstration to "encircle the Presidential Mansion with a chain of purple and gold," they said. In spite of a cold, drenching rain, more than 1,000 women stood before the White House holding banners and signs in a silent vigil to demand a women's suffrage amendment. Photographs show banners asking questions like, "Mr. President how long must women wait for liberty?" Meanwhile, a mile or so away, Jeannette Rankin of Montana took her seat in the House of Representatives as the first woman to be elected to the United States Congress.

Paul continued the picketing after the inauguration. While Wilson might have been somewhat amused at first, his attitude changed with the picketers' persistence. The silent sentinels, as the women called themselves, were increasingly seen as an embarrassment to the administration. On April 2, Wilson told Congress that war against Germany was necessary so that the world would be "made safe for democracy." The picketers' banners pointed out the hypocrisy of fighting for democracy and freedom in Europe while denying it to women at home.

In June 1917, the District of Columbia police began arresting picketers for obstructing sidewalk traffic. The arrested women were sent to the Occoquan Workhouse in northern Virginia. In August, scuffles broke out at the gates of the White House as angry spectators assaulted suffragists while city police stood by. The picketing continued. On October 20, Alice Paul was arrested and sentenced to seven months in jail. She and her companions were held in solitary confinement and denied counsel. Paul went on a hunger strike and was violently force-fed. Authorities confined her to a psychiatric ward in an effort to discredit her.

On November 14, 30 women in Occoquan were beaten, threatened, and mistreated in what came to be known as the Night of Terror. The subsequent storm of critical publicity was such that the administration itself soon called for the release of all suffragist prisoners. Alice Paul had commemorative pins made for the women who went to prison for the cause. In December 1917, at a meeting in their honor, the picketers who had been jailed were presented with these small silver pins in the shape of prison doors with heart-shaped locks. The National Museum of American History now holds three of these Jailed for Freedom pins, including the one that belonged to Alice Paul.

Meanwhile, Carrie Chapman Catt, who distanced herself from Paul's picketing, appealed to Wilson to support a congressional vote on the women's suffrage amendment, and he did. The Senate rejected the amendment by two votes in 1918, but the following year finally passed the 19th Amendment, which stated, "The right of citizens of the United States to vote shall not be denied or abridged by the United States or by any State on account of sex." It was ratified in 1920. With the passage of the 19th Amendment, the right to active participation in American representative democracy had finally reached all adult citizens over 21.

Among those who spoke out for women's suffrage was Helen Keller, one of the most admired women of her time. Keller participated in suffragist rallies and marches and opposed Woodrow Wilson's reticence to endorse women's rights. Keller was an advocate for a number of causes. She strongly supported the formation of labor unions, became a member of the Socialist Party, and joined the radical Industrial Workers of the World, better known as the Wobblies. She was a friend of birth control advocate Margaret Sanger. She believed strongly in justice for African Americans and supported the National Association for the Advancement of Colored People. She was also a founding member of the American Civil Liberties Union.

Now, whatever one might think of Keller's politics, she gained widespread respect for her personal achievements in overcoming her physical disabilities. Helen Keller was born on an Alabama plantation in 1880 to a veteran Confederate officer and a Southern socialite. Helen lost both her sight and her hearing at 19 months old when she suffered so-called brain fever, probably either scarlet fever or meningitis.

Helen grew up a sheltered and difficult child, always throwing tantrums, smashing things, kicking, biting, and scratching. Her parents felt pressure to give up on the prospect of Helen having anything like a fulfilling life. Then one day, her mother read an article about Laura Bridgman, another deaf and blind girl, who learned to write and communicate through sign language. A physician put Helen's mother in touch with Alexander Graham Bell, who, as we saw in an earlier lecture, had developed new technologies for teaching the deaf. Bell suggested the Perkins School for the Blind, where Bridgman had studied. The school's director suggested a tutor named Anne Sullivan. Anne Sullivan herself was vision-impaired woman and former Perkins student.

Sullivan moved into a small cottage on the family's property to live with Helen. Sullivan's early attempts at finger spelling—signing words into

Helen's palm—were a failure. Then one day Sullivan spelled out w-a-t-e-r as she ran pump water over Keller's hand. Helen had a breakthrough moment and spelled the word back to Sullivan.

That opened up the floodgates for Helen, who became a quick and obsessive learner. Within a year, Keller and Sullivan relocated to Boston to attend the Perkins School. Keller learned to read Braille, use a typewriter, and lip-read, following Bell's method of placing her finger on Sullivan's lips and throat. With Sullivan always at her side, Keller attended the Wright-Humason School for the Deaf in New York and the Cambridge School for Young Ladies in Boston before gaining entrance to Radcliffe College, where admirer Mark Twain helped arrange payment for her tuition. In 1904, Helen Keller became the first deaf and blind person to receive a college degree in the United States.

It was during Keller's school years that she and Sullivan traveled to Washington, DC and received this watch, now in the collections of the National Museum of American History. It was a gift from John Hitz, a former Swiss diplomat, who was serving as the superintendent of Alexander Graham Bell's Volta Bureau.

The elegant gold and brass timepiece was manufactured in Switzerland in about 1865. Its face has the usual hour and minute hands, with a smaller inset second timer. There's a stem for winding and a loop, or a bow, for attaching it to a chain. But what is unusual and might be mistakenly taken for a simple decorative feature are pin-like studs protruding from the case surrounding the dial, one for each hour. If we take a look at the back of the watch, we see something different. We see that at the back of the case there is a revolving hand in the shape of an elaborately decorated arrow. Called a touch watch, the device was designed to enable a person to tell time by feeling the watch instead of just looking at it. The user would line up the back arrow with the pins to determine the hour and estimate the minutes. Now, a diplomat like Hitz would use one to tell time discreetly while engaged in a meeting. The watch never even had to leave his pocket.

It's a mundane thing, looking at a watch, and if you aren't visually impaired, well, maybe you take telling the time for granted. But for Keller, this watch was invaluable. This simple watch with these modifications allowed her to have a new measure of independence, and she treasured this watch for the remainder of her life.

Keller learned to speak and become a popular lecturer, as well as the prolific author of more than a dozen books. Until her death in 1968, she traveled the world as an advocate for those with disabilities, raising public consciousness as well as funds. She visited 35 countries on five continents, where her eloquence, insight, and warmth not only challenged but exploded preconceptions of the disabled as limited human beings. With Sullivan's collaboration, Keller learned to communicate with mainstream audiences, who discovered that she had a lot to say, not only about the rights of the disabled, but about the welfare of all humankind.

Among the Smithsonian's most prized artifacts are those of another woman who extended the boundaries of achievement and achieved great fame—Amelia Earhart. Earhart is, without a doubt, the most famous female pilot in American history, and she vies with Charles Lindberg and the Wright Brothers for the title of the most famous pilot in American history—period. But let me be clear, she was not America's first female pilot.

At the National Air and Space Museum, we accord that honor to Bessica Raiche. On September 16, 1910, she made the first accredited solo flight by a woman in the United States, in a bamboo and silk Wright-style flyer that she and her husband built in their living room. There were literally hundreds of women involved in the pioneering days of flight as pilots, engineers, and even as barnstorming stuntwomen. They were the epitome of the new woman so admired by the suffragists.

Earhart certainly fit the new woman mold. Growing up in Kansas in the wake of the Wright brothers' first flight, Earhart exhibited no shortage of independence. She learned auto repair and attended college; she worked a variety of jobs, including nurse, social worker, telephone company clerk, truck driver, photographer. She took her first flight as a passenger in California in December 1920 and afterward declared, "As soon as I left the ground, I knew I myself had to fly." Her first instructor was a woman, Mary Neta Snook, who gave her lessons in a Curtiss Jenny.

Earhart purchased a plane and began flying in competitions with other women pilots. Thanks to publisher George Putnam, she flew across the Atlantic as a passenger in 1928. Putnam became her manager and companion, and a few years later, her husband. He promoted her heavily in the 1929 Women's Air Derby, the first all-female transcontinental competition, which proved a media sensation. She finished third. That same year, she helped to found the Women Pilots Association.

Charles Lindbergh had become America's hero in his solo flight across the Atlantic. Earhart was determined to replicate that flight and become the nation's flying heroine. In 1930, she bought this Vega 5B, now in the National Air and Space Museum, and called it her Little Red Bus. The Vega was sturdy, roomy, streamlined, and fast, the first plane designed by the new Lockheed company. It came to be favored by pilots seeking to set speed and distance records.

On May 20 to the 21, 1932, Earhart took off alone from Harbour Grace, Newfoundland, Canada, in this Vega heading for France. She fought fatigue, a leaky fuel tank, and a cracked manifold that spewed flames out the side of the engine cowling. Ice formed on the Vega's wings and caused a sudden 3,000-foot descent to just above the waves. Realizing she was on a course far north of France, she landed in a farmer's field in Northern Ireland.

Later, in 1932, Earhart made the first solo nonstop flight by a woman across the United States, also in this plane. She flew 2,447 miles from Los Angeles to Newark, New Jersey, establishing a women's record of 19 hours and 5 minutes.

In 1937, Earhart set her sights on an around-the-world flight. On May 20, 1937, she took off from Oakland, California in a new twin-engine Lockheed 10E Electra. This time, she brought a navigator, Fred Noonan. By June 29, they had flown across Africa, the Middle East, South Asia, and Australia to a landing in New Guinea. On July 2 they took off for tiny Howland Island for refueling. A U.S. Coast Guard cutter heard Earhart's radio transmissions as she approached the area, but the plane never arrived. Despite a massive search, the plane was never found, and Earhart and Noonan were declared lost at sea.

We have a number of items associated with Earhart in addition to the Vega, her flight coat, goggles, for example. But perhaps none is more telling than this trophy, which now rests in the National Air and Space Museum. This is the Stinson trophy that Earhart was among the first women to compete for. Had she completed her round-the-world flight, she very well may have come back to win this trophy. Thus, it's a reminder both of her skill and determination in making that flight, as well the premature loss her disappearance represented. Americans, and indeed, people around the world, were shocked by her loss. Earhart's unsolved disappearance has continued to spawn a wide variety of theories that sometimes overshadows her true contribution as a pioneer of aviation.

Another pioneering woman celebrated in the collections of the Smithsonian is Julia Child, who revolutionized American home cooking in the 1960s. For much of American history, cooking for one's family was regarded as women's work and largely a utilitarian pursuit. Homemakers had to prepare meals efficiently and well, given limited time and resources. If there was any flair to cooking, it typically came around special, holiday meals. Truly exceptional cooking, say, like classical French cuisine with its time-consuming sauces and exacting preparation methods, had largely been viewed as the purview of the professional chef. These chefs were almost always male, and they inhabited the kitchens of elite restaurants, men's dining clubs, or wealthy households, not the average American home.

But Julia Child changed that. By using her own kitchen as a classroom and turning food preparation into charming and entertaining televised performances, she demystified haute cuisine. Her 700-page book, co-authored with Simone Beck and Louisette Bertholle, was published the as Mastering the Art of French Cooking in 1961. A surprising and whopping success, it sold more than 100,000 copies in its first year. Moving to Cambridge, Massachusetts, Julia appeared on an educational television program in the Boston area, and this led to an 11-year run as The French Chef, which was produced by WGBH-TV.

The show was a huge hit. Julia's verve, talent, and unique persona engaged and encouraged viewers. Men and women alike tuned in to turn humdrum menus into masterpieces. Functional kitchens became studios for the culinary arts. Julia's show recast the act of cooking as a refined, middle-class, cultural pursuit and a worthy avenue of creativity, especially women's creativity.

Now, why were Julia Child's book and television program so successful? Well, I think the time was right. Jackie Kennedy, of French background and elegant taste, was in the White House, adding glamour to American public life. Maybe Child's cooking provided a broadly accessible pathway for women to identify with First Lady and President Kennedy, as Julia herself suggested decades later. Alternatively, maybe Julia had turned the kitchen into a place for intelligence, talent, and mastery, a domestic setting where many women, denied a skilled job in the workforce, could nonetheless seek personal growth and fulfillment. Or maybe the exploration of French cuisine represented the hankering for adventurous new experiences and signaled the cultural turn of the 1960s away from the conventional and toward the foreign and exotic.

Julia was also, quite simply, an excellent teacher. She believed that anyone could, as the title of her book suggested, master the art of French cooking. She skillfully used drama, and comedy, exaggeration, and props as teaching tools. She had a rare ability to break a technique down into its fundamental parts, demonstrate it to an audience, and show them how to apply that technique to an entire culinary world. Mistakes were treated as learning experiences; nothing was life or death in the kitchen. And she approached cooking not as a chore, but as an act of joy, a joy her viewers wanted to share.

For several of the later shows, Julia welcomed her viewers into her Cambridge home kitchen. Indeed, it became the historical artifact of Julia Child's life's work. The kitchen was no ordinary one. It had been specially designed by Julia and her husband, Paul. The counters had to stand several inches higher than usual in order to accommodate Julia's 6 foot 3 inch height. Paul traced the outline of each pot on the pegboard walls so that every utensil would have its own place in the zone where it would be used. The large six-burner Garland range allowed for the simultaneous preparation of several dishes. On the other hand, the kitchen looked lived in, a real person's kitchen. Julia called it the beating heart of the household.

In 2001, Julia was planning to leave Cambridge for a retirement home in Santa Barbara, California. Several people close to Julia and the Smithsonian urged that the museum look at the kitchen with an eye toward a donation. The three curators from the Smithsonian's National Museum of American History arrived at Julia's Cambridge home to undertake the task of collecting something from her kitchen. But after interviewing Julia and documenting the kitchen, they realized the care, the organizational style, and even the curatorial sensibilities that had gone into composing the kitchen. This was a work of culinary artistry. They wanted to acquire the whole kitchen, including the kitchen sink!

The kitchen was meticulously taken apart, transported, and then reconstituted in the American history museum in 2002. It has been an immense hit. The kitchen has become a popular pilgrimage stop for foodies, a reminder of how the talented woman stirred delight and creativity in American culture.

The remarkable women I have just discussed are only a few of the many women who have left their mark on American history. After all, women's history is everyone's history. Their courage, their efforts, their talents have touched all our lives. In subsequent lectures, we'll see how other remarkable American women have made major contributions to our national life at crucial points in our history.

The Power of Portraits
Lecture 18

There is a long and dramatic record of how the famous and infamous in American history have fashioned their own public image, how those images accord or contrast with portrayals by others, and how broader social dynamics of the time play out in such image making. Indeed, with more than 10,000 portraits, the Smithsonian's National Portrait Gallery is devoted to the matter. As you will learn in this lecture, images of Pocahontas, Frederick Douglass, Abraham Lincoln, and Rosie the Riveter speak simultaneously to the high values Americans place on individualism as well as on achieving an important national purpose.

Portrait of Pocahontas

- One of the portraits in the National Portrait Gallery depicts a young woman whose image received immense attention when it was first crafted—and has been imagined and reimagined repeatedly over the past 400 years. Simon van de Passe's engraving identifies her as Matoaka, the daughter of Prince Powhatan, emperor of Virginia Algonquians, and notes her baptism to the Christian faith as Rebecca, currently wife to John Rolfe. The world, however, better knows her by her nickname, Pocahontas, the "playful one."

- The engraving, based on an oil painting, was included in *Baziliogia, a Book of Kings*, which was not so much a book as a collection of prints or a catalog. Buyers could select their choices, which would then be compiled and bound, with a made-to-order title page, into an individual volume.

- The story of Pocahontas and of this image is closely entwined with the early history of Jamestown, the first permanent English settlement in America. In 1606, a group of English entrepreneurs gained a royal charter from King James I as the Virginia Company of London, with the right to settle colonies in the middle-Atlantic region of America. The company sold stock to raise funds to buy and equip ships and then enticed people to make the journey with promises of gold and riches.

- In December 1606, three ships—the *Susan Constant*, the *Discovery*, and the *Godspeed*—set out from England with 144 men and boys aboard. In April 1607, they made landfall and soon after settled on an uninhabited island surrounded by what they named the James River. The group was undermanned and ill prepared to form a viable settlement. Most of the group were inexperienced at hard manual labor and lacked the skills needed to survive. They nonetheless felled trees and built a primitive fort with a stockade fence.

Portrait of Pocahontas

- Equipped with matchlock muskets, they had firepower to defend themselves against Indian attack—surrounded as they were by about 14,000 Algonquian natives led by a paramount leader, Chief Powhatan. The Algonquians grew maize, beans, and squash; fished; hunted small game and deer; and lived in settled villages. The colonists, on the other hand, failed to clear land and plant crops in time for harvest, leading to a food shortage later that year that resulted in the deaths of about one-third of the settlers.

- That first winter, one of the more able settlers, 28-year-old John Smith, was captured by a band of Indians and was brought to Chief Powhatan. What happened next varied in Smith's own written accounts and has become the stuff of legend over the ensuing years, but, basically, facing physical harm and even death, he was saved by the compassionate action of Chief Powhatan's teenage daughter Pocahontas.

- Additional ships arrived in Jamestown in 1608 to reprovision the colony. Smith emerged as a leader in Jamestown. He proved a good negotiator, trader, and diplomat, improving relations with the Powhatan. Pocahontas would visit the fort, play with the children, and bring provisions. Nonetheless, despite Smith's best efforts, Jamestown still lacked a viable food supply.

- While away from Jamestown on a trading trip in 1609, Smith was severely injured in a gunpowder explosion and went back to England. Pocahontas heard that he had died. What followed was a period of raiding between the colonists and the Powhatan, with Jamestown suffering a massive food shortage during the winter of 1609 to 1610 called the "starving time." So many colonists died that by the spring, the survivors had abandoned Jamestown altogether, retreating downriver.

- When a relief ship, the *Deliverance*, arrived in 1610 with provisions and new settlers, it found that only 61 of about 500 colonists remained. Aboard was a new governor and one of the Virginia Company's largest shareholders, Lord De La Ware, who persuaded the survivors to return to Jamestown. Among the new settlers was a planter, John Rolfe, who carried with him tobacco seeds from the Caribbean for planting in the colony.

- Back in England, the Virginia Company knew that it had a problem. Jamestown was an economic failure returning no profit. So, the Company promoted the colony as an extension of England's might and prestige among world powers. It presented to investors the idea that Jamestown would help them convert "heathen" Indians to the Christianity of the Church of England.

- Nonetheless, warfare between Jamestown and the Powhatan continued. In 1613, in an attempt to compel Chief Powhatan to return captured settlers, weapons, and tools, colonists took Pocahontas hostage. It took months to arrange an exchange, during which time Pocahontas was held in the nearby settlement of Henricas, where she learned English, converted to Christianity, and was baptized as Rebecca by an English minister.

- She also met the pious John Rolfe, who was just starting to find success cultivating tobacco on his nearby farm. Pocahontas decided to stay with the English and marry Rolfe. Their marriage, as well as peace between the Powhatan and the colonists, came in 1614. The newlywed gave birth the next January to a son, Thomas.

- In an effort to show investors that Jamestown was a success, the Virginia Company had the Rolfes travel to England in 1616. Pocahontas was presented as the now-Christianized and civilized Indian princess. She met King James I and was briefly reunited with John Smith, whom she was astonished to find still alive. In 1617, as the Rolfes began their voyage back to Virginia, Pocahontas took ill at Gravesend in Kent, England, where she died and is buried.

- That the engraving of Pocahontas was included in a collection of images of British monarchs and notables conveyed the idea that American Indians, even the daughter of a native emperor, could become civilized and be incorporated into the English world. The portrait of Pocahontas's transformation indicated that Jamestown had succeeded as a British colony in America, a notion vital to the Virginia Company's marketing strategy.

Photo of Frederick Douglass

- Frederick Douglass was a dedicated social reformer, brilliant orator, insightful author, savvy statesman, and talented leader of the abolitionist movement. He was born into slavery in Maryland in 1818 and then escaped to New York and thereafter to Massachusetts. In 1845, he published his first autobiography, *Narrative of the Life of Frederick Douglass, an American Slave*, to critical acclaim. Douglass went on to lecture internationally, publish newspapers and pamphlets, and become the foremost spokesperson against slavery.

- Douglass was keenly aware of how visual images of African Americans in books, newspapers, and other publications were used to shape stereotypes about their purported racial inferiority and subservience so as to justify slavery and low social position.

Frederick Douglass Ambrotype Photo

- Douglass witnessed the early development of photography and commented on its ability to shape and reshape images of black men and women. Douglass believed that photography could be a widely democratizing medium. Photography, he saw, could be used to improve the perceptions and treatment of African Americans by presenting people as they really were.

- Douglass took his own advice in sitting and posing for photographs. He was perhaps the most photographed African American of the 19th century. In a rare ambrotype photograph from about 1856 in the collection of the National Portrait Gallery, Douglass is impeccably and formally dressed, on par with the most distinguished Americans of the day. This was no accident. He projects a distinguished, serious, intense presence.

Abraham Lincoln's Hat

- Although he was six feet four inches tall and towered over most of his contemporaries, Abraham Lincoln chose to stand out even more by wearing high stovepipe hats. While frontier values of honesty and hard work might have helped get Lincoln elected president, he would need to project sophistication and an elevated stature to meet the nation's challenges during the Civil War.

- Lincoln acquired his most famous top hat from J. Y. Davis, a Washington DC hatmaker. The hat was made of silk fibers over a paper base and fabric lining, decorated with a three-eighths-inch silk ribbon and a small metal buckle.

- After its purchase, Lincoln added a three-inch silk grosgrain ribbon mourning band in memory of his deceased son, Willie, who died in 1862. The band showed that like other parents—in the North and South—who were mourning their sons, albeit lost in war, the president, too, was mourning the loss of his son.

Abraham Lincoln's Hat

- Lincoln wore his most famous top hat for the last time on Friday, April 14, 1865. The Civil War had ended five days before with General Robert E. Lee's surrender to General Ulysses S. Grant at Appomattox Court House. Lincoln had preserved the Union and freed the slaves. He had recently celebrated his second inaugural and planned to take in a performance of *Our American Cousin* at Ford's Theatre with his wife, Mary Todd, and their guests, Clara Harris and her fiancé, Union officer Major Henry Rathbone.

- On that Good Friday morning, Confederate loyalist John Wilkes Booth, learning that the president would attend the play, joined with other conspirators to put in place a bold plan to kidnap and assassinate key Union leaders.

- In the evening, Lincoln donned his hat when he took a carriage ride from the White House to the nearby theater. He arrived late—the play was already in progress, but the action stopped as the audience greeted the president. He took his chair in the presidential box and placed his hat on the floor beside him.

- During the third act of the play, Booth made his way to the presidential box and shot Lincoln in the back of the head. The grievously wounded Lincoln was taken to the Petersens' boardinghouse across the street. Treatment by physicians proved futile, and he died shortly after seven o'clock the next morning.

- Just after Lincoln's death, mourners descended on Ford's Theatre and the Petersens' house. They sought items associated with Lincoln's martyrdom—bloodied bandages and linens from his deathbed, locks of his hair, moldings from the theater's box. Henry was worried about the hat becoming a relic of what he regarded as irrational veneration. He had it stored in the castle's basement.

- The American public did not see the hat again until 1893—well after Henry's death—when the Smithsonian lent it to an exhibition hosted by the Lincoln Memorial Association near Ford's Theatre. Throughout the 20th century, Lincoln's hat was often in public view and became an iconic visual symbol of the 16th president. It is one of the most treasured and popular items on display at the Smithsonian.

"We Can Do It!" Poster

- Created by J. Howard Miller, the "We Can Do It!" poster is arguably America's most famous World War II–era home-front poster. It depicts a muscular and determined—though attractive and shapely—female factory worker wearing lipstick and makeup and patriotically outfitted in a red and white bandanna and blue work shirt. She says, "We can do it!"—which speaks both to the determination of the country to win the war and to the role American women played in that effort by working in the defense industries.

- Posters—colorful lithographic prints on cheap paper, designed for short-term display—evolved as a form of popular advertising art in the late 19th century. They came of age as a propaganda tool during World War I. By the time America entered World War II in 1941, the persuasive art of the poster had been refined, and the messages were even more widespread, all reminding Americans in one way or another that it was everyone's duty to support the war effort.

"We Can Do It!" Poster

- When Westinghouse made this original print, it did not name the woman—nor did Miller, the artist. Miller had been hired by Westinghouse Electric Corporation's War Production Coordinating Committee to develop a series of images for the company's wartime production campaign. The posters were intended to keep up morale among workers.

- The "We Can Do It!" poster, along with other efforts, encouraged women to succeed in manufacturing and factory jobs that had been considered "man's work" until then. The poster projected the idea of female patriotism expressed through manual labor in factories.

- The name "Rosie the Riveter" was attached to this image much later. It came from a 1942 song written by Redd Evans and John Jacob Loeb. Rosie was a fictional female factory worker laboring for the war effort. The upbeat song was recorded by big band leader Kay Kyser.

- Numerous depictions of "real Rosies" followed as reporters and publicists found workers named Rose performing heavy-duty manual tasks in factories across the United States. Other characters also emerged—Winnie the Welder, for example—to call attention to the various roles played by women in military production.

- As nearly as can be determined, the woman in Miller's poster was a 17-year-old cellist named Geraldine Hoff, later Geraldine Doyle, who worked at a metal-pressing plant near Ann Arbor, Michigan, during the war. Miller was inspired by a United Press photograph of her, hard at work, her makeup flawless, her hair bound up in a polka-dot bandana.

- The "We Can Do It!" poster seems so iconic today, but it was not widely distributed at the time. To the contrary, it was displayed in Pittsburgh and some Midwestern Westinghouse factories for just two weeks or so in February 1942 and was seen by relatively few workers.

- The poster was "rediscovered" and revived well after the World War II era. In the 1970s, large numbers of women were once again entering the workforce in a variety of roles, finding their way in male-dominated professions and workplaces. It was at this point that the poster was apocryphally identified with Rosie the Riveter, who was regarded as an inspirational figure. From the 1980s onward, the image became the subject of veneration, alteration, and parody.

Featured Objects

Portrait of Pocahontas

Frederick Douglass Ambrotype Photo

Abraham Lincoln's Hat

"We Can Do It!" Poster

Suggested Reading

Bird and Rubenstein, *Design for Victory*.

Douglass, *Narrative of the Life of Frederick Douglas*.

Townsend, *Pocahontas and the Powhatan Dilemma*.

White, *A. Lincoln*.

The Power of Portraits
Lecture 18—Transcript

We live in an era of Facebook and selfies, where we take for granted the ability, and even the desirability of shaping our own image. It would be a mistake, however, to think that because we do this with contemporary technologies like the Internet and smartphones that somehow this is a new impetus for Americans. There's a long and dramatic record of how the famous and infamous in American history have fashioned their own public image, how those images accord or contrast with portrayals by others, and how broader social dynamics of the time play out in such image-making. Indeed, the Smithsonian has a whole museum—the National Portrait Gallery—devoted to the matter. With more than 10,000 portraits, this is essentially a collection of visual biographies, a record of how Americans have seen themselves since our earliest documented history.

One of those portraits depicts a young woman whose image received immense attention when it was first crafted and has been imagined and re-imagined repeatedly over the past 400 years. Simon van de Passe's engraving identifies her as Matoaka, the daughter of Prince Powhatan, emperor of the Virginia Algonquians, and notes her baptism to the Christian faith as Rebecca, currently wife to John Rolfe. The world, however, knows her by her nickname—Pocahontas—the playful one.

She is portrayed in the stylish dress of the English nobility of the time, with an elaborate bodice, collar lace, and a high hat. Her pose is firm and cool; her sharp features and shaded skin tone suggest her Native Powhatan identity. The engraving, based upon an oil painting, was included in Baziliogia, a Book of Kings, which was not so much a book as a collection of prints or a catalog, and buyers could select their choices, which would then be compiled and bound, with a made-to-order title page, into an individual volume. The title page of this compilation is dated 1618, a year after Pocahontas died.

The story of Pocahontas and this image is closely entwined with the early history of Jamestown, the first permanent English settlement in America. In the opening years of the 17th century, England trailed the Spanish, Dutch, Portuguese, and French in the exploration and establishment of profitable colonies in the New World. In 1606, a group of English entrepreneurs gained a royal charter from King James I as the Virginia Company of London, with the right to settle colonies in the middle-Atlantic region of America. The company sold stock to raise funds to buy and equip ships. The enterprise was a profit-making investment, and some 1,700 people purchased shares. The company then enticed people to make the journey with promises of gold and riches.

In December 1606, three ships—the Susan Constant, the Discovery, and the Godspeed—set out from England with 144 men and boys aboard. In April 1607 they made landfall and soon after settled on an uninhabited island surrounded by what they named the James River. While defensible from attack by natives, the island was a very poor choice, small, swampy, mosquito-ridden, and it really lacked good drinking water.

The group was under-manned and ill-prepared to form a viable settlement. Those seeking gold or an easy life were sorely disappointed. Most were inexperienced at hard manual labor and lacked the skills needed to survive. Nonetheless, they felled trees and built a primitive fort with a stockade fence. Equipped with muskets, matchlock muskets, they had firepower to defend themselves against Indian attack, surrounded as they were by some 14,000 Algonquian natives led by a paramount leader Chief Powhatan. The Algonquians grew maize, beans, and squash; fished; hunted small game and deer; and lived in settled villages. Encounters with colonists varied from skirmishes to the Powhatans actually providing food and even lavish feasts for the settlers. The colonists, on the other hand, failed to clear land and plant crops in time for the harvest, leading to a food shortage later that year that resulted in the deaths of about one-third of the settlers.

That first winter, one of the more able settlers, 28-year-old John Smith, was captured by a band of Indians and was brought to Chief Powhatan. What happened next varied in Smith's own written accounts and has become the stuff of legend over the ensuing years, represented in numerous, even fanciful, ways, but basically, facing physical harm and even death, he was saved by the compassionate action of Chief Powhatan's teenaged daughter Pocahontas.

Additional ships arrived in Jamestown in 1608 to re-provision the colony. New settlers established glassmaking works, the first forms of manufacture in the colony. And Smith emerged as a leader in Jamestown. He proved a good negotiator, a good trader, and diplomat, improving relationships with the Powhatan. And Pocahontas would visit the fort, play with the children, bring provisions. Nonetheless, despite Smith's best efforts, Jamestown still lacked a viable food supply.

While away from Jamestown on a trading trip in 1609, Smith was severely injured in a gunpowder explosion and went back to England. Pocahontas heard he had died. What followed was a period of raiding between the colonists and the Powhatan, with Jamestown suffering a massive food shortage during the winter of 1609 to 10. It was called the starving time. So many colonists died that by that by the spring, the survivors had abandoned Jamestown altogether, and they had retreated down the river.

When a relief ship, the *Deliverance*, arrived in 1610 with provisions and new settlers, it found that only 61 of some 500 colonists remained. Aboard was a new governor and one of the Virginia Company's largest shareholders, Lord De La Ware, who persuaded the survivors to return to Jamestown. Among the new settlers was a planter, John Rolfe, who carried with him tobacco seeds from the Caribbean for planting in the colony.

Back in England, the Virginia Company knew it had a problem. Jamestown was an economic failure returning no profit; it needed to entice new investment, and it did so by appealing to patriotism. The Company promoted the colony as an extension of England's might and prestige among world powers. It presented to investors the idea that, well, Jamestown would help convert heathen Indians to the Christianity of the Church of England.

Nonetheless, warfare between Jamestown and the Powhatan continued. In 1613, in an attempt to compel Chief Powhatan to return captured settlers, weapons, and food, colonists took Pocahontas hostage. It took months to arrange an exchange, during which time Pocahontas was held in the nearby settlement of Henricas, where she learned English, converted to Christianity, and was baptized Rebecca by an English minister. She also met the pious John Rolfe, who was just starting to find success cultivating tobacco on his nearby farm. Pocahontas decided to stay with the English and marry Rolfe, who loved her and wanted to save her soul. Their marriage, as well as peace between the Powhatan and the colonists, came in 1614. The newlyweds gave birth the next January to a son the named Thomas.

In an effort to show investors that Jamestown was a success, the Virginia Company had the Rolfes travel to England in 1616. Pocahontas was now presented as the Christianized and civilized Indian princess, in line with the Company's marketing strategy. She met King James I; she attended important events and was briefly reunited with John Smith, whom she was astonished to find still alive. His public show of respect for her, as well as the creation of the portrait from which this engraving was made, served the Company's needs.

In 1617, as the Rolfes began their voyage back to Virginia, Pocahontas took ill at Gravesend in Kent, England, where she died and is buried. That this engraving of Pocahontas in fashionable English garb was included in a collection of images of British monarchs and notables conveyed the idea that American Indians, even the daughter of a native emperor, could become civilized and be incorporated into the English world. The portrait of Pocahontas's transformation indicated that Jamestown had succeeded as a British colony in America, a notion vital to the Virginia Company's marketing strategy. Yet, however co-opted by the artist, or the intent of the Virginia Company, something of Pocahontas's character comes through. She fixes the viewer with a penetrating, intelligent gaze. There's historical evidence that Pocahontas was not a passive victim of the English, but instead, was headstrong, self-assured, and even acerbic young woman. She was a smart, capable, well aware of her position in bridging Native and European worlds.

Interestingly, the National Portrait Gallery has a painting of Pocahontas by an unknown artist, based upon either the engraving or the original 1618 portrait. This version is clearly a corruption of the original. But you can see what is probably the first of many flights of fancy regarding how Pocahontas would be mis-represented in the future, in advertisements, and theme parks, children's books and animated films. In accord with the vision of the Virginia Company's managers, Pocahontas's skin tone is lightened;

her features less angular, much more Anglicized. She is being made into a dignified, Christianized, English lady.

The ability to visually depict and represent people can be a mechanism of social control. That was clear to Frederick Douglass, who lived some 200 years after Pocahontas. Douglass was a dedicated social reformer, a brilliant orator, insightful author, savvy statesman, and a talented leader of the abolitionist movement. He was born into slavery in Maryland in 1818 and then escaped to New York and thereafter to Massachusetts. In 1845, he published his first autobiography, *Narrative of the Life of Frederick Douglass, an American Slave* to critical acclaim. Douglass went on to lecture internationally, publish newspapers and pamphlets, and become the foremost spokesperson against slavery.

Douglass was keenly aware of how visual images of African Americans in books, newspapers, and other publications were used to shape stereotypes about their purported racial inferiority and subservience so as to justify slavery and low social position. He attacked depictions of blacks "with features distorted, lips exaggerated—forehead low and depressed—and the whole countenance made to harmonize with the popular idea of Negro ignorance, degradation and imbecility."

Douglass witnessed the early development of photography and commented on its ability to shape and reshape images of black women and men. Douglass believed that photography could be a widely democratizing medium. He said, "The humblest servant girl can now see a likeness of herself, such as noble ladies and even royalty itself could not purchase 50 years ago." Photography, he saw, could be used to improve the perceptions and the treatment of African Americans by presenting people as they really were.

So Douglas advised blacks to present themselves carefully, with good, strong character, so that they could overcome white prejudices, and, he was, of course, very conscious of his own image. Reviewing Wilson Armistead's *A Tribute for the Negro*, a book arguing for the capabilities of blacks, Douglass noted that his own engraved image bore a "much more kindly and amiable expression, than is generally thought to characterize the face of a fugitive slave."

In Douglass's second autobiography, *My Bondage and My Freedom*, he corrected that impression with an engraving, drawn from an earlier daguerreotype photograph, in which Douglass looks much more serious and even angrily defiant. Douglass took his own advice in sitting and posing for photographs. He was perhaps the most photographed African American of the 19th century. In this rare ambrotype photograph from about 1856 in the collection of the National Portrait Gallery, Douglass is impeccably and formally dressed, on par with the most distinguished Americans of the day. This was no accident. He projects a dignified, serious, and intense presence.

Much of Douglass's effort after the beginning of the Civil War entailed convincing President Abraham Lincoln to end slavery and allow blacks the full rights of citizenship, including the vote and armed service in the military. Lincoln, not unlike Douglass, was also a master in crafting his own public image. And though he was six-foot-four-inches tall and towered over most of his contemporaries, Abraham Lincoln chose to stand out even more by wearing high stovepipe hats.

Silk hats were stylish and popular in the 1850s. Silk had been replacing beaver fur as the preferred hat material in America for several decades. The husband of Britain's Queen Victoria, Prince Albert, wore a top hat, and it became a symbol of upper-class respectability. In America, silk hats signaled a more urbane presence than fur caps, felt bowler hats, and other headwear typically worn in the United States. While frontier values of honesty and hard work might have helped get Abraham elected president, he would need to project sophistication and an elevated stature to meet the nation's challenges during the Civil War.

Now let's take a careful look at this hat. This is an exact 3D print of Abraham Lincoln's top hat. It was a made with the precise use of a laser scanner at the Smithsonian, recording every aspect of the hat in the Smithsonian's collection and then literally printing it out not in silk, but in a synthetic material, layer by layer, using pretty sophisticated software and equipment. So, look inside. What don't you see? Well, you don't see a tag. Lincoln's hat was typical of clothing of the time; it's not marked for size. Most clothing in pre-industrial America, Lincoln's hat included, was custom-made for a particular individual, either at home or by a specialized artisan. Like shoes, hats were made on wooden forms called lasts. A specific hat maker would have a series of lasts, but one maker's lasts were not necessarily the same size as another's. A customer would try a hat on for fit rather than look for a specific size. And while Abraham Lincoln's hat was not labeled as such, it would today correspond to a size $7^{1}/_{8}$.

Lincoln acquired his most famous top hat from J. Y. Davis, a Washington DC hat maker. The real hat is made of silk fibers over a paper base and fabric lining, decorated with a $^{3}/_{8}$-inch silk ribbon and a small metal buckle. After its purchase, Lincoln added this three-inch silk ribbon mourning band in memory of his deceased son, Willie, who had died in 1862. The band, the mourning band, showed that Lincoln was mourning his son like other parents, both North and South, were mourning their sons who were lost in the war. It was a statement that Lincoln was making of personal loss and also one of public empathy.

Lincoln's associates did not particularly like him wearing this tall top hat; it made him an even larger target for snipers. But Lincoln persisted and wore top hats for battlefield visits, including at Gettysburg. Lincoln wore this hat for the last time on Friday, April 14, 1865. The Civil War had ended five days before with General Robert E. Lee's surrender to General Ulysses S. Grant at Appomattox Court House. Lincoln had preserved the Union and freed the slaves. He had recently celebrated his second inaugural and had every reason to enjoy a welcome break. Lincoln planned to take in a performance of *Our American Cousin* at Ford's Theatre with his wife, Mary Todd. On that Good Friday morning, Confederate loyalist John Wilkes Booth, learning that the president would attend the play, joined the other conspirators to put in place a bold plan to kidnap and assassinate key Union leaders.

In the evening, Lincoln donned his hat when he took his carriage ride from the White House to the nearby theater. He arrived late; the play was already in progress. But the action stopped as the audience greeted the president. He took his chair in the presidential box, and he placed his hat on the floor beside him.

During the third act of the play, Booth made his way to the presidential box and shot Lincoln in the back of the head. The grievously wounded Lincoln was taken to the Petersens' boardinghouse across the street. Treatment by physicians proved futile, and he died shortly after seven o'clock the next morning.

Lincoln, upon his death, was immediately treated as a Christian martyr by many. Just as with saints and other religious figures, the relics associated with Lincoln not only took on historical significance, but also carried spiritual power as emblems of his sanctity. And just after Lincoln's death, mourners literally descended on Ford's Theatre and the Petersens' house, and they sought items associated with Lincoln's martyrdom—bloodied bandages and linens from his death bead, locks of his hair, moldings from the theater's box, even the wall paper.

Now, at the Smithsonian, when the hat came to the Smithsonian two years later, Joseph Henry, the head of the Smithsonian did not want to display the hat because he was worried that if he put it on display, that too would become the subject of this outpouring of what he regarded as kind of quasi religious fervor. So he thought that would be come an object of irrational veneration, and he had the hat stored in the Smithsonian's basement. The American people did not see that hat again until 1893, well after Henry's death, when the Smithsonian lent it to an exhibition hosted by the Lincoln Memorial Association near Ford's Theatre. Throughout the 20th century, Lincoln's hat was often on public view and became an icon, a visual symbol of the 16th president. It is one of the most treasured and popular items on display at the Smithsonian.

Lincoln's hat is, of course, not the only item illustrating the careful crafting of a president's image. In a previous lecture, we examined the detailed posing, the positioning, and the composition of George Washington's portrait by Gilbert Stuart, as well as the way Eisenhower suggested the redesign of the army jacket in order to communicate style and savvy.

These images were deeply patriotic in nature, as was this one created by J. Howard Miller. It is arguably America's most famous World War II-era home-front poster. It depicts a muscular and determined, though attractive and shapely, female factory worker wearing lipstick and makeup and patriotically outfitted in a red and white bandana and blue work shirt. She says, "We can do it!" Which speaks both to the determination of the country to win the war and the role American women played in that effort by working in the defense industries.

Posters, colorful lithographic prints on cheap paper designed for short-term display, evolved as a popular form of advertising art in the late 19th century. They came of age as a propaganda tool during World War I. By the time America entered World War II in 1941, the persuasive art of the poster had been refined, and the messages were even more widespread, all reminding Americans in one way or another that it was everyone's duty to support the war effort. Now, I'll bet that if I ask you who the woman is depicted in this poster you'd probably say, "Rosie the Riveter." If you would, you'd be incorrect, at least partially so, and so let me explain.

When Westinghouse made this original print, it did not name the woman, nor did Miller, the artist. Miller had been hired by Westinghouse Electric Corporation's War Production Coordinating Committee to develop a series of images for the company's wartime production campaign. The posters were intended to keep up morale among workers. The "We Can Do It!" poster, along with other efforts, encouraged women to succeed in manufacturing and factory jobs that had been considered "man's work" until then. The poster projected the idea of female patriotism expressed through manual labor in factories. The name "Rosie the Riveter," was attached to this image much later. It actually came from a 1942 song written by Redd Evans and John Jacob Loeb. Rosie was a fictional female factory worker laboring for the war effort. The upbeat song was recorded by big band leader Kay Kyser and became a national hit with its signature "brrrrrr" in the lyrics, simulating a riveting machine. The song goes, "She's making history, working for victory. Rosie, brrrrrrrrrr, the riveter." Numerous depictions of real Rosies followed as reporters and publicists found workers named Rosie performing heavy-duty manual tasks in factories across the United States. Other characters also emerged—Winnie the Welder, for example—to call attention to the various roles played by women in military production.

So, this leaves us with two questions. Who was the woman in this portrait? And who were the women she represented? Well first, as nearly as can be determined, the woman in Miller's poster was a 17-year-old cellist named

Geraldine Hoff, later Geraldine Doyle, who worked at a metal-processing plant near Ann Arbor, Michigan. During the war, Miller was inspired by a United Press photograph of her, hard at work, her makeup flawless, her hair bound up in a polka-dot bandana.

But Geraldine was just one of millions of women who joined the manufacturing labor force when American men went off to fight in World War II. And this was a significant cultural shift from the previous few decades. The stigma against working women had grown during The Depression, when women's labor was seen as taking jobs away from men. Women's manual labor was also associated with unladylike behavior. Now, recruitment posters, advertisements, and even songs had to convey the idea of women's wartime labor as a supportive affirmation of the traditional family, not a critique of it.

Some of the women who filled those jobs had worked in factories before but had lost their jobs during The Depression. Still others had held civilian jobs, like telephone operators, and laundresses, and cooks, and farm workers. Now they left those positions, sometimes crossing the country to take on jobs in the new shipyards and munitions factories. The factories often brought people together across lines of race and class to work together against a common foe.

This poster seems so iconic to us today, but it was not widely distributed at the time. To the contrary, it was displayed in Pittsburgh and some Midwestern Westinghouse factories for just two weeks or so in February 1943 and seen by relatively few workers. The We Can Do It poster was rediscovered and revived well after the World War II era. In the 1970s, large numbers of women were once again entering the workforce in a variety of roles, finding their way in male-dominated professions and workplaces. It was at this point that the poster was apocryphally identified with Rosie the Riveter. Rosie was regarded as an inspirational figure, transformed from the midcentury perky tomboy into the precedent-setting champion for modern women seeking empowerment in the workforce. From the 1980s onward, the image became the subject of veneration, alteration, and even parody.

So, think about the image of Rosie. It was up only in a few factories for a few weeks more than 60 years ago. Statistically, very few women were actually engaged in heavy duty manufacturing. And yet the image itself has a lasting vitality, simply but powerfully conveying the importance of the working woman and connecting the aspirations of a strong, self-assured, person with the greater good of the country. It's an image that in many ways, like that of Pocahontas, Douglass, and Lincoln, speaks simultaneously to the high values Americans place on individualism, as well as on achieving an important national purpose.

Two Centuries of American Style

Lecture 19

America has had its share of outsized celebrities whose styles have captured the public's imagination both at home and abroad and have shaped what might be called our national character. Artifacts they have left behind and in the collections of the Smithsonian help reveal who they were and what they reflected about our nation. As you will learn in this lecture, the optimism and spirit, in the face of considerable challenge, displayed by Benjamin Franklin, Andrew Carnegie, Babe Ruth, Muhammad Ali, Louis Armstrong, and Jackie Kennedy reflect something essential about the way in which we are American.

Benjamin Franklin

- Just as George Washington fought for independence on American soil, Benjamin Franklin battled in France as the American commissioner, essentially the first ambassador. Franklin's mission was to secure French support for the Revolutionary War effort.

- French aid, particularly at sea, was essential for an American victory. Britain's naval force was the strongest in the world. Its ships could blockade Colonial ports, transport soldiers along the Atlantic Coast, and bombard Washington's military positions with impunity. The French, if willing, would provide a counterweight to the British advantage.

- Franklin arrived in France as a celebrity in December 1776, less than six months after helping to draft the Declaration of Independence. He was America's most renowned personality, and the French were fascinated by his erudition and lack of pretension.

- Contributing to Franklin's popularity was a fur cap he wore to keep warm. To the French, this embodied the frontier spirit and reinforced their belief that Americans were somehow closer to nature than Europeans. French intellectuals at the time were positing ideas about human nature, natural rights, and the state. Franklin obliged their curiosity with his fur-capped appearances and the principles embedded in such writings as the Declaration of Independence. In contrast to the notoriously elaborate wigs and hats worn by France's Queen Marie Antoinette and the crown of King Louis XVI, Franklin's cap became a symbol of freedom—a cap of liberty.

- In 1777, Franklin prevailed upon General Washington to employ an outspoken French supporter of American independence and ideals as the revolutionary commander's aide-de-camp. This man was Marquis de Lafayette, who Franklin thought could help obtain French support.

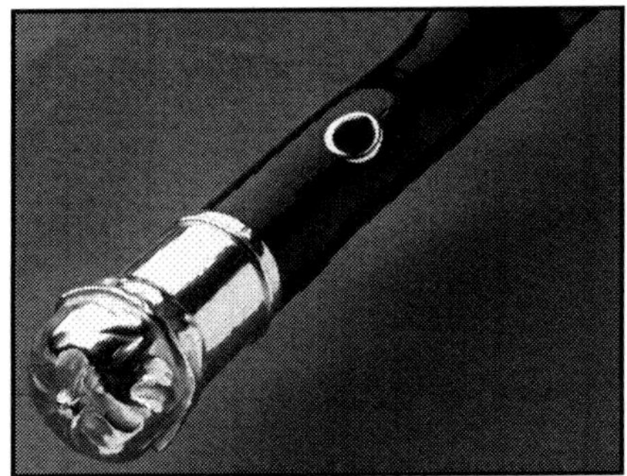

Benjamin Franklin's Cane

- He was right. In 1778, Franklin secured military and trade treaties allying the United States and France against Britain. The French agreed to recognize the revolutionary government, provide military support and supplies, and encourage other nations to help. Four days later, Britain declared war on France.

- Franklin's diplomatic work conjoined with his social life. An accomplished composer and musician, Franklin played several instruments and was a fixture in the salons of Paris. He also regularly attended the theater. Among his admirers was Maria Anna, the Countess of Forbach. She was an unabashed supporter of the American cause.

- The countess and Franklin dined together, and they also corresponded. The countess sought Franklin's help to obtain a commission for her nephew to serve in Washington's army. She was also friendly with Lafayette, who kept her abreast of the war's progress. The countess's two sons, Christian and William, both served with Lafayette toward the war's end.

- French participation proved decisive at the Battle of Yorktown, which effectively ended the war. Coordinating strategy with Washington, France sent 29 warships and more than 10,000 troops, forcing the surrender of British General Cornwallis. After that success, Franklin, the countess, and Lafayette celebrated together in Paris.

- The countess gave Franklin a walking stick as a very special gift. At the top of the walking stick is a gold orb in the shape of a fur cap—Franklin's cap. This walking stick is on exhibit at the National Museum of American History.

Andrew Carnegie

- Andrew Carnegie, the great steel magnate and philanthropist, is as known today for his charitable gifts as for building an industry. Carnegie's home on Fifth Avenue exemplifies the man behind the 19th-century rise of American industrial might. His residence was among the first in the city constructed from steel.

- Given that this alloy of iron and carbon was the source of the fortune that distinguished him as among the richest men in the world, the mansion—when completed in 1902—was an apt advertisement for American industry and ingenuity during the Gilded Age. Today, Carnegie's New York City mansion is run as the Cooper-Hewitt Smithsonian Design Museum.

- Born in 1835 to a handloom weaver, Carnegie was a self-made man. Carnegie's family immigrated from Scotland to western Pennsylvania in 1848. At the age of 13, Carnegie starting work as a bobbin boy in a cotton factory near Pittsburgh. A variety of jobs led to his eventual position as superintendent of the Western Division of the Pennsylvania Railroad.

- In 1864, Carnegie purchased an iron mill, the Cyclops Iron Company, which he merged into a succession of ironworks to form Union mills, which was poised to supply iron—and, later, steel—for America's great industrial expansion after the Civil War.

Andrew Carnegie

- Carnegie equipped his plants with early Bessemer furnaces that turned iron into large quantities of steel. Harder and less brittle than iron, poured steel became the elixir of American industrialization. Carnegie became enormously wealthy by investing in the entire supply chain. By the 1890s, Carnegie Steel Company was a giant.

- Meanwhile, in 1887, Carnegie married 30-year-old Louise Whitfield, a New York woman 21 years his junior. A daughter came a decade later. In 1901, Carnegie sold his company to fellow mogul John Pierpont Morgan for 480 million dollars, equivalent today to about 13 billion dollars. Morgan, a New York financier and industrialist, consolidated Carnegie's mills and other properties into U.S. Steel, the nation's first billion-dollar company.

- The Astors, Goulds, Morgans, Rockefellers, and Vanderbilts are among the families made wealthy by America's boom during the latter half of the 19th century. They built palatial houses in New York, Chicago, Cleveland, St. Louis, and Buffalo, as well as mansions in Newport, Palm Beach, and Long Island.

- Mansions were architectural billboards. They symbolized American ascendancy in the world as the United States became an industrial powerhouse, racing ahead of Europe. There long had existed the feeling that the wild frontier nation was culturally inferior to Europe. These exorbitant homes, with their industrial conveniences and appurtenances, positioned their owners as modern-day aristocracy, successors to Europe's fading nobility.

- To American workers, the estates demonstrated the stunning power of the men who controlled their livelihoods. Some believed that the leaders of the nation's railroads, ships, banks, coal, steel, and oil industries had unfairly amassed their wealth—that they were "robber barons."

- Carnegie, while publicly lumped into this group, was distinct. He had a strong philanthropic ethic and was not normally ostentatious. Beginning in the 1880s, Carnegie donated money to build 3,000 public libraries in the United States and Scotland.

- He gave millions of dollars to establish the Carnegie Institute of Technology in Pittsburgh and the Carnegie Institution in Washington. His gifts were consistent with the vision he outlined in *The Gospel of Wealth*, published in June 1889.

- For his home, Carnegie chose a location well north of what then was considered the socially acceptable edge of town—around 70th Street. The estate had an enormous impact on its neighborhood, Prospect Hill, later renamed Carnegie Hill. The retired steel magnate acquired adjacent land and other nearby lots and parceled them out to people he knew, to control development around his home.

- Ironically, the steel beams so prominent in the Carnegie Mansion were also the architectural means to erect what Carnegie sought to keep out of his neighborhood: tall buildings. Steel-framed skyscrapers, like the Woolworth Building in 1913 and the Empire State Building in 1931, came to characterize the New York skyline and the modern city.

- After Carnegie died in 1919, his wife Louise donated some nearby properties to the Spence School and to the Church of the Heavenly Rest, to prevent a large apartment building from going up. In time, however, luxurious residences inside of the new steel skyscrapers supplanted European-style mansions as a symbol of New Yorkers' power and prestige.

- Louise Carnegie lived in the family home until her death in 1946. The Carnegie Corporation donated it to the Smithsonian in 1972. The Cooper-Hewitt Museum opened its doors in 1976, during the celebration of the bicentennial of the United States. It houses a collection of more than 217,000 design-related objects, from drawings, prints, and graphics to furniture, metalwork, lighting, glass, jewelry, textiles, and wallpaper.

Babe Ruth and Muhammad Ali

- In sports, it's difficult to think of two more outsized personalities than Babe Ruth and Muhammad Ali. Both were "bad boys" in their own way but favorites of fans. They had a huge impact on their respective sports and played significant roles in helping Americans focus attention on social issues of the day.

Babe Ruth

- Ruth was an American hero who led the New York Yankees to seven pennants and four World Series Championships, hitting more home runs and dominating the game like no one before him—and few since. He was also remarkably accessible to fans and youths. He signed baseballs for thousands, including one at the Smithsonian.

- After the 1919 Black Sox scandal, in which players were suspected of throwing a World Series—allegations never proven—it was Ruth, the Sultan of Swat, who restored faith in baseball as the national pastime.

- Muhammad Ali evoked larger-than-life status nearly a half-century later. Born Cassius Marcellus Clay Jr., he won a boxing gold medal at the 1960 Olympics in Rome. Then, with a loud mouth and grandiose style, he bested Sonny Liston in 1964 for the world heavyweight title.

Muhammad Ali's Boxing Gear

- When he donated his boxing gloves and robe to the Smithsonian in March 1976, Ali, true to character, told a packed American history museum that his artifacts were the most important in the place—never mind the Star-Spangled Banner, George Washington's sword, Lincoln's hat, or anything else. Along the way, this man had come to transcend boxing, race, and his own country.

- He became a Muslim, was outspoken about civil rights, and opposed the war in Vietnam. He was willing to be stripped of his heavyweight title in 1967 rather than be inducted into the Army. Arrested and found guilty of draft evasion, Ali appealed all the way to the U.S. Supreme Court, where his conviction was overturned in 1971, albeit on a technicality.

- He returned to boxing to win the world heavyweight crown two more times and became a globe-trotting advocate for tolerance and the eradication of poverty. He has been recognized as a United Nations Messenger of Peace, and he received Amnesty International's Lifetime Achievement Award. In 2005, Ali was bestowed the Presidential Medal of Freedom, the nation's highest civilian decoration.

Louis Armstrong

- Trumpeter Louis Armstrong played his coronet and trumpet in a new form of American music called jazz. The music gave its name to the Jazz Age of the 1920s, and internationally it underscored the 1960s civil rights movement.

- Born in New Orleans in 1901, Armstrong was a key figure in blending various influences black and white, city and country, spiritual and secular into this new, distinct American art form. Armstrong and the music traveled up the Mississippi River from the post–Civil War South to Chicago, New York, and then around the world.

- Jazz was America's entrée to many countries during the Cold War. Its very essence reflected the ability to combine sounds grown of African, European, and other strains in improvisational ways. Jazz came to symbolize cultural fluidity and freedom of expression. Armstrong was one of its greatest proponents, and his trumpet has well earned its place in the Smithsonian.

- Armstrong enjoyed a long career—he knocked the Beatles off the *U.S. Billboard Hot 100* in 1964 with the Grammy-winning Broadway musical tune "Hello Dolly." Ever cheerful, jovial, and polite in public, Armstrong served as America's cultural ambassador, a strong counterweight to images of the "ugly American" during the period.

Jackie Kennedy

- Unlike presidents, first ladies of the United States are not elected, but Jackie Kennedy's command of the world stage began the day of her husband's inauguration, and she's never really left it. Jacqueline Lee Bouvier Kennedy, the daughter of a wealthy New York stockbroker, arrived in the nation's capital as the "Inquiring Camera Girl" for the *Washington Times-Herald* newspaper. She was beautiful, had style, and was glamorous.

- John Fitzgerald Kennedy, the scion of a wealthy Boston Irish family, had barely defeated Vice President Richard M. Nixon in the November 1960 election. On inauguration day, January 20, 1961, the 43-year-old Harvard-educated Democrat became the youngest elected president in American history. He replaced Dwight D. Eisenhower, 70, who at the time was the oldest.

- As if to drive home the transition of generations, Kennedy's wife had just given birth to the couple's second child and, at 31, was more than a decade younger than her husband. The Kennedys as a couple embodied the youthful orientation of a new generation of Americans, especially at the inaugural balls, a custom initiated in the early days of the republic.

- The Kennedys presided over five inaugural balls. Jacqueline Kennedy looked stunning, almost ethereal, in a silk white sheath gown of *peau d'ange*, or angel's skin, beneath a sleeveless white silk chiffon overblouse. Fashionably thin and projecting confidence, Jackie had the bearing of an haute couture model.

- In fact, her dress, designed by Ethel Frankau of Bergdorf Custom Salon, was based on Mrs. Kennedy's sketches and suggestions. The bodice was embroidered in silver thread and encrusted with brilliants. The gown's sleek, streamlined, monochromatic appearance reflected a very modern sensibility.

- As first lady, Jacqueline Kennedy led efforts to brighten dreary White House furnishings, artwork, and interior design. She supported the formation of the White House Historical Association to undertake a redecoration, and in February 1962, she invited the American people to see the results. In an unprecedented network television tour of the presidential mansion, she welcomed millions of viewers to what she called "the people's house."

Jackie Kennedy's Inaugural Ball Gown

- She promoted White House performances by the nation's artists and was an advocate for historical preservation. One building she saved was the former Corcoran Gallery of Art, across the street from the White House. The Corcoran had moved out decades before, and the building was slated for demolition. The building was turned over to the Smithsonian and eventually reopened as the Renwick Gallery.

- As other first ladies had, Jacqueline Kennedy donated her inaugural gown to the Smithsonian to become part of its First Ladies Collection. It was a tradition begun in 1912 with the receipt of the Empire-style gown of Helen Herron Taft, wife of the 27th president, William H. Taft. Over time, the collection became one of the Smithsonian's most popular exhibitions.

- Following the president's assassination in Dallas on November 22, 1963, Mrs. Kennedy stood next to Vice President Lyndon B. Johnson as he took the oath of presidential office. She demonstrated incredible poise and fortitude in helping to guide her family and the nation through the shock.

- With an eye toward history, Jackie planned the state funeral. And she lovingly held her young children as they mourned the loss of their father—and as America mourned the demise of its spirited, youthful leader. The Kennedys symbolized both the promise of the nation and its travails. Her husband's death cut short the exuberance of a new era, but she persisted through remarriage, a second widowhood, and a third act as a books editor for major publishing houses in New York.

Featured Objects

Benjamin Franklin's Cane

Andrew Carnegie's Mansion

Babe Ruth's Baseball

Muhammad Ali's Boxing Gear

Louis Armstrong's Trumpet

Jackie Kennedy's Inaugural Ball Gown

Suggested Reading

Armstrong, *Louis Armstrong.*

Bowles, Schlesinger, and Mellon, *Jacqueline Kennedy.*

Brands, *The First American.*

Two Centuries of American Style

Lecture 19—Transcript

In traveling around the world and listening to what people have to say about Americans, you often hear words like "casual," "friendly," "caring," "direct," "natural," and "showy," "rude," "spoiled," "egotistical." These descriptions reflect cultural bearing and ways of acting, the projection of personality through dress, décor, and demeanor. In short, character; style.

Americans are too diverse a people to be of one particular personality type, but the country has had its share of out-sized celebrities whose styles have captured the public's imagination both at home and abroad and shaped what might be called our national character. Artifacts they've left behind and in the collections of the Smithsonian help reveal who they were, and what they reflected about our nation. Take Benjamin Franklin's walking stick, on exhibit At the National Museum of American History. Franklin himself described it as, "My fine crab-tree walking stick, with a gold head curiously wrought in the form of the cap of liberty …," He wrote those words in his codicil to his Last Will and Testament in 1789. As he contemplated his life and role in crafting the new republic of the United States, Franklin made his final bequest. Franklin willed his cane "to my friend, and the friend of mankind, General Washington. If it were a sceptre, he has merited it, and it would become it."

What does this walking stick tell us about the American personality during Revolutionary times? What did it tell Franklin's contemporaries about Benjamin Franklin and about the new United States? Well, just as George Washington fought for independence on American soil, Franklin battled in France as the American commissioner, essentially the first ambassador. Franklin's mission was to secure French support for the Revolutionary War effort. French aid, particularly at sea, was essential for American victory. Britain's naval force was the strongest in the world; its ships could blockade Colonial ports, transport soldiers up and down the Atlantic Coast and bombard Washington's military positions with impunity.

The French, if willing, would provide a counterweight to the British advantage. Franklin arrived in France as a celebrity in December 1776, less than six months after helping to draft the Declaration of Independence. He was America's most renowned personality—a statesman, a scientist, and a man of cultural and civic accomplishment respected at home and abroad. The French were fascinated by his erudition and lack of pretension. They came out in droves to see him. Franklin was taken aback by all of the attention. In a letter to his daughter, he wrote, "My picture is everywhere, on the lids of snuff boxes, on rings, on busts. Your father's face is now as well known as the man in the moon."

Contributing to Franklin's popularity was a fur cap he wore to keep warm. To the French, this embodied the frontier spirit and reinforced their belief that Americans were somehow closer to nature than Europeans. French intellectuals at the time were thinking about ideas about human nature, about natural rights, and the state. Franklin obliged their curiosity with his fur-capped appearances and the principles embedded in such writings as the Declaration of Independence. In contrast to the notoriously elaborate wigs and hats worn by France's Queen Marie Antoinette and the crown of King Louis XVI, Franklin's cap became a symbol of freedom, a cap of liberty.

In 1777, Franklin prevailed upon George Washington to employ an outspoken French supporter of American independence and ideals as the revolutionary commander's aide-de-camp. The man was the Marquis de Lafayette, whom Franklin thought could help obtain French support.

He was right. In 1778, Franklin secured military and trade treaties allying the United States and France against Britain. The French agreed to recognize the revolutionary government, provide military support and supplies, and encourage other nations to help. Four days later, Britain declared war on France. Franklin's diplomatic work conjoined with his social life. An accomplished composer and musician, Franklin played several instruments and was a fixture in the salons of Paris. He also regularly attended the theater.

Among his admirers was Maria Anna, the Countess of Forbach. She was an unabashed supporter of the American cause. From humble beginnings, the countess had risen to become one of the grand ladies of France and a patron of the arts. She and Franklin dined together, shared a passion for chess, and they corresponded. The countess cherished her relationship with the American and sought his help to obtain a commission for her nephew to serve in Washington's army. She was also friendly with Lafayette, who kept her abreast of the war's progress. The countess's two sons, Christian and William, both served with Lafayette toward war's end. They were known to George Washington and were key officers under French General Rochambeau's command in Virginia.

French participation became decisive at the Battle of Yorktown, which, effectively, ended the war. Coordinating strategy with Washington, France sent 29 warships and more than 10,000 troops, forcing the surrender of British General Cornwallis. After that success, Franklin, the countess, and Lafayette celebrated together in Paris. The countess gave Franklin the walking stick as a very special gift. If you look closely at the top of the walking stick, you'll see a gold orb in the shape of a fur cap—Franklin's cap.

This Founding Father Franklin cherished that walking stick. In this relatively simple object, something about the personality of both Franklin and Washington is revealed, as by extension is the essence of early America. These revolutionaries fought a king and resisted the temptation to rule as royalty. What they accomplished was the transformation of a colonial frontier into a constitutional republic, ruled by its people. The liberty fur cap adorning Franklin's walking stick conveys a powerful message about America's national character at its inception.

Other Americans followed Franklin in achieving broad fame and leaving artifacts as telltale signatures of their personalities. Andrew Carnegie, the great steel magnate and philanthropist, is among them. The author of "The Gospel of Wealth" is as known today for his charitable gifts as for his building an industry. Carnegie's home on Fifth Avenue exemplifies the man behind the 19th-century rise of American industrial might. His residence was among the first in the city constructed from steel. Given that this alloy of iron and carbon was the source of the fortune that distinguished him as among the richest men in the world, the mansion, when completed in 1902, was an apt advertisement for American industry and ingenuity during the Gilded Age. We have one of Carnegie's artifacts at the Smithsonian; now, it's a very large artifact. It is his New York City Mansion. We run it as the Cooper-Hewitt Smithsonian Design Museum.

Carnegie was a self-made man. Born in Scotland in 1835, the son of a handloom weaver, Carnegie's family immigrated to western Pennsylvania in 1848. The young man wasted no time, starting work as a bobbin boy in a cotton factory near Pittsburgh at the age of 13. Carnegie moved on to serving as a messenger and telegraph operator for Western Union and then in a variety of jobs leading to superintendent of the Western Division of the Pennsylvania Railroad.

In 1864, Carnegie purchased an iron mill, the Cyclops Iron Company, which he merged into a succession of ironworks to form Union mills, which was poised to supply iron, and later steel, for America's great industrial expansion after the Civil War. Carnegie equipped his plants with early Bessemer furnaces that turned iron into large quantities of steel. Harder and less brittle than iron, poured steel became the elixir of American industrialization. Carnegie got enormously rich by investing in the entire supply chain, from coal and iron ore, to the railroads and ships that transported raw materials, to his factories, and then to the market. By the 1890s, Carnegie Steel Company was a giant.

Meanwhile, in 1887, Carnegie married 30-year-old Louise Whitfield, a New York woman 21 years his junior. A daughter came a decade later. Louise wanted a large garden and fresh air for her child, so Carnegie directed his architects to build "the most modest, plainest, and most roomy house in New York." He could afford it. In 1901, Carnegie sold his company to fellow mogul John Pierpont Morgan for $480 million, equivalent today to about $13 billion. Mellon's share was more than $200 million, equal to about $5.5 billion. Morgan, a New York financier and industrialist, consolidated Carnegie's mills and other properties into U.S. Steel, the nation's first billion-dollar company.

The Astors, Goulds, Morgans, Rockefellers, and Vanderbilts are among the families made wealthy by America's boom during the later half of the 19th century. They built palatial houses in New York, Chicago, Cleveland, St. Louis, and Buffalo, as well as mansions he euphemistically called cottages in Newport, Palm Beach, and Long Island. Writer and humorist Mark Twain coined the term "the Gilded Age," signifying a coat of gold paint, to signal the enormous wealth and splendor exhibited by this new class of Americans.

Of course, it also highlighted how materialism constituted a thin veneer that masked serious social and economic problems.

But mansions were architectural billboards of sorts. They symbolized American ascendancy in the world as the United States became an industrial powerhouse, racing ahead of Europe. There long had existed the feeling that the wild frontier nation was culturally inferior to Europe. These exorbitant homes, with their industrial conveniences and appurtenances, positioned their owners as modern-day aristocracy, successors to Europe's fading nobility. To American workers, the estates demonstrated the stunning power of the men who controlled their livelihoods. Some believed the leaders of the nation's railroads, ships, banks, coal, steel, and oil industries had unfairly amassed their wealth, that they were, essentially, robber barons. Carnegie, while publicly lumped into this group, was distinct. He had a strong philanthropic ethic and was not normally ostentatious. In "The Gospel of Wealth," published in June 1889, he wrote, "The problem for our age is the proper administration of wealth, so that the ties of brotherhood may still bind together the rich and poor in harmonious relationship."

Beginning in the 1880s, Carnegie donated money to build three thousand public libraries in the United States and Scotland. He gave millions of dollars to establish the Carnegie Institute of Technology in Pittsburgh and the Carnegie Institution in Washington. His gifts were consistent with the vision he outlined in the wealth gospel, though his manifesto clearly states that "in bestowing charity, the main consideration should be to help those who will help themselves."

For his home, Carnegie chose a location well north of what was then considered the socially acceptable edge of town—around Seventieth Street, Manhattan. The ballroom of wealthy socialite Caroline Astor, which could hold 400 people, was the yardstick by which New York society measured status. Carnegie was adamant that his house would never have a ballroom. The mansion's exterior was designed in Georgian Revival style, perhaps to resemble the baronial estates Carnegie aspired to as a boy in Scotland. It was built with a steel frame, consisting of I- or H-beams, with flanges at 90-degree angles that make the mansion particularly sturdy.

Inside, the residence had innovative central heating and cooling with extensive boilers and an elaborate coal-delivery system, as well as an Otis elevator. Other flourishes included a teak parlor designed by Lockwood de Forest and an Aeolian organ played every morning as Carnegie rose and dressed. About 20 servants maintained the household and outdoor garden. The estate had an enormous impact on its neighborhood, Prospect Hill, later renamed Carnegie Hill. The retired steel magnate acquired adjacent land and other nearby lots and parceled them out to people he knew to control development around his home. Ironically, the steel beams so prominent in the Carnegie Mansion were also the architectural means to erect what Carnegie sought to keep out of his neighborhood—tall, tall buildings. Steel-framed skyscrapers, like the Woolworth Building in 1913 and the Empire State Building in 1931 came to characterize the New York skyline and the modern city.

After Carnegie died in 1919, his wife Louise donated some nearby properties to the Spence School and to the Church of the Heavenly Rest to prevent a large apartment buildings from going up in a way that would have overshadowed her beloved garden. In time, however, luxurious residencies inside of the new steel skyscrapers supplanted European-style mansions and their yards and gardens as a symbol of New Yorkers' power and prestige.

Louise Carnegie lived in the family home until her death in 1946. The Carnegie Corporation donated it to the Smithsonian 1972. And the Cooper-Hewitt museum opened its doors in 1976 during the celebration of the bicentennial of the United States. It houses a collection of more than 200,000 design-related objects, from drawings, prints, and graphics to furniture, metalwork, lighting, glass, jewelry, textiles, and wallpaper. I suspect that the museum's emphasis on creativity, innovation, and design, would have appealed to its owner, the one-time Western Union messenger boy who preached The Gospel of Wealth.

In sports, it's hard to think of two more outsized personalities than Babe Ruth and Muhammad Ali. Both were "bad boys" in their own way but favorites of fans. They had a huge impact upon their respective sports and played significant roles in helping Americans focus attention on the social issues of the day. Ruth was an American hero who led the New York Yankees to seven pennants and four World Series Championships, hitting more homeruns and dominating the game like no one before him—and few since. He was also remarkably accessible to fans and youth. Ruth, who had a difficult childhood in his own right, drank, gambled, caroused, even as a professional athlete. Nonetheless, he visited orphanages and hospitals, and treated children with remarkable empathy. He signed baseballs for thousands, including this one at the Smithsonian. After the 1919 Black Sox scandal, in which players were suspected of throwing a World Series—allegations never proven—it was Ruth, the Sultan of Swat, who restored America's faith in baseball as the national pastime.

Muhammad Ali evoked larger-than-life status nearly a half century later. Born Cassius Marcellus Clay Jr., he won a boxing Gold medal at the 1960 Olympics in Rome. Then, with a loud mouth and grandiose style, he bested Sonny Liston in 1964 for the world title. When he donated his boxing gloves and robe to the Smithsonian in March 1976, true to character, Ali told a packed American history museum that his artifacts were the most important in the place, never mind the Star Spangled Banner, George Washington's sword, Lincoln's hat or anything else. Along the way, this man, the grandson of a slave raised in a middle-class African-American household in Louisville, Kentucky, had come to transcend boxing, race, and his own country.

He became a Muslim, was outspoken about civil rights, and opposed the war in Vietnam. He was willing to be stripped of his heavyweight title in 1967 rather than be inducted into the Army. Arrested and found guilty of draft evasion, Ali appealed all the way to the U.S. Supreme Court, where his conviction was overturned in 1971, albeit on a technicality. He returned to boxing to win the world heavyweight crown two more times and became a globe-trotting advocate for tolerance and the eradication of poverty. He has been recognized as a United Nations Messenger of Peace, and he received Amnesty International's Lifetime Achievement Award. In 2005, Muhammad Ali was bestowed the Presidential Medal of Freedom, the nation's highest civilian honor.

Trumpeter Louis Armstrong also swung from the lip, playing his cornet and trumpet in a new form of American music called jazz. The music gave its name to the era Babe Ruth played in, the Jazz Age of the 1920s. And internationally, it underscored the 1960s civil rights movement.

Born in New Orleans in 1901, Armstrong was a key figure in blending various influences—black and white, city and country, spiritual and secular—into this new, distinct American art form. Armstrong and the music literally traveled up the Mississippi River from the post-Civil War South to Chicago, New York, and then, around the world. Jazz was America's entrée to many countries during the Cold War. Its very essence reflected the ability to combine sounds grown of African, European, and other strains in improvisational ways. Jazz came to symbolize the cultural fluidity and freedom of expression of America. Armstrong was one of its greatest proponents, and his trumpet has well earned its place in the Smithsonian.

Armstrong enjoyed a long career, and, he knocked the Beatles off the U.S. Billboard Hot 100 in 1964, four decades after his first recording with the Grammy-winning Broadway musical tune "Hello Dolly." Ever cheerful, jovial, and polite in public, Armstrong served as America's cultural ambassador, a strong counterweight to images of the time of the "ugly American."

Armstrong also saw some ugliness, though, at home during his career when he performed with black and white musicians, for mixed audience, and during the era of segregation. Though not usually outspoken on political matters, he did speak out in September 1957 when on the orders of the governor of Arkansas, the National Guard surrounded a high school in Little Rock, blocking nine African-American students from entering the classrooms. Armstrong criticized the action, saying, "It's getting almost so bad a colored man hasn't got any country." A week later, President Dwight D. Eisenhower sent 1,200 U.S. troops to Little Rock to escort those students to school. "God bless you," Armstrong wired the president.

Unlike presidents, first ladies of the United States are not elected, but Jackie Kennedy's command of the world stage began the day of her husband's inauguration took place, and she never really left it. Jacqueline Kennedy, the daughter of a wealthy New York stockbroker who arrived in the nation's capital as the Inquiring Camera Girl for the Washington Times-Herald newspaper, was beautiful. She had style. And she was glamorous. John F. Kennedy, the scion of a wealthy Boston Irish family, had barely defeated Vice President Richard Nixon, in the November 1960 election. On inauguration day, January 20, 1961, this 43-year-old Harvard-educated Democrat became the youngest elected president in American history, replacing Dwight D. Eisenhower, age 70, who at the time was the oldest.

As if to drive home the transition of generations, Kennedy's wife had just given birth to the couple's second child, and at only 31 years old was more than a decade younger than her husband. It was a bone-chilling 22 degrees in Washington; a nor'easter storm had hit the day before, and the Army had been called out to clear eight inches of snow. President Eisenhower drove with Kennedy to the Capitol building for the inaugural ceremonies. Eisenhower, bundled in an overcoat and scarf, looked aged and dignified. Kennedy, taking off his overcoat, appeared young and exuberant; contralto Marian Anderson sang the national anthem; Robert Frost recited his poem, "The Gift Outright"; and Chief Justice Earl Warren administered the presidential oath over the Fitzgerald family Bible.

Kennedy's speech charted new frontiers and optimistic possibilities for a strong, humane, and generous America. He said, "Let the word go forth … that the torch has been passed to a new generation of Americans." The Kennedys as a couple embodied this youthful orientation, especially at that night's inaugural balls, a custom initiated in the early days of the republic. The Kennedys presided over five inaugural balls. Jackie Kennedy looked stunning, almost ethereal, in a silk white sheath gown of peau d'ange, or angel's skin, beneath a sleeveless white silk chiffon over blouse.

Fashionably thin and projecting confidence, Jackie had the bearing of an haute couture model. In fact, her dress, designed by Ethel Frankau of Bergdorf Custom Salon, was based on Mrs. Kennedy's sketches and her suggestions. The bodice was embroidered in silver thread and encrusted with brilliants. The gown's sleek, streamlined, monochromatic appearance reflected a very modern sensibility. The contrast between the youthful first lady and her immediate predecessor, the prim Mamie Eisenhower who favored mauve and floral prints, was dramatic. Photographers had a field day, and images of Jackie circled the globe.

As first lady, Jacqueline Kennedy led efforts to brighten the dreary White House furnishings, artwork, and interior design. She formed the White House Historical Association to undertake a redecoration, and in February,

1962, she invited the American people to see the results. In an unprecedented network television tour of the presidential mansion, she welcomed millions of viewers to see what she called "the people's house." She promoted White House performances by the nation's artists and was an advocate for historical preservation. One building she saved was the former Corcoran Gallery of Art, across the street from the White House. The Corcoran had moved out decades before, and the building was slated for demolition. The building was turned over to the Smithsonian, and eventually reopened as the Renwick Gallery.

As other first ladies had, Jacqueline Kennedy donated her inaugural gown to the Smithsonian to become part of its First Ladies Collection. It was a tradition begun in 1912 with the receipt of the Empire-style gown of Helen Herron Taft, wife of the 27th president, William Taft. After this gift, other former first ladies and their descendants donated inaugural apparel. Over time, the collection became one of the Smithsonian's most popular exhibitions.

Jacqueline Kennedy proved exceedingly popular around the world, so much so that President Kennedy, after a state visit to France to see his counterpart, Charles de Gaulle, jokingly introduced himself to the press as, "the man who accompanied Jacqueline Kennedy to Paris."

Following the president's assassination in Dallas on November 22, 1963, Mrs. Kennedy stood next to Vice President Lyndon B. Johnson as he took the oath of office. She demonstrated incredible poise and fortitude in helping to guide her family and the nation through the shock. With an eye toward history, Jackie planned the state funeral. And she lovingly held her young children as they mourned the loss of their father, and as America mourned the demise of its spirited, youthful leader. The Kennedys symbolized both the promise of the nation and its travails. Her husband's death cut short the exuberance of a new era, but she persisted through remarriage, through a second widowhood, and even a third act as a books editor for major publishing houses in New York.

Her personality, her bearing, generosity of spirit endeared Jackie Kennedy to the public. Like Franklin, Carnegie, Ruth, Ali, Armstrong Jackie Kennedy's optimism and spirit, in the face of considerable challenge reflected something we think is essential about the way in which we are American.

Hollywood—The American Myth Machine
Lecture 20

Myths and folktales may be products of the imagination, but nonetheless, they have helped guide, engage, and even amuse people for generations. With new communications technologies, our stories could reach ever-larger audiences. And, as you will learn in this lecture, the heart of American mythmaking for the past century has been Hollywood. From Mickey Mouse to Dorothy Gale, and from Kermit the Frog to the *Star Wars* droids, we see the creation of imagined places and characters that not only provide a commentary on our daily life, but also an aspirational vision of our life and our future.

Mickey Mouse

- Perhaps the most famous of Hollywood's mythological characters is Mickey Mouse, who became a worldwide icon because of the union of imagination with technology, innovation with entrepreneurship, and individual vision with American populism.

- A young Walt Disney was traveling by railroad with his wife, Lillian, from New York to Los Angeles in early 1928 when he had a creative insight. He had just lost an important film contract. He had to develop a new character for his fledging animation studio, or go under. "I had this mouse in the back of my head," he recalled, "because a mouse is a sort of a sympathetic character in spite of the fact that everybody's frightened of a mouse." Disney wanted to call the mouse Mortimer, but his wife thought it sounded too pompous. She suggested "Mickey" instead.

- But Mickey had to be drawn. That job fell to Ub Iwerks, Disney's cartoonist, chief animator, and occasional business partner. Iwerks came up with the characteristic use of circles for Mickey's head and ears and his limber, flexible, evocative body ripe for animation. Iwerks also drew Minnie, Mickey's female companion, in a similar fashion.

- Disney quickly produced two cartoon shorts: *Plane Crazy* and *The Gallopin' Gaucho*. Animation was tedious work—a six-minute cartoon required about 40,000 drawings. To make the work more efficient, animators drew Mickey on sheets of transparent celluloid, called cels, that could be placed on and moved across drawings of backgrounds while being filmed in order to create the appearance of sequential action.

- Both cartoons were silent films, as was typical of the time. While some short films had a primitive audio track, it was the success of *The Jazz Singer*, starring Al Jolson and released in October 1927, that gave filmgoers a new cinematic experience. By 1928, theaters were installing sound equipment so that they could carry the popular new talkies.

- Disney thought that the new audio innovation could work for him. He and his team developed a third Mickey Mouse feature, called *Steamboat Willie*. It was a very loose derivative of Buster Keaton's *Steamboat Bill Jr.*, a silent movie released earlier in the year.

- The question for Disney in making *Steamboat Willie* was whether the audience would believe that drawings could whistle, play instruments, and dance to music. In order to make them believe, the animation had to be closely synchronized with sounds. This would give Mickey a personality and convey humanlike traits.

- To achieve this audiovisual illusion, musicians tried to play along with the animation, but they couldn't keep up. So, Disney filmed and projected a bouncing ball on a screen for the musicians so that they could visualize the beats as they played. The technique worked.

- Disney premiered *Steamboat Willie* in New York City on November 18, 1928; it ran for two weeks at the Colony Theater, playing before the movie *Gang War*. The Disney short was a hit. The use of synchronized soundtracks with the creative animation helped Mickey Mouse develop into the most popular cartoon character of the time, winning Disney an Academy Award in 1932.

- In 1929, Mickey spoke for the first time, with Disney providing the voice—a role he would fulfill for almost two decades. Mickey's personality and appearance evolved a bit over the years, and he acquired a stable of new cartoon friends and colleagues—Goofy, Donald Duck, and Pluto, among others—who provided new stories and themes.

- But the other key to Mickey's success was Disney's business and marketing savvy. Disney started a fan club for Mickey in 1929 that within a few years had about 800 chapters and a million children as members. In 1930, Mickey starred in a newspaper comic strip that was widely syndicated and ran for decades.

- After successful shorts and full-length feature films, comic books, publications, and television followed, including the memorable *Mickey Mouse Club*. This was not an entirely new idea. Beatrix Potter, at the turn of the 20th century, had created stuffed Peter Rabbit dolls to sell along with her books, and by the 1930s, other famous characters soon had their own lines of merchandise.

- Disney recognized this trend, and Mickey was heavily merchandised. In fact, Mickey Mouse lunch boxes are part of the Smithsonian's collections. Thanks to Mickey's success, the Walt Disney Company became an American and worldwide entertainment enterprise.

Dorothy Gale

- Dorothy Gale was the lead character, played by Judy Garland, in the 1939 Metro-Goldwyn-Mayer film *The Wizard of Oz*, which won several Academy Awards and introduced the hit song "Over the Rainbow." The fantasy tale was based on L. Frank Baum's 1900 novel *The Wonderful Wizard of Oz*. Baum's book and its 13 sequels previously had been made into a cartoon, a stage musical, and several silent motion pictures before studio chief Louis Mayer purchased the film rights for 75,000 dollars.

- Mayer envisioned a film made primarily for children, but he quickly realized that he would have to sell a lot of tickets to adults to recoup his investment. Although 11-year-old Shirley Temple was perhaps Mayer's first choice for the role, the lead went to the 16-year-old and very adult-sounding Garland. This helped broaden the film's appeal to teens and young adults.

- Several decades later, Louis Mayer sensed that the story would strike a particularly resonant chord in a country struggling with despair and uncertainty in the wake of the Depression and the Dust Bowl, as well as the looming threat of war in Europe. Americans needed reassurance and self-confidence. They would find it in a film that would demonstrate the triumph of the honest, traditional values of the rural heartland, through the filter of fantastic, magical powers inherent in the slippers.

- Aside from their symbolic meaning, the ruby slippers—like Mickey Mouse—were tied to changes in storytelling technology. In Baum's story and in original and early scripts for the movie, the slippers are silver. But in one of the script revisions, the slippers were described as "ruby."

- The movie was among the first to use an innovative technology for color filmmaking. Walt Disney had produced *Snow White and the Seven Dwarfs* in Technicolor, and it became the top-grossing film of 1938. Mayer, envious of Disney's success, put his money on *The Wizard of Oz* with its rich visual imagery.

- When filmed under the brutally bright lights needed for the Technicolor filming, the silver slippers would appear a washed-out gray. A ruby red color would be visually striking. The job of making the shoes fell to Gilbert Adrian, MGM's chief costume designer. After several experiments, Adrian came up with two alternatives. One pair of slippers was covered with red sequins and faux jewels and equipped with ornate curled toes. These became known as the Arabian test shoes and were used only in test photographs of the costumes.

- Another approach was to dye a commercially manufactured basic pair of silk pumps red. A red silk fabric sewn with rows of approximately 2,3000 crimson-colored sequins was then attached to the shoe. But bright red appeared orange on screen, so dark burgundy sequins were used. In October 1938, Adrian added the butterfly-shaped, sequined red leather bows on top of the slippers, which helped convey Dorothy's youth and innocence.

- It is estimated that there were between 6 and 10 pairs of slippers made for Garland and her stand-in, Bobbie Koshay—though only 4 pairs, plus the test shoes, are known to now exist. The shoes differed slightly in size, depending on whether they would be featured in close-ups, for walking, or for dancing. The Smithsonian's pair was used for dancing sequences.

- Although their sequins are now fading, the slippers have not lost their fame. They are among the most popular items on display at the National Museum of American History, where they continue to remind viewers that there is magic in everyday life, as well as in Hollywood.

Kermit the Frog

- Unlike some far-off fantasyland, the home of a green puppet frog named Kermit was on Sesame Street, in an inner-city urban neighborhood, reflecting America's predominantly urban population in the 1970s. But unlike the negative, racially tinged stereotypes seen elsewhere, Sesame Street was presented as a friendly, nurturing place.

- The show introduced children nationwide to an extended family of White, African American, and Latino "neighbors," as well as Big Bird, Grover, Oscar the Grouch, Bert and Ernie, the Cookie Monster, and more—puppets whose quirks led to lessons in tolerance and negotiating differences.

- *Sesame Street* proved to be a landmark, demonstrating that television could serve a profound educational purpose. *Sesame*

Street could teach the alphabet, numbers, directions, songs, and lessons about geography, science, art, history, and just about everything through the colorful puppet characters, varied human hosts, and outstanding guests. The show revolutionized children's television; it made learning entertaining and fun.

- Kermit was key to the show's success. Many saw Kermit as an alter ego of his creator, Jim Henson—serious and softly assertive, talented but not overbearing, sometimes frustrated, but always trying to bring out the best in others.

- In 1955, as a freshman at the University of Maryland, Henson helped create a puppet show called *Sam and Friends* for television station WRC-TV in Washington DC. That show included a simple character made of cloth retrieved from his mother's discarded spring coat—with half Ping-Pong ball eyes. Although this character, now residing at the Smithsonian, was not yet called a frog, this was, indeed, the forerunner to Kermit.

- *Sam and Friends* led to television appearances on *The Tonight Show* and *The Ed Sullivan Show*. In the early 1960s, Henson and his wife formed Muppets, Inc., and with writer Jerry Juhl and puppeteer Frank Oz, they developed a variety of puppet characters. By 1969, Children's Television Workshop (CTW) asked Henson to work on a new children's series for public television—*Sesame Street.*

- *Sesame Street* was CTW's first production. And it was a smash it. Not only did *Sesame Street* fulfill CTW's educational mission, but it was also timely and hip—culturally in tune with the baby-boomer adults who would watch the show with their young children.

- Kermit, like Mickey Mouse, evolved over time. He became more finely developed with a green felt fabric skin and a mouth of red cloth and pink tongue. The puppet's body is hollow, allowing for hand operation and manipulation; steel wires support the arms, while the stuffed legs hang loosely.

- *Sesame Street* gave birth to one of the most popular and the first truly international hit television series, *The Muppet Show.* The show introduced a whole new cast of characters, including Miss Piggy, who became a huge star and the love interest of Kermit. The Muppets then went to Hollywood for a series of films. And Kermit's message of self-acceptance, tireless patience, and enduring friendship traveled far beyond America's borders.

R2-D2 and C-3PO

- As Henson was helping us build a better world here on Earth, another creative genius, George Lucas, was contemplating how humans might get along with machines and other forms of life in other galaxies. The vehicle for his musings was *Star Wars*. The original movie and the series it spawned proved a massive commercial success and a global phenomenon.

- The story provided a futuristic vision of a universe richly populated with an assortment of intelligent life but still engaged in the age-old struggle between good and evil. Audiences were intrigued by the richness of the fictional universe Lucas had created and by the film's superior special effects.

- From Darth Vader and Luke Skywalker to Yoda, Princess Leia, Obi-Wan Kenobi, Han Solo, and Chewbacca, *Star Wars* is chock-full of intriguing characters. When audiences first met these characters in 1977, *Star Wars* seemed like something entirely new. But one could argue that part of the film's success is how it was able to draw on older ideas from many different sources and combine them in new ways.

- Lucas acknowledged his debt to the timeless tale of a young hero's journey to adulthood that appears in so many cultures all over the world. Lucas was also influenced by the serialized science fiction melodramas of the 1930s known as "space operas." These epic stories often involved one man fighting against an unspeakably powerful foe—saving the world and getting the girl, of course.

- Another strong influence on Lucas was an international one. Lucas was a great admirer of the Japanese director Akira Kurosawa, and especially his 1958 film, *The Hidden Fortress.* That film opens with a scene that will seem familiar to any *Star Wars* fan: Two peasants—one tall, one shorter—trudge across a desert. They have just survived a terrible battle. And as they walk, they argue about whose fault it is that they're lost.

- Lucas pays homage to this comical duo with the most endearing of *Star Wars*'s characters: the droids, short for androids, named R2-D2 and C-3PO. The Smithsonian's collections include the R2-D2 and C-3PO costumes from *Return of the Jedi*, the third film in the series, released in 1983. Both costumes relied on a combination of electronic gadgetry and the actors' own motions to create two very different droids with distinctly human personalities.

- In the films, R2-D2 is a helpmate created to interface with computers and service starships on behalf of humans. He communicates with expressive squeals and head spins, lumbers around on stubby legs, and repeatedly saves the lives of his human masters. Actor Kenny Baker wore the R2-D2 costume. The costume has a body of aluminum and epoxy, built up with fiberglass cloth over a layer of foam, and the head is spun aluminum.

- C-3PO, R2-D2's sidekick and character foil, is called a "protocol droid." More humanoid than R2-D2 in form, movement, and character, C-3PO interfaces with the diverse cultures of Lucas's imaginary galaxy as a robotic translator and diplomat. The C-3PO costume was worn by actor Anthony Daniels. The torso is made of fiberglass; the legs combine leotard, socks, and fiberglass; the arms are aluminum; and the pelvis and feet are rubber.

- C-3PO was a less-complicated costume to operate than R2-D2 but required more character acting. Combined, the duo is more personable than calculating, more comical than threatening, and thus a refreshing alternative to the more sinister robots of much science fiction literature and film.

- The *Star Wars* films have made great entertainment, but they have also become a cultural touchstone—not only for avid fans, but also now for several generations of Americans. The droids are more than movie stars in these films; they are indicators of the place robots might occupy in the human experience.

Featured Objects

Mickey Mouse

Dorothy's Ruby Slippers

Kermit the Frog

R2-D2 and C-3PO

Suggested Reading

Finch, *The Art of Walt Disney*.

Jones, *Jim Henson*.

Rinzler, *The Making of* Star Wars.

Stillman and Scarfone, *The Wizard of Oz*.

Hollywood—The American Myth Machine
Lecture 20—Transcript

Myths and folktales are deeply rooted in the human experience. They are found in all societies the world over. They may be products of the imagination, but nonetheless, they've helped guide, engage, and even amuse people for generations. Traditionally, myths and folktales arise from oral tradition, stories told around a fire, on a trek across the bush, at a temple or pilgrimage site, and were only later expressed in art or in writing.

Native American groups developed a rich oral culture of myths, legends, and folktales. From generation to generation, these tales helped promulgate a sense of tribal and communal identity. Later, European settlers, enslaved Africans, immigrants, and exiles from around the world who came to the United States brought their traditions and their stories with them and created new ones. Sea chanties, Br'er Rabbit stories, the tall tales of lumberjacks, cowboy poetry, Appalachian ballads, and countless other ways of expressing human foibles and heroism, moral lessons and wisdom are still with us, found in communities and enclaves across the land.

But a nation that quickly grew to include hundreds of millions of people could hardly sit around the campfire and tell its stories. And with new communications technologies, we didn't have to. Our stories could reach ever-larger audiences—millions and now even billions—generation after generation, and the heart of American myth making and myth purveying for the past century has been Hollywood.

Perhaps the most famous of Hollywood's mythological characters is, surprisingly, neither a soaring eagle nor some supernatural being, Instead, it's a mouse. And that mouse would become a world-wide icon because of the union of imagination with technology, innovation with entrepreneurship, and individual vision with American populism.

A young Walt Disney was traveling by railroad with his wife, Lillian, from New York to Los Angeles in early 1928 when he had a creative insight. He had just lost an important film contract. He had to develop a new character for his fledgling animation studio, or go under. "I had this mouse in the back of my head," he recalled, "because a mouse is a sort of sympathetic character in spite of the fact that everybody's frightened of a mouse." Disney wanted to call his mouse Mortimer, but his wife thought it sounded too pompous. She suggested "Mickey" instead.

But Mickey had to be drawn. And that job fell to Ub Iwerks, Disney's cartoonist, chief animator, and occasional business partner. Iwerks came up with the characteristic use of circles for Mickey's head and ears and his limber, flexible, evocative body, ripe for animation. Iwerks also drew Minnie, Mickey's female companion, in a similar fashion. Disney quickly produced two cartoon shorts; Plane Crazy, in which the animated Mickey tries to imitate "Lucky Lindy" and fly, as the real Charles Lindbergh did the year before, and Gallopin' Gaucho.

Animation was tedious work; a six-minute cartoon required some 40,000 drawings. To make the work more efficient, animators drew Mickey on sheets of transparent celluloid, called cels, like this one at the Smithsonian. These cels could be placed upon and moved across drawings of backgrounds while being filmed in order to create the appearance of sequential action.

Both cartoons that Disney created were silent films, as was typical of the time. While some short films had a primitive audio tracks, it was really the success of The Jazz Singer starring Al Jolson released in October 1927 that gave filmgoers a new cinematic experience. By 1928, theaters were installing sound equipment so they could carry the popular new talkies. Disney thought this new audio innovation could work for him. He and his team developed a third Mickey Mouse feature called Steamboat Willie. Steamboat Willie was a very loose derivative of Buster Keaton's Steamboat Bill Jr., a silent movie released earlier that year.

The question for Disney in making Steamboat Willie was whether the audience would believe that drawings could whistle, play instruments, and dance to music. In order to make them believe, the animation had to be very closely synchronized with sounds. This would give Mickey a personality and convey human-like traits, like curiosity, anger, and mischievousness. To achieve this audiovisual illusion, musicians tried to play along with the animation, but when they did so, they found they couldn't keep up. So

Disney filmed and projected a bouncing ball on a screen for the musicians so they could visualize the beats as they played. The technique worked.

Disney premiered Steamboat Willie in New York City on November 18, 1928. It ran for two weeks at the Colony Theater, playing before the movie Gang War. No one remembers Gang War, but the Disney short was a big hit. In the seven-minute cartoon, Mickey pilots a steamboat and fights with the oafish Captain Pete; he gets animal passengers and a late-arriving Minnie on board and then plays a frenetic duet with Minnie. He angers the captain, who consigns him to peeling potatoes. Mickey whistles in time with the soundtrack whistle. The ship's steam horns go off in sync with the sound effects. When Mickey and Minnie play their "Turkey in the Straw" duet using pots, pans, animal tails, teeth, and other body parts as instruments, their movements are exactly attuned to the music. The scenes were not only credible, they were technically sophisticated, aesthetically engaging, and just plain funny. The use of synchronized soundtracks with the creative animation helped Mickey Mouse develop into the most popular cartoon character of the time, winning Disney an Academy Award in 1932.

Mickey's personality evolved over the years. Always positive, he went from hero to victim, sometimes cheerful, sometimes shy. He could be the mischievous loner, the determined inventor, the hopeful suitor, or the responsible leader. In 1929, Mickey spoke for the first time, with Walt Disney providing the voice, a role he'd fulfill for almost two decades. Mickey's appearance evolved a bit over the years, and he acquired a stable of new cartoon friends and colleagues named Goofy, Donald Duck, and Pluto, among others who provided new stories and new themes.

But the other key to Mickey's success was Disney's business and marketing savvy. Disney started a fan club for Mickey in 1929 that within a few years had some 800 chapters and one million children as members. In 1930, Mickey starred in a newspaper comic strip that was widely syndicated and ran for decades. After successful shorts and full-length feature films, comic books, publications, and television followed, including the memorable *Mickey Mouse Club*. This was not an entirely new idea. Beatrix Potter, at the turn of the 20th century, had created stuffed Peter Rabbit dolls to sell along with her books, and by the 1930s, other famous characters soon had their own lines of merchandise—Buster Brown, Raggedy Ann, Little Orphan Annie. Even former President Theodore Roosevelt got in on the act, giving his name to the Teddy Bear.

Disney recognized this trend, and Mickey was heavily merchandised, appearing as a toy, on watches, lunch boxes, and scores of other goods, including video games, all with special appeal to young children. We have some of those really characteristic lunch boxes, which are part of the Smithsonian's collection. In this scene, we have Mickey instructing a class of younger mice. The caption on the chalkboard reads "school days." And then there's this lunchbox; we see Mickey conducting a *Mickey Mouse Club* band, evoking a country and western theme, in this case, for the Mouseketeers. And these were the types of ways we see that Mickey was integrated into every part of children's lives. He was seen everywhere. Thanks to Mickey's success, the Walt Disney Company became an American and worldwide entertainment enterprise.

A global success of this magnitude always attracts attention, and challenges, and even critics, and the lovable mouse was no exception. For some years, and even in some quarters, "Mickey Mouse," as an expression, was used pejoratively to indicate a lack of substance or shallow consumerism, and Disney's famous mascot has sometimes been taken as a negative symbol of American cultural expansion and even domination.

But Walt Disney harbored no such pretensions about Mickey. He said,

> "All we ever intended for him or expected of him was that he should continue to make people everywhere chuckle with him and at him. We didn't burden him with any social symbolism; we made him no mouthpiece for frustrations or harsh satire. Mickey was simply a little personality assigned to the purpose of laughter."

If Mickey was created to make Americans laugh, Dorothy Gale was created to comfort and re-assure. Dorothy Gale was the lead character, played by Judy Garland, in the 1939 Metro-Goldwyn-Mayer film, *The Wizard of Oz*. In the film, she wore these ruby slippers, one of the most famous Hollywood props of all time. The fantasy tale was based on L. Frank Baum's novel, *The*

Wonderful Wizard of Oz, written in 1900. Baum's book and its 13 sequels previously had been made into a cartoon, a stage musical, and several silent motion pictures before studio chief Louis Mayer purchased the film for a whopping 75,000 dollars. Mayer envisioned a film made primarily for children, but he quickly realized that he would have to sell a lot of tickets to adults to recoup his investment. Although 11-year-old Shirley Temple was perhaps Mayer's first choice for the film, she did not work out. Instead, the lead went to the 16-year-old, and very adult-sounding, Judy Garland, which actually helped broaden the film's appeal to teens and young adults.

You know the film. Dorothy from a farm in Kansas is caught in a tornado and lands in the fantastic land of Oz. The ruby slippers, delivered by a Good Witch, carry Dorothy along a yellow brick road, accompanied by her dog, Toto, and faithful companions—the Scarecrow, the Tin Man, and the Cowardly Lion. They survive a staggering array of challenges thrown at them by a Wicked Witch and arrive at the dazzling Emerald city to seek wisdom from the Wizard. They discover that the Wizard is a charlatan, but Dorothy finds that the slippers hold the key to her finding happiness and her way back home.

Some scholars argue that Baum's original story was actually an allegory for American monetary policy at the turn of the century, with the main characters representing different American interests, and the Emerald City being Washington; the Wizard being the president; the yellow brick road, the gold standard; and so on. Now, whatever you think of this interpretation, and surely there are good arguments both for and against it, it shows how the original novel was already taking on some of the qualities of a myth—A magical, fantastical story that helped people think about contemporary problems.

Several decades later, Louis Mayer sensed that the story would strike a particularly resonant chord in a country struggling with despair and uncertainty in the wake of the Depression and the Dust Bowl, as well as the looming threat of war in Europe. Americans needed reassurance and self confidence. They would find it in a film that would demonstrate the triumph of the honest, traditional values of the rural heartland, through the filter of fantastic, magical powers inherent in the slippers.

Aside from their symbolic meaning, the ruby slippers, like Mickey Mouse, were tied to changes in story-telling technology. In Baum's story and in original and early scripts for the movie, the slippers are silver. But in one of the script revisions, a new stage direction was inserted, "the ruby slippers appear on Dorothy's feet, glittering and sparkling in the sun."

But what caused that change? The answer was Technicolor. The movie was among the first to use this innovative technology for color filmmaking. Technicolor was invented by three men, two of whom were Massachusetts Institute of Technology graduates, hence the "Tech" refers to their alma mater. Walt Disney had produced Snow White and the Seven Dwarfs in Technicolor, and it became the top-grossing film of 1938. Mayer, envious of Disney's success, put his money on *The Wizard of Oz* with its rich visual imagery. He came up with the idea of beginning the film on the tornado-ravaged prairie in sepia-tinted black and white in order to contrast it with the jaw-dropping, spectacularly colorful Land of Oz shot in three-strip Technicolor film.

When filmed under the brutally bright lights needed for the Technicolor filming, the silver slippers would appear a washed-out gray; a ruby red color would be visually striking.

The job of making the shoes fell to Gilbert Adrian, MGM's chief costume designer. An already-manufactured pair of leather shoes sprayed with shiny patent-leather-looking paint turned out to be visually flat and unsatisfactory. After several other experiments, Adrian came back with two alternatives. One pair was a distinctly exotic-looking pair of slippers resembling something from a Middle Eastern fantasy. The slippers were covered with red sequins, and faux jewels, and equipped with ornate curled toes. These became known as the Arabian Test Shoes and were used only in test photographs of the costumes.

Another approach was to dye a commercially manufactured basic pair of silk pumps red. A red silk fabric sewn with rows of approximately twenty-three hundred crimson-colored sequins was then attached to the shoe. But bright red appeared orange on-screen, and so dark burgundy, almost brown, sequins were used. In October 1938, two weeks before the film shooting started,

Adrian added the butterfly-shaped, sequined red leather bows on top of the slippers, which helped convey Dorothy's youth and innocence.

We think there were somewhere between six to ten pairs of slippers made for Garland and her stand-in, Bobbie Koshay, though only four pairs plus the test shoes are known to now exist. The shoes differed slightly in size, depending on whether they would be featured in close-ups, for walking, or for dancing. And our curators know that the Smithsonian's pair was used for dancing sequences because they have a layer of felt on the soles that helped muffle the sounds of shoe leather on the soundstage floor. The film won several Academy Awards and introduced the hit song "Somewhere Over the Rainbow," in which Garland imagined an idyllic paradise where, as the song says, "the dreams that you dare to dream really do come true." Although their sequins are now fading, the slippers have not lost their fame. They are among the most popular items on display at the National Museum of American History, where they continue to remind viewers that there is magic in everyday life, as well as in Hollywood.

Three decades after Americans followed Dorothy in Oz, they became enamored of a green puppet frog named Kermit, first on television and then in the movies. Unlike some far-off fantasy land, Kermit's home on *Sesame Street*, an inner-city urban neighborhood, reflected America's predominantly urban population in the 1970s. But unlike the negative, racially-tinged stereotypes seen elsewhere, *Sesame Street* was presented as a friendly, nurturing place. The show introduced children nationwide to an extended family of White, African American, and Latino neighbors, as well as Big Bird, Grover, Oscar the Grouch, Bert and Ernie, the Cookie Monster, and more, puppets whose quirks led to lessons in tolerance and negotiating difference.

Sesame Street proved to be a landmark, demonstrating that television could serve a profound educational purpose. *Sesame Street* could teach the alphabet, numbers, directions, songs, lessons about geography, science, art, history, just about everything, through the colorful puppet characters, varied human hosts, and outstanding guests. The show revolutionized children's television. *Sesame Street* made learning entertaining and fun.

Kermit was key to the show's success. He played a television reporter or commentator, a straight man, or even a lecturer. Many saw Kermit as the alter ego of his creator, Jim Henson, serious and softly assertive, talented but not overbearing, sometimes frustrated, but always trying to bring out the best in others.

Henson was fascinated by Burr Tillstrom's *Kukla, Fran and Ollie*, a popular show he watched as a child on TV in the 1950s. In 1955, as a freshman at the University of Maryland, he helped create a puppet show called *Sam and Friends* for television station WRC-TV in Washington DC. That show included a simple character made of cloth retrieved from his mother's discarded spring coat with half Ping-Pong-ball eyes. Though this character, residing at the Smithsonian, Henson was able to express the character that became the forerunner to Kermit; it wasn't quite a frog yet. But Henson studied commercial design and textile arts in college as he developed his puppets and his characters. Like Disney's approach to Mickey Mouse, Henson wanted his puppets to be alive and have personalities. He preferred cloth hand-and-rod puppets to wooden marionettes for their more lifelike, fluid motion.

Sam and Friends led to television appearances on *The Tonight Show* and *The Ed Sullivan Show*. In the early '60s, Henson and his wife formed Muppets, Inc., and with writer Jerry Juhl and puppeteer Frank Oz, they developed a variety of puppet characters. By 1969, Children's Television Workshop, or CTW, asked Henson to work on a new children's series for public television, and that became *Sesame Street*.

CTW was at the forefront of educational television in the United States. It was a nonprofit organization created in the late 1960s by journalist and public television producer Joan Ganz Cooney. She was dismayed by the lack of quality television programming for children, and she was convinced that it was possible to use television to teach. *Sesame Street* was their very first production, and it was a smash it. Not only did *Sesame Street* fulfill CTW's educational mission; it was also timely and hip. It was culturally in tune with the baby-boomer adults who would watch the show with their young children—me included.

Kermit, like Mickey Mouse, evolved over time. He became more finely developed with green-felt fabric skin and a mouth of red cloth and pink tongue. He acquired a scarf that accentuated his head and covered a seam, but he retained his Ping-Pong-ball eyes. The puppet's body is hollow, allowing for hand operation and manipulation; steel wires support the arms, while Kermit's stuffed legs hang loosely.

Kermit's personality is perhaps best expressed in one of his most famous songs, "Bein' Green," written by composer Joe Raposo. It addressed the difficulty—and the joy—of being different. Kermit wonders whether it would be better to be yellow, or red, or gold and ultimately finds reasons to be proud of being green, which, he concludes, is beautiful. Kermit's message, it not only appealed to young children, teaching self-confidence and tolerance, but also to many adults who saw in it the simple message of the civil rights movement.

Sesame Street gave birth to one of the most popular and the first truly international hit television series, *The Muppet Show*. The show introduced a whole cast of characters, including Miss Piggy, who, though she began the show as a mere chorus pig, became a huge star, and, of course, the love interest of Kermit.

The Muppets then went to Hollywood for a series of films. And Kermit's message of self-acceptance, tireless patience, and enduring friendship traveled far beyond America's borders. Whether he is called Cocas o Sapo in Portuguese, la Rana René in Latin America, or Kamel in Arabic, he is a friend to generations of young and old in scores of countries around the world. And as Henson was helping us build a better world here on Earth, another creative genius, George Lucas, was contemplating how humans might get along with machines and other forms of life in other galaxies. The vehicle for his musing was *Star Wars*. The original movie and the series it spawned proved a massive commercial success and a global phenomenon.

The story, which purported to take place "a long time ago," actually provided a futuristic vision of a universe richly populated with an assortment of intelligent life but still engaged in the age-old struggle between good and evil. Audiences were intrigued by the richness of the fictional universe

Lucas had created and by the film's superior special effects. Space battles, exotic humanoid species, and a startling array of robots all seemed so real. From Darth Vader, and Luke Skywalker, to Yoda, Princess Leia, and Obi-Wan Kenobi, Han Solo, and Chewbacca, *Star Wars* is chock-full of intriguing characters.

When audiences first met these characters in 1977, *Star Wars* seemed like something entirely new. But one can argue that part of the film's success is how it was able to draw on older ideas from many different sources and combine them in new ways. Lucas acknowledged his debt to the timeless tale of a young hero's journey to adulthood that appears in so many cultures all over the world. Lucas was also influenced by the serialized science fiction melodramas of the 1930s known as space operas. These epic stories often involved one man fighting against an unspeakable, powerful foe and saving the world and, of course, getting the girl as well.

Another strong influence on Lucas was an international one. Lucas was a great admirer of the Japanese director Akira Kurosawa, and especially his 1958 film, *The Hidden Fortress*. That film opens with a scene that will seem familiar to many *Star Wars* fans: Two peasants—one tall, one short—trudge across a desert. They've just survived a terrible battle, and as they walk, they argue about who's at fault and why they're lost.

Lucas pays homage to this comical duo with the most endearing of *Star Wars*' characters—the droids—short for android, named R2-D2 and C-3PO. The Smithsonian's collections include the R2-D2 and C-3PO costumes from the Return of the Jedi, the third film in the series, released in 1983. Both costumes relied on a combination of electronic gadgetry and the actors' own motions to create these two very different droids with distinctly human personalities.

R2-D2 looks more like a small, fancy blue-and-white garbage can than a human being. In the films, R2-D2 is a helpmate, created to interface with computers and service starships on behalf of humans; he's a highly competent technician who effectively and efficiently performs complicated tasks well beyond human capability. Though visibly a machine, he has a personality that alternates between comic and courageous. He communicates with expressive squeals and head spins; he lumbers around on stubby legs and repeatedly saves the lives of his human masters.

Actor Kenny Baker wore the R2-D2 costume. Baker was of sufficiently small stature to fit inside the 44-inch-high unit. The costume has a body of aluminum and epoxy, built up with fiberglass cloth over a layer of foam, and the head is of spun aluminum. The entire costume still weighed 68 pounds.

The costume's head is removable. There's a small seat inside, with a seat belt. It's equipped with a handle for the actor to control the movement of the head. There are two six-volt battery packs for powering and blinking the winker lights and the other fiber optic displays on opposite sides of the head. The robot's power source also enabled the body to rock forward and backward. Baker could put his feet in the droid's hollow "feet" to steady himself while doing this. Small zippered boots in these hollowed areas allowed Baker to secure himself.

C-3PO, R2-D2's sidekick and character foil, is called a protocol droid in the series. More humanoid than R2-D2 in form, movement, and character. C-3PO interfaces with the diverse cultures of Lucas's imaginary galaxy as a robotic translator and diplomat. C-3PO is talkative and tentative, sometimes even meek and cowardly, a good counterpoint to the terser, braver, and more certain R2-D2.

The C-3PO costume, worn by actor Anthony Daniels, is five foot eight and weighs thirty pounds. The torso is made of fiberglass; the legs combine a leotard, socks, and fiberglass; the arms are aluminum; and the pelvis and feet are rubber. The sole of C-3PO's boots imitated that of the Apollo 11 astronauts; an homage to the feat of man walking on the moon. C-3PO was a less-complicated costume to operate than R2-D2 but required more character acting. Combined, however, the duo is more personable than calculating, more comical than threatening, and thus an interesting alternative to the more sinister robots of much of the science fiction literature and film that we experienced in the post-World War II era.

The *Star Wars* films have made great entertainment, but they've also become a cultural touchstone, not only for avid fans, but now for several generations of Americans. The droids are more than movie stars in these films; they are indicators of the place robots might occupy in the human experience.

From Mickey to the Ruby Slippers, from Kermit the Frog to these droids, we see the creation of imagined places and characters that provide a commentary on our daily life, our ups and our downs, our highs and our lows, but also, they provide an aspirational vision of our life and maybe our future.

The Hope Diamond—America's Crown Jewel
Lecture 21

This lecture focuses on the Hope Diamond, which is now enshrined in the redesigned Harry Winston Gallery at the Smithsonian—delighting and intriguing millions of visitors annually. The brown paper box it was mailed in (now called the Hope Diamond wrapper) has long been a treasured item in the National Postal Museum, illustrating the trust the famous jeweler placed in the U.S. Postal Service to deliver the mail. In this lecture, you will learn more about the incredible story of one of the most famous diamond in the world.

The Hope Diamond

- On Monday morning, November 10, 1958, mailman James Todd picked up a plainly wrapped package at Washington DC's general post office and drove about a mile west on Constitution Avenue to deliver it to the addressee—Dr. Leonard Carmichael at the Smithsonian's National Museum, now the National Museum of Natural History.

- The package came from Harry Winston, a Fifth Avenue jeweler in New York City. His staff had packed and wrapped it up and handed it to a Winston worker, a former policeman, who then took the subway to the general post office in Manhattan and mailed it. The postage was only 2 dollars and 44 cents, but registry and insurance—for a million dollars—brought the total up to 145 dollars and 29 cents.

- In this box was the 45-carat blue Hope Diamond, one of the largest and most famous diamonds in the world. This was no publicity stunt. Harry Winston had been sending large, precious diamonds in the mail since he went into business in the 1930s. He felt that while they were in the mail, he had the whole U.S. government protecting his gems.

- At the museum, Secretary Carmichael—who was the head of the Smithsonian—and a crowd of officials, notables, and the press gathered for the delivery. The diamond was presented by the jeweler's wife, Edna Winston. The gem was put in a new display case, and though it looks old fashioned today, it was at the time an important addition to the museum's modernization program.

- Harry Winston, who possessed some of the world's largest and most interesting diamonds, was donating the Hope for what amounted to patriotic reasons. The son of Jewish immigrants from the Ukraine, Winston had a great appreciation for the American dream. He believed that his donation would stimulate others to give their gems, too, and over time he turned out to be right.

- Winston had bought the Hope Diamond at the estate sale of Washington socialite Evalyn Walsh McLean in 1949. He got the Hope and 72 other pieces of jewelry for a bargain price of just over a million dollars. At that time, Winston was envisioning a whole new market for his product.

- Before the 1880s, diamonds were very rare and associated with royalty and enormous wealth. They were not given as engagement rings or as tokens of enduring love until the late 19th and early 20th centuries. The marketing of diamonds picked up after World War II, largely through South Africa's DeBeers Company.

- In 1948, DeBeers's public relations agency N. W. Ayer came up with a way to correlate the value of diamonds with love. One of their copywriters, a woman named Frances Gerety, came up with one of the world's most enduring marketing slogans: "Diamonds are forever."

- A few years later, in 1953, *Gentlemen Prefer Blondes* became a hit film starring Marilyn Monroe as Lorelei Lee. In the best-known song from that film, "Diamonds are a Girl's Best Friend," Monroe sang about the enduring value of diamonds. Covered in sparkling diamonds, she pauses in the song and says seductively to the camera, "Talk to me Harry Winston, tell me all about it." Winston's name had become synonymous with diamonds.

The Hope Diamond

- The Hope Diamond was part of Winston's sales pitch. He told his elite, wealthy, Fifth Avenue clientele that the bigger and clearer the diamond, the greater and more pure the love. The more elaborate the setting and rarer the color, the more intense and valued the romance. Simply put, the Hope was good for business. Its fame brought people in to his Fifth Avenue shop, and it lent prestige to his own stature among a very wealthy international clientele.

- Winston also used the Hope as the centerpiece of something he created in the early 1950s called the Court of Jewels. Winston would ship his largest and most well-known diamonds around the country to be used for charity events. Local models and high-society women would wear the gems for benefit luncheons, performances, and exhibits to raise money for a host of good causes. For Winston, the Hope was a fabulous, regal gem that attracted attention and donations for charity. He thought that if it went to the Smithsonian, it could help the country show its status.

- The day that the diamond came to the Smithsonian, Secretary Carmichael hailed the Hope as a wonderful scientific specimen. But no one really bought that—even though it was true. The public came to see the diamond because it was famous. In fact, attendance at the museum immediately doubled. What drew them was the diamond's notoriety.

- There had been, over the years—even decades—numerous stories about how the Hope Diamond carried an ancient curse. Several commentators questioned the wisdom of accepting it. If the Smithsonian was the national museum and it acquired the Hope Diamond, then the country would own it. Would the American people be cursed?

- This was during the Cold War, and public anxiety was high. Many letter writers told the Smithsonian and President Eisenhower to "turn the diamond down" and "don't accept the Hope." But many discounted the idea of a curse.

- Then, in the months that followed, James Todd, the postman who delivered the Hope, suffered a series of misfortunes. His wife died, his leg was crushed, his dog was strangled, and his house burned down. All of a sudden, a lot of people became more interested in the possibility of a curse.

- Research conducted at the Smithsonian over the years has uncovered that the curse story was made up, a modern folktale elaborated by French jeweler Pierre Cartier in Paris in 1910 to entice Evalyn Walsh McLean to buy the gem. Cartier wove together a number of different strains from historical accounts, a British novel, and stories from *The New York Times* and *The Times* to concoct his tale. He attributed deaths, revolutions, bankruptcy, and divorce to the stone's malevolent curse.

The History of the Diamond

- The Hope Diamond's history is fascinating. The blue diamond had originally been a roughly cut gem of about 112 carats when French diamond merchant Jean Baptiste Tavernier first acquired it in the Golconda region of India in the mid-1600s. At that time, India was the only known source of diamonds in the world—they had not yet been discovered in Brazil or South Africa.

- There were all sorts of stories told about how diamonds were obtained, stories that went back to ancient times, but it was Tavernier who actually went to see the diamond mines firsthand and who came back with the fullest descriptions of them. He also bought hundreds of diamonds, often trading them for pearls he acquired in the Middle East on the way.

- Portuguese, French, Dutch, German, and English dealers and merchant traders flocked to India to procure diamonds, but no one acquired more gems or made better deals than Tavernier. He made six trips to India between about 1630 and 1670.

- Returning to France after one of those trips in 1668, he met with King Louis XIV of France at the newly built Versailles palace. Tavernier sold the king the 112 carat blue diamond along with about 200 other diamonds.

- Louis XIV accumulated the greatest collection of crown jewels on the continent. European gem cutters, influenced by Renaissance ideas of using optics and geometry to manipulate light, had learned how to cut diamonds to predictably alter the stone's reflective and refractive properties, basically to let the light out of the diamond. They used diamond dust and a "secret ingredient"—olive oil on a wheel—so that they could cut raw diamonds into particular shapes.

- Louis XIV had Tavernier's blue diamond cut down from a roughly shaped 112 carats into a symmetrical, beautiful gem of 67 carats that sparkled and shined. It was recorded in the royal inventory and renamed the French Blue. It was valued at about 3.6 million dollars in today's currency. Louis XIV wore it simply from a ribbon hanging from his neck or in a brooch.

- The diamond passed down as part of the French crown jewels to Kings Louis XV and Louis XVI. These two kings wore the diamond as part of their knightly decoration, the Order of the Golden Fleece.

- There are apocryphal stories that it was worn by Queen Marie Antoinette, but there is no evidence of that. When she and her husband were imprisoned after the outbreak of the French Revolution, the crown jewels were put in a warehouse, publicly exhibited, and, in September 1792, stolen.

- When Napoleon became emperor of France, he swore to recover all the French crown jewels, including the blue diamond. But he could not find the French Blue. The gem went missing for about 20 years, until a smaller 45-carat blue diamond turned up in London in 1812 in the possession of an English diamond merchant Daniel Eliason. He did not document where it came from, but there was speculation that it was cut down from the French Blue.

- Eliason sold the blue diamond to British King George IV. Some call it the George Blue Diamond. George IV celebrated the diamond as a trophy for defeating his enemy Napoleon. He wore the blue diamond in a new golden fleece decoration.

- The British king, though, was a spendthrift who almost bankrupted the throne. So, after the king's death in 1830, his executor, the Duke of Wellington, had to sell the blue diamond to pay off debts. He sold it to Henry Philip Hope—a great diamond collector. Hope set the diamond in a medallion with a hanging pearl. He simply called the blue diamond "number 1." But after some years, it became known as the Hope Diamond.

The Curse of the Diamond

- In 1887, the diamond was inherited by Lord Francis Hope, Henry Philip Hope's great-grandnephew. Francis bet badly on horses and business enterprises. He lost his fortune and, after a series of court cases, was allowed to sell the Hope Diamond. It was purchased by a New York jeweler, Joseph Frankel's Sons Co., in 1902.

- Frankel's hoped to make a quick sale and a big profit, because they had put up much of their business capital to buy it. Instead, the overvalued diamond sat in their vault. The 1907 Bankers' Panic—

basically a recession—took its toll on the company. Frankel's was going bankrupt. The Hope Diamond was sold, at a bargain price, to other diamond dealers, finally coming to the Cartier brothers in Paris.

- In 1910, Cartier approached Evalyn and Ned McLean, an immensely wealthy couple who had bought a large diamond from Cartier when they vacationed in Paris after their marriage. Cartier weaved an elaborate tale about how the diamond was cursed by a Hindu god, and Evalyn was entranced by the story. She decided to buy the diamond.

- Evalyn wore the diamond at extravagant parties, paraded the diamond around Washington, and made much of it publicly—until 1919, when her 10-year-old son was struck down and killed by a car near their Washington DC estate. Newspapers proclaimed that the Hope Diamond really was cursed.

- The curse story was only amplified by ensuing events: Ned McLean went insane, and the family lost their ownership of *The Washington Post* in bankruptcy, despite Evalyn trying to use the Hope Diamond as collateral for a loan.

- Evalyn pawned the Hope Diamond in 1932 in order to hire an investigator to track down the kidnappers of Charles Lindbergh's baby. The remaining money was to be used for a possible ransom. The money was not needed, however, and she got the diamond back.

- Over the years, Evalyn used the diamond for charitable purposes as Washington's grand social maven. Seeing or holding it was the prize for buying a raffle ticket or attending a benefit. In 1946, another tragedy struck. Evalyn's daughter Evie committed suicide. Evalyn died in 1947, and the estate sold the Hope Diamond to Harry Winston.

The Diamond and the Smithsonian

- A decade later, the diamond arrived at the Smithsonian. It came with the setting crafted by Cartier—16 one- to one-and-a-half-carat diamonds and a necklace of 46 diamonds set in platinum. The Hope Diamond itself weighed 45.52 carats.

- Although the Smithsonian had the diamond, others wanted it, including Charles de Gaulle, the president of France. He wanted to do what Napoleon could not—reunify the French crown jewels, albeit for a temporary exhibition, at the Louvre Museum in 1962. Because the consensus among gemologists and historians was that the Hope had been cut from the French Blue, the Louvre wanted the Hope for the exhibit.

- The French approached the Smithsonian for the loan. The Smithsonian's curators were very reluctant. Not having the Hope Diamond on display would hurt museum attendance. But even more so, Smithsonian curators wondered what would happen if it didn't come back. The Smithsonian denied the request.

- Then, First Lady Jacqueline Bouvier Kennedy called Secretary Carmichael asking that the Hope be sent to Paris. The secretary called the Smithsonian chancellor—the chief justice of the Supreme Court, Earl Warren. They decided to accede to Jackie's request.

- In May 1962, the Hope Diamond was sent to the Louvre to be reunited with the French Crown Jewels. It was displayed as a gem without a setting—as the descendant stone of the French Blue. The exhibit proved immensely popular. At the end of its month-long stay in Paris, the Hope returned to the Smithsonian.

- In December, the French reciprocal gift came to the United States. It was a painting of an intriguing woman with an enigmatic smile—she was the *Mona Lisa,* by Leonardo da Vinci. The *Mona Lisa* was shown at the National Gallery of Art in Washington and at the Metropolitan Museum of Art in New York, seen by more than a million and an half visitors.

- Since that time, curators at the Smithsonian, chiefly Jeff Post, have conducted numerous scientific studies of the diamond. In essence, the gem is a biopsy of the earth. It formed as crystallized carbon about 90 miles below the earth's surface about a billion years ago. It rose to the surface relatively slowly, up through a volcanic vent on India's Deccan plateau, and then was carried by rivers and streams to the alluvial field where it was mined.

- The Hope's blue color comes from a small number of boron atoms mixed in with crystallized carbon. The diamond is not of a uniform quality; it has a grain and various zones of different shades of blue. It is the largest known blue diamond in the world, and scientific and technical studies have confirmed that it was formerly larger still, as it was most likely cut from the French Blue, which in turn was cut from the stone Tavernier acquired in India.

- The Hope Diamond also has a distinct property: After exposure to ultraviolet light, it phosphoresces a bright red-orange. Scientists believe that this is a result of the interaction of boron atoms with other trace elements.

Featured Objects

The Hope Diamond

The Hope Diamond Wrapper

Suggested Reading

Kurin, *Hope Diamond.*

———, *Madcap May.*

The Hope Diamond—America's Crown Jewel
Lecture 21—Transcript

On Monday morning, November 10, 1958, mailman James Todd picked up a plainly wrapped package at Washington, DC's general post office and drove about a mile west on Constitution Avenue to deliver it to the addressee—Dr. Leonard Carmichael at the Smithsonian's National Museum, now the National Museum of Natural History.

The package came from Harry Winston, a Fifth Avenue jeweler in New York City. His staff had packed and wrapped it up and handed it to a fellow worker, a former policeman, who then took it on the subway to the general post office in Manhattan and mailed it. As you can see, the postage was $2.44, but registry and insurance—for a million dollars—brought the total up to $145.29.

In this box was the 45-carat blue Hope Diamond, one of the largest and most famous diamonds in the world.

Now, this was no publicity stunt. Harry Winston had been sending large, precious diamonds in the mail since he went into business in the 1930s. He felt that while they were in the mail, he had the whole U.S. government protecting his gems. At the museum, Secretary Carmichael, who was the head of the Smithsonian, and a crowd of officials, notables, and the press gathered for the delivery. The diamond was presented by the jeweler's wife, Edna Winston, because Harry avoided crowds and didn't want his picture taken. In fact, Harry's insurance company discouraged public appearances because that would keep would-be thieves from identifying him.

The gem was put in a new display case, something I call the "ship's portal" installation, and though it looks old-fashioned to us today, it was at the time, an important addition to the museum's modernization program. Winston, who possessed some of the world's largest and most interesting diamonds, was donating the Hope for what amounted to patriotic reasons. The son of Jewish immigrants from the Ukraine, Winston had a great appreciation for the American dream. And why not? Starting out working in his father's jewelry stores in New York and Los Angeles, he had become wildly successful and was widely known as the "King of Diamonds."

Winston felt that the United States, after World War II, was now a world power and should, therefore, have an outstanding collection of jewels. The United States, unlike France, England, or Russia, had no kings or queens, so it had to rely on its citizens—people like himself—to make the donations that would build such a collection. Winston believed his donation would stimulate others to give their gems too, and over time, he turned out to be right.

The Hope Diamond had been good to Winston. He'd bought it at the estate sale of Washington socialite Evalyn Walsh McLean in 1949. He got the Hope and 72 other pieces of jewelry for a bargain price of just over $1 million. At that time, Winston was envisioning a whole new market for his product. American men and women had just come through a terrible period in history—the Great Depression followed by World War II. They were now ready and anxious to rebuild the economy and their lives, settle down, get married, raise a family. And Harry was ready to sell them diamonds.

Before the 1880s, diamonds were very rare and associated mainly with royalty and enormous wealth. They were not given as engagement rings or as tokens of enduring love until the late 19th and early 20th centuries. The marketing of diamonds picked up after World War II, largely through South Africa's DeBeers Company. In 1948, DeBeers' public relations agency N. W. Ayer came up with way to correlate the value of diamonds with love. One of their copywriters, a woman named Frances Gerety, had been reading Anita Loos's 1925 novel, *Gentlemen Prefer Blondes*. That novel's heroine, Lorelei Lee, somewhat cynically notes, "Kissing your hand may make you feel good, but a diamond and a sapphire bracelet lasts forever." Well, Gerety took that line, removed the cynicism, and came up with one of the world's most enduring marketing slogans—"Diamonds are Forever."

A few years later, in 1953, *Gentlemen Prefer Blondes* became a film starring Marilyn Monroe as Lorelei Lee. In the best-known song from that film, "Diamonds are a Girl's Best Friend," Monroe sang about the enduring value of diamonds in juxtaposition to ladies aging, losing their charms, and shapes. Now, outfitted in her slinky-tight pink dress, covered in sparkling diamonds, with moist red lips, she pauses in the song and says seductively to the camera, "Talk to me Harry Winston, tell me all about it." Winston's name had become synonymous with diamonds.

The Hope Diamond was part of Winston's sales pitch. He told his elite, wealthy, Fifth Avenue clientele that the bigger and clearer the diamond, the greater and more pure the love. The more elaborate the setting and rarer the color, the more intense and valued the romance. Simply put, the Hope was good for business. Its fame brought people into his Fifth Avenue shop, and it lent prestige to his own stature among a very wealthy international clientele.

Winston also used the Hope as the centerpiece of something he created in the early 1950s called the Court of Jewels. Winston would ship his largest and most well-known diamonds around the country to be used for charity events. The Hope anchored the tours of amazing diamonds to towns large and small; it even went to Toronto and Cuba. In some places, six decades later, there are still shrines commemorating the Hope's visit to their community.

Local models and high-society women would wear the gems for benefit luncheons, performances, and exhibits to raise money for a host of good causes. I've actually personally met some of the ladies who wore these gems in the 1950s, and decades later, they still remembered the excitement of doing so.

For Winston, the Hope was a fabulous, regal gem that attracted attention and donations for charity. Now, he thought, if it went to the Smithsonian, it could help the country show its status. Now, that day, when the diamond came to the Smithsonian, Secretary Carmichael hailed the Hope as a wonderful scientific specimen. But no one really bought that, even though it was true. The public came to see the diamond because it was famous. In fact, attendance at the museum immediately doubled. What drew them was the diamond's notoriety.

There had been, over the years—even decades—numerous stories about how the Hope Diamond carried an ancient curse. Several commentators questioned the wisdom of accepting the diamond. If the Smithsonian was the national museum of the United States and it acquired the Hope Diamond, then the country would own it. Would the American people then be cursed? Now remember, this was during the cold war, and public anxiety was high. Turn down the diamond; don't accept the Hope, many letter writers wrote the Smithsonian and even President Eisenhower. Cartoonists parodied the idea of the United States and Uncle Sam being cursed.

Of course, many discounted the idea of a curse. And then, in the months that followed, James Todd, that postman who delivered that package, suffered a series of misfortunes. His wife died; his leg was crushed; his dog was strangled; and his house burned down. All of a sudden a lot of people became more interested in the possibility the cursed Hope Diamond. Well, as we've done the research over the years at the Smithsonian, we've found that the curse story was made up, a modern folktale elaborated by French jeweler Pierre Cartier in Paris in 1910 in order to entice Evalyn Walsh McLean to buy the gem. Cartier wove together a number of different strains from historical accounts, a British novel, stories from the New York Times and the London Times, and with that he concocted his tale. He attributed deaths, revolutions, bankruptcy, and divorce to the stone's malevolent curse.

Now, while the curse story is made up, it also reveals of the diamond's history, which, really, is fascinating. The basic story goes like this. The blue diamond had originally been a roughly cut gem of about 112 carats when French diamond merchant Jean Baptiste Tavernier first acquired it in the Golconda region of India in the mid-1600s. At that time, India was the only known source of diamonds in the world; they hadn't yet been discovered in Brazil or South Africa. There were all sorts of stories told about how diamonds were obtained, stories that went back to ancient times and were retold by the likes of people like Marco Polo. But it was Tavernier who actually went to see the diamond mines first hand and who came back with the fullest descriptions of them. He also bought hundreds of diamonds, often trading them for pearls he acquired in the Middle East on the way.

The Indians had very elaborate ideas about gemstones. They believed that gemstones had protective powers. They did not cut gemstones the way we do. Instead, they tended to preserve as much of the stone as they could, only cutting out cracks and other imperfections. This, it was believed, maximized their ability to protect one from evil influences. Basically, the idea was that gems absorbed negative influences and contained them in the stone, kind of like a Pandora's box. Rulers wore lots of diamonds and other gems—the bigger the better. And that would provide them the most protection. Other Indians wore smaller talismans with smaller gems and different gems for the same purpose.

Portuguese, French, Dutch, German, and English dealers, and merchant traders flocked to India to procure diamonds, but no one acquired more gems or made better deals than Tavernier. He made six trips to India between about 1630 and 1670. Returning to France after one of those trips in 1668, he met with King Louis XIV of France at the newly built Versailles palace. Tavernier sold the king the 112 carat blue diamond, along with about 200 other diamonds. A big, blue diamond like this was incredibly rare, and the king's artist drew a diagram of the diamond to record the acquisition.

Now, recall, Louis XIV was called the Sun King, and if you have been to Versailles, you know why. He viewed his reign as one of enlightenment, of letting in the light of divine kingship, of letting knowledge, and beauty, and the arts shine. At Versailles, you see the glass of chandeliers exquisitely cut to reflect and refract the light. You see mirrors and windows and the dazzling use of light in the architecture and the décor.

Well, for diamonds, it was the same thing. Louis XIV accumulated the greatest collection of crown jewels on the continent. European gem cutters, influenced by Renaissance ideas of using optics and geometry to manipulate light, had learned how to cut diamonds predictably, and they would alter the stone's reflective and refractive properties, basically, to let the light out of the diamond and let it shine. They used diamond dust and a very secret ingredient at the time to cut diamonds. It was Olive oil put on a wheel, and so they would cut diamonds, raw diamonds, into particular shapes.

Louis XIV had Tavernier's blue diamond cut down from a roughly shaped 112 carats into a symmetrical, beautiful gem of 67 carats—and it sparkled, and shined. It was recorded in the royal inventory and renamed the French Blue. It was valued at about 3 and 3.6 million dollars in today's currency. Louis XIV wore it simply from a ribbon hanging from his neck or in a brooch.

The diamond passed down as part of the French crown jewels to kings Louis XV and Louis XVI. These two kings wore the diamond as part of their knightly decoration, something called the Order of the Golden Fleece.

There are apocryphal stories that the diamond, this blue diamond, was worn by Queen Marie Antoinette, but there is absolutely no evidence of that. When she and her husband were imprisoned after the outbreak of the French Revolution, the crown jewels were put in a warehouse, publicly exhibited, and then, in September 1792, stolen. When Napoleon later became emperor of France, he swore to recover all the French crown jewels, including the blue diamond. But he failed. He could not find the French Blue.

The French Blue diamond went missing for some 20 years until a smaller 45-carat blue diamond turned up in London in 1812 in the possession of an English diamond merchant named Daniel Eliason. Eliason didn't say where it came from, but there was speculation that it was cut down from the French Blue. This 45 carat blue diamond, as drawn in a document of the time, is the same one that is in the Smithsonian today.

Eliason sold the blue diamond to British King George IV, and some called it the George Blue Diamond. George IV celebrated the diamond as a trophy for defeating his enemy Napoleon. He wore the blue diamond in a new golden fleece decoration. The British king, though, was a spendthrift who almost bankrupted the throne. So after the king's death in 1830, his executor, the Duke of Wellington, had to sell the blue diamond to pay off his debts. He sold it to Henry Philip Hope, a great diamond collector.

Hope set the diamond in a medallion with a hanging pearl. He simply called the blue diamond "number 1." But after some years, it became known as the Hope Diamond. The Hope family was among England's wealthiest. They'd aided American colonial commerce and helped finance the Louisiana Purchase. They accumulated land, castles, Dutch and Flemish paintings, and other riches. But in the course of a few generations, they squandered that great wealth.

In 1887 the diamond was inherited by Lord Francis Hope, Henry Philip Hope's great-grandnephew. Francis bet badly on horses, business enterprises, and an American showgirl wife, May Yohé. He lost his fortune and his wife, and after a series of court cases was allowed to sell the Hope Diamond. It was purchased by New York jeweler Joseph Frankel's Sons in 1901. Frankel's hoped to make a quick sale and a big profit, as they'd put up much of their business capital to buy the Hope diamond. Instead, the over-valued diamond sat in their vault. In the 1907 Bankers' Panic, basically a recession, took its toll on the company. Frankel's was diamond rich but cash poor and going bankrupt.

The first stories about the Hope Diamond being unlucky came in the financial pages of the New York Times in 1908; the chronicle noted that the gem was responsible for Frankel's failure. Other newspapers in Washington and London picked up the story and made it increasingly elaborate, speaking of the baleful influences and power of the mysterious rays that emanated below the glittering surface of the diamond that unleashed evil upon those who possessed it. These stories blamed the executions of Louis XVI and Marie Antoinette, Hope's bankruptcy and divorce, and Frankel's collapse on the malevolent influence of the blue diamond.

The Hope Diamond was finally sold, at a bargain price, to other diamond dealers, finally coming to the Cartier brothers in Paris. Pierre Cartier was enchanted with the novel The Moonstone, written decades earlier by English author Wilkie Collins. In Collins' story, a large, yellow diamond had formed the eye of an idol of a Hindu deity in a temple in India. The diamond literally embodied the power of the god. There it rested until it was looted by a Muslim conqueror and taken to his treasury. Then years later, British colonial soldiers looted the treasury in battle, taking the diamond back to England. There, tragedy, murder, kidnapping, insanity followed the possession of the ill-gotten gem. The god had cursed the stone; an evil force would emanate rays from the stone and strike misfortune upon all who owned it until the gem was properly returned to the deity back in India. Finally, Indian Hindu priests retrieved the diamond and brought it back home. Now, this story by Collins was basically a cautionary tale about divine or supernatural payback for the immorality of colonialism.

These were the historical and fictional elements that Cartier combined when he approached Evalyn and Ned McLean in 1910. Cartier already had a relationship with the immensely wealthy couple; he had sold them a large diamond when they vacationed in Paris after their marriage. Cartier applied the Moonstone story to the Hope Diamond, telling the couple it was cursed by a Hindu god, and embellished a bit more, blaming the French the Turkish and other revolutions on its baleful influence.

Evalyn was entranced by Cartier's story, and she decided, later, to buy the diamond. The McLeans were among the richest families in the United States, owning banks, real estate, and the *Washington Post*. McLean, Virginia is named after the family. They owned some of Washington's most luxurious and valuable real estate, in addition to homes in Newport Rhode Island, Bar Harbor, Maine and Palm Beach, Florida. They exemplified the later years of the Gilded Age, using, flaunting, and even, some would say, wasting their gigantic fortune on over-the-top conspicuous consumption.

Evalyn wore the diamond at extravagant parties, paraded the diamond around Washington, and made much of it publicly, until 1919. It was then that her 10-year-old son, Vinson, was struck down and killed by a car near their Washington DC estate. Newspapers proclaimed, well, maybe that the Hope Diamond really was cursed, and they wondered who would next be struck by the diamond's malignant light rays. It was as if all the negative energy that was locked up in the uncut diamond had now been unleashed upon its possessors because of the cutting. Pandora's box, so to speak, had been opened. The story of the curse appealed to the public and resonated with other curse stories of the era about the Titanic and Egyptian mummies. The idea was that somehow the wealthy, who had flaunted their wealth by obtaining the treasurers of others, were now getting their comeuppance from higher supernatural powers.

The curse story was only amplified by ensuing events. Ned McLean went insane, and the family lost the *Washington Post* in bankruptcy, despite Evalyn trying to use the Hope Diamond as collateral for a loan. Evalyn actually pawned the Hope Diamond in 1932 in order to hire an investigator to track down the kidnappers of Charles Lindbergh's baby. The remaining money was to be used for a possible ransom. The money wasn't needed, however, and she got the diamond back.

Over the years, Evalyn used the diamond for charitable purposes as Washington's grand social maven. Seeing or holding it was the prize for buying a raffle ticket or attending a benefit. She lent the diamond to brides as "something blue." She even had her great dane, Mike, wear the diamond around his neck. In Evalyn's autobiography, she expressed her ambivalence about the Hope Diamond, sometimes pooh-poohing the curse and other times wondering if the curse was payback for money and time misspent and frittered away. In 1946, another tragedy struck. Evalyn's daughter Evie committed suicide. Evalyn died in 1947, and the estate sold the Hope Diamond to Harry Winston.

A decade later, the diamond came to the Smithsonian. When it did, it was given an acquisition number, just like every other Smithsonian object. The Hope Diamond is #217868. This diamond that you see here, by the way, is a high quality replica. The original is far too valuable to travel from its home at the Smithsonian. It came with the setting crafted by Cartier and 16 one- to one-and-a-half-carat diamonds surrounding the main blue stone. It's set in platinum, and the Hope Diamond itself weighs 45.5 carats. Now, though the Smithsonian had the diamond, others wanted it too, including Charles de Gaulle, the president of France. He wanted to do what Napoleon could not, reunify the French crown jewels, albeit for a temporary exhibition, at the Louvre Museum in 1962. Since the consensus among gemologists and historians was that the Hope Diamond had been cut from the French Blue, the Louvre wanted the Hope for its exhibition.

The French approached the Smithsonian for the loan. The Smithsonian curators were very reluctant. Not having the Hope Diamond on display would hurt museum attendance. But even more so, Smithsonian curators wondered, what if it didn't come back? The Smithsonian said no. The French promised they'd make a dramatic loan in return. The Smithsonian stood firm in its opposition. Then things changed. First Lady Jacqueline Kennedy called Secretary Carmichael asking that the Hope be sent to Paris. The secretary called the Smithsonian chancellor, the chief justice of the Supreme Court, Earl Warren. They discussed the matter and decided to accede to Jackie's request. She wrote a note that we have in the Smithsonian archives, "Thank you. Thank you. Thank you." In May 1962, the Hope Diamond was sent to the Louvre to be reunited with the French Crown Jewels. It was displayed as a gem without a setting as the descendant stone of the French Blue. The exhibit proved immensely popular. At the end of its month-long stay in Paris, the Hope came back to the Smithsonian. In December, the French reciprocal gift came to the United States. It was a painting of an intriguing woman with an enigmatic smile; she was the Mona Lisa by Leonardo da Vinci. The Mona Lisa was shown at the National Gallery of Art in Washington and at the Metropolitan Museum of Art in New York, seen by more than a million and an half visitors who waited in lines for hours to see the masterpiece.

Since that time, curators at the Smithsonian, chiefly my colleague Jeff Post, have conducted numerous scientific studies of the diamond. In essence, the gem is a biopsy of the earth. It formed as crystallized carbon about 90 miles below the earth's surface about a billion years ago. It rose to the surface relatively slowly up through a volcanic vent on India's Deccan plateau and then was carried by rivers and streams to the alluvial field where it was eventually mined.

The Hope's blue color comes from a small number of boron atoms mixed in with the crystalized carbon. The diamond is not of a uniform quality; it has a grain and various zones of different shades of blue. It is the largest known blue diamond in the world, and scientific and technical studies have confirmed that it was formerly larger still, as it was most likely cut from the French Blue, which in turn was cut from the stone Tavernier acquired in India. The Hope Diamond also has a very distinct property. After exposure to ultraviolet light, it phosphoresces a bright red-orange. Though not fully understood, scientists believe that this is the result of the interaction of boron atoms with other trace elements, but it's a very eerie effect.

And the curse? Well, as curator Jeff Post says, "Since the arrival of the Hope diamond, the National Gem Collection has grown steadily in size and stature and is today considered by many to be the finest public display of gems in the world. For the Smithsonian Institution, the Hope diamond has obviously been a source of good luck." Great generosity has flowed from Winston's philanthropic interest. Following Winston, Mrs. John Logan donated the 423 carat Logan Sapphire. Marjorie Merriweather Post donated the Napoleon necklace and the 31-carat Blue Heart Diamond. Leonard and Victoria

Wilkinson gave the 68 carat Victoria Transvaal diamond; Janet Annenberg Hooker gave a large emerald and suite of yellow diamonds, and so on.

The Hope Diamond is now enshrined in the redesigned Harry Winston Gallery at the Smithsonian, delighting and intriguing millions annually. And that brown paper box it came in? Well, that's long been a treasured item in our National Postal Museum, illustrating the trust the famous jeweler placed in the U.S. postal service to deliver the mail.

Sing Out for Justice—American Music

Lecture 22

The history of protest music in the United States is long and rich, extending to the early 19th century. In the mid-20th century, American protest music took on perhaps its greatest social significance, when it became associated with three particular movements: for civil rights, for justice for the economically downtrodden, and against the Vietnam War. As you will learn in this lecture, the music of Marian Anderson, Woody Guthrie, and Bob Dylan captured the attention and the imagination of two generations dissatisfied with prejudice, injustice, and greed.

Marian Anderson

- One of the earliest and most extraordinary events in the nascent civil rights movement took place on the National Mall in Washington DC on Easter Sunday, April 9, 1939. African American contralto Marian Anderson performed an unprecedented open-air concert on the steps of the Lincoln Memorial to a huge live audience and to millions more over the radio.

- The mink coat she wore on that chilly spring evening—now a part of the Smithsonian's Anacostia Community Museum collection—became a symbol of the day, reminding all that the concert took place outdoors, not by initial design, but because Marian Anderson had been denied an indoor stage at Constitution Hall because she was African American.

- The coat attests to the fact that a narrow act of racial prejudice had been transformed into a public performance that commanded national respect. The fact that it was a mink coat—a recognized symbol of high status for women at the time—also illustrates that despite stereotypes and obstacles, an African American woman could transcend entrenched social and cultural barriers to achieve fame, fortune, and success.

- Marian Anderson was born around 1897 and grew up in South Philadelphia. She sang for various community groups, such as the People's Choral Society, where her prodigious talents were recognized and supported not only by the community, but also by visiting artists, who mentored and encouraged her.

- After graduating high school, Anderson applied to an all-white Philadelphia music academy but was turned away after being told, "We don't take colored." So, she studied with a private tutor and, in 1925, won a singing contest that earned her a performance with the New York Philharmonic.

- Anderson's career took off from there. In 1928, she made her debut at Carnegie Hall. Still, very few American theaters and opera companies would allow Anderson to perform. Undaunted, Anderson embarked on a singing tour of Europe. The acclaim received from European critics established her reputation in the United States.

- In 1934, Sol Hurok, famed theatrical impresario, became Anderson's manager, and with his clout and her reputation, the walls of racial segregation began to crumble. Anderson gave perhaps five or six dozen concerts a year in the United States and gave a private performance for Franklin and Eleanor Roosevelt at the White House in 1936. But while on tour, she sometimes faced discrimination—denied a room at a whites-only hotel or a table at a restaurant. But while Anderson faced these indignities on the road, her studio recordings became big sellers.

- For Easter 1939, Anderson was scheduled to perform in Washington DC in a concert sponsored by historically black Howard University. The search for a venue was complicated, because Anderson was sure to draw an enormous crowd, with fans of all races, but the nation's capital was still a segregated town.

- The city government denied Anderson use of Central High School, because it was a white school and its policies forbade admission to an integrated audience. The denial provoked petitions and outrage among black leaders, the black community, and liberal white supporters. But the Supreme Court's 1896 *Plessey v. Ferguson* decision, which had made "separate but equal" the law of the land, gave any venue, public or private, the right to turn Anderson away, so these protests were ignored.

Marian Anderson's Mink Coat

- Sol Hurok then tried to book Constitution Hall, which was administered by the Daughters of the American Revolution (DAR), an organization of women representing descendants of Revolutionary War officers, officials, and soldiers. The DAR was a segregated organization that did not admit black members, even though about 5,000 black soldiers fought in George Washington's Continental Army. The DAR turned Anderson down, claiming that the hall was booked. But it became apparent that they did not want to host a black performer or an integrated audience. Their refusal produced more protests.

- Eleanor Roosevelt, who had become a member shortly after her husband became president, resigned from the DAR. Eleanor Roosevelt's example brought the issue national attention. Hundreds of other members resigned from the DAR.

- The Roosevelts, working with Hurok and the National Association for the Advancement of Colored People, approached Secretary of the Interior Harold Ickes. He arranged to hold the concert under the auspices of the National Park Service at the Lincoln Memorial. The plan immediately captured the national imagination.

- The day of the concert, crowds began to arrive before dawn. About 500 uniformed officers patrolled the National Mall. The crowd swelled to more than 70,000 people, black and white. At 5 pm, Anderson took her place on the steps, adorned in her mink coat and matching hat. She was introduced by Secretary Ickes, who stood before an assemblage of microphones broadcasting across the United States as well as to Canada and Mexico.

- Anderson removed her hat and began her first selection, "America." A hush of silence fell over the crowd as she concluded; many were moved to tears. Anderson then sang two arias. When she sat down for a break, the audience erupted in an outpouring of emotion and appreciation. The second half of her performance included several spirituals, and she closed the concert with the resonant "Nobody Knows the Trouble I've Seen." Then, briefly, Anderson addressed her audience, without politics or commentary.

- After the Lincoln Memorial concert, Anderson went on to enjoy a full and acclaimed career. Her farewell performance tour began at Constitution Hall and ended at Carnegie Hall. The famous mink coat she wore at the Lincoln Memorial for that Easter day concert in 1939 came to the Smithsonian after her death, donated by her nephew, James DePriest, the longtime conductor of the Oregon Symphony. It was recently joined at the Smithsonian by another item—the dress she wore that day, also donated by her family.

Woody Guthrie

- Woodrow Wilson Guthrie was born in 1912 in Okemah, Oklahoma. He learned to play the harmonica and guitar as a youth, and although he thought of himself as a musical vagabond, he was a voracious reader and a member of both the high school band and the glee club. When he was 19, he went to live in Texas, married young, and started a family.

- But this was the early 1930s, the era of the Great Depression and the Dust Bowl. The already strained economy of the southern Great Plains was struck by an ecological disaster. Guthrie joined thousands of other Dust Bowl refugees and headed to California looking for work and opportunity. This migration of poor, rural working people trying to escape despair for an unknown but hopeful future stimulated much of his early songwriting.

- Guthrie settled in Los Angeles, playing traditional hillbilly and folk music on a radio program as well as his own songs based on his migration experience. His prolabor views unnerved radio station sponsors, so Guthrie headed east to New York, where he was introduced to the political urban folk music scene, where his views were more welcomed.

- Early in 1940, Guthrie became frustrated hearing Kate Smith's version of Irving Berlin's "God Bless America" repeatedly on the radio. He found it syrupy and overly celebratory. As he traveled across the country, he had seen firsthand too much poverty, homelessness, and joblessness—many people who did not seem to be so blessed. On February 23, 1940, Guthrie wrote his response.

- Guthrie first titled the song "God Blessed America for Me" and used it as the last line of each stanza, but then he crossed it out, replacing it with "This Land Was Made for You and Me." Guthrie's lyrics were populist but hard-hitting. While the song celebrated the breadth and diversity of the United States, its natural beauty and bounty, and a profound democratic sense that all Americans owned the country, it also addressed tough issues—the Depression, the disparity of wealth, and economic and social injustice.

- Around that time, Guthrie met Pete Seeger and the two became lifelong friends, traveling across the United States, engaging in spirited discussions, performing in concerts, taking up causes, and recording albums together. They lived in a communal house in Greenwich Village and sponsored and participated in hootenannies—or rousing folk music singing parties—as the

Almanac Singers. They both penned and sang pro-union, protest, and peace songs.

- They were against the entry of the United States into World War II, but once Germany invaded the Soviet Union, they became pro-war and anti-Nazi. Guthrie joined the U.S. Merchant Marine. He also wrote songs about the conflict. A piece of sheet music for the song he titled "Round Up the Nazis" is housed in the Smithsonian's Folkways Archives.

- On leave in March 1944, Guthrie visited the New York City studio of Moses Asch, then the founder and operator of Asch Records, a small independent label that later would be absorbed into Asch's life's work, Folkways Records. Asch and Guthrie's mutual respect for the ability of song and speech to express raw human experience made them friends.

- In April 1944, Guthrie came in to Asch's studio six different times and recorded at least 150 songs—a fraction of the 3,000 songs he wrote. In the last session, Guthrie recorded "This Land Is Your Land."

- Asch didn't issue the recorded song until 1951, and when he did, it was for a children's record on the Folkways label. It was a 1946 "cleaned-up" version, excluding Guthrie's original, Socialist-sounding lyrics about private property and lines of people outside the relief office. Instead, the recorded version, with the first stanza repeated as a chorus, was catchy and upbeat.

- The publisher, Ludlow Music, allowed the song to be included in school music textbooks for free as a promotional strategy. Music and classroom teachers found it an easy song for their students to learn and sing as a group. It became immensely popular—some even called it an alternative national anthem.

- In the 1960s, it became popular with the folk music revival and later with the antiwar protest movement. It has been covered by hundreds of musicians, and it has been translated into numerous languages.

In a recording from the Smithsonian Folkways collection, the great American folk artist Ella Jenkins leads a children's chorus in singing the song, in honor of the American bicentennial.

- The original 1944 shellac master recording of Guthrie singing the song in Asch's studio is in the Moses and Frances Asch Folkways Collection in the Ralph Rinzler Folklife Archives at the Smithsonian Center for Folklife and Cultural Heritage—along with hundreds of other Guthrie masters and the tens of thousands of recordings Asch produced in his career and later donated to the Smithsonian.

- On the master, the title of the song is written in pencil as "This Land Was Made for You and Me." The recording shows its age—it's even decomposing chemically. But thanks to Smithsonian archivists and sound engineers, it has been preserved. They've even been able to play it—once—make a new recording, and hear Guthrie's voice intone for a fair share of this land for the common man.

Bob Dylan

- Guthrie influenced a generation of American singer-songwriters. One, most exceptionally, was a Jewish kid born Robert Zimmerman in 1941 and raised in the Iron Range region of Minnesota. In high school in the mid-1950s, he played the new rock-and-roll music. As he matured, he was attracted to American folk music, with its depth of emotion and themes of despair and struggle. He was particularly drawn to the lyrics of Woody Guthrie.

- In 1961, he arrived in New York City and made a pilgrimage to visit Guthrie, who was hospitalized at the time with Huntington's disease. He modeled himself after the famed balladeer, as someone whose music would tackle the serious issues of the day.

- After arriving in New York, Robert Zimmerman changed his name to Bob Dylan. He began performing in coffeehouses in Greenwich Village. When Dylan opened at Gerde's Folk City for the Greenbriar Boys, he caught the attention of *New York Times* music critic Robert Shelton, who wrote a laudatory review that attracted strong public attention.

- Although Dylan had sought to record for Asch and Folkways Records, just like Guthrie, he was instead signed by John Hammond to Columbia Records. At the same time, he recorded for other labels using several pseudonyms. His first 1962 Columbia album, *Bob Dylan*, included folk, blues, and gospel tunes and two original songs. While the album was by no means a hit, it introduced audiences to his characteristic voice.

- Dylan's second album, *The Freewheelin' Bob Dylan*, released in 1963, earned him a reputation as a creative singer-songwriter and protest singer. With the albums that followed, Dylan became the leading singer-songwriter for the emerging counterculture of the 1960s, and by mid-decade, Dylan songs—such as "Blowin' in the Wind," "The Times They Are A-Changin'," and "Mr. Tambourine Man"—were standards at concerts and protest demonstrations. Within a few years, Dylan was ascribed to be the voice for a generation questioning the social and political status quo.

- As Dylan's career progressed, he began to express reservations about his own status within the American folk music movement. In 1964's "It Ain't Me, Babe," he seems to reject the role of the people's balladeer. In the 1965 album *Bringing It All Back Home*, Dylan experimented with musical styles and themes, venturing into love ballads, irony, and a more electrified sound—later termed "folk rock"—that disappointed traditionalist fans. Nevertheless, the album demonstrated Dylan's artistic virtuosity and was tremendously influential.

- In 1966, at the height of his success, Dylan was in a terrible motorcycle accident and took some time to recover. To fill the void, Columbia Records decided to release a greatest hits album. John Berg, Columbia's art director, asked graphic designer Milton Glaser to create a poster of Dylan that would be included in the album.

- Glaser found inspiration for the Dylan poster from a self-portrait created by Marcel Duchamp, the French surrealist painter. Duchamp's 1957 self-portrait showed his silhouetted head in a white square set into a black border. Glaser used a similar composition, but reversed it, representing Dylan's head facing left in black against a white background.

- To this design, Glaser added his own 1960s twist: He turned Dylan's wild and unkempt hair into vividly colored, swirling ribbons. This suggested the psychedelic imagery coming out of the counterculture of the West Coast. Dylan's kinetic, colored hair contrasts sharply with the flat black-on-white profile, animating what would otherwise be a rather stark representation. The result is a portrait that seems simple yet exudes profound dignity. Glaser added a bold typeface with the simple one-word legend "Dylan." The poster, and the album, became instant hits, selling 6 million copies.

Featured Objects

Marian Anderson's Mink Coat

Woody Guthrie's original sketches and handwritten sheet music to "Round Up the Nazis"

Milton Glaser's *Bob Dylan* Poster

Suggested Reading

Arsenault, *The Sound of Freedom*.

Dylan, *Chronicles*.

Guthrie, *Bound for Glory*.

Sing Out for Justice—American Music

Lecture 22—Transcript

The history of protest music in the United States is long and rich, extending to the early 19th century. Before the Civil War, the spiritual songs of American slaves, like "Go Down Moses," expressed their religious faith, but also called up their suffering and their longing for freedom. Abolitionists composed anthems, like "The Fugitive's Song," to sing at rallies and protests. The women's suffrage movement had songs like "Daughters of Freedom" and "Shall Women Vote?" Some of these have become classics; some are long forgotten. But there is no doubt that Americans have always blended politics and song.

In the mid-20th century, America protest music took on perhaps its greatest social significance when it became associated with three particular movements. These were the movements for civil rights, for justice for the economically downtrodden, and against the Vietnam War. One of the earliest and most extraordinary events in the nascent civil rights movement took place on the National Mall in Washington, DC on Easter Sunday, April 9, 1939. African American contralto Marian Anderson performed an unprecedented open-air concert on the steps of the Lincoln Memorial to a huge live audience and to millions more over the radio.

The mink coat she wore on that chilly spring evening—this mink coat, now a part of the Smithsonian's Anacostia Community Museum's collection—became a symbol of the day, reminding all that the concert took place outdoors, not by initial design, but because Marian Anderson had been denied an indoor stage at Constitution Hall because she was African American. The coat attests to the fact that a narrow act of racial prejudice had been transformed into a public performance that commanded national respect. The fact that it was a mink coat, a recognized symbol of high status for women at the time, also illustrates that despite stereotypes and obstacles, an African American woman could transcend entrenched social and cultural barriers to achieve fame, fortune, and success.

Marian Anderson was born around 1897 and grew up in South Philadelphia. She was fortunate to live in a neighborhood that, while not wealthy, was culturally diverse and intellectually rich. She sang for various community groups, like the People's Choral Society, where her prodigious talents were recognized and supported not only by the community, but by visiting artists, who mentored and encouraged her. After graduating high school, Anderson applied to an all-white Philadelphia music academy but was turned away after being told, "We don't take colored." So she studied with a private tutor, and in 1925 won a singing contest that earned her a performance with the New York Philharmonic.

Anderson's career took off from there. In 1928, she made her debut at Carnegie Hall. Still, very few American theaters and opera companies would allow Anderson to perform. Undaunted, Anderson embarked on a singing tour of Europe, where she performed for such dignitaries as King Gustav of Sweden and King Christian of Denmark. The acclaim received from European critics established her reputation in the United States. Composer Jean Sibelius and others were moved by her contralto voice and deep, soulful renditions; she formed lasting relationships in the international classical music community.

In 1934, Sol Hurok, famed theatrical impresario, became Anderson's manager, and with his clout and her reputation, the walls of racial segregation began to crumble. Anderson gave perhaps five or six dozen concerts a year in the United States and gave a private performance for Franklin and Eleanor Roosevelt at the White House in 1936. But while on tour, she sometimes faced discrimination, denied a room at a whites-only hotel or a table at a restaurant. She preferred to drive from city to city, rather than travel by segregated train. And such segregation was not limited to the South; Albert Einstein hosted her after she was refused accommodation in Princeton, New Jersey, before a performance at the university. But while Anderson faced these indignities on the road, her studio recordings became big sellers.

For Easter 1939, Anderson was scheduled to perform in a Washington, DC concert sponsored by historically black Howard University. The search for a venue was complicated, because Anderson was sure to draw an enormous crowd, with fans of all races, but the nation's capital was still a segregated town. A church venue did not work out, and the auditorium at a black high school was too small. The city government denied Anderson use of Central

High School, because it was a white school and its policies forbade admission to an integrated audience. The denial provoked petitions and outrage among black leaders, the black community, and liberal white supporters. But the Supreme Court's 1896 *Plessy v. Ferguson* decision, which had made "separate but equal" the law of the land, gave any venue, public or private, the right to turn Anderson away, so these protests were ignored.

Sol Hurok then tried to book Constitution Hall, which was administered by the Daughters of the American Revolution, the DAR, an organization of women representing descendants of Revolutionary War officers, officials, and soldiers. The DAR was a segregated organization that did not admit black members, even though some 5,000 black soldiers had fought in George Washington's Continental Army. The DAR turned Anderson down, claiming that the hall was booked. But it became readily apparent that they did not want to host a black performer or an integrated audience. Their refusal produced more protests.

Eleanor Roosevelt, who had become a member shortly after her husband became president, spoke out, saying, "To remain as a member implies approval of that action, and therefore, I am resigning." Eleanor Roosevelt's example brought the issue national attention. Hundreds of other members resigned from the DAR. Some local branches distanced themselves from DAR's decision, while others vocally supported it. The Roosevelts, working with Hurok and the National Association for the Advancement of Colored People, approached Secretary of the Interior Harold Ickes. He arranged to hold the concert under the auspices of the National Park Service at the Lincoln Memorial. The plan immediately captured the national imagination.

The day of the concert, crowds began to arrive before dawn. They came prepared with blankets, umbrellas, and raincoats, as the weather promised to be cold and wet. Police were in full force; some 500 uniformed officers patrolled the National Mall. The crowd swelled to more than 70,000 people, black and white. Anderson arrived by train at Union Station in the early afternoon and was hosted at the home of Gifford Pinchot, a Roosevelt adviser and former Republican governor of Pennsylvania, before arriving at the Memorial. A simple wave of her hand brought forth thunderous applause.

At 5:00 pm Marian Anderson took her place on the steps of the Lincoln Memorial adorned in her mink coat and matching hat. She was introduced by Secretary Ickes, who stood before an assemblage of microphones broadcasting across the United States, as well as to Canada and Mexico. He said, "In this great auditorium under the sky, all of us are free."

Anderson removed her hat, and began her first selection—"America." Closing her eyes, then opening them and gazing upward to the sky, she sang, "My country 'tis of Thee, / Sweet Land of Liberty / of thee we sing." Let's listen to her.

A hush of silence fell over the crowd as she concluded; many were moved to tears. No one applauded right away, sensing that to do so would have been an intrusion on a truly sacred moment. Anderson then sang two arias. When she sat down for a break, the audience erupted in an outpouring of emotion and appreciation.

The second half of her performance included several spirituals, and she closed the concert with the resonant "Nobody Knows the Trouble I've Seen." Then briefly, Anderson addressed her audience. Without politics or commentary, she humbly apologized for not being a good speaker and thanked them sincerely for their attention and appreciation. After the Lincoln Memorial concert, Anderson went on to enjoy a full and acclaimed career. She entertained the troops during World War II and finally appeared at the DAR's Constitution Hall for a Red Cross benefit concert in 1943. In 1955, she became the first African American to perform at the Metropolitan Opera in New York. She sang at the presidential inaugurations of both Dwight D. Eisenhower and John F. Kennedy. She served as a U.S. representative to the UN Human Rights Committee and as a goodwill ambassador. She toured the world and also inspired other classical artists of color.

Active in the civil rights movement, she returned to the Lincoln Memorial with the Reverend Dr. Martin Luther King Jr. to sing for the March on Washington in 1963. And when she did her farewell performance tour, she began it at Constitution Hall and completed it at Carnegie Hall. The famous mink coat she wore at the Lincoln Memorial for that Easter day concert in 1939 came to the Smithsonian after her death, donated by her nephew, James

DePriest, the longtime conductor of the Oregon Symphony. It was recently joined at the Smithsonian by another item, the dress she wore that day, also donated by her family.

For Marian Anderson, the very act of singing and doing it in a particular place was itself a matter of justice in the face of historic racial discrimination. A contemporary of Anderson's, Woody Guthrie, had an entirely different style, the folk idiom of the singer-songwriter, and his songs attacking greed, bigotry, and injustice were far more direct and more cutting.

Woodrow Wilson Guthrie was born in 1912 in Okemah, a small town in Oklahoma. His father was a businessman involved in real estate, newspaper writing, and local and state politics. Guthrie's mother, a teacher for the Creek Indians, was afflicted with Huntington's disease, a serious and ultimately fatal neurological disorder, and she was committed to an asylum when Guthrie was a teenager.

Guthrie learned to play the harmonica and guitar as a youth, and although he thought of himself as a musical vagabond, he was a voracious reader and a member of both the high school band and the glee club. When he was 19, he went to live in Texas; he married young and started a family. But this was the early 1930s, the era of the Great Depression and the Dust Bowl. The already strained economy of the southern Great Plains was struck by an ecological disaster. This area was ideal for livestock grazing, in good years. But it had been converted to grain cultivation. The native grasses that locked the topsoil in place were gone. So when a severe drought and strong spring winds hit this already arid climate, "black blizzards" of windblown soil rendered the area almost uninhabitable. It took a decade of replacing and replanting the grasses and building windbreaks—all with federal aid—for the land to recover.

Meanwhile, Guthrie joined thousands of other Dust Bowl refugees, derisively known as Okies no matter where they were from, and headed off the plains to California looking for work and opportunity. The migration of poor, rural working folks trying to escape despair for an unknown but hopeful future stimulated much of Guthrie's early songwriting. Let's get a sense of

Guthrie's distinctive early musical style from this clip of him performing the folk standard "John Henry." That's Guthrie—unadorned, straight, and raw.

Guthrie settled in Los Angeles, playing traditional hillbilly and folk music on a radio program, and he played his own songs as well, based on his migration experience. His pro-labor views unnerved radio station sponsors, so that Guthrie ended up heading back east to New York, where he was introduced to the political urban folk music scene, and, where his views, frankly, were more welcomed.

Early in 1940, he became frustrated hearing Kate Smith's version of Irving Berlin's "God Bless America" repeatedly on the radio. Berlin was a Russian Jewish immigrant, who, like Guthrie, had come from a background of poverty and deprivation. He had first composed the song in 1918 but never released it. In 1938, seeing the dark storm clouds of war gathering over Germany and Europe, Berlin brought it out and revised it. He wanted that song to convey his hope for peace and his love and gratitude to his adopted country.

Smith premiered the song on radio on the anniversary of World War I's Armistice Day that year, backed by a full orchestra playing a very dramatic arrangement, a more bold and boastful interpretation than Berlin had really intended. The song became very popular, but it annoyed Guthrie, who found it somewhat syrupy and over celebratory. As he traveled across the country, Guthrie had seen firsthand too much poverty, homelessness, and joblessness, many people who did not seem to be so blessed.

On February 23, 1940, Guthrie wrote his response. Guthrie first titled the song "God Blessed America for Me" and used it as the last line of each stanza, but then crossed it out, replacing it with "This Land Was Made for You and Me." Guthrie's lyrics were populist, but hard-hitting. On one hand, the song celebrated the breadth and diversity of the United States; its natural beauty and bounty; and a profound, democratic sense that all Americans owned the country. On the other hand, the song addressed tough issues—the Depression, the disparity of wealth, and economic and social justice.

Guthrie's drawings express the same issue. Here, for example, we have from the Smithsonian's archives some of Guthrie's original drawings. Here's one that shows a sign with "private property" indicating that people should "keep out" Now, around this time, Guthrie met Pete Seeger, and the two became lifelong friends, traveling across the United States, engaging in spirited discussions, performing in concerts, taking up causes, and recording albums together. They lived in a communal house in Greenwich Village and sponsored and participated in hootenannies, or rousing folk music singing parties, as the Almanac Singers. They both penned and sang pro-union, protest, and peace songs.

They were against the entry of the United States into World War II, but once Germany had invaded the Soviet Union, they became pro-war and anti-Nazi. Guthrie wrote, "This machine kills fascists" on each of his guitars and joined the U.S. Merchant Marine. He also wrote songs about the conflict. Here's a piece of sheet music, in his hand, from the Folkways Archives for a song he titled "Round Up the Nazis"

On leave in March 1944, Guthrie visited the New York City studio of Moses Asch, then the founder and operator of Asch Records, a small independent label that would later be absorbed into Asch's life's work, Folkways Records. Asch was a Jewish immigrant from Poland who approached music as a documentarian, not as a performer or political activist. But Asch and Guthrie's mutual respect for the ability of song and speech to express raw human experience made them friends. Asch would record everything Guthrie wanted to sing, and whenever Guthrie needed money to spend, Asch would dole some out.

In April 1944, Guthrie came into Asch's studio six different times and recorded at least 150 songs, a fraction of the 3,000 songs he wrote. Asch was interested mainly in Guthrie's labor, war, anti-fascist, and children's songs. He regarded Guthrie foremost as a poet, and Guthrie's song was poetic outpouring at its best.

In the last session, Guthrie recorded "This Land Is Your Land." The master was a ten-inch disk made out of blackened shellac—magnetic audiotape had not yet been invented. Asch recorded at 78 rpm, meaning the disk could not hold more than three minutes of music, and the song clocked in at two minutes and forty-three seconds. Asch didn't issue the recorded song until 1951, and when he did, it was for a children's record on the Folkways label. It was a 1946 cleaned-up version of the song that excluded Guthrie's original, Socialist-sounding lyrics about private property and lines of people outside the relief office. Perhaps most poignantly, the excluded sixth stanza notes the hunger of his fellow citizens and asks, "Is this land made for you and me?" These lyrics did not accord with either the period or the audience. Instead, the recorded version, with the first stanza repeated as a chorus, was catchy and upbeat.

The publisher, Ludlow Music, allowed the song to be included in school music textbooks for free as a promotional strategy. Music and classroom teachers found it an easy song for their students to learn and sing as a group. It was sung at camps and by all sorts of youth groups, and became immensely popular; some even called it an alternative national anthem.

In the 1960s, it became popular with the folk music revival, and later the antiwar protest movement. It's been covered by hundreds of musicians, like Bob Dylan and Peter, Paul, and Mary, and It's been translated into numerous languages. Bruce Springsteen and Pete Seeger performed it at the Lincoln Memorial for the 2009 inaugural concert of President Barack Obama, and the original 1944 shellac master recording of Guthrie singing the song in Asch's studio is in the Moses and Frances Asch Folkways Collection in the Ralph Rinzler Folklife Archives at the Smithsonian Center for Folklife and Cultural Heritage, along with hundreds of other Guthrie masters and the tens of thousands of recordings Asch produced in his career and later donated to the Smithsonian.

On the master, the title of the song is written in pencil as "This Land Was Made for You and Me." The recording shows its age; it's even decomposing chemically. But thanks to Smithsonian archivists and sound engineers, it's been preserved. We've even been able to play it—once—and make a new recording, and hear Guthrie's voice intone for a fair share of this land for the common man.

Guthrie influenced a generation of American singer-song writers. One, most exceptionally, was a Jewish kid born Robert Zimmerman in 1941 and raised on the Iron Range region of Minnesota. In high school in the mid-1950s, he played the new rock-and-roll music. But as he matured, he was attracted to American folk music, with its depth of emotion and themes of despair and struggle. He was particularly drawn to the lyrics of Woody Guthrie, and in 1961 he arrived in New York City and made a pilgrimage to visit Guthrie, who was hospitalized at the time with Huntington's disease. He modeled himself after the famed balladeer and as someone whose music would tackle the serious issues of the day. After arriving in New York, Robert Zimmerman changed his name to Bob Dylan. He began performing in coffeehouses in Greenwich Village. When Dylan opened at Gerde's Folk City for the Greenbriar Boys, he caught the attention of the New York Times music critic Robert Shelton, who wrote a laudatory review that attracted strong public attention.

Though Dylan had sought to record for Asch and Folkways Records, just like Guthrie, he was instead signed by John Hammond to Columbia Records. At the same time, he recorded for other labels using several pseudonyms. His first 1962 Columbia album, Bob Dylan, included folk, blues, and gospel tunes and two original songs. While the album was by no means a hit, it introduced audiences to his characteristic voice. Joyce Carol Oates said that though he sounded "as if sandpaper could sing, the effect was dramatic and electrifying." Coupled with acoustic guitar and harmonica, Dylan's voice was viewed as authentic, much in the way Guthrie had been received by the previous generation.

Dylan's second album, The Freewheelin' Bob Dylan, released in 1963, earned him a reputation as a creative singer-songwriter and protest singer. That year, he performed at the Newport Folk Festival for the first time and visited the Highlander Research and Education Center in Tennessee, a social justice leadership training organization. It was at Highlander that "We Shall Overcome," a black gospel tune, was adapted by Zilphia Horton, Guy Carawan, and Pete Seeger, and started to become popular in the Civil Rights Movement. Dylan performed at concerts with Pete Seeger, the Freedom Singers, and other activists.

In August 1963, Dylan performed with Marian Anderson; Mahalia Jackson; Peter, Paul and Mary; and Joan Baez at the Lincoln Memorial on the National Mall for the March on Washington. They provided musical selections prior to the Reverend Dr. Martin Luther King Jr.'s "I Have a Dream" speech.

With the albums that followed, Dylan became the leading singer-songwriter for the emerging counterculture of the 1960s, and by mid-decade, Dylan songs like "Blowin' in the Wind," "The Times They Are A-Changin'," and "Mr. Tambourine Man" were standards at concerts and protest demonstrations. Dylan's simple aesthetic of powerful poetry, simple guitar chords, and expressive harmonica riffs had exceptional appeal. Within a few years, Dylan was ascribed to be the voice for a generation, questioning the social and political status quo.

As Dylan's career progressed, he began to express reservations about his own status within the American folk music movement. In 1964's "It Ain't Me, Babe" he seems to reject the role of the people's balladeer. In the 1965 album Bringing It All Back Home, Dylan experimented with musical styles and themes, venturing into love ballads, irony, and a more electrified sound, later termed "folk rock," that disappointed traditionalist fans. Nevertheless, the album demonstrated Dylan's artistic virtuosity and was tremendously influential.

In 1966, at the height of success, Dylan was in a terrible motorcycle accident and took some time to recover. To fill the void, Columbia Records decided to release a greatest hits album. John Berg, Columbia's art director, asked graphic designer Milton Glaser to create a poster of Dylan that would be included in the album. Glaser was a young designer who had studied art at New York's Cooper Union and in Italy on a Fulbright scholarship. He was familiar with a broad range of European and American approaches to graphic representation. Glaser found inspiration for the Dylan poster from a self-portrait created by Marcel Duchamp, the French surrealist painter. Duchamp had his heydays in the early 20th century, but it was being rediscovered by the American pop artists of the 1960s.

Surrealism was an artistic movement of the early 20th century that was heavily influenced by Freudian psychology and principles of mental free association, a philosophy that was, frankly, a good fit with the 1960s counterculture. Pop art, on the other hand, was then a contemporary movement, a sort of anti-art, that sought to represent familiar, everyday objects in unfamiliar aesthetic ways as a critique of mass production and commercialism.

Duchamp's 1957 self-portrait showed his silhouetted head in a white square set into a black border. Glaser used a similar composition, but reversed it, representing Dylan's head facing left in black against a white background. To this design Glaser added his own 1960s twist; he turned Dylan's wild and unkempt hair into vividly colored, swirling ribbons. This suggested the psychedelic imagery coming out of the counterculture of the West Coast, the evocations of LSD hallucinogenic experiences, the Day-Glo decorative paintings of author and activist Ken Kesey and his Merry Pranksters, San Francisco's Fillmore theater posters, and the light shows that were the hallmark of Grateful Dead and the Jefferson Airplane.

Dylan's kinetic, colored hair contrasts sharply with the black-on-white profile, animating what would otherwise be a stark representation. The result is a portrait that seems simple, yet exudes profound dignity—Dylan as a modern philosopher-poet with gravitas, and yet of the new age. Glaser added a bold typeface with the simple one-word legend "Dylan." The poster and the album became instant hits, selling some six million copies.

The music of Bob Dylan, Woody Guthrie, and Marian Anderson captured the attention and the imagination of generations dissatisfied with prejudice injustice and greed. One of the strongest testaments to the power of song was made by the actor and playwright Ossie Davis, who, as a student at Howard University, was in the crowd for Marian Anderson's Lincoln Memorial Concert that Easter day. Looking back on the experience, he said that listening to her "All of a sudden, I had a transformation that was almost of a religious nature. Ah, something in her singing, something in her voice, something in her demeanor entered me and opened me up … Marian Anderson on that particular day, opened the doors of my prison, and I walked out a free man." Music really can change the world.

Exploring the Land, Exploring the Universe

Lecture 23

The desire to explore—to search beyond the horizon—seems like one of those characteristics that is deeply ingrained in American culture. Perhaps it comes from the construction of our national mythology. For hundreds of years, generations of Americans grew up with the idea of a persistent and intrepid Columbus journeying across the Atlantic to discover and explore a new world. As you will learn in this lecture, the age of exploration is far from over. The Smithsonian's national museums hope to stimulate the next generation to ask questions in increasingly sophisticated ways—and even inspire the explorers among them to help answer them.

The Lewis and Clark Expedition

- On the orders of President Thomas Jefferson, Meriwether Lewis and William Clark ventured out across the North American continent to explore and map what would become the expanse of the United States. But Lewis and Clark's expedition was not just a mapmaking venture—although the maps they made were important. It was a mission of diplomacy and scientific discovery. And none of it would have been possible without their compass, which today rests in the Smithsonian.

- Made in Philadelphia by craftsman Thomas Whitney, the compass cost Meriwether Lewis five dollars—worth maybe about 100 dollars today. Lewis also purchased three other, cheaper compasses as he prepared for a daunting transcontinental journey.

- Lewis and Clark's mission was to explore the Louisiana Territory, which was purchased from Napoleon in 1803. A region of more than 800,000 square miles, it would later become Arkansas, Missouri, Iowa, Oklahoma, Kansas, Nebraska, almost all of South Dakota, most of Montana, Wyoming, Colorado, Louisiana, Minnesota, and parts of Texas and New Mexico.

- Meriwether Lewis had served in the commonwealth militia and then the U.S. Army, where he was a commissioned lieutenant. He was a naturalist of sorts, adept at survival in the wild, and also somewhat knowledgeable about and sensitive to the cultures of American Indians. Lewis chose a fellow soldier, William Clark, to share command of the expedition. Clark had joined the militia as a teenager to fight Indians on the frontier after the Revolutionary War and rose to become an officer.

- They led a group of almost three dozen men, called the Corps of Discovery. The Corps' mission was to explore the new territory, establish trade and sovereign relationships with American Indian tribes, and find a route to the Pacific Ocean so that the United States could lay claim to the Oregon Territory. Jefferson encouraged the expedition to make maps, observe natural phenomena, and chart the geology, flora, fauna, and resources of the region.

- At Jefferson's direction, Lewis started buying items in the late spring of 1803, among them the compasses, thermometers, a portable microscope, a brass scale, and hydrometers for testing liquid density. There were also other navigation instruments besides the compasses. Jefferson personally tutored Lewis in making celestial observations and had Lewis study with the leading mathematicians and scientists of Philadelphia.

- The Corps of 33 soldiers and William Clark's lifelong slave, an African American named York, were equipped with rifles, ammunition, gunpowder, knives, medicine, mosquito netting, tools and nails, writing implements, kettles and cooking implements, lamps, axes, saws, adzes, fish hooks, and Peace Medals to give to Indian leaders. After staging in the Illinois Territory, the Corps embarked on May 14, 1804, from outside St. Louis on their expedition up the Missouri River. They had a large 55-foot keelboat equipped with sail, oars, and poles and two smaller craft.

- They possessed copies of roughly drawn, incomplete, and inaccurate maps and accounts composed by previous travelers.

Following Jefferson's instructions, they took detailed note of particular landmarks and river confluences.

- The Corps used the compass and other instruments to chart their course, using a technique called dead reckoning to determine geographic position by use of a compass, a clock, and astronomical charts. The use of the compass and other navigational devices required skill, patience, calculating acumen, and time—as did their daily composition of maps charted on the period's equivalent of graph paper.

- Over the summer of 1804, the Corps journeyed westward up the Missouri River, passing what are now Kansas City and Omaha. They built Fort Mandan to winter in what is now North Dakota and met a French Canadian fur trapper and his Shoshone wife, Sacagawea. She then helped translate and guide them through parts of their journey.

- The Corps crossed the Continental Divide in the Rockies and followed the Clearwater River to the Snake River and then to the Columbia River and passed what is now Portland to the Pacific Ocean. They wintered in Oregon and then headed back east. The group split up at the Continental Divide and reunited in August 1806 at the confluence of the Yellowstone and Missouri Rivers. They made it back to St. Louis by September 23.

- Amazingly for the time, only one member of the Corps died during the journey. They returned with immense knowledge, having discovered about 200 new species of flora and fauna. The Corps met leaders from about two dozen American Indian tribes and described dozens more. The many accurate maps—about 140 of them—facilitated subsequent discoveries and settlement in the new territory.

- When Lewis and Clark arrived back in St. Louis in September 1806, few of their instruments survived the journey—but the pocket compass was among them. Clark kept it as a memento and then gave it to a friend. It was handed down in that family and ultimately came to the Smithsonian. Other Lewis and Clark materials—specimen sheets, field notes, and maps—are in other institutions, and they give us a wonderful sense of how these brave explorers did their painstaking work.

- In the decades following the Lewis and Clark Expedition, the vast Louisiana territory was settled, and the nation expanded. By the turn of the 20th century, the United States had become a continental nation, stretching from the Atlantic to the Pacific coasts, and with the addition in 1959 of Alaska and Hawaii as the 49th and 50th states, the United States had stretched even further.

The Space Race

- On October 4, 1957, the Soviet Union successfully launched an intercontinental ballistic missile carrying a basketball-sized satellite named Sputnik. This was the first manmade object to be placed into Earth's orbit, traveling at about 17,000 miles per hour about 500 miles above Earth.

- Sputnik's launch came as a surprise to many Americans, and there was widespread anxiety that the United States had lost its technological superiority on the world's stage. A month later, the Soviets launched a much larger Sputnik 2 with a dog aboard as a passenger, suggesting that manned space flight was not too far behind. The Cold War had now moved into space.

- The United States, through the armed services, had been working on its own satellite launch programs, but unsuccessfully. President Dwight D. Eisenhower formed the National Aeronautics and Space Administration (NASA) as a civilian government agency on October 1, 1958. Its first mission, Mercury, was to put an American into orbit.

- NASA designed and built a small nose-cone capsule that could be launched into space atop a rocket. The challenge, aside from achieving a successful launch and orbit, would be to return the astronaut to Earth alive, unlike the Russian dog, which had died during her journey.

- NASA chose its astronauts after reviewing about 500 active military test pilots. The final list of candidates went through grueling medical and fitness tests. The chosen "Mercury Seven" became instant American heroes. The astronauts participated in a rigorous training program.

- In September 1959, the Soviets crashed a 177-pound capsule called Luna 2 on the surface of the moon, and the following month, they used the Luna 3 orbiter to photograph the moon's hidden far side. The United States appeared to be falling further behind.

- But in January 1961, NASA launched Ham, a four-year-old Cameroonian chimpanzee, on a suborbital space flight in a Mercury capsule. This enabled NASA scientists to assess the effects of space travel on a living creature as a prelude to human flight. More importantly, the capsule returned Ham to Earth alive after a 16-minute flight. Ham then took up residence at the Smithsonian's National Zoo for 17 years before retiring to live out his days at the North Carolina Zoo.

- Americans planned to send a manned rocket, *Freedom 7*, into space in March 1961. But technical problems delayed the launch, and on April 12, Soviet cosmonaut Yuri Gagarin became the first person in space and also the first to orbit Earth. Weeks later, the United States launched astronaut Alan Shepard into space on a suborbital flight that took 15 minutes and 22 seconds.

- Soon after, President Kennedy addressed Congress, challenging it to fund a program that would give the United States the undisputed lead in the exploration of space. Less than 60 years after the Wright brothers' first powered flight wobbled a few feet off the ground for a few moments, the notion of landing a man on the moon was still the stuff of science fiction. The sheer ambition of Kennedy's goal sent a determined and visionary message to the American public about space as the new American frontier.

- On February 20, 1962, 41-year-old former jet fighter pilot John Glenn was propelled into space from Cape Canaveral, Florida. Glenn's space capsule, the *Friendship 7*, was fabricated by McDonnell Aircraft Corporation.

- Glenn made three orbits in *Friendship 7* over the course of a flight that was just about five hours from liftoff to splashdown. He was strapped into a form-fitting fiberglass seat designed to ease the accelerations of launch and reentry. He kept in touch by radio with Mercury Mission Control at NASA and its worldwide network of ground stations in places as far away as Zanzibar and Australia.

- Glenn was able to report on observations from space, monitor his physical condition, and conduct a few experiments. He engaged the manual controls to adjust the heading of the spacecraft in orbit and to ensure proper functioning of his heat shield, which would protect him upon reentry into Earth's atmosphere.

- Glenn safely reentered the atmosphere nearly 20 miles above Earth's surface. *Friendship*'s parachute deployed at about 11,000 feet. Glenn splashed down in the Atlantic Ocean and was picked up by the USS *Noa*. The capsule was pulled up on deck, where Glenn fired the explosive hatch and exited to the crew's and the country's acclaim.

- *Friendship 7* went on what became known as its fourth orbit—a goodwill tour around the world. It arrived at the Smithsonian in November 1962 and was placed on display; in 1976, it was moved into the National Air and Space Museum, which opened on the National Mall for the Bicentennial of the United States.

- Seven years later, NASA met President Kennedy's great challenge. The Apollo program brought mankind to the Moon on July 21, 1969, when Neil Armstrong exited the Apollo 11 Lunar Module and set foot on that heavenly body. Armstrong and his crew documented their journey, took samples, and made it safely home with valuable new knowledge.

The Space Shuttle Program

- NASA didn't rest on its achievements. The idea of a reusable spacecraft gained traction in the 1970s and resulted in a fleet of space shuttles—an orbiter attached to solid rocket boosters with an external fuel tank. The Mercury and Apollo spacecraft used ablative heat shields that burned away upon reentry, rendering the craft unusable. The shuttles were covered with insulating ceramic tiles that could absorb the heat of multiple reentries.

- An aircraft initially called *Constitution* was built as a test shuttle. Fans of the popular television show *Star Trek* petitioned to rename the vehicle *Enterprise*, the name of the fictional starship in the series. In 1977, *Enterprise* completed a series of test flights at Edwards Air Force Base in California and then went on to carry out other tests until it was retired to the National Air and Space Museum in 1985.

- A fleet of four space shuttles was built and went into operation: *Columbia*, *Challenger*, *Discovery*, and *Atlantis*. *Columbia* was the first of these to launch, on April 12, 1981. Although tragedy would eventually strike both *Columbia* and *Challenger*, resulting in the loss of both the shuttles and their crews, the shuttle program continued for more than 30 years and 135 missions.

- *Discovery* became the workhorse of the space shuttle fleet, executing every type of mission the shuttle was meant to fly. Entering service in 1984, *Discovery* completed 39 missions and spent a total of 365 days in space, traveling more than 148 million miles, orbiting Earth more than 5,800 times at about 17,500 miles per hour.

- In 2004, President George Bush had announced that the space shuttle program had fulfilled its mission and would come to an end. The shuttle program's final mission, designated STS-135, was

Space Shuttle *Discovery*

complete when the shuttle *Atlantis* touched down at Kennedy Space Center on July 21, 2011.

- In 2012, *Discovery* was flown to the Smithsonian's Udvar-Hazy Center, dramatically circling the nation's capital before landing at the museum and beginning its second life as an educational and inspirational museum object.

- But American exploration of the most distant frontiers has not ended. NASA landed *Curiosity*, an unmanned vehicle, on Mars to document that planet's landscape and continues to send American astronauts to the International Space Station in cooperation with other nations, while the Cassini probe explores the outer reaches of our solar system.

The Giant Magellan Telescope

- The Smithsonian's astrophysicists are active in working with an international consortia building the Giant Magellan Telescope

Giant Magellan Telescope

(GMT), which will allow scientists to explore the furthest reaches of the universe and see back close to the beginning of time.

- It is being built high in the Atacama Desert mountain region of Chile in South America, 8,500 feet above sea level on Las Campanas Peak. The air there is especially clear and dry. Its isolation from human civilization means that the skies are dark, making it an ideal location for astronomical observations.

- The GMT is the product of our supercomputer-enabled advanced knowledge of astrophysics. It will provide astronomers an unprecedented surface for collecting light from stellar observations. Scientists will be able to see faint objects that are unobservable today.

- The GMT is capable of receiving light waves from the depths of the universe, as far away as 76 sextillion miles. Astoundingly, this means that we will be able to look very far back in time—because the light we will see would have taken about 13 billion years to arrive on Earth. That's about a billion years after the big bang and roughly 9 to 10 billion years *before* Earth even formed. The resultant images will be about 10 times sharper than those currently obtained by the Hubble Space Telescope—at this time the most advanced telescope we have.

- The GMT will improve scientific understanding of exploding stars, supernovas, and gamma-ray bursts. It will enable astronomers to image planets in orbits around other stars and help astrophysicists determine their chemical composition. It will also help scientists probe black holes in unprecedented detail and test theoretical models of such little-understood phenomena as dark energy and dark matter. It may even help us find other life in the universe.

Featured Objects

Lewis and Clark's Compass

Mercury *Freedom* Capsule

Space Shuttles *Enterprise* and *Discovery*

Giant Magellan Telescope

Suggested Reading

Bizony, *The Space Shuttle.*

Carpenter, Cooper, Glenn, Grissom, Schirra, Shepard, and Slayton, *We Seven.*

Lewis and Clark, *The Journals of Lewis and Clark.*

Exploring the Land, Exploring the Universe
Lecture 23—Transcript

The desire to explore, to search beyond the horizon, seems like one of those characteristics deeply ingrained in American culture. Perhaps it comes from the construction of our national mythology; for hundreds of years, generations of Americans growing up with the idea of the persistent and intrepid Columbus journeying out across the Atlantic to discover and explore the new world.

Perhaps just as legendary in our national consciousness is the journey of Lewis and Clark, who on the orders of President Thomas Jefferson ventured out across the North American continent to explore and map what would become the expanse of the United States. But Lewis and Clark's expedition was not just a map-making venture, although the maps they made were surely important. It was a mission of diplomacy and scientific discovery. And none of it would have been possible without their compass, which today rests in the Smithsonian.

Though it might appear modest to us today, this silver-plated compass was an important navigational instrument. The device fits well in the palm of a hand, and it boasts a leather carrying case and a securing strap. Mounted with screws in a small, square mahogany case, it features a silver-plated brass rim that is divided into degrees and eight numbered sections, or octants. A paper dial is recessed within the case, and two small brass sight vanes protrude from either side of it. Not as accurate as a modern GPS—maybe—but if you want to head west like Lewis and Clark, a compass can still get you there.

Made in Philadelphia by craftsman Thomas Whitney, this compass cost five dollars, worth maybe about $100 today. Lewis also purchased three other, cheaper compasses as he prepared for a daunting transcontinental journey. Lewis and Clark's mission was to explore the Louisiana Territory. As we discussed in the first lecture, the Louisiana Territory was purchased from Napoleon in 1803. A region of more than 800,000 square miles, it would later become Arkansas, Missouri, Iowa, Oklahoma, Kansas, Nebraska, almost all of South Dakota, most of Montana, Wyoming, Colorado, Louisiana, Minnesota, and parts of Texas and New Mexico.

Napoleon had envisioned this land as part of a French empire in the Americas but gave up the idea following slave revolts and an independence movement in Haiti. The United States had only expected to buy New Orleans from the French; it was a port that would anchor America's trade up and down the Mississippi River. Napoleon's offer to sell the whole territory startled the American government. Although the constitutionality of the purchase was questionable, Jefferson went ahead with the purchase anyway. The strategic boost it would give the young nation trumped his reservations. And besides, the price was right—about $15 million, or a mere $.03 per acre. With the purchase, the size of the United States immediately doubled, and its westward expansion was assured.

Meriwether Lewis, born in Virginia, had served in the commonwealth militia and then the U.S. Army, where he was a commissioned a lieutenant. He was a naturalist of sorts, adept at survival in the wild, and also somewhat knowledgeable about and sensitive to the cultures of American Indians. Lewis chose a fellow soldier, William Clark, to share command of the expedition. Clark had joined the militia as a teenager to fight Indians on the frontier after the Revolutionary War and rose to become an officer.

They led a group of almost three dozen men, called the Corps of Discovery. The Corps' mission was to explore the new territory; establish trade and sovereign relationships with American Indian tribes; and find a route to the Pacific Ocean so the United States could lay claim to the Oregon Territory. Jefferson encouraged the expedition to make maps, observe natural phenomena, chart the geology, flora, fauna, and resources of the region.

At Jefferson's direction, Lewis started buying items in the late spring of 1803, among them the compass, thermometers, a portable microscope, a brass scale, and hydrometers for testing liquid density. There were also other navigation instruments besides the compasses. These included Hadley's quadrant, a set of plotting instruments to make maps, a theodolite for measuring angles, a set of planispheres to identify stars and constellations, and artificial horizons to measure distances. Jefferson personally tutored Lewis in making celestial observations and had Lewis study with the leading mathematicians and scientists of Philadelphia.

The Corps of 33 soldiers and William Clark's lifelong slave, an African American named York, was equipped with rifles, ammunition, gunpowder, knives, medicine, mosquito netting, tools, nails, writing implements, kettles, cooking implements, lamps, axes, saws, adzes, fish hooks, as well as Peace Medals to give to Indian leaders. After staging in the Illinois Territory, the Corps embarked, on May 14, 1804, from outside St. Louis on their expedition up the Missouri River. They had a large 55-foot keelboat equipped with sail, oars, and poles, and two smaller craft.

They possessed copies of roughly drawn, incomplete, and inaccurate maps and accounts composed by previous travelers. Following Jefferson's instructions, they took detailed note of particular landmarks and river confluences, so that, as Jefferson put it, "they may with certainty be recognized hereafter." The Corps used the compass and other instruments to chart their course, using a technique called dead reckoning to determine geographic position by use of a compass, a clock, and astronomical charts. This type of mapping required one first to determine geographic position in terms of latitude and longitude. Latitude was most easily determined by using the sextant to locate the North Star at night and then, by determining angles, calculating a distance from the pole onto the globe.

Computing longitude was more complex; it required the use of an accurately wound clock, observing the position of the sun at noon, determining the plane of the horizon, and calculating the difference from Greenwich Mean Time. Local time was also calculated by observing the moon's position in the sky relative to other stars and then comparing that to readings in a nautical almanac. The use of the compass and other navigational devices required skill, patience, calculating acumen, and time, as did their daily composition of maps charted on the period's equivalent of what we know today as graph paper.

Over the summer of 1804, the Corps journeyed westward up the Missouri River, passing what are now Kansas City and Omaha. They built Fort Mandan to winter in what is now North Dakota, and met a French Canadian fur trapper and his Shoshone wife, Sacagawea. She then helped translate and guide them through parts of their journey. We don't know what Sacagawea looked like, but she has been commemorated on the U.S. dollar coin.

The Corps crossed the Continental Divide in the Rockies and followed the Clearwater River to the Snake River and then to the Columbia River and passed what is now Portland to the Pacific Ocean. They wintered in Oregon and then headed back east. The group split up at the Continental Divide and reunited in August 1806 at the confluence of the Yellowstone and Missouri rivers. They made it back to St. Louis by September 23.

Amazingly for the time, only one member of the Corps died during the journey. They returned with immense knowledge, having discovered some 200 new species of flora and fauna. The Corps met leaders from about two dozen American Indian tribes, and described dozens more. The many accurate maps—some 140 of them—facilitated subsequent discoveries and the settlement in the new territory.

When Lewis and Clark arrived back in St. Louis in September 1806, few of their instruments survived the journey, but the pocket compass was among them. Clark kept it as a memento, and then gave it to a friend. It was handed down in that family and ultimately came to the Smithsonian. Other Lewis and Clark materials—specimen sheets, field notes, and maps—are in other institutions, and they give us a wonderful sense of how these brave explorers did their painstaking work.

In the decades following the Lewis and Clark Expedition, the vast Louisiana territory was settled, and the nation expanded. By the turn of the 20th century, the United States had become a continental nation, stretching from the Atlantic to the Pacific coasts, and with the addition in 1959 of Alaska and Hawaii as the 49th and 50th states, we've stretched even further. Had we reached our limit? Was there any new frontier to explore? Well, as it turned out, there was, and it would require the bravery and foresight of the Lewis and Clark expedition, but a lot more scientific and technical sophistication. And like Lewis and Clark, to achieve this goal, Americans had to look to the stars.

On October 4, 1957, the Soviet Union successfully launched an intercontinental ballistic missile carrying a basketball-sized satellite named Sputnik. This was the first man-made object to be placed into Earth's orbit, traveling at about 17,000 miles an hour some 500 miles above

Earth. Sputnik's launch came as a surprise to many Americans, and there was widespread anxiety that the United States had lost its technological superiority on the world's stage. A month later, the Soviets launched a much larger Sputnik 2 with a dog aboard as a passenger, suggesting that manned space flight was not too far behind. The Cold War had now moved into space.

The United States, though, through the armed services, had been working on its own satellite launch programs, but unsuccessfully. President Dwight D. Eisenhower formed the National Aeronautics and Space Administration—NASA—as a civilian government agency on October 1, 1958. Its first mission, Project Mercury, was to put an American into orbit. NASA designed and built a small nose-cone capsule that could be launched into space atop a rocket. The challenge, aside from achieving a successful launch and orbit, would be to return the astronaut, a Greek for star sailor, to Earth alive, unlike the Russian dog, who had died during her journey.

At NASA, aeronautical engineers pioneered the idea of a conical spacecraft with a cylindrical nose. It had a broad, flat base covered by a heat shield made of fiberglass and resin. This would create a shock wave to slow down the spacecraft as it plunged back toward Earth, while protecting the astronaut and equipment inside from the intense heat of the reentry.

NASA chose its astronauts after reviewing some 500 active military test pilots. The final list of candidates went through grueling medical and fitness tests. The chosen Mercury Seven, as they were called, became instant American heroes. The astronauts participated in a rigorous training program. As former test pilots, they insisted on playing a role in the design of the craft. For example, the astronauts insisted on a window over their heads so they could actually see out from their seated positions. They also made suggestions about the interior layout so they could more easily and effectively operate manual controls should any of the automated systems fail.

In September 1959, the Soviets crashed landed a 177-pound capsule called Luna 2 on the surface of the moon, and the following month they used the Luna 3 orbiter to photograph the moon's hidden far side. The United States appeared to be falling further behind. But in January 1961, NASA launched

Ham, a four-year-old Cameroonian chimpanzee, on a suborbital space flight in a Mercury capsule. This enabled NASA scientists to assess the effects of space travel on a living creature as a prelude to human flight.

More importantly, the capsule returned Ham to Earth alive after a 16-minute flight. Ham, by the way, then took up residence at the Smithsonian's National Zoo for 17 years before retiring to live out his days at the North Carolina Zoo.

Americans planned to send a manned rocket, Freedom 7, into space in March 1961. But technical problems delayed the launch, and on April 12, Soviet cosmonaut Yuri Gagarin became the first person in space, and also the first to orbit Earth. Weeks later, the United States launched astronaut Alan Shepard into space on a suborbital flight that took 15 minutes and 22 seconds.

Soon after, President Kennedy addressed Congress, challenging it to fund a program that would give the United States the undisputed lead in the exploration of space:

> I believe that this nation should commit itself to achieving the goal, before this decade is out, of landing a man on the Moon and returning him safely to the Earth. No single space project in this period will be more impressive to mankind, or more important for the long-range exploration of space; and none will be so difficult or expensive to accomplish.

This was a bold statement, much more so than sending Lewis and Clark to traverse the continent. Less than 60 years after the Wright brothers' first powered flight wobbled a few feet off the ground for a few moments, the notion of landing a man on the moon was still the stuff of science fiction. The sheer ambition of Kennedy's goal sent a determined and visionary message to the American public about space as the new American frontier.

February 20, 1962, 41-year-old former jet fighter pilot John Glenn was propelled into space from Cape Canaveral, Florida. Glenn's space capsule, the Friendship 7, was fabricated by McDonnell Aircraft Corporation. Its skin and structure were made of titanium, with nickel-steel alloy and beryllium shingles. It was a small spacecraft, about 6 feet across at its base and a bit over 11 feet long, weighing barely more than a ton and a half. The capsule was so compact that the astronauts joked, "You don't get into it, you put it on."

Glenn made three orbits in Friendship 7 over the course of a flight that was just about five hours from liftoff to splashdown. He was strapped into a form-fitting fiberglass seat designed to ease the accelerations of launch and reentry. He kept in touch by radio with Mercury Mission Control at NASA and its worldwide network of ground stations in places as far away as Zanzibar and Australia.

Glenn was able to report on observations from space, monitor his physical condition, and conduct a few experiments. He took pictures out of the window using two cameras and a jury-rigged pistol grip to accommodate his bulky space gloves. He engaged the manual controls to adjust the heading of the spacecraft in orbit and to ensure proper functioning of his heat shield. If the heat protection did not work, Glenn knew the last thing he'd feel would be a pulse of heat at his back before he burned up upon his reentry into Earth's atmosphere. But the heat shield held, of course, and Glenn safely reentered the atmosphere nearly 20 miles above Earth's surface. Friendship's parachute deployed at about 11,000 feet, and Glenn splashed down in the Atlantic Ocean and was picked up by the USS *Noa*. The capsule was pulled up on deck, where Glenn fired the explosive hatch and exited to the crew's and the country's acclaim, including a congratulatory call from President Kennedy.

Friendship 7 went on what became known as the fourth orbit, which is really a goodwill tour around the world. It arrived at the Smithsonian in November 1962 and placed on display; in 1976, the space capsule was moved into the National Air and Space Museum, which opened up on the National Mall for the Bicentennial of the United States. It was a testament to America's spirit of discovery.

Seven years later, NASA met President Kennedy's great challenge. The Apollo program brought mankind to the Moon on July 21, 1969, when, as we've discussed, Neil Armstrong exited the Apollo 11 Lunar Module and set foot on that heavenly body. One can only imagine what it was like for Lewis and Clark to look upon the vast, seemingly endless Pacific Ocean as the fulfillment of their journey. And now, here was Neil Armstrong standing on the surface of the Moon, looking out at the Earth—a small, isolated blue planet afloat in the unimaginable expanse of outer space. Just like the Corps of Discovery, Armstrong and his crew documented their journey and took samples, in this case, Moon rocks, and made it safely back home with valuable new knowledge.

And like those earlier generations of explorers, NASA did not rest on its achievements. The idea of reusable spacecraft gained traction in the 1970s and resulted in a fleet of space shuttles, an orbiter attached to solid rocket boosters with an external fuel tank. The Mercury and Apollo spacecraft used ablative heat shields that burned away upon reentry, rendering the craft unusable. The shuttles were covered with insulating ceramic tiles that could absorb the heat of multiple re-entries. Also, shuttles could land on a runway rather than crashing into the sea, as previous capsules had done. But because jet engines for atmospheric flight were sacrificed to meet cost and weight limits, the shuttle had to glide to its landing without power. It would have only one chance to land safely, no wave-offs, no fly-arounds.

An aircraft initially called Constitution was built as a test shuttle. Fans of the popular television show Star Trek petitioned to rename the vehicle Enterprise, the name of the fictional starship in the TV series. In 1977, Enterprise completed its flight tests at Edwards Air Force Base in California and then went on to carry out other tests, until it was retired to the National Air and Space Museum in 1985.

A fleet of four space shuttles was built and went into operation—*Columbia, Challenger, Discovery* and *Atlantis*. *Columbia* was the first of these to launch, on April 12, 1981. Although tragedy would eventually strike both *Columbia* and *Challenger*, resulting in the loss of both the shuttles and their crews, the shuttle program continued for just over 30 years and 135 missions.

Discovery became the workhorse of the space shuttle fleet, executing every type of mission the shuttle was meant to fly. Entering service in 1984, it is the size of a Boeing 737 airliner—122 feet long with a 78-foot wingspan and a vertical stabilizer 57-feet high. Its aluminum airframe is covered with silica/ceramic thermal protection tiles.

Discovery completed 39 missions and spent a total of 365 days in space, traveling more than 148 million miles, orbiting the Earth more than 5,800 times at about 17,500 miles per hour. *Discovery* delivered the Hubble Space Telescope into orbit; it repaired and redeployed planetary exploration craft; it supported laboratory space research missions; and it re-supplyed the International Space Station. *Discovery* held a special place in the space program; 184 different astronauts and 32 different commanders, including two women commanders, served as crew for its flights. It returned John Glenn to space in 1998, and it returned the United States to space after the tragic losses of Challenger and Columbia.

In 2004, President George Bush had announced that the Space Shuttle program had fulfilled its mission and would come to an end. The shuttle program's final mission, designated STS-135, was completed when the shuttle Atlantis touched down at Kennedy Space Center at 5:57 a.m. on July 21, 2011. In 2012 *Discovery* was flown to the Smithsonian's Udvar-Hazy Center, dramatically circling the nation's capital, and, as you can see from this video taken by the staff here, briefly passing over The Great Courses' studio before landing at the museum adjacent to nearby Dulles Airport, where, in the museum, it began its second life as an educational and inspirational museum object.

But American exploration of the most distant frontiers has not ended. NASA landed Curiosity, an unmanned vehicle, on Mars to document that planet's landscape, and continues to send American astronauts on to the International Space Station in cooperation with other nations, while the Cassini probe explores the outer reaches of our solar system.

Meanwhile, the Smithsonian's own astrophysicists are active in working with an international consortia building what we call the Giant Magellan Telescope. This instrument, which will probably never fit into one of our museums, will allow scientists to explore the furthest reaches of the universe and see back close to the beginning of time. It's being built high in the Atacama Desert mountain region of Chile in South America, 8,500 feet above sea level on Las Campanas Peak. The air there is especially clear and dry. Its isolation from human civilization means the skies are dark, making it an ideal location for astronomical observations.

We've come a long way in the two centuries since the dead-reckoning of Lewis and Clark's compass. The Giant Magellan Telescope is the product of our supercomputer-enabled advanced knowledge of astrophysics. The Giant Magellan Telescope will consist of seven 28-foot-diameter segments, with six of them surrounding a central segment. Each of the segments consists of a precisely cast honeycombed-glass mirror weighting 18 tons and so finely polished in a parabolic shape that it is exact to one millionth of an inch. Segments are coordinated and calibrated though the use of complex instrumentation and computer software, enabling them to work together, essentially, as one extremely large 80-foot diameter telescope.

This telescope will provide astronomers with an unprecedented surface for collecting light from stellar observations. Scientists will be able to see faint objects that are unobservable today. The Giant Magellan Telescope will be so powerful, it could allow a person to see the equivalent of a candle flame on the Moon. But, we will be able to see a lot more. You know, light travels at about 186,000 miles per second. When we look up in the daylight sky, we are not seeing the sun as it currently is but as it was 8 minutes ago; that's how long it takes for the light from the sun to travel the 93 million miles to the Earth.

The Giant Magellan Telescope is capable of receiving light from the depths of the universe, as far away as 76 sextillion miles—that's a 76 with 21 zeros after it. Astoundingly, this means that we'll be able to look very far back in time, because the light we will see would have taken some 13 billion years to arrive on Earth. That's about a billion years after the big bang, and roughly 9 to 10 billion years before Earth even formed.

The resultant images will be about 10 times sharper than those currently obtained by the Hubble Space Telescope, at this time, the most advanced telescope we have.

The Giant Magellan Telescope will improve scientific understanding of exploding stars, supernovas, and gamma-ray bursts. It will enable astronomers to image planets in orbits around other stars, and help astrophysicists determine their chemical composition. It will also help scientists probe black holes in unprecedented detail and test theoretical models of such little-understood phenomena as dark energy and dark matter. It may even help us find other life in the universe.

The Giant Magellan Telescope will provide a new celestial window on a much larger universe. Just as explorers like Magellan thought they had found in America a New World, and Lewis and Clark mapped it, this magnificent telescope will tell us much more about our planet, and no doubt, many new ones. It promises to open up many new chapters in the history of our nation and the world, and help address the most profound human questions we have: Where are we? How did we get here? Where might we be going?

The age of exploration is far from over. The Smithsonian's national museums hope to stimulate the next generation, to ask those questions in increasingly sophisticated ways, and even inspire the explorers among them to help answer them, not only understanding history, but making it!

"All Men Are Created Equal"—Civil Rights

Lecture 24

"We hold these truths to be self-evident, that all men are created equal, that they are endowed by their Creator with certain unalienable Rights, that among these are Life, Liberty, and the pursuit of Happiness." As a nation, we've sometimes struggled to realize these ideals, set forth in the Declaration of Independence. But if we look at American history and the experience of its people over time, we see a nation and society that is vital and robust, one that created vast opportunities and widespread successes for a population of incredible diversity in many ways.

The Declaration of Independence

- The Declaration of Independence was written to explain the decision of the Continental Congress, that a set of colonies in North America had declared themselves sovereign and united states—independent from Great Britain and free from the rule of its monarch, King George III.

- General George Washington had been leading an army against the British for almost a year by the time the Congress gathered in Philadelphia to discuss the nation's future. So, the Declaration of Independence was not so much an act of war as it was a result of it.

- Both the war and the Continental Congress were responses to the so-called Intolerable Acts or Coercive Acts of 1774, which the British passed to subdue the citizens of Massachusetts in the wake of the Boston Tea Party. These acts closed the port of Boston, dissolved the elected government of Massachusetts, and extradited all royal officials accused of crimes to Britain for trial. These acts, and many other grievances, are described in detail in the Declaration.

- In September 1774, 12 colonies sent delegates to Philadelphia to form the First Continental Congress. At first, Congress existed to communicate with one voice the colonists' needs and grievances to the British crown, but as time passed, it became the temporary, de facto government of the United States.

- The Congress did not form with the intent to declare independence. They began with an embargo of British goods and then coordinated military resistance to British occupation and aggression. The Second Continental Congress convened in May 1775, and in July, they attempted to make peace with George III one last time, but the king refused to receive their petition.

- By the next summer, sympathies within the Congress had shifted, and declaring independence seemed the only choice. The call for a declaration was made by delegate Richard Henry Lee of Virginia on June 7, 1776. Congress voted in favor of his resolution on July 2.

- The actual declaration was drafted by a group called the Committee of Five. This group included Benjamin Franklin of Pennsylvania, John Adams of Massachusetts, Robert Livingston of New York, Roger Sherman of Connecticut, and Thomas Jefferson of Virginia—the initial and primary drafter. Jefferson based the Declaration on his

Declaration of Independence

1774 argument against British taxation, published as *A Summary View of the Rights of British America.*

- Jefferson worked on a portable, hinged mahogany desk that he designed himself and had crafted by Philadelphia cabinetmaker Benjamin Randolph. Jefferson later gave the desk to his grandson-in-law. The family later donated the desk to the Smithsonian.

- Franklin improved Jefferson's initial "sacred and undeniable" truths to the more elegant "self-evident." The committee then presented the draft to the Continental Congress, which, to Jefferson's chagrin, reduced it by a quarter, improved its grammar, and removed Jefferson's complaint that Britain had foisted slavery upon the colonies.

- On July 4, 1776, the revised wording of the Declaration of Independence was approved, and the handwritten document was sent to the nearby Philadelphia printer, John Dunlap, for publication. That night, Dunlap set the Declaration in type and printed about 200 copies in broadside, a kind of one-sided bulletin or poster intended to be read aloud or displayed briefly and then discarded.

- These first copies of the Declaration of Independence were sent around the country, to England, and to General Washington in New York to be read to the troops and raise their spirits. Public readings occurred outside Independence Hall in Philadelphia as well as in other cities and towns of the colonies.

- Only 26 copies of Dunlap's first printing are still known to exist. While some of Jefferson's earlier drafts have been preserved, the actual handwritten manuscript of the final draft—what was read and approved by Congress on July 4—has disappeared.

- Nonetheless, the Declaration became, over time, the model for proclaiming the rights of women, workers, farmers, and others. The Constitution articulated the law of the land and the nature of governance, but the Declaration articulated the principles and philosophies that made the Constitution possible.

- The copy of the Declaration familiar to most people is not the original July 4 broadside. It is the so-called engrossed version, a large sheet of parchment upon which the text of the Declaration of Independence was handwritten by the clerk of the Congress, Timothy Matlack. Congress ordered this copy on July 19, and it took a few weeks to prepare. It was signed by most of the delegates in August and features the famous oversized John Hancock signature, along with 55 others.

- By 1820, the ink on the engrossed version of the Declaration of Independence was fading. Secretary of State John Quincy Adams, charged with caring for our national documents, did not want to lose this singular American treasure. He commissioned printer William Stone to create an engraving of the document so that accurate facsimiles could be printed and distributed throughout the country.

- Experts believe that Stone create what was called a "press copy" by moistening the surface of the original so that some of its ink would be transferred onto a copper plate, which was then etched and used as the master to print copies. It took Stone three years to do the etching. Congress paid Stone to print 200 copies on parchment. Stone actually printed 201, saving one for himself. This copy was donated to the Smithsonian by his widow in 1888.

- The engrossed original, not surprisingly, lost some ink in Stone's process and suffered additional damage from decades of exposure to sunlight and oxygen. Now the property of the National Archives, the Declaration remains on display, but to slow its decay, in 2001, conservators encased it in a titanium and aluminum case filled with inert argon gas. Most facsimiles around today, sold in stores, and used in classrooms are based on the Stone copies.

The Ku Klux Klan

- The ideals of equality and freedom articulated in the Declaration have faced numerous challenges over the course of the last two centuries. Enslaved Africans were hardly equal or free. Women were not equal to men—they were denied certain rights. Nonwhites were denied the right to become naturalized citizens; Native Americans were rounded up, forcibly relocated, and even deliberately starved.

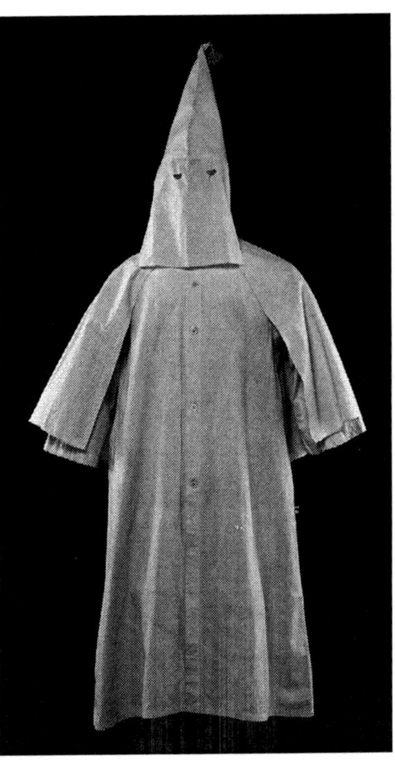

Ku Klux Klan Robe and Hood

- At the end of the American Civil War, the program of laws and amendments known as Reconstruction attempted to bring the promise of freedom to the nation's former slaves. The Thirteenth, Fourteenth, and Fifteenth Amendments to the Constitution outlawed slavery, expanded citizenship and voting rights to all adult men regardless of race, and ensured the equal protection of citizens under the law. The Reconstruction program improved public schools, rebuilt the railroads, found land and jobs for freed slaves, and ensured the electoral process and other civic activities in the Southern states.

- Between 1865 and 1877, African Americans won Southern seats in Congress. Coalitions of black freedmen and Northern politicians dominated the governments of former slave states. They worked to ensure that the new civil rights laws remained in force and to prevent reprisals against former enslaved blacks.

- There was certainly a degree of coercion in Reconstruction. Many in the South—and even in the border and northern states—saw various federal measures as radical, punitive, and corrupt. The states reacted by legislating new "black codes" to reinstitutionalize some aspects of slavery.

- Angry planters and former Confederates formed a number of secret groups to lash out against civil rights laws in a campaign of intimidation, terrorism, and murder. One of the most notorious of these groups was the Ku Klux Klan, founded by Confederate veterans in Pulaski, Tennessee, in late 1865.

- The Klan adopted hoods and robes to hide their identities. It grew to perhaps 500,000 members, all white men. Attempts were made to organize the Klan around a codified dogma with a quasi-military structure, but local groups remained largely independent.

- By 1870, Congress passed several Force Acts, which enabled district attorneys to prosecute Klan violence as federal crimes, and the movement went dormant. This worked for a while, but within a few years, an underground network began to reemerge.

- The so-called Compromise of 1877 gave Rutherford Hayes the U.S. presidency over Samuel Tilden after a disputed national election, in return for effectively ending federal intervention in the South. This returned segregationist, white, so-called redeemer Democrats to power in the South. Violence against blacks continued and even intensified, often with local government support.

- Southern state legislatures began to dismantle Reconstruction. Collectively called Jim Crow laws, new legislation promoted racial segregation and discrimination in all aspects of life. They reinforced segregation of black and white in all public facilities. Jim Crow laws overcame voting rights by instituting state-level poll taxes, literacy tests, and residency and document requirements that made it difficult if not impossible for many blacks to participate in elections.

- These formal Jim Crow laws in the South were echoed by informal cultural attitudes in the North. The result was a segregated society, with a disenfranchised black population facing restricted freedoms and unequal and diminished rights and opportunities.

- In 1896, the U.S. Supreme Court ruled in *Plessy v. Ferguson* that "separate but equal" was legal—that states could designate separate public services and amenities for blacks and whites as a matter of policy, as long as the services were equivalent. Of course, they were not.

- As America entered the 20th century, Washington DC was a deeply segregated city. Only the federal workforce and federal facilities in the nation's capital were integrated. When Woodrow Wilson became president in 1913, he changed this situation—for the worse. One of his first acts was to resegregate the workforce of government agencies and the White House.

- In 1915, a new version of the Klan was founded in Atlanta, Georgia. The new Klan was organized more formally than the old one, recruiting members as if it were just another fraternal organization. The Klan grew to perhaps 5 million members by the time of its grand parade down Pennsylvania Avenue in Washington DC on September 13, 1926.

- This time, the Klan's agenda was largely anti-black, anti-immigrant, anti-Semitic, and anti-Catholic and also attacked southern and eastern European immigrants who had fled war and poverty at home and found factory jobs in America.

- In the South, in particular, violence escalated once again, including floggings and brandings of their targets. Scandals, criminal behavior, and errant leadership were gradually uncovered by the press, and determined opposition by such groups as the National Association for the Advancement of Colored People eroded membership and residual public sympathies by the early 1930s. In 1947, the state of Georgia revoked the Klan's national corporate charter.

- The Klan revived again during the civil rights movement of the 1960s. But their campaign of terror could not stop the march of freedom. And while the Klan still exists, since the 1980s, their numbers have continued to decline.

- Despite their near disappearance from contemporary life, the Klan's archetypal regalia is distinctive and widely recognized. Typically, it consists of a floor-length solid-white robe, sometimes decorated with a round badge bearing an insignia with a cross, and a white, sharply pointed hat that includes a full-faced cloth mask with eyeholes. The Smithsonian has several Klan robes, capes, and hoods in its collection.

The Greensboro Four

- A lunch counter and its stools were installed in the Woolworth's department store at 132 South Elm Street in Greensboro, North Carolina, in 1938, when the store first opened. Lunch counters in department stores were a way for chain-store managers to get shoppers to stick around and spend a bit more money.

- The counters also became a place where people in the community would congregate. This was the case for the large Woolworth's in Greensboro, with its long L-shaped counter accommodating more than 60 seats. A section of the Greensboro Woolworth's original counter is now at the Smithsonian.

- In Greensboro, as in much of the South, while blacks could shop at Woolworth's, Jim Crow laws prevented them from eating at the

Greensboro Lunch Counter

counter—that was reserved for whites only. African Americans were served only at the take-out section of the counter.

- On Monday, February 1, 1960, four African American men—Franklin McCain, Ezell Blair Jr., Joseph McNeil, and David Richmond—entered the Greensboro Woolworth's and sat down on stools at the lunch counter. The four men were freshmen at the Agricultural and Technical College of North Carolina (A&T). They asked to be served and were refused. Instead of getting up and leaving, these men, later known as the Greensboro Four, launched a sit-in protest that lasted for six months.

- One of the four young men, Joseph McNeil, noted that the idea of a sit-in protest had been around for a while. He and his four friends agreed ahead of time that their protest would be nonviolent and that they would miss no classes. The students arrived at the Woolworth's at about 4:30 pm and stayed until closing, an hour later, without being served.

- The next day, the men returned to the store at about 10:30 am, this time joined by more than a dozen other A&T students, who all made small purchases in the store to establish that they were paying customers. The students again asked to be served, but were refused. As white customers left, black students took their places.

- The next day, scores of students from A&T showed up for the sit-in. In subsequent days, protesters were joined by students from Bennett College and three white coeds from Greensboro College, as well as black high school students. Whites taunted protesters, began to block the aisles, and tried to prevent blacks from taking seats at the Woolworth's counter. The police had to intervene to keep protesters and counterprotesters apart. Three white men were arrested.

- As negotiations between city officials and the students failed to end the protest, it garnered increasing national attention. By Saturday, hundreds of people crowded into the Woolworth's lunch counter area. The students agreed to a cooling-off period following a meeting with town and college officials so that a solution could be found. It wasn't. The Greensboro sit-in inspired similar protests in other North Carolina and southern cities.

- In March, President Dwight D. Eisenhower expressed his support for the rights of the students to be served under the law. The economic impact on Woolworth's was devastating. On July 25, it served its own black employees at the counter and, the next day, ended its segregation policies chain-wide. Hundreds of other stores followed suit as the impact of the Greensboro sit-in spread across the South, from lunch counters to other civic institutions.

- The students' courageous action inspired young blacks and others around the nation to advocate for their civil rights as equal citizens. It took many years and many other courageous actions to finally end segregation: Rosa Parks and the Montgomery bus boycott, the *Brown v. Board of Education* case argued by Thurgood Marshall, the marches and speeches of Dr. Martin Luther King, and the actions of many others.

Featured Objects

Declaration of Independence

Ku Klux Klan Robe and Hood

Greensboro Lunch Counter

Suggested Reading

Maier, *American Scripture.*

Morgan and Davies, eds., *From Sit-Ins to SNCC.*

"All Men Are Created Equal"—Civil Rights
Lecture 24—Transcript

"We hold these truths to be self-evident, that all men are created equal, that they are endowed by their Creator with certain unalienable Rights, that among these are Life, Liberty, and the pursuit of Happiness."

These words from the Declaration of Independence are among the most famous in the English language. They convey a powerful idea, one that the new-born nation was already fighting a war to uphold, one that its people would continue to fight for, at home and abroad, to this very day. These words, perhaps more than any others, define the American spirit.

The Declaration was written to explain the decision of the Continental Congress, that a set of colonies in North America had declared themselves sovereign and United States, independent from Great Britain and free from the rule of its monarch, King George III. General George Washington had been leading an army against the British for almost a year by the time the Congress gathered in Philadelphia to discuss the nation's future. So the Declaration of Independence was not so much an act of war, as rather, a result of it.

Both the war and the Continental Congress were responses to the so-called Intolerable Acts,, or Coercive Acts, of 1774, which the British passed to subdue the citizens of Massachusetts in the wake of the Boston Tea Party. These acts closed the port of Boston, dissolved the elected government of Massachusetts, and extradited all royal officials accused of crimes to Britain for trial. They also, in theory, allowed the governor of any colony to quarter British soldiers in private homes, although it is not known if this ever happened. But these acts, and many other grievances, are described in detail in the Declaration.

In September 1774, 12 colonies sent delegates to Philadelphia to form the First Continental Congress. Georgia was the only holdout; it would join the Second Continental Congress in 1775. At first, Congress existed to communicate with one voice the colonists' needs and grievances to the British crown, but as time passed, it became the temporary, de facto government of the United States.

It's important to note that the Congress did not form with the intent to declare independence. They began with an embargo of British goods; then coordinated military resistance to British occupation and aggression. The Second Continental Congress convened in May 1775, and in July, they attempted to make peace with George III one last time, but the king refused to receive their petition. By the next summer, sympathies within the Congress had shifted, and declaring independence seemed the only choice. The call for a declaration was made by delegate Richard Henry Lee of Virginia on June 7, 1776. Congress voted in favor of his resolution on July 2.

The actual declaration was drafted by a group called the Committee of Five. This group included Benjamin Franklin of Pennsylvania, John Adams of Massachusetts, Robert Livingston of New York, Roger Sherman of Connecticut, and the group's young intellectual firebrand, Thomas Jefferson of Virginia. The initial and primary drafter, Jefferson based the Declaration on his 1774 argument against British taxation, published as *A Summary View of the Rights of British America.*

Jefferson worked on a portable, hinged mahogany desk that he designed himself and had crafted by Philadelphia cabinetmaker Benjamin Randolph. Jefferson later gave the desk to his grandson-in-law with an inscription. It said, "Politics as well as Religion has its superstitions. These, gaining strength with time, may, one day, give imaginary value to this relic, for its association with the birth of the Great Charter of our Independence." The family later donated the desk to the Smithsonian, as Jefferson had predicted.

Franklin improved Jefferson's initial writings. Jefferson had written "sacred and undeniable" truths. Franklin edited it to the more elegant "self-evident." The committee then presented its draft to the Continental Congress, which, to Jefferson's chagrin, reduced it by about a quarter, improved its grammar, and removed Jefferson's complaint that Britain had foisted slavery upon the colonies.

On July 4, 1776, the revised wording of the Declaration of Independence was approved and the handwritten document was sent to the nearby Philadelphia printer, John Dunlap, for publication. That night, Dunlap set the Declaration in type and printed some 200 copies in broadside, a kind of one-sided bulletin, or poster, intended to be read aloud or displayed briefly and then discarded.

These first copies of the Declaration of Independence were sent around the country; they were sent to England, to George Washington in New York to be read to the troops and raise their spirits. Public readings occurred outside Independence Hall in Philadelphia, as well as in other cities and towns of the colonies.

Only 26 copies of Dunlap's first printing are still known to exist. While some of Jefferson's earlier drafts have been preserved; the actual handwritten manuscript of the draft that was read and approved by Congress on July 4, well, that's disappeared. Maybe one of you watching this lecture has it stuffed behind a picture in a frame, maybe stored with old documents in an attic, basement, or an old footlocker. We'd love to find that original Declaration of Independence.

The British government never gave an official response to the Declaration. George III gave a short speech about the American "troubles" later in the year, and his troops continued fighting against Washington's army. Others commented on Britain's behalf, charging that the signers were elite conspirators who had whipped up the sentiments of otherwise loyal colonists for their own private benefit. Some argued that the Declaration of Independence was hypocritical; how could the principle that "all men are created equal" be taken seriously when many of the signers owned slaves?

Nonetheless, the Declaration became, over time, the model for proclaiming the rights of women, workers, farmers, and others. Abraham Lincoln drew on the Declaration to justify the emancipation of the slaves, those abandoned by the founders' promise of liberty for all. Elizabeth Cady Stanton echoed the wording of the Declaration when helping to draft the Declaration of Sentiments in defense of women's rights. The Constitution articulated the law of the land and the nature of governance, but the Declaration of

Independence that articulated the principles and philosophies that made the Constitution possible.

Now, the copy of the Declaration familiar to most people is not the original July 4 broadside. It's rather the so-called engrossed version; that's a large sheet of parchment upon which the text of the Declaration of Independence was handwritten by the clerk of the Congress, Timothy Matlack. Congress ordered this copy on July 19, and it took a weeks for Matlack to prepare. It was signed by most of the delegates in August and features that famous oversized John Hancock signature, along with 55 others. At least one delegate probably didn't add his signature to this unique calligraphed engrossed version of the declaration until November.

By 1820, the ink on the engrossed version of the Declaration of Independence was fading. Secretary of State John Quincy Adams charged with caring for our national documents, did not want to lose this singular American treasure. He commissioned printer William Stone to create an engraving of the document so that accurate facsimiles could be printed and distributed throughout the country. Now remember, this was before photography was invented, so there were only a limited number of methods to make a copy. One was simply to trace the original onto another thin or relatively transparent piece of paper. Another was to create what was called a press copy. Experts believe Stone used the later method. He moistened the surface of the original so that some of its ink would be transferred onto a copper plate, which was then etched and used as the master to print copies. It took Stone three years to do the etching. Congress paid Stone to print 200 copies on parchment. Stone actually printed 201, saving one for himself, and that copy was donated to the Smithsonian by his widow in 1888.

The engrossed copy of the Declaration of Independence, not surprisingly, lost some of its ink in Stone's process, as making the copy literally pulled the ink off of the paper. Now, it suffered additional damage in the decades of exposure afterwards because of the sunlight and exposure to oxygen. Now the property of the National Archives, the Declaration remains on display, but to slow its decay, in 2001, conservators encased that engrossed copy of the Declaration of Independence in a titanium and aluminum case filled with inert argon gas. Most facsimiles around today, sold in stores and used in classrooms, are based upon the Stone copy.

The ideals of equality and freedom articulated in the Declaration have faced numerous challenges over the course of the last two centuries, as even many of the signers were aware. Enslaved Africans were hardly equal or free. Women were not equal to men, denied certain rights, including the right to vote in almost every state. Non-whites were denied the right to become naturalized citizens; and even the Declaration refers to Native Americans as "merciless Indian Savages." They were rounded up, forcibly relocated, and even deliberately starved.

At the end of the American Civil War, the program of laws and amendments known as Reconstruction attempted to bring the promise of freedom to the nation's former slaves. The Thirteenth, Fourteenth and Fifteenth Amendments to the Constitution outlawed slavery, expanded citizenship and voting rights to all adult men regardless of race, and ensured the equal protection of citizens under the law. The Reconstruction program improved public schools, rebuilt railroads, found land and jobs for freed slaves, and ensured the electoral process and other civic activities in the Southern states that formed the Confederacy.

Between 1865 and 1877, African Americans won Southern seats in Congress. Coalitions of black freedmen and Northern politicians dominated the governments of former slave states. They worked to ensure that the new civil rights laws remained in force and to prevent reprisals against former enslaved blacks.

There was certainly a degree of coercion in Reconstruction. Radical Republicans in the North controlled Congress and the national agenda, impeaching Lincoln's successor Andrew Johnson and gaining the support of President Ulysses S. Grant. The U.S. Army imposed martial law in parts of the South. Southern states could not regain representation in Congress unless they approved the Fourteenth Amendment. Lucrative government contracts were often awarded to Northern companies and to political supporters of the Grant administration, including Union officers. Many in the South, and even in the border and some even in northern states, saw various federal measures as radical, punitive, and even corrupt.

The states reacted by legislating new, what we called, black codes to re-institutionalize some aspects of slavery. Such laws criminalized vagrancy or unemployment for African Americans, forcing them, as punishment, to work for free or for low wages. These codes restricted other civil liberties, in some cases denying blacks the ability to own property, carry firearms, or even marry.

Angry planters and former Confederates formed a number of secret societies to lash out against civil rights laws in a campaign of intimidation, terrorism, and murder. One of the most notorious of these groups was the Ku Klux Klan, founded by Confederate veterans in Pulaski, Tennessee, in late 1865. The name came from the Greek word kyklos, meaning “circle” or “clan.” With its connotations of antiquity, kinship, and militant unity, they adopted hoods and robes to hide their identities, and some also claimed they represented the ghosts of slain Confederates seeking revenge. The Klan grew to perhaps 500,000 members, all white men. Attempts were made to organize the Klan around a codified dogma with a quasi-military structure, but local groups remained largely independent.

By 1870, Congress passed several Force Acts, which enabled district attorneys to prosecute Klan violence as federal crimes, and the movement went dormant. That worked for a while, but within a few years an informal underground network began to reemerge.

The so-called Compromise of 1877 gave Rutherford Hayes the U.S. presidency over Samuel Tilden after a disputed national election in return for effectively ending federal intervention in the South. This returned segregationist, white, so-called redeemer Democrats to power in the South. Violence against blacks continued and even intensified, often with local government support. More than three thousand blacks were lynched by the Klan and similar groups in the United States between 1882 and 1920.

Southern state legislatures began to dismantle Reconstruction. Collectively called Jim Crow laws, new legislation promoted racial segregation and discrimination in all aspects of life. They reinforced segregation of black and white in public facilities, with separate bathrooms, eating places, railroad cars, schools, and so on. Jim Crow laws overcame voting rights by instituting state-level poll taxes, literacy tests, residency and document requirements that made it difficult, if not impossible, for many blacks to participate in elections. These formal Jim Crow laws in the South were echoed by informal, cultural attitudes in the North. The result was a segregated society with a disenfranchised black population facing restricted freedoms, unequal and diminished rights and opportunities.

In 1896 the U.S. Supreme Court ruled in Plessy v. Ferguson that "separate but equal" was legal, that states could designate separate public services and amenities for blacks and whites as a matter of policy as long as the services were equivalent. Of course, they weren't. As America entered the 20th century, Washington DC, where Abraham Lincoln had first emancipated the slaves, was a deeply segregated city. Only the federal workforce and federal facilities in the nation's capital were integrated.

When Woodrow Wilson became president in 1913, he changed this situation—for the worse. One of his first acts was to re-segregate the workforce of government agencies and the White House. Although a progressive on many issues, Wilson harbored racist attitudes and was a strong supporter of segregation. As president of Princeton University, he had refused to integrate the school. As president of the United States, he once said that for African Americans, "Segregation is not a humiliation but a benefit."

In 1915, a new version of the Klan was founded in Atlanta, Georgia, inspired in no small part by the widespread popularity of D. W. Griffith's epic silent film, *The Clansman*, which was later retitled *The Birth of a Nation*. This film offered a heroic depiction of the Reconstruction-era Klan and their white supremacist agenda. The film was based on a novel and play written by Thomas Dixon, a classmate of Woodrow Wilson's, who also arranged for the film's screening at the White House.

The new Klan was organized more formally than the old one, recruiting members as if it was another fraternal organization. It gave recruiters a share of the initiation fee and the charge paid by each new recruit for his robe and hood. It had a formal national and state structure and produced a constitution for its so called knights, or members. The Klan grew to perhaps five million members by the time of its grand parade down Pennsylvania Avenue in Washington, DC, on September 13, 1926.

The Klan reflected the various regional tensions of the times. In the South, it was fueled by racism. But it also found a home in the cities of the North and the Midwest, feeding off the social tensions of urban industrialization and vastly increased immigration. The Klan even made its way to Canada.

This time, the Klan preached what he called “One Hundred Percent Americanism”; its agenda was largely anti-black, anti-immigrant, anti-Semitic, and anti-Catholic and also attacked southern and eastern European immigrants who had fled war and poverty at home and found factory jobs in America. Allied with white fundamentalism, the Klan also supported Prohibition and capitalized on fears about the perceived loosening of public morals in the so-called Jazz Age by recruiting members for a women’s auxiliary.

In the South, in particular, violence escalated once again. The Klan adopted a burning wooden Latin cross as an emblem of its alleged Christian mandate and used it as a means of intimidation. Scandals, criminal behavior, errant leadership of the Klan, and gradual uncovering of issues by the press, all undermined the Klan’s effectiveness, including opposition by such groups as the National Association for the Advancement of Colored People, basically, over a number of years, the Klan’s membership started to go down, and so did residual public sympathies, By the early 1930s, the Klan was in severe decline, and by 1947, the State of Georgia revoked the Klan’s national corporate charter.

The Klan revived again during the civil rights movement of the 1960s. They are believed to be responsible for the murders of many individual activists and more than 100 bombings during that decade. But their campaign of terror could not stop the march of freedom. And while the Klan still exists, since the 1980s, their numbers have continued to decline. Despite their near-disappearance from contemporary life, the Klan’s archetypal regalia, sometimes called the glory suit by Klansmen, is distinctive and widely recognized. Its historical origins are unclear; some believe it harkens to religious fraternal and penitential organizations, others to the costuming in Griffith's film. Typically it consists of a floor-length solid-white robe, sometimes decorated with a round badge bearing an insignia with a cross, and a white, sharply pointed hat that includes a full-faced cloth mask with eyeholes. The basic costume, which has some rank-based and regional variations, was designed both to disguise and to intimidate.

The Smithsonian has several of these Klan robes, capes, and hoods in its collection. While not treasured by museum curators or visitors, the Klan robes and hoods in the Smithsonian's collection provide poignant and necessary reminders of a history of intolerance and persecution, now, largely overcome because of acts of decency, bravery, and humanity celebrated by such items such this one—the Greensboro lunch counter.

This lunch counter and its stools were installed in the Woolworth's department store at 132 Elm Street in Greensboro, North Carolina in 1938 when the store first opened. They were essentially the same as those found in hundreds of communities across the nation. Lunch counters in department stores were a way for chain-store managers to get shoppers to stick around and spend a little bit more money. The counters also became a place where people in the community would congregate, catch up on the news, gossip, and even transact some business. This was the case for the large 25,000-square-foot Woolworth's in Greensboro, with its long L-shaped counter accommodating more than 60 seats.

A section of the Greensboro Woolworth's original counter is now at the Smithsonian. On the surface, this is a very ordinary, even mundane, object, and yet this one tells a most profound story, one of how African Americans sought to realize the dream called for in the Declaration of Independence, that all men are created equal and entitled to life, liberty, and the pursuit of happiness.

In Greensboro, as in much of the South, while blacks could shop at Woolworth's, Jim Crow laws prevented them from eating at the counter; that was reserved for whites only. On Monday, February 1, 1960, four African

American men entered the Greensboro Woolworth's and sat down on stools at the lunch counter. Until that moment, the stools had never been occupied by black customers. The four men, Franklin McCain, Ezell Blair Jr., Joseph McNeil, and David Richmond, were freshmen at the Agricultural and Technical College of North Carolina. They simply asked to be served, and they were refused. Instead of getting up and leaving, these men, later known as the Greensboro Four, launched a sit-in protest that lasted for six months.

Greensboro had been the site of a variety of civil rights activities in the 1950s. Protests had been mounted over inferior schools for blacks as well as a whites-only public swimming pool. The local chapter of the National Association for the Advancement of Colored People had led efforts to desegregate the municipal golf course. The Reverend Martin Luther King Jr. came to Greensboro in 1958 and gave a sermon at the chapel of Bennett College, a liberal arts college for black women, when he was not allowed to speak anywhere else in town.

One of the four young men, Joseph McNeil, would later recall the impetus for the students' sit-in protest. McNeil's family lived in New York, and he found the bus journeys from the north to the south especially disturbing. He said, "In Philadelphia I could eat anywhere in the bus station. By Maryland, that had changed. … I was still the same person, but I was treated differently."

The idea of a sit-in protest, he noted, had been around for a while. He and friends agreed ahead of time that their protest would be nonviolent and that they would miss no classes. The students arrived at that Woolworth's at about 4:30 p.m. on the first day and stayed until closing—without being served.

The next day, the men returned to the store at a10:30 in the morning, this time joined by more than a dozen other A&T students, who all made small purchases in the store to establish that they were, indeed, paying customers. A photographer with the Greensboro News & Record took a photo of four students at the counter: McNeil and McCain, along with William Smith and Clarence Henderson. That photograph was published on the front page of the newspaper and became widely circulated.

The students again asked to be served, but were refused. As white customers left, black students would take their place at the counter. The students spoke softly and read at the counter. They left after noon, but promised to return the next day with more and more students, for weeks, if necessary, until they were served.

The next day, scores of students from A&T—about one-third of them women—showed up for the sit-in. In subsequent days protesters were joined by students from Bennett College and three white coeds from Greensboro College, as well as black high school students. Whites, some carrying Confederate flags, taunted protesters, they began to block the aisles, and they tried to prevent blacks from taking seats at the Woolworth's counter. The police had to intervene to keep protesters and counter-protesters apart, and three white men were arrested.

As negotiations between city officials and the students failed to end the protest, it garnered increasing national attention. By Saturday, hundreds of people crowded into the Woolworth's lunch counter area. A bomb threat led to the store's evacuation, and so the protest moved down the street to the Kress store, which then had to close.

The students agreed to a cooling-off period following a meeting with town and college officials so that a solution could be found. It wasn't. And when the protests resumed, outside picketers joined in, and the black adult population began an economic boycott of downtown stores. The Greensboro sit-in inspired similar protests in other North Carolina and southern cities.

In March, President Dwight D. Eisenhower expressed his support for the rights of the students to be served under the law. The economic impact on Woolworth's was devastating. And finally on July 25 it served its own black employees at the counter, and then the next day ended its segregation policies chain-wide. Hundreds of other stores followed suit as the impact of the Greensboro sit-in spread across the South, from lunch counters to other civic institutions.

The students' courageous action inspired young blacks and others around the nation to advocate for their civil rights as equal citizens. It took many years and many other courageous actions to finally end segregation: Rosa Parks and the Montgomery bus boycott, the Brown v. Board of Education case argued by Thurgood Marshall, and the marches and speeches of Dr. Martin Luther King, and the actions of many others, who, to quote the closing words of the Declaration, "pledged their lives, their fortunes, and their sacred honor" to the cause of civil rights. And their example continues to inspire us.

Whatever their assumptions, whatever their blind spots, America's founders got it right. In the Declaration of Independence they created a charter for people to pursue their potential as human beings. They enshrined ideas of equality and freedom into the culture of a new nation. They established democracy as the basis of its governance. They recognized the importance of knowledge, tolerance, innovation, and creativity.

As a nation we've sometimes struggled to realize those ideals, and sometimes we've have had to face wars and tragedies, great maladies and economic crises. But if we look at American history and the experience of its people over time, we see a nation and society that is vital and robust, one that created vast opportunities and widespread successes for a population of incredible diversity in all sorts of ways.

America has taken mankind to the Moon, and promulgated noble ideas and profound influence around the planet. As you've seen and heard in these lectures, at the Smithsonian—your Smithsonian—we preserve a record of all that so that current and future generations can learn from their predecessors, and make the country and the world even better. I'm proud to play a role in that work, and I thank you for your attentiveness during these lectures. I hope you've enjoyed hearing them as much as I've enjoyed giving them, and I thank you for your support.

Bibliography

Anderson, Chris. *Makers: The New Industrial Revolution.* New York: Crown Business, 2014. This book, from one of the leaders of the "maker movement," discusses the potential impacts of such new technologies as 3-D printing on the future of American industry.

Anderson, Nancy K., and Linda S. Ferber. *Albert Bierstadt: Art and Enterprise.* Manchester, VT: Hudson Hills, 1991. This large-format art book from the Brooklyn Museum can be a bit difficult to find, but it offers both magnificent reproductions of Bierstadt's work and a terrific analysis of Bierstadt the showman.

Armstrong, Louis. *Louis Armstrong, In His Own Words: Selected Writings.* Edited by Thomas Brothers. New York: Oxford University, 1999. A glimpse into the mind of the genius musician, revealing his views on his art and his experiences of segregation and the civil rights movement.

Arsenault, Raymond. *The Sound of Freedom: Marian Anderson, the Lincoln Memorial, and the Concert That Awakened America.* New York: Bloomsbury, 2009. The story of that remarkable concert in even richer detail, set in the broader context of the civil rights movement.

Barr, Luke. *Provence, 1970: M. F. K. Fisher, Julia Child, James Beard, and the Reinvention of American Taste.* New York: Clarkson Potter, 2013. For an experience of Julia Child's recipes, one should turn to *Mastering the Art of French Cooking*. However, for an argument about her influence on American culture, this is a terrific starting point.

Barratt, Carrie Rebora, and Ellen G. Miles. *Gilbert Stuart.* New York: Metropolitan Museum of Art, 2004. A thorough look at the life and work of the creator of the Lansdowne portrait.

Berg, A. Scott. *Lindbergh.* New York: Berkley, 1999. Widely considered the definitive biography.

Berlin, Ira, Joseph Patrick Reidy, and Leslie S. Rowland. *Freedom's Soldiers: The Black Military Experience in the Civil War*. New York: Cambridge University, 1998. This stirring history of the Civil War is based on the firsthand accounts of African American soldiers like Christian Fleetwood.

Berner, Brad K. *The Spanish-American War: A Documentary History with Commentaries*. Madison, NJ: Fairleigh Dickinson, 2014. A collection of primary-source documents that helps immerse the reader in the atmosphere of the times, including the response to the explosion of the *Maine*.

Binder, Frederick. *All the Nations under Heaven*. Columbia History of Urban Life. New York: Columbia University, 1996. In the shadow of the Statue of Liberty, New York City became the most diverse city in the United States. In this way, the city offers a living laboratory of the urban immigrant experience. In this book, the author chronicles 200 years of that experience, from the 1790s to the 1990s.

Bird, William L. Jr., and Harry R. Rubenstein. *Design for Victory: World War II Posters on the American Home Front*. Princeton, NJ: Princeton Architectural Press, 1998. A look at World War II poster art through the Smithsonian's collections.

Bizony, Piers. *The Space Shuttle: Celebrating Thirty Years of NASA's First Space Plane*. Minneapolis, MN: Zenith, 2011. A detailed history, with images, of each of the shuttle program's 135 missions, with a balanced analysis of its triumphs and mistakes. Includes technical specifications and diagrams.

Bowles, Hamish, Arthur M. Schlesinger, and Lambert Mellon. *Jacqueline Kennedy: The White House Years: Selections from the John F. Kennedy Library and Museum*. New York: Bulfinch, 2001. An analysis of Jacqueline Kennedy as a style icon.

Bradford, William. *Of Plymouth Plantation*. Garden City, NY: Dover, 2006. A firsthand account of the settlement of Plymouth from one of the colony's leaders. Of course, the eponymous rock is conspicuously absent.

Brands, H. W. *The Age of Gold: The California Gold Rush and the New American Dream*. New York: Anchor, 2003. A readable yet scholarly account of how the California gold rush not only drove Americans west, but also profoundly altered the American character.

———. *The First American: The Life and Times of Benjamin Franklin*. New York: Anchor, 2002. An engaging biography of America's first elder statesman.

Buhite, Russell D., and David W. Levy, eds. *FDR's Fireside Chats*. Norman: University of Oklahoma, 2010. The complete text of all 31 of Roosevelt's radio addresses.

Carpenter, M. Scott, Gordon L. Cooper, John H. Glenn, Virgil I. Grissom, Walter M. Schirra, Alan B. Shepard, and Donald K. Slayton. *We Seven: By the Astronauts Themselves*. Reprint ed. New York: Simon & Schuster, 2010. Originally published in 1962 and reprinted for the 50th anniversary of the Mercury program, the original Mercury Seven tell their story in their own words.

Chernow, Ron. *Washington, A Life*. New York: Penguin, 2010. A comprehensive recent biography of America's first president that pays thorough attention to his pre-Revolution career.

Clinton, Catherine. *Harriet Tubman: The Road to Freedom*. New York: Back Bay Books, 2005. Between the mid-1940s and the early 21st century, the only new biographies of Tubman being published were for the juvenile market. Thankfully, that has changed, and this is one of several great offerings now available.

De Monchaux, Nicholas. *Spacesuit: Fashioning Apollo*. Cambridge, MA: MIT, 2001. The full story of the Apollo space suit, layer by layer.

Douglass, Frederick. *Narrative of the Life of Frederick Douglas, An American Slave*. New York: Penguin, 2014. First published in 1845, this is one of the best known of all American slave narratives and is well worth reading, not only as the biography of a remarkable man, but also as an introduction to the genre.

Dylan, Bob. *Chronicles*. New York: Simon & Schuster, 2005. Less like a memoir and more like a blog in book form, this autobiography reveals Dylan in a very Dylanesque fashion and may surprise even long-time fans.

Eisenhower, David. *Eisenhower at War 1943–1945*. New York: Random House, 1986. A detailed biography of Eisenhower's war years. Although written by his grandson, the book manages to maintain objectivity and offers an invaluable personal perspective.

Finch, Christopher. *The Art of Walt Disney: From Mickey Mouse to the Magic Kingdoms and Beyond*. New ed. New York: Harry N. Abrams, 2011. The gang is all here, from Mickey to Disney's latest digital creations. There is also a 1973 edition that focuses more on the (earlier) films and less on the theme parks and spin-offs.

Goldstone, Lawrence. *Birdmen: The Wright Brothers, Glenn Curtiss, and the Battle to Control the Skies*. New York: Ballantine, 2014. This book picks up the Wrights' story after their success at Kitty Hawk, when they had to defend their invention against Curtiss and others. It also tells the thrilling story of the early years of flight and the barnstorming daredevils who took to the skies.

Gorrow, Teena Ruark, and Craig A. Koppie. *Inside a Bald Eagle's Nest: A Photographic Journey through the American Bald Eagle Nesting Season*. Atglen, PA: Schiffer, 2013. This collaboration between a teacher and a raptor biologist provides a unique view of this magnificent animal—wonderful for adults and children.

Gray, Charlotte. *Reluctant Genius: Alexander Graham Bell and the Passion for Invention*. New York: Arcade, 2011. More than the biography of the inventor, it is the biography of the family that helped him succeed and the many inventions brought forth by his remarkable mind.

Greenberg, Joel. *A Feathered River across the Sky: The Passenger Pigeon's Flight to Extinction*. New York: Bloomsbury, 2014. A comprehensive look at the complicated set of forces that led to the pigeon's extinction. Compelling and sobering.

Greenwald, Alice M., and Clifford Chanin, eds. *The Stories They Tell: Artifacts from the National September 11 Memorial Museum*. New York: Skira Rizzoli, 2013. This book, released in advance of the museum's opening, pairs 28 objects from the museum with essays by staff members explaining their origins—in spirit, very similar to this course.

Gustavson, Todd. *Camera: A History of Photography from Daguerrotype to Digital*. New York: Sterling Signature, 2012. Not a history of photographs but a history of the cameras themselves, using the collection of machines and diagrams from the George Eastman House collection.

Guthrie, Woody. *Bound for Glory*. Reissued ed. New York: Plume, 1983. Guthrie's autobiography (in this edition, with an introduction by his close friend Pete Seeger), it is also a sort of precursor to the road novels of the beat generation. An excellent introduction to the man and his work.

Halpin, Marjorie M. *Totem Poles: An Illustrated Guide*. Vancouver: University of British Columbia, 1981. This brief volume by a respected anthropologist is nonetheless one of the best introductions available to the history and iconography of totem poles.

Hickey, Donald R. *The War of 1812: A Forgotten Conflict, Bicentennial Edition*. Champaign: University of Illinois, 2012. A comprehensive history of America's least-understood war.

Hirasuna, Delphine, Terry Heffernan, and Kit Hindrichs. *The Art of Gaman: Arts and Crafts from the Japanese American Internment Camps 1942–1946*. New York: Ten Speed, 2005. A beautiful and moving collection of internment camp art.

Horton, James Oliver, and Lois E. Horton. *Slavery and the Making of America*. New York: Oxford University, 2006. The history of slavery in

America told through the real-life stories of those who were enslaved. Some of the subjects were famous, some were not so famous—but all are worth hearing.

Jefferson, Thomas. *The Jefferson Bible, Smithsonian Edition: The Life and Morals of Jesus of Nazareth*. Edited by Janice Stagnitto Ellis. Introduction by Harry Rubenstein and Barbara Clark Smith. Washington DC: Smithsonian Books, 2011. This is the edition used in the course, with all of Jefferson's edits and the ravages of time preserved. Possibly the best edition for Jefferson scholars—or the scholarly minded—to possess.

Jones, Brian Jay. *Jim Henson: The Biography*. New York: Ballantine, 2013. An honest look at the man behind the Muppets.

Jones, Cleve, and Jeff Dawson. *Stitching a Revolution: The Making of an Activist*. New York: HarperOne, 2001. The story of the AIDS quilt told by those who created it.

Keller, Helen. *The Story of My Life: The Restored Edition*. Edited by James Berger. New York: Modern Library, 2004. A classic autobiography, this particular edition includes some of Keller's later writings, both autobiographical and political.

Kimbro, Enda, Julia G. Costello, and Tevvy Ball. *The California Missions: History, Art and Preservation*. Conservation & Cultural Heritage Book 8. Los Angeles: Getty Conservation Institute, 2009. Although focused on the missions of California, this beautifully photographed book contains excellent examples of mission art and architecture, as well as descriptions of mission life.

Kisseloff, Jeff. *The Box: An Oral History of Television, 1929–1961*. New York: Viking, 1995. Hundreds of interviews with the pioneers of television, plus relatives of the television's inventors.

Kluger, Jeffrey. *Splendid Solution: Jonas Salk and the Conquest of Polio*. New York: Penguin, 2006. A history of both the science and the politics behind the creation of the polio vaccine.

Kurin, Richard. *Hope Diamond: The Legendary History of a Cursed Gem*. New York: Harper Perennial, 2007. A complete history of the diamond at the heart of the Smithsonian's National Gem Collection—all the myths, all the facts, all the science.

———. *Madcap May: Mistress of Myth, Men, and Hope*. Washington DC: Smithsonian, 2012. May Yohe was one of the many fabulous figures whose life was touched by the Hope Diamond. A story of Gilded Age excess—and proof that, at least for one woman, the diamond was not such a curse.

———. *The Smithsonian's History of America in 101 Objects*. New York: Penguin, 2013. The book that inspired this course, it includes many of the same objects (although often examined from a slightly different perspective) and several others not covered. Full of rich photographs and insider stories about the Smithsonian and its history.

LaPointe, Ernie. *Sitting Bull: His Life and Legacy*. Layton, UT: Gibbs Smith, 2009. Sitting Bull's grandson recounts the great warrior's biography from the perspective of family and tribal oral history.

Leepson, Marc. *What So Proudly We Hailed: Francis Scott Key, A Life*. Basingstoke, UK: Palgrave Macmillan, 2014. A brief biography of the author of our national anthem, covering not only his role in the Battle of Baltimore, but also his later—somewhat controversial—role in the abolitionist movement.

Levy, Jacques E. *Cesar Chavez: Autobiography of La Causa*. Minneapolis: University of Minnesota, 2007. Levy was a journalist who spent six years with Chavez and several more writing and researching this book. The result is an invaluably accurate account of Chavez's beliefs—helpful in understanding immigrant workers' perspectives, even if you disagree with Chavez's positions.

Lewis, Meriwether, and William Clark. *The Journals of Lewis and Clark*. Edited by Bernard DeVoto. Wilmington, MA: Mariner, 1997. The jointly kept journals of these two explorers provide an incomparable record of the

Louisiana Territory and the American West before its settlement by European American colonists. An enlightening read.

Maier, Pauline. *American Scripture: Making the Declaration of Independence*. New York: Vintage, 1998. Maier is heavily concerned with demythologizing and deromanticizing the writing of the Declaration, but she never denies its importance as a work of political philosophy, nor its place in American history. Dense and thought provoking.

Masur, Louis P. *Lincoln's Hundred Days: The Emancipation Proclamation and the War for the Union*. Cambridge, MA: Belknap, 2012. This tightly focused historical account examines the 100 days between the release of the first draft of the Emancipation Proclamation and the date it went into effect in its final form. It considers the many events that could have affected the success or failure of emancipation as an act of war.

May, Elaine Tyler. *America and the Pill: A History of Promise, Peril, and Liberation*. New York: Basic Books, 2011. A history of oral contraceptives told from the perspective of women who have used them. While decidedly pro-pill, it gives an honest voice to how the pill has and has not fulfilled various hopes and fears in American society.

Morgan, Iwan, and Philip Davies, eds. *From Sit-Ins to SNCC: The Student Civil Rights Movement in the 1960s*. Gainesville: University Press of Florida, 2012. A collection of academic essays that sets the events in Greensboro in the context of the larger student-driven portion of the civil rights movement.

Muller, Eric L, ed. *Colors of Confinement: Rare Kodachrome Photographs of Japanese American Incarceration in World War II*. Documentary Arts and Culture. Published in association with the Century for Documentary Studies at Duke University. Chapel Hill: The University of North Carolina, 2012. Sixty-five photographs and explanatory essays capturing life at the Heart Mountain Relocation Center in Wyoming.

Norman, Donald A. *The Design of Everyday Things*. New York: Basic Books, 2002. Have you ever wondered how a Steve Jobs or a George

Eastman makes complicated technology into user-friendly tools? This book explains the role of designers in manufacturing.

O'Malley, Gregory E. *Final Passages: The Intercolonial Slave Trade of British America, 1619–1807*. Published for the Omohundro Institute of Early American History and Culture, Williamsburg, Virginia. Chapel Hill: The University of North Carolina, 2014. A by-the-numbers economic history of the early slave trade in North America—but no less harrowing for all that. If you want to grasp the economic drivers of the triangle trade, this is your starting point.

Page, Jake. *In the Hands of the Great Spirit: The 20,000-Year History of American Indians*. New York: Free Press, 2004. A history of the many Native American peoples from the earliest archeological evidence to today.

Pauketat, Timothy R. *Cahokia: Ancient America's Great City on the Mississippi*. Penguin Library of American Indian History. New York: Penguin, 2010. A great introduction to one of North America's most influential and widespread pre-Columbian civilizations.

Prange, Gordon W. *At Dawn We Slept: The Untold Story of Pearl Harbor*. 60th anniversary ed. New York: Penguin, 2001. Exhaustively detailed and full of haunting photographs, this is a comprehensive assessment not only of the day, but also of the causes and aftermath.

Pursell, Carroll. *The Machine in America: A Social History of Technology*. Baltimore: Johns Hopkins University, 2007. This book explores the early Industrial Revolution in America and features some of the tools that could only be discussed briefly in the course—examples of which can be found in the Smithsonian's museums.

Pykles, Benjamin C. *Excavating Nauvoo: The Mormons and the Rise of Historical Archaeology in America*. Critical Studies in the History of Anthropology. Lincoln: University of Nebraska, 2010. The interests of historians and researchers sometimes come into conflict with the people to whom that history belongs. The story of the excavation of Nauvoo is an interesting lesson in both the work of archeologists and the sensitive issues they often confront.

Rich, Doris L. *Amelia Earhart*. Washington DC: Smithsonian, 1996. A classic biography discussing Earhart as a pilot, a celebrity, and an activist.

Rinella, Steven. *American Buffalo: In Search of a Lost Icon*. New York: Spiegel & Grau, 2009. A modern American adventurer goes on a hunt for bison in Alaska and comes face to face with history. Not for the faint of heart, Rinella's account is sometimes frightening, sometimes grisly, sometimes darkly humorous, and even occasionally thought provoking.

Rinzler, J. W. *The Making of* Star Wars*: The Definitive Story Behind the Original Film*. New York: LucasBooks, 2007. Released for the 30th anniversary of the first *Star Wars* film (or "Episode IV," depending on your perspective), this photo-packed book by a LucasFilm insider is not just a fan's dream; it's also full of original interviews and documents—a real glimpse into cinematic history.

Rose, Kenneth D. *One Nation Underground: The Fallout Shelter in American Culture*. New York: New York University, 2004. This book examines the popular view toward nuclear war and fallout shelter construction without stooping to insult those who lived through this tumultuous time. A thoughtful and thorough work.

Rouse, Parke, and Parke Rouse Jr. *The Great Wagon Road: From Philadelphia to the South*. Petersburg, VA: Dietz, 1992. Aimed at a younger audience and arguably as much folklore as history, this is nonetheless a very readable account of a rarely treated subject: the early history of the Conestoga wagon.

Seidensticker, John, and Susan Lumpkin. *Giant Pandas*. New York: Harper, 2007. A photo-packed look at these marvelous creatures by two National Zoo employees—two people who know these animals intimately.

Snow, Richard. *I Invented the Modern Age: The Rise of Henry Ford.* New York: Scribner, 2013. A dual biography of the Model T Ford and the man who invented it.

Standage, Tom. *The Victorian Internet: The Remarkable Story of the Telegraph and the Nineteenth Century's On-line Pioneers*. 2nd ed. New York: Bloomsbury, 2014. This charming book not only details the history of the telegraph but also society's response to it.

Stillman, William, and Jay Scarfone. *The Wizard of Oz: The Official 75th Anniversary Companion*. New York: Harper Design, 2013. More entertaining than scholarly, this is nonetheless a must for any *Oz*-phile's library.

Taylor, Frederick. *The Berlin Wall: A World Divided, 1961–1989*. New York: Harper Perennial, 2008. An analysis of the forces that created and destroyed the Berlin Wall that places the structure at the heart of the Cold War.

Taylor, Lonn, Jeffrey Brodie, and Kathleen Kendrick. *The Star-Spangled Banner: The Making of an American Icon*. Washington DC: Smithsonian, 2008. A history of the flag by the curators who oversaw its restoration.

Townsend, Camilla. *Pocahontas and the Powhatan Dilemma: The American Portraits Series*. New York: MacMillan, 2005. This book considers Pocahontas as a sort of early diplomat between the Native Americans and the English colonists.

Utley, Robert M. *Sitting Bull: The Life and Times of an American Patriot*. New York: Holt, 2008. An award-winning biography by the former chief historian of the National Park Service.

Varon, Elizabeth R. *Appomattox: Victory, Defeat, and Freedom*. New York: Oxford University, 2013. This work not only considers the events leading up to the treaty and the men who signed it, but also the long-term implications for Reconstruction as well.

Walker, J. Samuel. *Prompt and Utter Destruction: Truman and the Use of Atomic Bombs Against Japan*. Chapel Hill: The University of North Carolina,

2005. Perhaps no event in the 20th century is more mired in controversy than the bombings of Hiroshima and Nagasaki. Walker's admirable effort cuts through the emotion to the facts behind Truman's decision making while never denying the terrible costs of either choice.

Walton, Mary. *A Woman's Crusade: Alice Paul and the Battle for the Ballot.* Basingstoke, UK: Palgrave Macmillan, 2010. A personal and detailed assessment of Paul as a thinker and leader.

White, Ronald C., Jr. *A. Lincoln: A Biography.* New York: Random House, 2010. This enormous and highly respected biography delves into the issue of Lincoln's public image, as well as his political skill.

Wolmar, Christian. *The Great Railroad Revolution: The History of Trains in America.* New York: PublicAffairs, 2013. A noted historian of Britain's railways takes on American railroad history.

Image Credits

Front Cover:

George Washington's Uniform, 1789, Wool (overall material), metal (overall material) [buff wool rise-and-fall collar, buff cuffs and lapels, buff lining, metal buttons], 72 X 36 X 36 in (182.88 X 91.44 X 91.44 cm), National Museum of American History, Kenneth E. Behring Center, Smithsonian Institution, Cat. No. 16148, Accession: 13152.

Star-Spangled Banner, Mary Pickersgill, 1814, Baltimore Maryland, United States, Wool (overall material), 30 X 34 foot (9.144 X 10.3632 m.), National Museum of American History, Kenneth E. Behring Center, Smithsonian Institution, Cat. No. 13649, Accession: 54876.

Liberty Enlightening the World, Frédéric Auguste Bartholdi, 1884, painted terracotta, tin (crown), 46 X 12 X 11 in (116.8 X 30.5 X 28.0 cm), Smithsonian American Art Museum, Smithsonian Institution; transfer from the U.S. Capitol, XX76.

Hope Diamond, cushion antique brilliant with a faceted girdle and extra facets on the pavilion, platinum setting surrounded by sixteen white pear-shaped and cushion-cut diamonds designed by Pierre Cartier, 1910, length: 25.60 mm., width: 21.78 mm., depth: 12.00 mm., weight: 45.52 carats, National Museum of Natural History, Smithsonian Institution; gift of Harry Winston Inc.

Abraham Lincoln's Top Hat, J.Y. Davis, mid-19th century, United States: Washington, D.C., silk, paper, 7 X 10 ¾ X 12 in. (17.78 X 27.305 X 30.48 cm), National Museum of American History, Kenneth E. Behring Center, Smithsonian Institution, transfer from the War Department, Cat. No. 9321, Accession: 38912.

Bald Eagle, National Zoological Park, Smithsonian Institution. Photograph Jessie Cohen, National Zoological Park, Smithsonian Institution.

Lecture 1:

Star-Spangled Banner, Mary Pickersgill, 1814, Baltimore Maryland, United States, Wool (overall material), 30 X 34 foot (9.144 X 10.3632 m.), National Museum of American History, Kenneth E. Behring Center, Smithsonian Institution, Cat. No. 13649, Accession: 54876.

Lecture 2:

George Washington's Uniform, 1789, Wool (overall material), metal (overall material) [buff wool rise-and-fall collar, buff cuffs and lapels, buff lining, metal buttons], 72 X 36 X 36 in (182.88 X 91.44 X 91.44 cm), National Museum of American History, Kenneth E. Behring Center, Smithsonian Institution, Cat. No. 16148, Accession: 13152.

***George Washington* (Lansdowne Portrait),** Gilbert Stuart (3 Dec 1755-July 1828), 1796, Germantown, Pennsylvania, United States, oil on canvas, Stretcher: 97 ½ X 62 ½ in (247.6 X 158.7 cm), Frame:111 5/8 X 76 ½ X 7 in (283.5 X 194.3 X 17.8 cm), National Portrait Gallery, Smithsonian Institution. Acquired as a gift to the nation through the generosity of the Donald W. Reynolds Foundation, Object No. NPG.2001.13.

Lecture 3:

Hide Painting of Saint Anthony of Padua, Franciscan B , 1720, United States: New Mexico, Tesuque. Painting, hide, tanned, paint, 20 ½ X 15 9/16 X 3/16 in (52 X 39.5 X .5 cm), National Museum of American History, Kenneth E. Behring Center, Smithsonian Institution; gift of Dr. J. Walter Fewkes, Cat. No. 176401, Accession: 31785.

Plymouth Rock Fragment, granite, Plymouth, Massachusetts, United States, 2 ¾ X 4 ¼ X 7/8 in. (6.985 X 10.795 X 2.2225 cm.), National Museum of American History, Kenneth E. Behring Center, Smithsonian Institution; gift of Mrs. Virginia L.W. Fox. Cat. No. 012058, Accession 52309.

***Thomas Jefferson-Life and Morals of Jesus of Nazareth*,** Thomas Jefferson, ca. 1820, United States, Leather (overall material), paper (overall material), 8 3/8 X 5 1/8 X 1 in (21.2725 X 13.0175 X 2.54 cm), National Museum of American History, Smithsonian Institution. Cat. No.158231, Accession: 147182.

Sunstone Capital or Mormon Sun Stone, 1844**,** Nauvoo, Illinois, United States, White fossiliferous limestone**,** 53 X 72 X 18 in (134.6 X 182.9 X 45.7 cm)**,** National Museum of American History, Kenneth E. Behring Center, Smithsonian Institution; purchase from Historical Society of Quincy & Adams County, Quincy, Illinois. Cat. No. 1989.0453.01, Accession: 1989.0453.

Lecture 4:

Eli Whitney's Cotton Gin Model, Eli Whitney, 1790, Georgia, United States, 10 X 17 ½ X 14 in. (25.4 X 44.45 X 35.56 cm), National Museum of American History, Kenneth E. Behring Center, Smithsonian Institution**,** Cat. No. TE*T8756.

Harriet Tubman's Hymn Book-*Gospel Hymns No. 2*, P.P. Bliss and Ira D. Sankey, c. 1876, ink on paper, 8 3/16 X 5 3/8 X 9/16 in. (20.7963 X 13.6525 X 1.42875 cm.), National Museum of African American History and Culture, Smithsonian Institution; gift of Charles L. Blockson, Accession: 2009.50.25.

Lecture 5:

Emancipation Proclamation "Pocket Copy," Published by John Murray Forbes, 1862, United States of America, Ink on paper (fiber product)**,** 3 ¼ X 2 1/8 in. (8.3 X 5.4 cm)**,** National Museum of African American History and Culture, Smithsonian Institution**,** Accession: 2012.40.

Christian Fleetwood's Medal of Honor, 1862, bronze, silk, 4 ¼ X 2 1/16 X ¼ (10.795 X 5.23875 X 0.635 cm), National Museum of American History, Kenneth E. Behring Center, Smithsonian Institution, Cat. NO.: AF*046054.1, Accession: 178781.

Lecture 6:

Colt Holster Model Paterson Revolver (No. 5), Colt's Patent Firearms Manufacturing Company, ca. 1839, Paterson, New Jersey, United States, Iron (overall material), wood (overall material), Measurements: overall: 5 X 13 ¾ X 1 ½ in (12.7 X 34.925 X 3.81 cm), National Museum of American

History, Kenneth E. Behring Center, Smithsonian Institution, Cat. No. 251084, Accession: 48865.

Among The Sierra Nevada, California, Albert Bierstadt, 1868, Sierra Nevada Mountains, California, United States, oil on canvas, Measurements overall: 72 X 120 1/8 in (183 X 305 cm). Frame: 96 ¼ X 144 3/8 X 7 ¼ in (244.5 X 366.7 X 18.4 cm), Smithsonian American Art Museum, Smithsonian Institution; Bequest of Helen Huntington Hull, granddaughter of William Brown Dinsmore, who acquired the painting in 1873 for "The Locusts," the family estate in Dutchess County, New York, Accession: 1977.107.1.

Lecture 7:

Clovis Stone Points, Drake Cache,Colorado, United States, National Museum of Natural History, Smithsonian Institution. Top Row, Left to Right: cat. nos. A561339, A561337, A561329, A561332, A561331, A561338, and A561340. Bottom Row, Left to Right: Catalog numbers A561327, (un-numbered), A561328, A561330, A561333, and A561334. Image by Marcia Bakry, Smithsonian Institution.

Copper Plate (Human Figure), Etowah, AD. 1300-1375, Cartersville, Bartow County, Georgia, United States, *Repoussé* sheet Copper, 12.9921 X 9.44882 in. (33 X 24 cm.), National Museum of Natural History, Smithsonian Institution, Cat. No. A91117, Accession: 014255.

Totem Pole, 2001-2012, David Boxley and David Robert Boxley, red cedar, latex paint, 22 feet (6.7056 m.), National Museum of the American Indian, Smithsonian Institution, Accession: 26/8612, Photo by R.A. Whiteside, Smithsonian Institution. © David Boxley.

Lecture 8:

Conestoga Wagon, 1840-1850, Pennsylvania, United States, wood and iron, 17' 10" X 12' 6", Blue body, red running gear, decorative ironwork, National Museum of American History, Kenneth E. Behring Center, Smithsonian Institution, Cat. No. 321453, Accession: 243296.

Steam Locomotive, John Bull, Robert Stephenson and Company, 1831, United Kingdom: England, Newcastle upon Tyne, Assembled in Camden, New Jersey, United States, iron, wood, copper, brass, 11 ½ ft. X 7 ½ ft. X 36 ¼ ft. (3.5052 X 2.286 X 11.049 m), National Museum of American History, Kenneth E. Behring Center, Smithsonian Institution, Cat. No. 180001, Accession: 15804.

Lecture 9:

Morse-Vail Telegraph Key, Samuel Finley Breese Morse and Alfred Vail, 1844, Morristown, NJ, wood, brass, 3 X 2 X 6.75 in., (7.62 X 5.08 X 17.145 cm), National Museum of American History, Kenneth E. Behring Center, Smithsonian Institution, Cat. No. 181411, Accession: 31652.

RCA TRK-12 Television Set, 1939, Radio Corporation of America (RCA) Corporation, United States of America, Wood, glass, Metal, plastic, Measurements: overall 40 ¾ X 34 ½ X 20 ½ in. (103.505 X 87.63 X 52.07 cm.), National Museum of American History, Kenneth E. Behring Center, Smithsonian Institution; gift from Col. Frank E. Mason, Cat. No. 326100, Accession: 258911.

Lecture 10:

Liberty Enlightening the World, Frédéric Auguste Bartholdi, 1884, painted terracotta, tin (crown), 46 X 12 X 11 in (116.8 X 30.5 X 28.0 cm), Smithsonian American Art Museum, Smithsonian Institution; transfer from the U.S. Capitol, XX76.

Azada de Mango Corto-Short Handled Hoe (owned by Librado Hernandez Chavez, father of Cesar), 1936, San Jose, California, United States, Metal (blade material), welded to metal neck, wood (handle material), 5 X 16 in. (12.7 X 40.64 cm), overall; 4 X 6 in. (10.16 X 15.24 cm), blade, National Museum of American History, Kenneth E. Behring Center, Smithsonian Institution; gift of Rita Chavez Medina, Cat. No. 1998.0197.01, Accession: 1998.0197.

Cesar Chavez's union jacket, 1980s-1990s, California, United States, Polyester (shell material), nylon (lining material), 26 X 25 in. (66.04 X 63.5cm), National Museum of American History, Kenneth E. Behring Center, Smithsonian Institution; gift of Helen Chavez, Cat. No. 1993.0409.01, Accession: 1993.0409.

Lecture 11:

1846_Howe Jr.'s Sewing Machine Patent Model, 1846, Elias Howe Jr., Cambridge, Massachusetts, United States , metal, wood, 12 X 9 X 11 in. (30.48 X 22.86 X 27.94 cm), Cat. No. T.6050, Accession: 48865.

Bernice Palmer's Kodak Brownie Camera, 1912, Eastman Kodak Company, Rochester, New York, United States, Wood, glass, pated metal, and copper alloy, Measurements: overall: 5 ¼ X 4 X 6 ¼ in (13.335 X 10.16 X 15.875 cm), National Museum of American History, Kenneth E. Behring Center, Smithsonian Institution; gift of Bernice Palmer Ellis, Cat. No. 1986.0173.38, Accession: 1986.0173.

Lecture 12:

Bald Eagle, National Zoological Park, Smithsonian Institution. Photograph Jessie Cohen, National Zoological Park, Smithsonian Institution.

Ling-Ling and Hsing-Hsing Pandas, National Zoological Park, Smithsonian Institution; gift by the people of the People's Republic of China to the people of the United States Photo by Jessie Cohen, Smithsonian Institution.

Lecture 13:

1903 Wright Flyer (or Wright Brothers' Kitty Hawk Flyer), 1903, Wilbur and Orville Wright, Dayton Ohio, United States, Spruce and ash, covered with muslin, Wingspan: 40 ft 4 in (12.3m), Length: 21 ft (6.4 m), Height: 9 ft 3 in (2.8 m), Weight, empty: 605 lb (274 kg), National Air and Space Museum, Smithsonian Institution; gift of the Estate of Orville Wright, Inv. No. A19610048000. Photo by Dane Penland, Smithsonian Institution.

Neil Armstrong, Apollo 11 pressure suit A7-L,1969, ILC Industries, Inc., United States of America, overall materials: beta cloth, rubber, nylon, plastic connectors, aluminum (red, blue), neck ring: aluminum wrist locking rings, aluminum (red, blue), zipper: brass with neoprene gasket, overall dimensions 5ft 6 15/16 in X 2 ft. 8 5/16 X 11 in (170.02 X 82 X 28 cm), National Air and Space Museum, Smithsonian Institution, Inv. No. A19730040000. Photo by Mark Avino, Smithsonian Institution.

Lecture 14:
Boeing B-29 Superfortress *Enola Gay*, 1945, Boeing Aircraft Co., Martin Co., Omaha, Nebraska, United States, polished overall aluminum finish, overall: (354.330 X 1188.97 in.) (900 X 3020 cm), 29 ft. 6 5/16 in. X 99 ft. 1 in., 71825.9 lb. (32580 kg), National Air and Space Museum, Steven F. Udvar-Hazy Center, Smithsonian Institution, A19500100000. Photo by Dane Penland, Smithsonian Institution.

Fallout Shelter, Universal Tank & Iron Works, Inc., ca. 1955, Indianapolis, Indiana, United States, (15 X 13 X 10 ft. (4.572 X 3.9624 X 3.048 m), steel, National Museum of American History, Kenneth E. Behring Center, Smithsonian Institution; gift of Timothy L. and Vera R. Howey. Cat. No. 2005.0051.04, Accession: 2005.0051.

Lecture 15:
Bugle from the USS *Maine*, before 1898, metal, 4 X 14 X 2 ½ in (10.16 X 35.56 X 6.35 cm), National Museum of American History, Kenneth E. Behring Center, Smithsonian Institution, Cat. No. 31188, Accession: 66761.

USS *Oklahoma* duplex handstamp, 1941, Hawaii, United States, Wood, rubber, (wooden handle): 1 ½ X 2 9/16 X 3 ¾ in (3.8 X 6.5 X 9.5 cm), (rubber stamp): 1 3/8 X 2 ¾ X ½ in (3.5 X 7 X 1.3 cm), National Postal Museum, Smithsonian Institution, Accession: 1992.2002.369.

Lecture 16:
Salk Polio Vaccine, Mahoney Strain, Jonas E. Salk, 1952, Pittsburgh, Pennsylvania, United States, Vaccine residue, polio virus (drug active ingredients), Measurements overall: 2 3/16 X 7/8 in (5.5 X 2.3 cm), National Museum of American History, Kenneth E. Behring Center, Smithsonian

Institution, Cat. No. 221419.04, Accession: 221419.04. **Salk Polio Vaccine, Saukett Strain,** Jonas E. Salk, 1952, Pittsburgh, Pennsylvania, United States, Vaccine residue, polio virus (drug active ingredients), Measurements overall: 2 3/16 X 7/8 in (5.5 X 2.3 cm), National Museum of American History, Kenneth E. Behring Center, Smithsonian Institution, Cat. No. 221419.05, Accession: 221419.05. **Salk Polio Vaccine, MEF-1 Strain,** Jonas E. Salk, 1952, Pittsburgh, Pennsylvania, United States, Vaccine residue, polio virus (drug active ingredients), Measurements overall: 2 9/16 X 1 1/8 in (6.5 X 2.8 cm), National Museum of American History, Kenneth E. Behring Center, Smithsonian Institution, Cat. No. 221419.06, Accession: 221419.06. **Jonas Salk's Syringe,** Becton, Dickinson and Company, ca. 1950, glass (plunger material), glass (barrel material), glass (tip, force material), steel (handle material), metal, steel (needle material), overall: 4 1/8 X 1 1/8 X 3/8 in. (10.4 X 2.8 X 1 cm), National Museum of American History, Kenneth E. Behring Center, Smithsonian Institution, Cat. No. 221419.07, Accession: 221419.

Wagner DialPak Patent Model (Prototype Pill Dispenser and Patent) David P. Wagner, 1962, United States, Paper, plastic, staples, pencil, double-faced transparent tape, National Museum of American History, Kenneth E. Behring Center, Smithsonian Institution, Cat. No. 1995.0057.01, Accession: 1995.0057.

AIDS memorial Quilt Panel, Gert McMullin, 1985-1990, San Francisco, California, United States, Textile, Measurements: overall: 35 11/16 X 70 7/8 X 3/16 in. (90.6 X 180 X .5 cm.), National Museum of American History, Kenneth E. Behring Center, Smithsonian Institution; in Memory of Roger Lyon. Gift of Gert "Cindy" McMullin, Cat. No. 1998.0254.01, Accession: 1998.0254.

Lecture 17:

"The Great Demand" Banner, ca. 1917, Probably Emma Louthan, United States, Yellow silk, applied purple silk letters, 67 X 65 in. (170.179 X 165.099 cm), National Museum of American History, Kenneth E. Behring Center, Smithsonian Institution; gift of Martin Gilmer Louthan in honor of his mother Marie Gilmer Louthan. Cat. No. 2009.0207.01, Accession: 2009.0207.

Helen Keller's Watch, ca. 1865, Rossel & Fils, Switzerland, Gold (watch case material), brass (watch movement material), Measurements: overall: watch 2 5/8 X 1 7/8 X ½ in (6.6675 X 4.7625 X 1.27 cm); overall case: 2 ½ X 2 ½ X ¾ in (6.35 X 6.35 X 1.905 cm), National Museum of American History, Kenneth E. Behring Center, Smithsonian Institution; gift of Phillips Brooks Keller & Mrs. Gordon Erwin, Cat. No. 335239, Accession: 314555.

Julia Child's Kitchen at the Smithsonian, National Museum of American History, Kenneth E. Behring Center, Smithsonian Institution; gift of Julia Child, Accession: 2001-0253. Additional related objects, gift of Philadelphia Cousins and the Trustees of the Julia Child Foundation, Accessions: 2009.0091 and 2012-0043.

Lecture 18:

Pocahontas, Unidentified artist, copy after the 1616 engraving by Simon van de Passe, After 1616, Oil on canvas, Stretcher: 30 ½ X 25 ½ X 1 in. (77.5 X 64.8 X 2.5 cm), Frame: 36 ½ X 31 ½ X 2 ½ in (92.7 X 80 X 6.4 cm), National Portrait Gallery, Smithsonian Institution; transfer from the National Gallery of Art; Gift of the A.W. Mellon Educational and Charitable Trust, Object number NPG.65.61.

Frederick Douglass, Unidentified Artist, 1856, Quarter-plate ambrotype, Image: 4 3/16 X 3 3/8 in (10.6 X 8.6 cm), Case (open): 4 11/16 X 7 ½ X ½ in (11.9 X 19.1 X 1.3 cm), National Portrait Gallery, Smithsonian Institution; purchased with funds from an anonymous donor, NPG.74.75.

Abraham Lincoln's Top Hat, J.Y. Davis, mid-19th century, United States: Washington, D.C., silk, paper, 7 X 10 ¾ X 12 in. (17.78 X 27.305 X 30.48 cm), National Museum of American History, Kenneth E. Behring Center, Smithsonian Institution, transfer from the War Department, Cat. No. 9321, Accession: 38912.

"We Can Do It!" [photolithograph], J. Howard Miller, ca. 1942, Glenshaw, Pennsylvania, United States of America, Paper, 22 X 17 in. (55.88 X 43.18 cm.), National Museum of American History, Kenneth E. Behring Center, Smithsonian Institution; purchase from J. Howard Miller. Accession: 1985.0851.

Lecture 19:
Benjamin Franklin's walking stick, ca. 1783, crabtree wood, gold cap, 46 ½ L X 1 3/8 D X 3/8 dia at tip, National Museum of American History, Kenneth E. Behring Center, Smithsonian Institution; transfer from United States Department of State. Accession: Cat. No. 032011, Accession: 68016.

Andrew Carnegie © Smithsonian Library of Congress, Prints and Photographs Division, LC-USZ62-88699.

Babe Ruth, Nickolas Muray, 1927 (printed 1978), Gelatin silver print, Image: 9 5/8 X 7 11/16 in (24.5 X 19.5 cm), Sheet: 9 15/16 X 8 in (25.2 X 20.3 cm), Mat: 22 X 16 in (55.9 X 40.6 cm), NPG.78.150. National Portrait Gallery; photo by Nickolas Muray; © Nickolas Muray Photo Archives.

Muhammad Ali's gloves, ca. 1974, Everlast, United States of America, Leather (overall material), fabric (overall material), Overall 10 ½ X 6 in (26.67 X 15.24 cm), National Museum of American History, Kenneth E. Behring Center, Smithsonian Institution; gift of Muhammad Ali, Cat. No. 1977.1073.01, Accession: 1977.1073.

Muhammad Ali's robe, ca. 1974, United States of America, Fiber, cotton (overall Material), Overall 47 X 23 in (119.38 X 58.42 cm), National Museum of American History, Kenneth E. Behring Center, Smithsonian Institution; gift of Muhammad Ali, Cat. No. 1977.1073.02, Accession: 1977.1073.

Jacqueline Kennedy's Inaugural Gown, Ethel Frankau of Bergdorf Custom Salon, 1961, Off-white silk chiffon over peau d'ange, embroidered with silver thread, National Museum of American History, Kenneth E. Behring Center, Smithsonian Institution; gift of Mrs. John F. Kennedy, Cat. No. 234793.01, Accession: 234793.

Lecture 21:
Hope Diamond, cushion antique brilliant with a faceted girdle and extra facets on the pavilion, platinum setting surrounded by sixteen white pear-shaped and cushion-cut diamonds designed by Pierre Cartier, 1910, length: 25.60 mm., width: 21.78 mm., depth: 12.00 mm., weight: 45.52 carats,

National Museum of Natural History, Smithsonian Institution; gift of Harry Winston Inc.

Lecture 22:
Marian Anderson's Mink Coat, maker unknown, mink, silk, 27 ½ X 47 X 4 in (69.85 X 119.38 X 10.16 cm), Anacostia Community Museum, Smithsonian Institution; gift of James DePriest on behalf of Marian Anderson, Accession: 1992.0034.0001.

Lecture 23:
Image of *Discovery* © NASA

Giant Magellan Telescope, Image courtesy of GMTO Corporation.

Lecture 24:
Declaration of Independence by Stone, printer's copy. William J. Stone, Engraving, 33 ¾ X 27 ¼ in. (85.725 X 69.215 cm), National Museum of American History, Kenneth E. Behring Center, Smithsonian Institution; gift of Mrs. E. J. Stone., Cat. No. 4685, Accession: 21086.

KKK Hood, 12 X 12 X 8 ½ in. (30.48 X 30.48 X 21.59 cm) , National Museum of American History, Kenneth E. Behring Center, Smithsonian Institution; gift from Mr. Kenton H. Broyles. Cat. No. 286282.08, Accession: 286282.

KKK Robe, 49 X 32 X 21 in. (124.46 X 81.28 X 53.34 cm), National Museum of American History , Kenneth E. Behring Center, Smithsonian Institution; gift of Kenton H. Broyles. Cat. No. 286282.06, Accession: 286282.

Greensboro Lunch Counter, F.W. Woolworth Co., 38 X 15 X 15 in (96.52 X 38.1 X 38.1 cm), National Museum of American History, Kenneth E. Behring Center, Smithsonian Institution, Cat. No. 1994.0156.01, Accession: 1994.0156.

Notes

Notes

Notes

Notes